APE CULTURE

PREFACE

At the beginning of this century a number of geoscientists and climate experts were so perplexed by the data they were faced with that they proclaimed a new period in the Earth's history: the Anthropocene. So what had happened? Since World War II, fundamental parameters of the terrestrial system had changed dramatically. Diagrams indicated an exponential rise in the development of carbon dioxide concentrations, water consumption, and the exploitation of resources, accompanied by a simultaneous reduction in biodiversity. The researchers characterized this development as a "big acceleration." Consequently, a system of material balances that had existed for millennia became increasingly unstable. Climate changes were followed by transformations in biosystems. The Earth threatened, and still threatens, to become an inhospitable place as a result of man's actions.

This is the historical context that the Haus der Kulturen der Welt has explored over the last three years in the *Anthropocene Project*, and within which an important part of the primate research from the second half of the twentieth century can be located. In light of the danger posed to the planet by humanity, the question can be posed: Who is this human? Where does she or he come from? What is her or his relationship to nature?

Primatology, as traced by Donna Haraway in her groundbreaking study *Primate Visions: Gender, Race, and Nature in the World of Modern Science*, has made a contribution towards answering this question in two ways: Firstly, through the work of (mostly female) researchers such as Jane Goodall, who set off to find the cradle of humankind in the seemingly undisturbed natural world at the very heart of Africa. By cohabitating with chimpanzees, Goodall was attempting to restore the broken bond with nature, seeking to evoke a unity between culture and nature that had been destroyed by a technology guided by science.

The other movement looked to the future: Primates in space flight were to signpost the route into an as yet undetermined future. When the Earth has been destroyed as a habitat, the journey into space remains the only alternative.

In the first case the nature/culture dualism had to be overcome. At the same time the colonial mindset denied the African population any role as actors, placing them instead on the side of nature. Only by such means was it possible to maintain the idea of nature unspoiled by human hand.

In contrast, in space flight the participating apes, followed by human beings, developed into cyborgs, becoming actors for whom the boundaries between technology and living beings had disappeared. Fusing with technology in space corresponded to the integration with nature at the heart of Africa.

The path to the origin of civilization as well as that leading to its future make clear how attempts to solve the destabilizations generated by the Anthropocene involve a repositioning of not only the categories of modernity, but also their classification systems.

It is the goal of the Haus der Kulturen der Welt to address precisely these shifts. A major role is played here by research from recent decades on the faculty of language, on the expression of emotions, but also on the use of tools by primates, thus dissolving the seemingly clear division between great apes and people, and evoking the question: How much person (culture) is there in apes (nature), or alternatively, how much ape (nature) is there in people (culture)? Or to put it differently: do we have to naturalize our image of humans and culturalize our picture of the apes somewhat?

I would like to extend warm thanks to the curators of this project, Hila Peleg and Anselm Franke.

Bernd Scherer,
Director of the Haus der Kulturen der Welt

INTRODUCTION

*"In the similarity of clowns to animals the likeness of humans to apes
flashes up; the constellation animal/fool/clown is a fundamental layer
of art."*
Theodor W. Adorno

Since antiquity, apes and monkeys have been used to reflect human
behaviors in both literary and artistic representations. In Christian
theology, apes were placed as inferior to man, just as man was to God.
In the Middle Ages, apes were first identified with evil, and later figured
as icons of degeneration. Sometimes apes were used to symbolize
man being entrapped by earthly and sensual desires. In art, they often
also symbolized an "inferior mimesis," as empty imitation, without
understanding and access to the spiritual dimension of human culture,
or a primordial, prehistoric animality that is overcome or suppressed
in humanity.

The figure of the ape in art is posed at the margins of recognized
human behavior. It has been used in two opposing ways: to reinforce
human social order through hierarchal degradation of the ostracized
"animal other," or to critique the pretence and hypocrisy of social order
and reveal its suppressed and unconscious aspects, and its mythological narratives.

Situated at the threshold of humanity and animality, and thus of
nature and culture, figures of apes do not merely serve as tokens
marking these divisions, but also frequently introduce slippage and
ambiguity into these borders and the convictions sustaining ordered
knowledge at large. This has found expression in a vast diversity of
cultural narratives casting apes as tricksters, as anti-civilization, and
as an ambigous figure.

"At least on a phenomenological level, sociality in most primates is prior
to individualism. It took all the resources of late-capitalist economic
theory to make the autonomous, competitive individual fill the primate
scientist's field of vision," writes Donna Haraway in her seminal study
Primate Visions from 1989—one of the major sources of inspiration for
this project. The primacy of sociality is established as a new paradigm
of study and application, turning the tables on many prior assumptions and patterns of explanation. An ever growing number of primatologists recognize that it is impossible to avoid entering into social
relationships with their research subjects. Indeed, for social beings,
there is no stepping out of the magic circle of sociality. This insight has
also redefined debates on objectivity in the sciences. The longstanding

dispute about anthropomorphic approaches to animal study, which
attribute humanlike characteristics to nonhumans, has gradually been
transformed into a differentiated tool and necessary prerequisite of
research.

However, some twenty-five years after Haraway wrote her study,
we can clearly discern that this turn towards sociality is not only
the result of struggles within culture and the field of primatology; it
also reflects a shift in economic paradigms. While indeed it is no longer
merely the alleged struggles for power and survival that drive and
dominate the debate about apes, it is the social nature of apes, and
processes of "social learning," "cooperation," and "empathy" that
have become prominent issues in primate research as in culture at
large. Just as throughout the twentieth century, apes acted as "psychobiological goldmines" (Robert Yerkes) that opened the gates to the
betterment, reconstruction, and exploitation of human "nature," so it
seems the interest in the fundamentals of primate sociality, to which
apes promise human access, has been stirred up at a time when
sociality itself is being turned into an economic resource, and the very
notions of "the social" and "society" are being redefined against the
background of technological developments.

The exhibition *Ape Culture* has been divided into two separate sections:
One part consists of contemporary works of art and films, some of
them produced for the occasion; a second section functions like an
annotated bibliography, consisting of scientific and cultural documents organized in sixteen thematic chapters that examine the history
of primatology, as well as the image of apes in popular culture, using
selected examples.

In this publication, the two sections have been reproduced and
documented, and are complemented by a series of commissioned
texts. An essay by Anselm Franke elaborates on the connection
between art, apes, and the changing paradigms of the "primacy
of sociality". Astrid Deuber-Mankowsky revisits Donna Haraway's
Primate Visions, situating its publication within the context of
primatology and political movements. An essay jointly written by
John Barker, Matthew Hyland, and Ines Doujak explores the connections between primate research and the ideology of work as well
as racism. Cord Riechelmann's essay addresses the basis of social
existence, the elementary need to form social bonds and to
communicate between individual bodies, and the impossibility
of reducing such dynamics to biological determinants.

Finally, we have Cord Riechelmann's interview with the primatologist
Christophe Boesch, in which we learn about the "golden barrier"
between humans and nonhumans, the internal lines of division within
primatology, and the role that the notion of "culture" plays in this field
of science. In the documentary portion of the exhibition,

Boesch and his collaborators have contributed a separate subsection containing their original research on the diversity of ape cultures, which is reproduced here in part.

We would like to thank all the artists and authors for their valuable contributions to the exhibition and this book.

Anselm Franke and Hila Peleg

Wallpaper from the installation *06 Kriminaloffe*, 2015
Ines Doujak in collaboration with John Barker
and Matthew Hyland

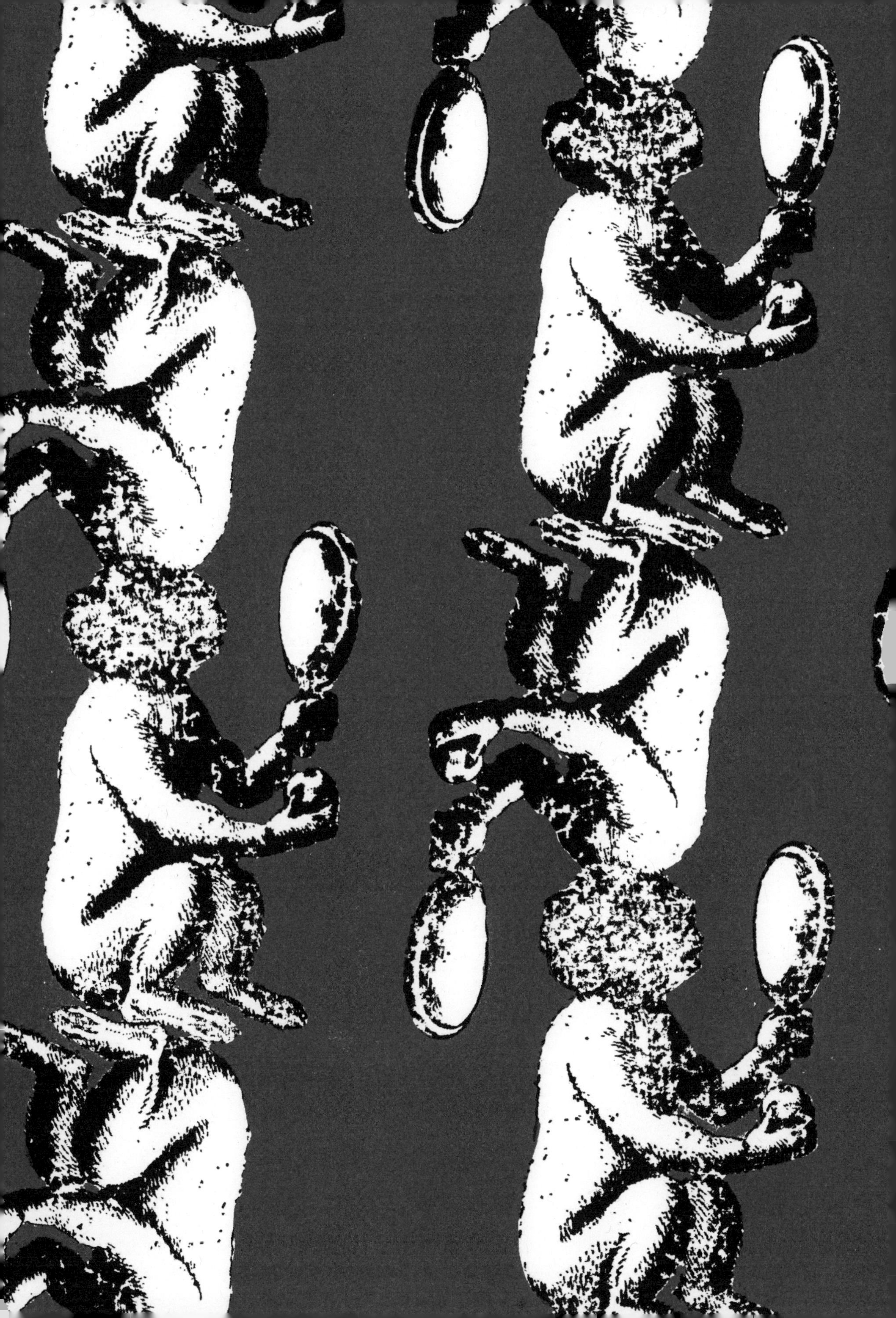

MIRRORS AT FRONTIERS

Anselm Franke

It is impossible to look at apes and monkeys, our "simian mirrors," without being captured affectively. On the one hand, we are drawn into a play between similarity and difference that lies at the core of mimetic processes and signification. Yet on the other, we are drawn into a web of narratives and imaginaries around the origins of humanity and society, and its relation to "nature." These two forces pull in opposite directions: The first destabilizes signifiers, and tends to undermine fixed meanings (which is why it is inevitable that we laugh when looking at apes), while the second draws a series of external and internal borders, reinforcing meaning and our own sense of self by assuring us of our own privileged place in nature.

Ape Culture is an exhibition that explores these modes of being captured and the uses and misuses of the "simian mirror." These issues are reflected in the exhibition's two parts: The section comprising artworks and films is about "signifying" apes, about how the politics of mimesis and desire in human society is brought into focus by the simian mirror, about imitative and mocking behavior that has so frequently been identified with apes and ape imagery, and about the way ape imagery can signify what society doesn't actually know about itself. The section consisting of historical and recent documents from science and popular culture concerns the narrative matrix and optics through which we look at apes, and how these optics and narratives reflect changing parameters of modern industrial and post-industrial societies. It also tells the story of how attempts (of various ideological color, but usually in the service of power) at modeling human society after some "primate pattern" have ultimately failed, since there is not "one nature" of "primate sociality." However, the exhibition also proposes that these attempts may now succeed thanks to the existence of algorithmic machines.

The exhibition also goes on to suggest, controversially, that apes and art, at least with respect to their cultural role, share a common trait: They open up the field of an expanded, "wild" semiosis, in which the foundations of what it means to be "social" are at stake. The terrain of this semiosis pertains to embodied knowledges, to gesture and nonlinguistic communication, to mimetic behavior, to the "being-in-communication" of organisms.

Ape Culture is also about the way apes and monkeys have been held prisoners of the mirror that they represent for us—and the prospect that they can emerge from behind this screen. The title Ape Culture is therefore not intended to be an authoritative assertion either of the uses of apes in human culture, or of what has recently come to be recognized within science as the "culture" of apes in their own right—although the latter is important and is also given due discussion in this publication. Instead, this exhibition as a whole is about the schizophrenic relationship between the different usages of the "simian mirror."

EVOLUTIONARY NARRATIVES AND
WHAT THE GAZE PRODUCES

Evolutionary tales and stories of origins, whether mythological or scientific, have always been used to explain the nature of sociality, to construct social norms, and, more often than not, to justify forms of coercion. There is certainly still a long way to go in dissociating knowledge of evolutionary processes from the social and political *function* of narrative in constructing social orders—and I do not wish to imply that such dissociation is possible, or that there could ever be totally "objective" knowledge of evolution. Instead, the process of dissociation we are concerned with here aims to highlight the nonidentity between the social function of such tales—which always bind together evidence that can potentially tell other stories—and the evolutionary processes, or whatever else may be the subject of scientific inquiry. Insisting on this nonidentity remains a central legacy of Darwinism, notwithstanding its reductionist, deterministic, and ideological appropriations.

Oscillating back and forth between the object of scientific inquiry and the function of narrative brings various levels of semiosis into relation with each other: cultural, scientific, natural. Instead of introducing us to a realm of definitive truths, it opens up a space of diverse potentiality—and also of politics. From within this space replete with potentiality we can begin to discern how narratives are not only historically contingent, but *performative*, actively shaping forms of being and being together, producing the very effects that they name. The narratives themselves may then come to be understood as *actors* in the evolution of human society, and the relation between narrativization and science then emerges as a central, future arena for the making and remaking of society. In this arena, all images act as mirror screens, dividing and connecting, producing an image of self by inscribing a set of differences, circumscribing a milieu. However, the art of making these mirror screens, and hence of making ourselves, can differ dramatically. This arena cannot do without mirrors, but we can achieve a degree of reflexivity over the means of their construction.[1]

The emotionally and ideologically charged stories of primatology constitute a royal road for the investigation of the process by which evolutionary narratives and stories of origin *create*—rather than merely reflect and solidify—forms of sociality. Such narratives both perform border functions and circumscribe a field of communicability, of what it means to be in-a-medium-of-communication. The starting point of this exhibition project has been the assertion that this performative character of narrative continuously throws us back, not merely onto the background of tacit assumptions, but moreover, onto a paradoxical primary condition of being-in-a-medium, a "milieu" of semiosis. This primary mediality of social beings always envelops them within milieus, as beings-in-relation, and as interpreters of environments. This means that as social beings we always construct and share a milieu with what we observe, although of course this milieu can be constructed in very different ways. It means we can never step outside the social circle of mediality as such, for even antisocial behavior (of whatever kind) inevitably communicates and remakes relations. However, the social is not a thing; it cannot

be objectified according to the protocol of the objectivist natural sciences (rather, it can only be approximated and translated into patterns that can then be used to frame interactions, as we currently experience in our technological environments). In classical positivism this dimension of the social, the awareness of mediatedness, relatedness, and the milieu disappears completely by virtue of a slight of hand—what one could call, with Bruno Latour, a *denial of mediation*.[2] It gives the observer seemingly unmediated direct access to both the fact and the dimension of universal knowledge.

The denial of mediation and the breakdown of sociality haunts the scientific study of primates. The first ever study of a nonhuman primate society illustrates this well, attempting as it does to present a picture of the "nature" of primate society, while actually portraying a complete breakdown of social structures in this very same society. This tale is set in London in the mid-1920s, where the newly established "Monkey Hill" in London Zoo was enormously popular with both visitors and the sensationalist press. It was perceived as a "window" into nature, the primate nature of society in particular. The monkeys in question were hamadryas baboons brought from Ethiopia—the very species held sacred by the ancient Egyptians and often found mummified in pharaonic graves, which today are recognized as having one of the most structured social systems of all primates. What visitors to London Zoo observed confirmed their expectations of the raw, wild, and untamed primate nature beneath the thin "veneer" of what was understood as "culture." It was exactly what an enlightened late Victorian expected from the "state of nature" at the height of the British Empire: a fierce and violent war over resources, power, and dominance. Within the space of just two years a third of the baboons had been brutally killed by other members of the group. Based on a nine-day study of this "baboon colony," Solly Zuckerman's influential 1932 book *The Social Life of Monkeys and Apes* sought to prove Freud's theory of sex as the primary social glue and drive, looking at the baboons as a "primal horde" held together by constant female receptivity."[3] He reached the erroneous conclusion that while a baboon society did exist, there was no such thing as society among all other primates that bred seasonally. The success of the book was due not least to the fact that it echoed the dominant views of the day, offering, amongst other things, seemingly plausible explanations of male dominance and female dependence.

However, since no observations of baboons in the wild had taken place, the role played by the Monkey Hill environment was not taken into account. Nature, such was the positivist belief, could be observed objectively as if from outside, just as history, or for that matter, primate life, could be exhibited in a museum or zoo and delivered to the gaze. The fact that any such gaze or scenography of the laboratory or exhibition already constitutes, a priori, a mediated and hence *social* relationship to the object observed was blanked out. Thirty to forty years passed before Zuckerman's findings were finally refuted. What he was describing was not the inexorable natural laws that underwrite society, but the contrary: a society in utter distress, a "social catastrophe." Field researchers demonstrated that baboons in the wild were seasonal, and showed few of the behavioral patterns they had displayed in London Zoo. The "nature" that had been constructed there was entirely unnatural, in the sense of not being innately given; rather, it was a symptomatic *product* of the social situation and "milieu," which created an object of knowledge devoid of social relations and reflexivity. It was as if one were to study the behavior of prison inmates as a means of determining the ultimate nature of humanity. [4]

This pattern, according to which objectified nature turns out to be an effect, a symptom produced by the denial of mediation, turns out to be persistent and widespread. The baseline assumption is that nature is initially asocial, and hence knowledge of nature must advance to the stratum of asociality, eclipsing mediation and casting nature in the image of the biological machine. This symptomatic image of nature looms large, particularly in an era of rationalist triumphalism, where the signifier reigns supreme, in patriarchal discipline and in the kingdom of knowledge, but also in the savage lands subjugated by Europeans. From this "nature" out there, the apes emerge as messengers of the jungle, that surplus

of mediation with its semiotic abundance and magic conflations, in which rationality and its distinctions break down and "humanity" as such is in jeopardy, enveloped by animality. Imported into Europe, apes were positioned at the trenchline in the battle of dualisms. There, at the frontier of the old confrontation where religion and idealism battled mechanistic materialism, the ape comes to stand for a whole set of divisions and transgressions—literally set at the limits, as a borderline image. But the borderline that is being pictured runs *within* the human being. The ape is merely a symbol for this internal division: a division between humans as people, on the one hand, and humans as organisms, on the other. [5] The ape becomes the operating image of the "anthropological machine," [6] which can be defined as the discursive mechanism, plus its corresponding institutional practices, by which the animal becomes internally and externally divided from the human. Moreover, it is the imaginary and narrative matrix that creates the category of the human in the first place, through a series of scissions and caesurae. This matrix is like a stage on which the figure of the human rises triumphantly. As long as we are under the spell of this matrix, all stories of origin tend to follow the same structure: that of the rise of humanity and of a specific subject (largely the alphabetic subject, the patriarchial autonomous subject), which emerged from brute nature and was initially seen as speechless and asocial. Within the ocean of this asocial nature there are mysterious islands of animal sociality; then there is the continent of human culture that has risen above determined nature, which came into being through human individuals merged into higher-order collectivities. However, these land masses constitute the exception in the dominant view, for initially there is no sociality in nature, and hence what we need to explain is its emergence and separation from "mere" animality. And while Darwinism, on the one hand, presents a challenge to this anthropological machine and its triumphalism, it ultimately consolidated the genre of evolutionary narratives that seek to explain the emergence of sociality and the rise of humanity from an initially asocial matter. The problem, obviously, was that in such narratives, the asocial then assumes the status of a baseline and "actual reality," marginalizing and delegitimizing the empirical primacy of sociality and instead granting patriarchial patterns the seal of a natural law.

Is it possible to exit the matrix provided by the anthropological machine? Giorgio Agamben suggests that in order to do so we must return to a point before the division is established—and rather than pondering the "metaphysical mystery of conjunction,"[7] we have to study "the practical or political mystery of separation": "What is man, if he is always the place—and at the same time, the result—of ceaseless divisions [...]?"[8] But how is it possible to return to the point "before" the division? To this end, I suggest that that the line itself be turned into a *Kippbild,* an invertible figure, which cannot be thought without the two halves that it produces. It is only at the line's meridian that such a point of prior mediality becomes thinkable, forming a vantage point from which to observe first the performative character of narratives; second, how they operate and create division; and third, how that division crafts a particular field of mediality.

In order to render the standard narrative of the evolutionary rise of humanity into a *Kippbild,* one has to resort to mythologies. This is in no sense designed to refute the facts of evolution or to appeal to higher truths—it is carried out in order to question the status of sociality in evolutionary narratives and their performative quality in enacting sociality. It allows us to observe the narrative matrix by constructing a vantage point that is both external to sociality and non-reductive. And that it also allows us to tackle tacit assumptions whose coercive logic may hold science and popular imagination in an iron grip, for it is now widely accepted that all data is interpreted in the light of its theoretical and sociohistorical background. The precondition for exploring these backgrounds is the potential for thinking things differently.

Perhaps the most poignant inversion of the direction prescribed by the workings of the anthropological machine can be found in the mythologies of what are called animist cultures. In a wide range of animist myths, sociality is primordial—precisely in the sense of a mediality and communicability "before" the divisions. There are numerous myths that speak of a time in which all beings shared a common language. This is concisely articulated in Amerindian ontologies, in an exact inversion of our own scientific mythology: The common basis of all beings is humanity or the soul, while it is in nature (bodies) that beings are discontinuous. What we have in common is thus not animality, but humanity. "Animals are ex-humans (rather than humans, ex-animals)."[9] Mythology is the account of how animals and other beings have become differentiated from the human, rather than how humanity has risen from and above animality. "The development of the universe, then, has been primarily a process of diversification, with mankind as the primal substance out of which many if not all of the categories of beings and things in the universe arose."[10]

My argument here is not that this is a more accurate description of evolution, but that it creates a different form of sociality. Once again, the stories we tell of origins and evolution are never identical to actual evolutionary processes, which in themselves are polysemic and multidirectional and never fit into narrative structures. They can only be approximated, tested against all forms of evidence, and are more or less ignorant of the facts. And the story itself has an evolutionary function. The use value of the reference to animist ontology and mythology in this case is that it places the question of sociality on different ground, namely that communicability and mediation are not uniquely human achievements tied to the linguistic signifier and symbolic order.

As a result, this reference opens up a field of expanded sociality and communicability, although the forms of mediation are by no means certain. Animist cosmologies, notes Eduardo Viveiros de Castro, may be thoroughly anthropomorphic, but certainly not anthropocentric[11]—communication can never be judged by the human standard, since animals and other beings do not speak human languages. This distinction matters, because the denial of mediation occurs with frequent reference to the fallacy of anthropomorphisation, and it is only recently that scientists have had the courage to defend anthropomorphism as a necessary prerequisite for an engagement with nonhuman social beings, and hence for what Donna Haraway calls "good science."[12] The attempt to avoid anthropomorphism by sacrificing it on the altar of detached objectivity has led to what primatologist Frans de Waal calls "anthropodenial,"[13] which is an impossible standpoint for anyone who has realized that not only are animals not machines, but that they have more in common with ourselves than with automata. It is impossible for humans to enter social relations without a degree of anthropomorphism, without the assumption that the other being may partake in emotional and cognitive processes similar to us. Only on this basis is it possible to acknowledge not similarity, but difference. However, it remains a difficult task to further qualify anthropomorphism in a move towards "good science"; anthropomorphism is intimately tied to the tacit background and the "milieu," and it is virtually impossible to articulate its always relational and processual truths in stable facts. The primordial mediality postulated here is never simply a given; it must be articulated and enacted, but it exists, as Cord Riechelmann writes in this volume, "by mere virtue of the fact that it [takes] place."[14] Is there anyone who, while watching Penny Patterson with Koko the "talking gorilla," has not marveled at Patterson's achievement in recognizing Koko's unique personality, powerfully displaying the forces of anthropomorphism as the basis for relating? At the same time, is there anyone who has not felt unease about the highly specific cultural norms of behavior that Patterson tries to impose as she interacts with Koko, treating American middle-class conventions as if they were the universal markers of humanity? Future progress in the field of evolutionary narratives—both as a political arena and an arena of potentiality —will mean reflectively engaging with the modes of sociality that narrative structures enable or prohibit.

The first part of the exhibition *Ape Culture* consists of sixteen walls displaying documents from science and popular culture. The different chapters on these walls engage with the primate image and the web of narratives and imaginaries around the origins of humanity and society. The signifier "ape" gradually shifts from an image of deficiency and the absence of rational mind, spirit, and understanding, to that of unobstructed primate nature that reveals to us the reality of nature underwriting the illusions of culture. Throughout the twentieth century, apes have thus served as a foil for the modeling of human society. Some primatologists, however, especially those who refuse to accept that results attained from apes in captivity are "objective," have radically altered the field and shed serious doubts on whether "we could easily make evolutionary models of human society based on our knowledge of primate relatives."[15] Not only have these primatologists carried out long-term field research in natural habitats that has revealed an almost shocking diversity of social systems among our genetic kin, they have also liberated a good deal of research from the grips of objectivism and biological determinism employed in the service of hegemonic ideologies, showing that genes do not determine behavior but rather are actively interpreted by organisms when interacting with their environments. In short, they have pushed the field towards what Stephen Jay Gould termed "biological potentiality."[16] The argument pursued over the course of the exhibition's sixteen walls, which are partially reproduced in this publication, is one that leads from the anthropological machine and the objectivist reign of signifiers to the realization of the primacy of sociality in primates, and hence towards an expanded field of semiosis and sociality.

And this expanded field of nonlinguistic communication is exactly what art shares with the ape complex. Which brings me back to the beginning, where I spoke about the two different usages of the "simian mirror," the two registers of being captured by ape images: the web of narratives surrounding evolution and origins, and the play between similarity and difference. The "simian mirror" not only makes us look into the image of our primate nature, it mirrors, above all, our own being-in-a-milieu of signification. This is what Kafka's ape stands for, as he addresses the academy: He acts as a mirror of the mimetic hierarchies and forms of behavior that cannot be spoken and addressed other than through the ape mirror.[17] They are subject to the ban imposed on what Michael Taussig has called the "public secret," namely non-articulable social knowledge, closely tied to subjection to power: *that which is generally known, but cannot be articulated.*"[18]

APES ON THE UNDERSIDE OF SIGNS
Mimetic behavior, in Kafka's ape, is not a sign of primitive wildness, but of pure survival in the face of the unconscious underside of human collectives, their means of exclusion, and the war they fight against "animality." In this context, animality refers not only to the danger of wild animals, but chiefly to *other* forms of sociality that, when seen from the outside, always look at us with their animal face. Kafka's ape uses "aping" as the only possible language to signify the boundary of sociality, and the politics that marks this boundary.

So what is this other side of the "simian mirror"? It mirrors processual mimesis, "communication about relationship and the material–semiotic means of relating."[19] It is about the "truth" of nonlinguistic communication, and it is equally about the expanded field of sociality and semiosis that is thus opened up.[20] The ape, in the sign of Kafka's mirror, is a mirror in which repressed dimensions of mimesis return— precisely those dimensions of signification and becoming on whose repression the myth of the autonomous, rational subject, who makes his world and himself, is based. It is an anti-ideological mirror, for this expanded field of mimetic social-related- ness is not part of the grand narrative of "production," according to which we are what we are through tool-use and the impression of form onto formless matter. The tie between capitalism and primatology begins with the disciplinary imperative of work, a connection developed by Ines Doujak, in her collabo- ratively written essay in this book, for the twentieth century and the biblical banishment from paradise which condemned humans to work. In the eight- eenth century an early illustration of great apes ties their speechlessness to the refusal to work: "The Javanese, however, say they can indeed speak, they only refrain from doing so in order that one does not force them to work."[21] This is the opposite strategy to that of Kafka's ape; it allows them to stay outside the "human" collective and the coercive "social contract" of productionist ideology and discipline, while for Kafka's "Rotpeter," learning to speak is an adaptive strategy, a case of the strategic use of the mimetic marshaled against his own milieu.[22] However, it certainly turns the tables nicely using the weapon of speechlessness.

The repression of animality, the repression of mimetic ritual; our own civilizational arsenal of myths and disciplinary institutions is built on these founda- tions, which enabled the potentially anarchic field of mediality to be enclosed and governed by a state and a legal framework, providing in turn the backdrop for factory discipline, among other things. The anthro- pologist Barbara Glowczewski has pointed out the degree to which gesture had been identified with an- imality, and hence separated from language proper: Everything that did not possess language in the linguistic sense was deemed "animal." According to Glowczewski, the Vatican banned deaf people from using sign language for over a century.[23] Frans de Waal adds that the potential for great apes acquiring the ability to speak was deemed to be such a threat that the Société de Linguistique de Paris banned all re- search into the origins of language in 1866.[24] However, the repression in these cases simply concerns other forms of being social, other forms of being, other forms of developing potentiality. The kernel of this repression is power over representation and meaning, a "limitation of possibilities."[25]

Gesture, of course, is central to art, as it lies at the core of nonlinguistic communication and the riddles of embodiment. Gesture leads us into the primordial stratum of mediality, the *sine qua non* of meaning. It speaks of a unity of content and expres- sion, of an "expressive substance" that ultimately causes dualist conceptions of the world to implode from within.[26]

Following Kafka's lead, there is a critical mimesis that leads us to an understanding of the politics of aping. Accordingly, the simian mirror is a mirror that reveals denied mediality, a subversive mirror with the ability to undermine the stable order and the syntax of knowledge and truth. "How are we to think about those decisive moments of physical and affective communication that precede and exceed interpretation, the sensation that comes before and goes beyond logic but is somehow logic's operative basis?"[27] This is the simian mirror as critical mimesis with the power to conflate and expose difference, functioning as a "reversed sign," a signifier that introduces slippage into the realm of signification. "The sensation that comes before and goes beyond logic,"[28] and the gesture and slippage of meaning; these are of course key elements of both aesthetics and art. Susan Buck-Morss has convincingly shown that philosophers have been so wary of "aesthetics" because it has little to do with the "trinity of Art, Beauty and Truth," belonging instead to the realm of the nervous system and "animal instincts," to the biological residue, to that part of the body that does not fully dissolve in the symbolic order and hence provides a locus of possible resistance.[29] In this realm of "the aesthetic," which is so intimately tied to embodiment, it is impossible not to assume a stance based on the primacy of mediality, rather than noncommunicative inert matter. It is impossible to understand—to use the language of Aby Warburg—how the transhistorical facts of the "social psychology" (his term for the modality specific to culture) have been coined at the margins in an initial process of distinction which constitutes the "phobic origins" of the civilizational process, without returning to the point "before the division."[30]

Thus we arrive at the expanded field of semiosis and sociability shared between the "ape" cast as a *Kippbild*, and "art." Of course, this proximity has often been noted, and Aby Warburg's endorsement of Darwin's *The Expression of the Emotions in Man and Animals* is frequently invoked in this context, namely that there is a fundamental continuity between animal and human means of communication. According to Erwin Panofsky, other-than-human creatures also use signs, but without grasping the logic of signifying. They also create imagery, but without grasping the process of making images. Art, for Panofksy, means dissociating the idea of the function from the means by which it is carried out. He is one of many who tried to grasp the human difference through the account of the Other. But he is also one of many who tried to come to terms with the wicked relation between the process of signifying, and the possible knowledge of this process.[31]

Hence art's use of the ape motif is not restricted to allegories of "mere aping,"[32] rather, it articulates a "politics of aping" that far exceeds imitation. By dissociating signs from functions and unleashing what is an excess of meaning or a potentially anarchic mediality, art throws us back onto the background assumptions that we carry with us at all times, onto the tacit dimension of bodily knowledge and the historical contingency of the senses. Art is the "simian mirror" that possesses the unique power to produce knowledge of the processes of signification and its medial basis, while also undermining fixed positions of the knower and known.

Art connects us back to the semiotic surplus, the realm of "biological potentiality," to a realm of polysemic play and "fiction" as an ontological realm in which the evolution of sociality is forged, and in which thinking can also be conceived as sensing, and sensing as semiosis. Aesthetics, once it is released from the evolutionary prison that only recognizes the pressures of natural selection, is a field of this kind of expanded semiosis. Indeed, there are increasing numbers of scientists who highlight the importance of the individual experience of animal organisms that have the power to change patterns of behavior and the "interpretation" of genetic code.[33] There has been a general recognition of variability in natural processes, the majority of which are attributable to "individual differences in experience"; this is something that even Edward Wilson, the founder of sociobiology, admits.[34] Authors such as Stephen J. Gould have opposed Wilson's otherwise deterministic and reductive sociobiology, insisting on the importance of evolutionary "by-products" and exuberances. There are those who, like Elisabeth Grosz,[35] recognize in Darwinian "sexual selection" an "inventive animal exuberance attaching to qualities of life, with no direct use-value or survival value."[36] Others have attempted to integrate forms of behavior into the evolutionary explanation that in the past had been completely excluded. This assigns them an evolutionary "function," namely the human interest in "fictional experience (in all media and genres) and other products of the imagination."[37] John Tooby and Leda Cosmides, representing an "evolutionary aesthetics," speak of aesthetics as the realm of the ludic, in which actions are not directly functional, consequential, or applicable to real-life situations.

Others see in animal play a form of metacommunication as a necessary basis of sociality, providing the "conditions of [human] language."[38] Accordingly, play is always playing with meaning, with bodily relations and imaginative scenarios. Play establishes a metacommunicative milieu, in which it is the aesthetic dimension of gesture that, by signifying actions without actually putting them into practice, "performs possibility."

> The prehuman, preverbal, embodied logic of animal play is already essentially language-like. It is effectively, enactively linguistic *avant la lettre*, as humans say in French. Why then shouldn't the opposite also be the case: that human language is essentially animal, from the point of view of the ludic capacities it carries, so intimately bound up with its metalinguistic powers? Think of humor. Why not consider human language a reprise of animal play, raised to a higher power? Or say that it is actually in language that the human reaches its highest degree of animality?[39]

Again, turning the tables on the narrative direction of the "anthropological machine" provides fertile ground for thinking sociality differently. It opens up our world to an expanded field of sociality, to 'domains that are extra-linguistic, non-human, biological, technological, aesthetic, etc."[40] It is the realm that Félix Guattari addressed in his concepts of enunciative assemblage and "machinic animism."[41] And it is a realm in which "bodily dispositions are semiotic even though they are not necessarily conscious or discursive. Semiosis is always embodied, even though some sign processes are more so than others. Furthermore, all sensing is already semiotic, even though it is not language like."[42] It is a field that witnesses a gradual re-assessment of "language" as a system of expression that pertains to all the senses, to what it means to be-in-a-medium.

This anti-Cartesian turn towards an expanded sociability and communicability, however, must be understood within a wider context. The current surge of animal studies is part of a larger, if somewhat polyphonous tendency that hints at larger tectonic shifts in the epistemic and ontological architectures. According to media philosopher Erich Hörl, we are currently experiencing a transformation that "implies a momentous redefinition of our entire objective condition and the place that we as subjects occupy therein."[43] Hörl speaks of how technology, having become environmental in the form of ubiquitous computing, undoes previous ontological hierarchies, and with it our "sense culture." The process of "experiencing the world and constructing sense" now takes place in the "technological condition," in which "human and non-human actors" are constantly merged and in which sense is produced "before the difference between subject and object." Quoting Serge Moscovici's work from the 1960s, Hörl describes what he terms the "technological condition" as the third historical stage of three "natural states". The first is an "organic natural order," in which humans give shape and meaning to external, inert, and passive matter: this is man the toolmaker. The second is the "mechanical natural state," in which humans are likened to machines and work becomes "instrumental," and at the center of which is "the transmission mechanism, which serves as the intermediary between the machine tool and the power source." The "third, cybernetic natural state" is dominated by "information and communication technologies," which the old opposition of form and matter no longer adequately describes. It is no longer "the forming of objects" that defines "work," but what Hörl calls "transinstrumental control performance." Contrary to Moscovici, Hörl notes that in this third condition it is not only the very concept of "work" that loses its central cultural position, but that we are experiencing a shift in the status and sense of objects (towards "active, communicating objects"), and undergoing a veritable technological "displacement of sense." Speaking with Félix Guattari (the "first theoretician of a technological unconscious"), we are entering into "a new post-significative order of sense." No longer can the unconscious be understood "in the traditional psychoanalytic framework derived from the culture of writing or as a matter of intrapsychic entities or linguistic signifiers, but rather only as assemblages of different semiotic and pragmatic dimensions that come from the most diverse, existential, media-technologically saturated territories."[44]

Erich Hörl suspects that the "ecologization" of thought has its roots not in a new approach and relation to nature, but in the media-technological "condition," in the "becoming-environmental" of technology. Is our contemporary "animism,"[45] the tendency to articulate flat ontologies, and the interest in animal studies, a mere symptom of a becoming-technological of the human socius, which changes our own relation to animal nature? And if so, in what way is this animal nature being changed?

Inevitably, primatology's shift toward sociality must be conceived as part of the larger turn towards the "posthuman." And we should remain mindful that a new ontological approach to the animal has not yet resulted in a change in the status of animals in human societies. As J. M. Coetzee insists, "we have been able to afford to cultivate compassion" only since we won the war that we had waged against the animals. It is a rather recent victory, only made possible "when we invented guns" after millions of years, but a definitive one.[46]

The discursive tendency to embrace expanded sociability makes us blind to the fault lines and frontiers of contemporary society—the process by which the socius itself is remade in the image of the machine. The link that ties primate bodies to exploitation and productionism is all but untied, even if the frontier of rationalization and valorization has moved deeper into the very essence of "socialness." The immediate historical backdrop to the current algorithmization of the social, which enforces a new alliance between animism and capital, is cybernetics. And it was cybernetics that pioneered the approach to the study of primate society as a "semiotic project." As Donna Haraway comments, the "cybernetic approach bridged linguistics, social psychology, biology, and increasingly, technology and computing

through the overarching concept of communication."[47] This emphasis on communication and the primacy of sociality, however, can play out in two entirely different directions: one that focuses on individuals, variation, and "biological potentiality," in the way that semiosis and interpretation give shape to forms of life and ever-changing milieus; and another, which circumvents individual experience and symbolic meaning altogether and instead computes patterns of interaction. One of the main discoveries of information theory was that brains are not necessary for communication. Sociality is currently being remade on a grand scale through forms of algorithmic factorization, resulting in technological environments in which the world itself becomes our simian mirror, at a time in which we increasingly inhabit our own digital bubble, encountering our own patterns, profiles, and preferences everywhere. However, underlying these personalized animistic worlds is the computation of "evolution" itself—the connection, for instance, that ties algorithms derived from game theory (used by the military and financial markets to predict behavior) to Evolutionary Stable Strategies that treat biosystems like "markets." Narrative has surrendered its power to the machine—which makes it no less powerful and dangerous in social realms. The ideologues of this techno-animism want to believe that evolution is increasingly in our hands, that in the algorithmically enforced world the combination of prediction and imaginary scenarios has the power to produce a new world. Hence the growing interest in primate sociality and phenomena of empathy not only reflects a shift away from ignorance and recognition, it is also indicative of the techno-economic frontier. If, as Donna Haraway states, "how meanings are constituted is the essence of politics"—for meanings cannot be wished into existence but are becoming enacted as materialized practice—then today's "material" is no longer "matter" in the old sense, but the "matter" of which sociality is made.

1   See Donna J. Haraway, "Animal sociology and a Natural Economy of the Body Politic," Parts I & II, *Signs: Journal for Women in Culture and Society*, vol. 4, no. 1, autumn 1978, pp. 21–60.

2   Bruno Latour, *We Have Never Been Modern*, tr. Catherine Porter (Cambridge, Massachussetts: Harvard University Press, 1993), pp. 32–35.

3   Solly Zuckerman, *The Social Life of Monkeys and Apes* (New York: Harcourt, Brace & Co., 1932).

4   See Alison Jolly, "The Bad Old Days of Primatology?" in *Primate Encounters: Models of Science, Gender, and Society*, Shirley C. Strum and Linda Marie Fedigan (eds.) (Chicago: University of Chicago Press, 2000), pp. 71–84; Donna Haraway, *Primate Visions: Gender, Race, and Nature in the World of Modern Science* (New York: Routledge, 1989), p. 101; Shirley C. Strum and Bruno Latour, "Redefining the social link: from baboons to humans," *Social Science Information*, vol. 26, no. 4, 1987, pp. 783–802; Hans Kummer, *In Quest of the Sacred Baboon: A Scientist's Journey*, tr. M. Ann Biederman-Thorson (Princeton: Princeton University Press, 1995).

5   See Tim Ingold, "Becoming Persons: Consciousness and Sociality in Human Evolution," *Cultural Dynamics*, vol. 4, no. 3, 1991, pp. 355–378.

6   Giorgio Agamben, *The Open: Man and Animal*, tr. Kevin Attell (Stanford: Stanford University Press, 2004), p. 35.

7   Referring to the conjunction between body and soul, living things and logos, animal nature and social or divine element. See Agamben, *The Open*, p. 16.

8   Ibid.

9   Eduardo Viveiros de Castro, "Exchanging Perspectives: The Transformation of Objects into Subjects in Amerindian Ontologies," *Common Knowledge*, vol. 10, no. 3, 2004, p. 465.

10   Gerald Weiss, "Campa Cosmology," *Ethnology*, vol. 11, no. 2, 1972, pp. 169–170.

11   De Castro, "Exchanging Perspectives," p. 465.

12   Donna Haraway, *Simians, Cyborgs, and Women: The Reinvention of Nature* (New York: Routledge, 1991), p. 98.

13   Frans de Waal, *The Ape and the Sushi Master: Cultural Reflections of a Primatologist* (New York: Basic Books, 2001), p. 69.

14   Cord Riechelmann, "An Ape Alone Is Not an Ape," in this volume.

15   Shirley C. Strum and Linda M. Fedigan, "Changing Views of Primate Society: A Situated North American View," in *Primate Encounters: Models of Science, Gender, and Society*, Strum and Fedigan (eds.) (Chicago: University of Chicago Press, 2000), p. 17.

16   Stephen J. Gould, "Biological Potentiality vs. Biological Determinism," in *Ever Since Darwin* (New York: W.W. Norton, 1977), pp. 251–259.

17   See Stefan Willer, " 'Imitation of Similar Beings': Social Mimesis as an Argument in Evolutionary Theory around 1900," *History and Philosophy of the Life Sciences*, vol. 31, no. 2, 2009, p. 209.

18   Michael Taussig, *Defacement: Public Secrecy and the Labor of the Negative* (Stanford: Stanford University Press, 1999), p. 5 [italics in original].

19   Donna J. Haraway, *When Species Meet* (Minneapolis: University of Minnesota Press, 2008), p. 26.

20   Ibid.

21   Christianus Emmanuel Hoppius, "Vom Thiermenschen," in *Des Ritter Carl von Linné Auserlesene Abhandlungen aus der Naturgeschichte, Physik und Arzney wissenschaft*, Carl Linnaeus (Leipzig: A. F. Böhme, 1776), p. 66.

22   See Willer, "Imitation of Similar Beings," pp. 209–211.

23   See the interview with Barbara Glowczewski as part of the long-term audiovisual research project *Assemblages* by Angela Melitopoulos and Maurizio Lazzarato, 2010. See also the transcript at http://www.e-flux.com/journal/assemblages-felix-guattari-and-machinic-animism.

24   See Frans de Waal, *The Ape and the Sushi Master: Cultural Reflections of a Primatologist*, (New York: Basic Books, 2001), p. 32.

25   Charles Sanders Peirce, *The Essential Peirce: Selected Philosophical Writings*, vol. 1, Nathan Houser and Christian Kloesel (eds.) (Bloomington: Indiana University Press, 1992), pp. 323–324.

26   Louis Hjelmslev, *Prolegomena to a Theory of Language*, tr. Francis J. Whitfield (Madison: University of Wisconsin Press, 1969), p. XX; see also the critical rereading by Felix Guattari, *Cartographies schizoana-lytiques* (Paris: Galilee, 1989).

27   Kenneth Surin, "The Sovereign Individual and Michael Taussig's Politics of Deface-ment," *Nepantla: Views from South*, vol. 2, no. 1, 2001, p. 205.

28   Ibid.

29   Susan Buck-Morss, "Aesthetics and Anaesthetics: Walter Benjamin's Artwork Essay Reconsidered," *October*, vol. 62, 1992, pp. 3–41, here pp. 6–7.

30   Aby Warburg, "The Absorption of the Expressive Values of the Past," tr. Matthew Rampley, *Art in Translation*, vol. 1, no. 2, 2009, pp. 273–283.

31   See Erwin Panofsky, "The History of Art as a Humanistic Discipline," in *The Meaning of the Humanities*, T. Greene (ed.) (Princeton: Princeton University Press, 1940), pp. 89–118; reprinted as the introduction to Panofsky's *Meaning in the Visual Arts* (Chicago:
University of Chicago Press, 1955), pp. 1–25, here p. 5.

32   Antonia Ulrich, "Äffen und NachschAff-en," kunsttexte.de, no. 2, 2005, http://www.kunsttexte.de/index.php?id=711&idartikel-=12359&ausgabe=12136&zu=121&L=1.

33   See Stuart A. Altmann & Jeanne Altmann, "The transformation of behaviour field studies,"*Animal Behaviour*, vol. 65, no. 3, 2003, pp. 413–423, here p. 423.

34   Edward O. Wilson, *The Insect Societies* (Cambridge, Massachusetts: Belknap Press, 1971, p. 165), quoted by Stuart A. Altmann & Jeanne Altmann, ibid., p. 417.

35   Elizabeth Grosz, *Becoming Undone: Darwinian Reflections on Life, Politics, and Art* (Durham: Duke University Press, 2011).

36   Brian Massumi, *What Animals Teach Us about Politics*, Durham: Duke University Press, 2014, p. 2.

37   Leda Cosmides and John Tooby, "Does Beauty Build Adapted Minds?" *SubStance: A Review of Theory and Literary Criticism*, vol. 30, nos. 1/2, 2001 (Special Issue: "On the Origin of Fictions"), pp. 6–25, here p. 7.

38   Massumi, *What Animals Teach Us about Politics*, p. 8.

39   Ibid. p. 8.

40   Félix Guattari, *Chaosmosis: An Ethico-Aesthetic Paradigm*, (Bloomington: Indiana University Press, 1995), p. 24.

41   See Angela Melitopoulos and Maurizio Lazzarato, "Machinic Animism," in *Animism* vol. I, Anselm Franke (ed.) (Berlin: Sternberg Press, 2010).

42   Eduardo Kohn, "How Dogs Dream: Amazonian natures and the politics of transspecies engangement, *American Ethnologist*, vol. 34, no. 1, 2007, pp. 3–24, here p. 19, footnote 10.

43   Erich Hörl, "The Technological Condition," tr. Anthony Enns, *Parrhesia*, no. 22, 2015, pp. 1–15, here p. 7, http://www.parrhesiajournal.org/parrhesia22/parrhesia 22_horl.pdf.

44   Ibid., p. 10.

45   N. Katherine Hayles, "RFID: Human Agency and Meaning in Information-Intensive Environments," *Theory, Culture & Society*, vol. 26, nos. 2/3, 2009, p. 48, referenced by Hörl, ibid., p. 9.

46   J. M. Coetzee, *The Lives of Animals*, Amy Gutmann (ed.) (Princeton: Princeton University Press, 2001), p. 59.

47   Haraway, *Primate Visions*, p. 101.

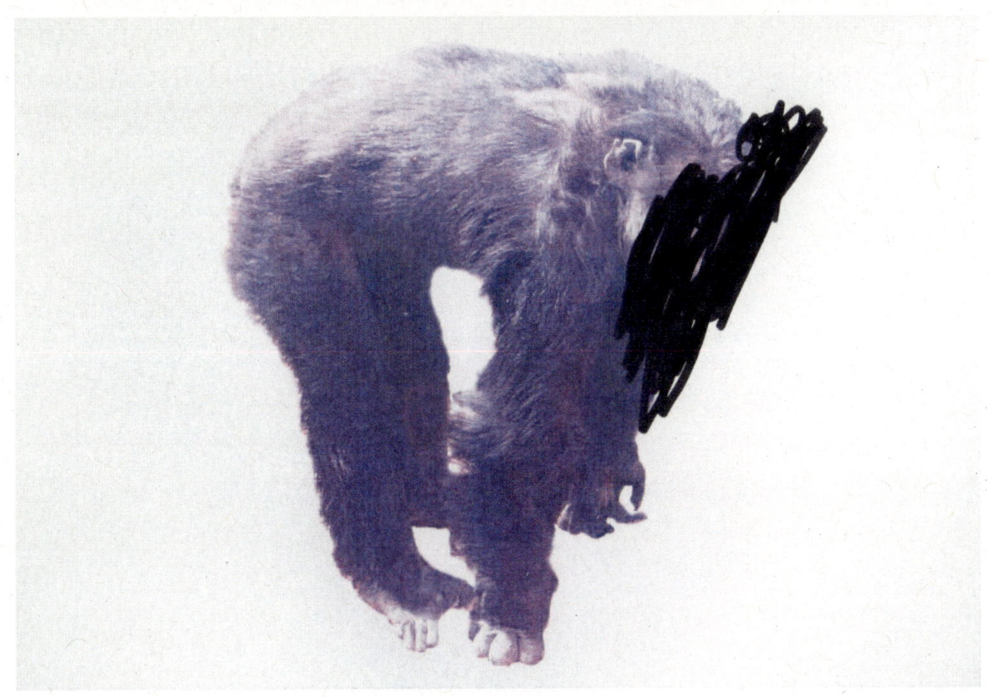

Image taken from an article by Aya Saito on drawing behavior of chimpanzees compared with that of human children.

WHERE THE HELL IS THE EXIT TO THIS FIELD

ON THE CONTINUED RELEVANCE OF DONNA HARAWAY'S HISTORY OF PRIMATOLOGICAL KNOWLEDGE

Astrid Deuber-Mankowsky

PRIMATE VISIONS
I want this book to be interesting for many audiences, and pleasurable and disturbing for all of us. In particular, I want this book to be responsible to primatologists, to historians of science, to cultural theorists, to the broad left, anti-racist, anti-colonial, and women's movements, to animals, and to lovers of serious stories.[1]

It was with these unusual wishes that the biologist and historian of science Donna Haraway delivered her study of almost five hundred pages on the history of primatology to the public in 1989. The fruit of ten years of intensive research, Haraway's *Primate Visions: Gender, Race, and Nature in the World of Modern Science* did in fact do more than any other publication to bring primatology to the attention of cultural and media studies. *Primate Visions* has proved a continuing source of inspiration for those studying culture and media, providing an introduction to the rich, diverse, and highly contested world of primatology and its objects of study. It has opened the door to chimpanzees, gorillas, orangutans, baboons, gibbons, and langurs; to their habitats in Africa, Asia, and South America; and to the historically momentous activities of laboratories situated in research institutions and universities across the United States.

It was true that *National Geographic* documentaries and movies on Jane Goodall and her chimpanzees in Tanzania, Dian Fossey and her fight for the mountain gorillas in Rwanda, and Birutė Galdikas and her research on orangutans in Borneo had already been presented to the broader consciousness and the media-consuming public before *Primate Visions* appeared in print. The images and stories of these female primatologists had been part of US-American popular culture since the 1960s. *Gorillas in the Mist* (Michael Apted, USA 1988), an Oscar-nominated biopic on Dian Fossey starring Sigourney Weaver, had been released the year before the publication of *Primate Visions*. The trailblazing 1965 documentary *Miss Goodall and the Wild Chimpanzees* had kicked off a series of TV specials produced by the National Geographic Society. And the documentary *Primate*, to cite one last example, a cinéma-vérité film directed by Frederick Wiseman in 1975 on the Yerkes National Primate Research Center in Atlanta, Georgia, had already presented the research laboratory as a cybernetic organism, designed to produce a controlled, rational, and reproductive system of knowledge in which anthropoids and prosimians functioned as data sources.

What was new in Haraway's *Primate Visions*, however, was the history of the links between primate research and the influential *National Geographic Society* on the one hand, and the industry of the military and space exploration program on the other and space exploration on the other. What was new was her analysis of the history of the imagined scenarios, the hopes for a better world and the fears of nuclear catastrophe, which were all associated with primary research on primates in the postwar era in the United States. What was new was the evidence indicating the extent to which the history of primatology was linked to the production and reproduction of differences along the power axes of race, class, and gender. And, finally, what was new was the proof of the degree to which the gender of the mostly white scientists shaped research on primates, leading up to the claim that primatology in the mid-1980s could be described as a genre of feminist theory.

In an analysis that was both vivid and carefully argued, Haraway showed that the important themes
and concerns of modern North America were reflected in the bodies and lives of animals. But monkeys
and apes act not only as mirrors for humans; Haraway emphasizes that their meaning is more than
symbolic, for they simultaneously serve researchers
as tools. As laboratory animals they have been—
and continue to be essential for basic research in
physiology, behavioral science, and the investigation
of social organizations. Their nervous systems and
reproductive systems provide the raw material
for fundamental biomedical research. Alluding to the
title of the famous 1925 book in which Robert Yerkes,
founder of experimental biopsychology and creator
of the primatology labs at Yale University, describes
his behavioral observations of two chimpanzees,
Haraway characterizes primates as "almost human."[2]
Like a picture puzzle, the word "almost" conceals the
ambivalence of presenting monkeys and apes, and
especially hominids, of course, both as mirror images
of humans and as animals and thus as the nonhuman
Other. Ascribing to its subject the status of being
'almost human," primatology was predestined to conduct research that promised to lead to a better understanding of the origin and nature of human beings
and simultaneously contribute to a better future
for them.

After World War II, with the rise of cybernetics
and the arrival of information science in the lab,
communication between organisms and machines
also became a central concern for primatological
research. Within this paradigm, communication was
understood as a medium of control, and organisms
and living beings were addressed much like machines
as self-maintaining systems. As a result, the boundaries between humans, machines, and animals col-
lapsed in dramatic fashion. As Haraway shows, where
before there had been allegedly natural differences,
the battles that now commenced featured recon-
stituted differences of an entirely different kind.
The branch of primatology that was starting to focus
on cognition and learning saw children, nonhuman
primates, and artificial intelligences as "almost minds"
that all had "almost human reason" at their disposal.
Even though primatology implicitly but persistently

dealt with the issue of what constitutes the status
of a fully human being, Haraway emphasized that the
discipline never posed the question of who or what
should be afforded "fully human status."

By making this complex network of relations visible,
Haraway's book granted cultural studies access to
the world and history of primatology. The majority of
both male and female primatologists, however, rejected her work. They felt that Haraway challenged
the authority of their science with her deconstructive
procedures and provocative combination of story-
telling and popular culture; of science, economics,
and politics; of the search for truth and the projection
of desires; and of knowledge and science fiction.
Believing that they were not being taken seriously,
they found the book "infuriating." In their eyes,
Haraway tried "to move physical anthropology (specifically primatology) into the realm of literary criticism,"
as a review in *American Journal of Primatology* put it
shortly after the publication of *Primate Visions*.[3]

The review in question is entitled "Partisan Primatology." The author, Susan Cachel, a professor of
physical anthropology and human evolution at Rutgers
University, was familiar with the quantitative procedures and data collection upon which research practice in primatology was based. Drawing upon her
experience as a scientist, Cachel concedes that it is
not easy to develop good research strategies and
produce adequate explanations for data captured in
the lab. And yet, as Cachel argues against Haraway,
for this very reason one should not rely on myth-pro-
ducing stories if one does not want to give up any
claim to being scientifically sound. Yet giving up this
claim was precisely *not* what the professor in the
renowned departments of the History of Consciousness and Feminist Studies at The University of
California, Santa Cruz, wanted to do. Haraway's goal
was not to abandon science. When she expressed
the hope that her work would be in the interest
of primatology, she had meant it in earnest. Haraway
wanted to contribute to a "better" science.
But what form would an improved science take?

A COMPLEX LITERATURE OF SURVIVAL
Primate Visions was not only the first carefully and
comprehensively researched history of primatological

knowledge in the United States in the twentieth century, it was also the first work of its kind to take into account the contested situation in which the young discipline found itself in the postwar era in the United States and which was charged in equal measure with hopes and expectations. Occupying the border zones between psychiatry and zoology, psychology and physical anthropology, behavioral science and the natural sciences, primatology was influenced by the cold war and placed in the service of exploring outer space, but it also stood at the center of desires for a better world and harmony with nature. The "almost human" subjects of primatology similarly traversed a liminal space marked by ambivalence and desire. The primates were, as Haraway shows with great sensitivity, part of a large research laboratory in which scientists influenced by cybernetics applied new information technologies in order to investigate the behavior and communication of living organisms and social organizations in both the closed spaces of research institutions and the open laboratories of natural habitats, i.e. out in the field. In the twentieth century, monkeys and apes occupied, as Haraway convincingly demonstrates, the border regions between the "potent mythic poles" of nature and culture.[4]

Haraway openly admits that her interest in primates stems from the importance attached to them in Western society. Primates "are popular, important, marvelously varied, and controversial."[5] Moreover, all of them—including human beings—are threatened. As the historian of science boldly claims, primatology in the late twentieth century may be understood as "part of a complex survival literature in global, nuclear culture."[6] While primatologists found the comparison of their science with sciencefiction literature in the late twentieth century irritating, it was, for Haraway, an expression of the high expectation she had of primatology as a mode of thinking and interacting with others. The others in question are not only the primates, but all agents female, male, or neuter who are viewed as nonhuman or almost human, including the Earth, which is of course no less threatened than the primates.

Through its research on monkeys and apes, primatology promises to provide insights into the origin of humanity. Origin stories, however, also always include statements about the future of the phenomena to which they give rise, as critical philosophy since Kant has shown in its modern and postmodern versions. Seen from this perspective, it is only consistent that, as Haraway analyzes the field as a site where the biopolitics of difference and identity are elaborated and contested for the members of industrial and postindustrial cultures, she also reads the texts of primatology as science fiction. Haraway thereby makes clear that she regards the analysis of implicit statements about the future of humanity in primatological texts as part and parcel of her task as a historian of science. If she orients her work towards the concerns of antiracist, anticolonial, and feminist movements, she does so in accordance with the methodological demand that the colonialist, racist, and sexist presuppositions unthinkingly embedded in the foundational history of primatology should be countered with a different, heterogeneous history that also respects the nonhuman primates in their differences.

PRIMATOLOGY: A FEMINIST SCIENCE?
Until the mid-1960s, the model of superiority, aggressiveness, and competitive behavior amongst male primates guided the reconstruction of the origins of man in primatology. Female primates were not even investigated as such. They appeared in primatology only as part of the nuclear family and in the union between mother and child.[7] It is not difficult to see how this model was to a large extent influenced by the patriarchal gender order of Western societies. In this early phase, primatology unthinkingly reproduced the idea that the female gender revolves entirely around the reproduction of the species and lacks its own proper history.

Sarah Blaffer Hrdy, a feminist primatologist, social biologist, and leading behavioral scientist, was not the first to expound the problematic nature of this view, but she did enjoy huge cross-disciplinary success when she published her study *The Women That Never Evolved* in 1981. The title of her book alludes to the fact that mainstream primatology had simply ignored the role of female primates in evolution. By way of counterargument, Blaffer Hrdy demonstrates that female monkeys and apes are not at all passive. Like male primates, the females seek a competitive advantage, are sexually active, choose their partners, compete with other females for rank and resources, and defend their offspring to the death. At the same time, female primates mate with the killers of their children if successful reproduction depends on it; they cooperate with other female animals to defend themselves, and not only do they accept promiscuity, but they also enjoy it themselves if the circumstances afford. Blaffer Hrdy's research led her to conclude that female primates are nowhere near as suppressed as they are within the species of *Homo sapiens*! Her advice to human women: they should study the behavior of their female relatives and acquaint themselves with their biological heritage so that they learn what they can do and take their fate into their own hands. Blaffer Hrdy's feminist intervention picks up on the sociobiological turn in North American behavioral biology, which no longer concentrated on the group but on the behavior of individuals. Sociobiology assumed that the goal of successfully reproducing one's genes determines this behavior. Evidently, the corresponding cost–benefit calculations in socio-biology were very much in tune with the neoliberal credo that was beginning to spread at the time in Western capitalist societies. Haraway highlights the feminist and scientific contributions of Blaffer Hrdy, but not without also pointing out the correlations between the applications of a calculus of optimization in both sociobiology and neoliberal late capitalism. In addition, Haraway comments critically on the fact that Blaffer Hrdy presupposes sexual difference as a biological fact and does not include, in her own analysis, the sex/gender system as a scientific con-struction, i.e. both an object and a condition of knowledge.

Blaffer Hrdy was only one among many other women primatologists in the late 1970s who began to concentrate on female primates in their research. Only a few of these primatologists described them-selves as feminist, but many of them agreed with the criteria that a feminist critique of the natural scienc-es had elaborated for the purpose of a feminist science: reflexivity; the consideration of the female standpoint; the reconceptualization of nature; the dissociation from dualism and reductionism; the understanding of scientific insight as a means of emancipation. "Reflexivity" means that scientific research takes into account the context in which it takes place. The reconceptualization of nature aims to understand nature as active, complex, and holistic. And dualistic and reductionist views should be super-seded by an outlook according to which the elements of nature form a continuum, rather than binary oppositions. The change that a significant number of female scientists in the United States ushered in with their primatological research in the early 1980s led Haraway to describe primatology as a "genre of feminist theory."[8]

PRIMATES IN THE MIRROR

The term "good science" appears twice within the (almost) 500-page-long *Primate Visions*. Both pas-sages appear in the third part of the book entitled "The Politics of Being Female: Primatology Is a Genre of Feminist Theory", in a chapter devoted to the works of the primatologist Linda Marie Fedigan. Today, Fedigan is a professor and Canada Research Chair in primatology and bioanthropology at the University of Calgary, and the past executive editor of the *American Journal of Primatology*. What was it, then, in Haraway's opinion that distinguished Fedigan's work of the 1970s and early 1980s as "good science"? Fedigan, who had initially studied cultural anthropology, did her PhD supervised by a student of the influential anthropologist and paleoanthro-pologist Sherwood Washburn. Her thesis was a study of social roles in a group of Japanese Arashiyama monkeys that had been brought from Japan to the United States in 1972 for research purposes. Besides the monkeys, the Japanese scientists also gave their colleagues in the United States genealogical charts and other data that they had collected over the course of eighteen years. Fedigan was thus able to base her research on an extensive set of data. In 1982, her PhD thesis appeared as a book under the title *Primate Paradigms: Sex Roles and Social Bonds*. As Fedigan told Haraway, however, she had originally wanted to call the publication *Primate Mirrors: Reflections on Sex Differences in Behaviour*.

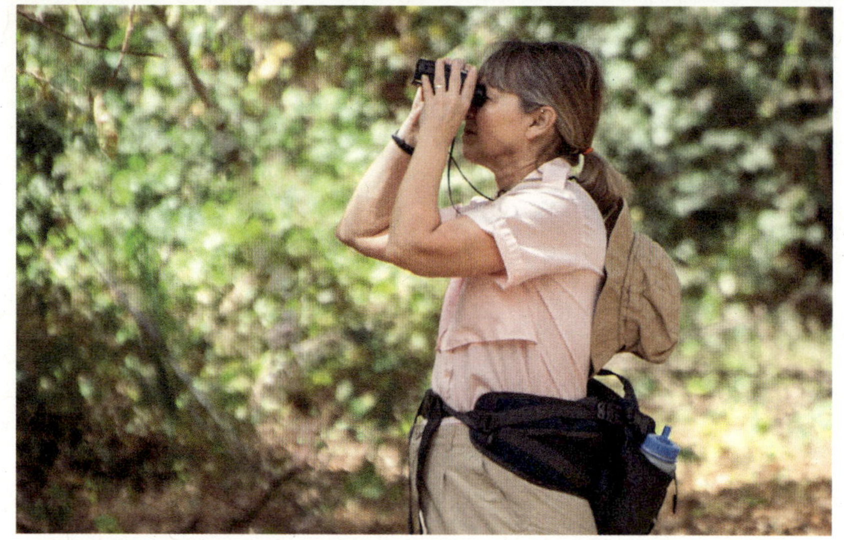

Even though Fedigan could not get the title accepted, it was important for Haraway to mention it for the original title points towards the criteria that characterize good science in the latter's opinion. The title namely avoids the common conception that biology is the basis of culture. As Haraway emphasizes, employing the concept of a mirror instead highlights the process by which historically situated human scientists very actively polish the reflecting surface on which the fantasies of both their own societies and their own bodies return in the images they produce of the animals. The play with the metaphors of the mirror, reflection, and reflecting indicates Fedigan's sensitivity for the imaginative powers of language.

According to Haraway, Fedigan's work on the lives of primates is "good science" not only because it is based on a rich set of carefully collected data, but also because she is conscious of the great power of metaphors and well-told stories and develops her argument on a sound theoretical and epistemological basis. In light of this, Fedigan distances herself from the idea that the animals she researched were ontologically or epistemologically passive resources, i.e. raw material for the production of scientific knowledge. In a similar vein, she criticizes the view that sex is the raw material for gender, and nature the basis of culture. As a result of this critique, Fedigan

carefully distinguishes between the reference to sexual difference on the one hand, and statements about human nature on the other, which play such a central role in bioanthropological histories of the origin of humanity.

Haraway notes approvingly that Fedigan distinguishes between different kinds of public, not only in view of the difference between the more limited public of the scientific community and the wider nonscientific public of the media, but also in relation to the various standpoints and orientations within scientific disciplines. In the introduction to *Primate Paradigms,* Fedigan thus expresses the hope that her book will speak to primatologists as well as representatives of women's and gender studies. She addresses both groups as experts, which is a sign of her experience in interdisciplinary research. For Haraway, "good science" also means that Fedigan employs the sex/gender system as a category for the analysis of power relations, rather than as something that could undergird bioanthropological histories of the origin of human culture. To sum up, "good science" would thus be a research practice that not only carefully applies the rules and methods of the relevant scientific discipline, but also takes into account the cultural, medial, social, and gender conditions of its own standpoint. It would not conceive of nature as a passive resource, would avoid reductionism and dualism, support complexity and diversity, and be sensitive to the power of dramatic stories and well-chosen metaphors.

It is not difficult to recognize in this catalogue the criteria for a feminist scientific practice put forward by feminist critics of science, such as Sandra Harding, Evelyn Fox Keller, Ruth Hubbard, Ruth Bleier, Anne Fausto-Sterling, Londa Schiebinger, Jane Flax, Nancy Hartsock, Helen Longino, and of course Haraway herself. Does this mean that a good science would be a feminist science, and vice versa?

Eight years after Haraway's *Primate Visions*, Linda Marie Fedigan published an article entitled "Is Primatology a Feminist Science?"[9] Fedigan takes up Haraway's chapter on primatology as a genre of feminist theory and asks why most of her primatologist colleagues rejected the book after they had heard of it through reviews in journals devoted to their discipline. Fedigan points out that her colleagues appear not to know that the study received the highest praise and was lauded in many other periodicals, including specialist journals of feminist studies, the history of science, and cultural studies. Indeed, not only did Evelyn Fox Keller, Ruth Hubbard, and Elvira Scheich pen enthusiastic reviews, but Anne Fausto-Sterling, writing in the *Journal of the History of Biology*, even begins her assessment with the assertion that *Primate Visions* changed her life and is among the most important books of the past twenty years.[10]

Fedigan confirms in her article that primatology has not only become particularly gender sensitive and gender inclusive since the 1980s, but the discipline has also implemented the other criteria that produce good science according to a feminist point of view. What is responsible for these changes, according to Fedigan, is the fact that an exceptional number of women primatologists have taken their research in the direction of a behavioral–ecological paradigm. Even though only a few of these scientists would have described themselves as feminist, this paradigm shift has nonetheless led to a rethinking—and critique—of androcentric prejudices. The question of why primatology so unanimously rejected Haraway's book thus becomes all the more pressing. Fedigan mentions that she has read forty reviews by representatives of the field, which all agreed in their sharp criticism of *Primate Visions*. She explains this reaction with the conjecture that most primatologists must have spurned Haraway's thesis that primatology is a politics. In another essay, Fedigan offers a different explanation for the critical reaction from within primatology, and it is this second argument that I would like to pursue a bit further. According to Fedigan, primatologists first had to get used to the idea that both their science and they themselves had become an object of research, and that they were now also being observed by people with pens and notebooks.[11] Indeed, twenty-five years ago the history of science as well as science and technology studies were young disciplines, with which no one had had much experience. If Haraway described primatology as a politics, then she did so not from within the discipline, but from the perspective of an epistemologist and historian of science. The latter do not study the same object as the primatologist. Georges Canguilhem, the French philosopher and founder of the epistemology of life sciences, emphasized that the object of science has nothing in common with the object of epistemology. The object of the history of knowledge is the historicity of scientific discourse.[12] For Haraway, however, a "good" science would hold the epistemological view on its practices in high esteem and share it. As she emphasizes, the natural sciences are no less the result of historical and cultural processes than the humanities, which implies that the scientific production of facts is from the very beginning entangled with historically and culturally situated values. Making these implicit values legible is one of the tasks Haraway set for herself in writing the history of primatology. It constitutes the political dimension of her study and is all the more explosive since primatology is a science at the center of public interest that has ties to the histories of colonialism, Western technology, and human sciences.

DIFFRACTIONAL THEORY AS A TECHNIQUE OF SEEING

From a contemporary perspective, *Primate Visions* is impressive not only because of the experimental dimension of the writing, but also because of its belief in the creativity of thought. When Haraway refers to the movements of the antiauthoritarian left, antiracist groups, and women's liberation and combines their concerns with the call for a better science, then her book betrays the kind of optimism in regards to the potential of thought that was last seen in the writings of Foucault and Deleuze/Guattari. Just think of Michel Foucault's last lectures in the early 1980s and his description of "the living body of philosophy" as an " 'essay'—which should be understood as the assay or test by which [...] one undergoes changes, and not as the simplistic appropriation of others for the purpose of communication."[13] Or recall *A Thousand Plateaus*, the transgressive work published in 1980 that Deleuze and Guattari cowrote under the influence of strong extraparliamentary movements on the left and that even today is a cult book for students who ceaselessly try to conjoin thought and politics. Incidentally, Georges Canguilhem's epistemology and thought had left its mark on all three of them, on Foucault no less than on Deleuze and Guattari.

In *A Thousand Plateaus*, Deleuze and Guattari had already assembled materials from very different spheres. In a multilayered structure, the authors integrated literature, music, historical events, and philosophy, and drew on disciplines such as ethnology, linguistics, geography, and their respective histories. Deleuze and Guattari included aspects from the histories of technology and mathematics, and incorporated photographs and sketches in their book. Haraway, by comparison, also refers to popular culture and the histories of advertising, pulp fiction, and television in her history of knowledge. She develops her argument with the help of metaphors and thinks in terms of images. As she writes in the introduction to her book, "I have tried to fill *Primate Visions* with potent verbal and visual images."[14]

In Haraway's work on primatology, techniques of seeing, presenting, and visualizing increasingly come to the fore. As these techniques ranging from photography to the diorama, from the documentary film to the Hollywood movie, and from the advertising clip to the capture and presentation of data gained in importance, so did the metaphor of vision. Given the central importance afforded to seeing and techniques of visualization in the life sciences,

Haraway demands that good science—and a good historiography of the sciences—bear the responsibility for the generative power of visual practices. With this in mind, she suggests that the scientific practice of seeing and the production of visions associated with the imagery of reflection and mirroring back should be replaced by a different practice of seeing and reconstructing histories, viz. a practice based on the methodology concealed in the technical process of diffraction. Both reflection and diffraction point towards optics, i.e. the study of light, "related to seeing." While reflection describes the return of a wavefront at an interface between two different media, diffraction designates the phenomena that occur when a wave encounters an obstacle or a slit. Both reflection and diffraction have to do with visualization and refer to technical procedures that played an important role in the histories of physics and the life sciences in the twentieth century. As techniques of visualization, moreover, both processes relate to the etymology of the concept of theory, which goes back to the Greek noun *theōría*, meaning a looking at, a viewing, or investigation. The Greek noun, in turn, is derived from the verb *theōreîn*. *Théa* is the view, and *horãn* means seeing.

Thanks to the X-ray diffraction images of DNA taken by the physicist Rosalind Franklin at the beginning of the 1950s at King's College, London, diffraction became crucially important for molecular genetics and the resulting genetic and reproductive technologies. Diffraction served as the basis for James D. Watson and Francis Crick when they built their models of DNA from atomic building blocks and modified them until they were compatible with the pattern of Franklin's X-ray images. The model that fitted was the double helix structure. The key to Haraway's metaphorical reference to the process is the fact that diffraction, unlike reflection, does not produce copies, but patterns. Diffraction does not follow the model of representation. It is not based on the difference between original and copy, but instead deals with belatedness and the binding nature of events that have taken place elsewhere and are always already past.

By playfully contrasting reflection and diffraction as different technical modes of making something visible, Haraway changes the perspective on the relation between science and epistemology. She opens the view onto the interrelations between science, media *dispositifs*, technical apparatuses, the history of philosophy, the will to knowledge, and the effective power of images and metaphors. According to Haraway, diffraction patterns can be read as traces recording the history of interactions, interferences, and differences, and she concludes that: "Diffraction is about heterogeneous history."[15]

APES IN EDEN, APES IN SPACE

Primate Visions can be read as an entire collection of heterogeneous histories. The book seeks to make visible the interferences between primatology, on the one hand, and a set of diverse histories, on the other, including the histories of communications theory, computer science, and the cold war; postcolonialism, racism, and changes in gender relations; and the switch of scientific paradigms from positivism and functionalism to sociobiology and behavioral ecology. The interferences examined also include the imagined scenarios, the hopes and fantasies, which played into the work with simians and contributed to the various *dispositifs* for the investigation of their behavior. As Haraway seeks to show, these scenarios are modeled on salvation narratives that live on, in a secularized form, in politics, science, scientific communication, science fiction, economics, and the mass media.

"Apes in Eden, Apes in Space" is the title of the chapter in which Haraway narrates the reinvention of primatology under the banner of communication at the beginning of the 1960s. This is an era when the young Jane Goodall takes up contact with wild chimpanzees in the Tanzanian jungle, and Allen and Beatrice Gardner teach a captive female chimpanzee American sign language, or AMESLAN, while scientists in New Mexico train simians as cyborgs and launch them into outer space. This is an era when space travelers (as personified by Yuri Gagarin) and astrochimps (as personified by the chimpanzee Ham) at one end of the world explore outer space in order to guide a traumatized postwar world threatened by the nuclear bomb towards a new, unwritten future, while at the other end of the world female primatologists like Jane Goodall study the behavior of simians in their natural habitat in the African jungle in order to get to the bottom of the origins of humanity. This is an era when the ecosystem is invented and the colonization of outer space begins. Characteristic of Haraway's diffractional procedure is the fact that she follows the trail of the interferences between these events and in the end describes the patterns that hold them together. As she shows by way of a circuitous route, at one end of time and space wild chimpanzees modeled communication for a civilized humanity that was both ecologically threatened and simultaneously endangered the ecosystem, while at the other end the extraterrestrial chimpanzee helped construe social and technical cybernetic communication systems that were supposed to allow the very same humanity

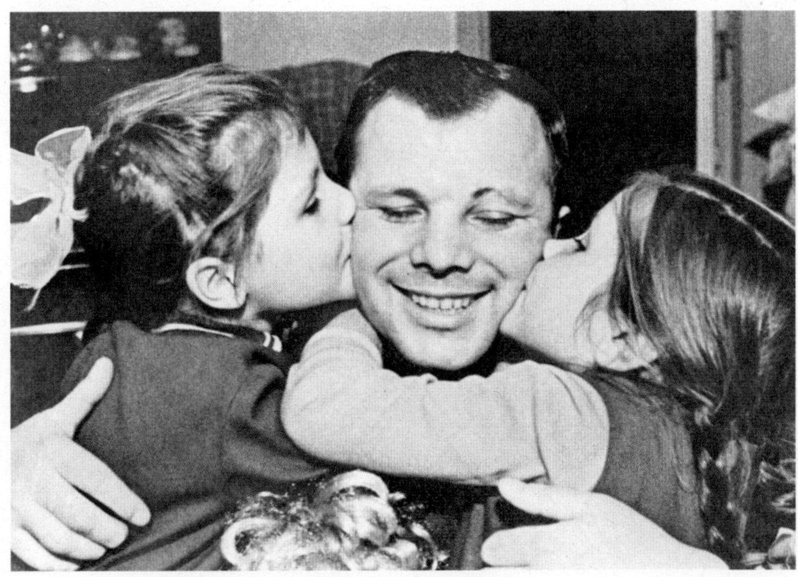

to escape into a better future made possible in the first place by the sociotechnical systems of the "information age."

It is interesting at this point to examine the case of Yuri Gagarin, the first cosmonaut and hero of the Soviet Union, who came from a family of simple farmers. On April 12, 1961, the twenty-seven-year-old Yuri Gagarin was the first human to travel into outer space, an occasion on which he turned towards the future and called for peace. During his orbit around the Earth he was promoted to major, and was subsequently dubbed the "Columbus of the Cosmos." Yet after his return he was only allowed to travel for propaganda purposes on behalf of socialism. Gagarin died in a plane crash in 1968 under circumstances that have never been fully explained.

"Circling the Earth, I marveled at the beauty of our planet. People of the world! Let us safeguard and enhance this beauty, not destroy it."

With these sentences, Yuri Gagarin gave expression to both the belief in progress and its fragility. As Haraway convincingly argues, it is precisely this ambivalence that links on the one hand the ecosystem and the fantasies revolving around it, and on the other hand outer space and the visions of the future associated with it. Thanks to his flight, Yuri Gagarin had acquired a star persona. He not only embodied the New Man and the heroism of socialism; as the "Columbus of the Cosmos" he was also the representative of a humanity that, 350 years after the conquest of America, was setting out to explore outer space and give itself a new future through the conquest of a new world. It is impossible to overestimate the role played by Gagarin as a hero of the Soviet Union and socialist space travel pioneer. Not only did he give interviews to newspapers, mostly in the socialist countries of the world, but he also appeared on television, and streets and schools were named for him throughout the Eastern Bloc.

And yet one thing was never mentioned on these propaganda trips: Yuri Gagarin was picked from all the other candidates not only because he had a calm demeanor, but also because he was short and therefore able to fit easily into a space capsule. Another thing that was never brought up was the fact that Gagarin the cosmonaut was in fact a cyborg.

Being a cyborg, however, is not compatible with the role of a hero, for cyborgs are complex self-regulating systems, and what matters for them are not heroic deeds, but rather functions and feedback. Cyborgs rely on control mechanisms and automated reactions instead of self-posited purposes and the autonomy of a self. As a cyborg, Gagarin had become part of a mechanical organism. After the Copernican Turn, Darwinism, and psychoanalysis, as Haraway aptly remarks, cybernetics and computer science inflicted a fourth narcissistic wound on humanity.

To be sure, the first cyborg was a hybrid creature consisting of a laboratory rat, an osmotic pump, and chemical substances periodically administered to the rat organism with the pump. However, the model for which Manfred E. Clynes and Nathan S. Kline invented the concept of the cyborg was addressed in regards to the space traveler. The hybrid creature—or rather, the feedback system—made up of a pump, pharmacology, and an organism was aimed at the biotechnical optimization of astronauts. The experiment was designed to test how organisms could be made more independent of their environment. What remained hidden behind the star persona of Yuri Gagarin was the kinship between the space traveler and the feedback systems called cyborgs. The affinity between astronaut and cyborg becomes obvious, however, once we compare the story of Gagarin with that of Ham. Ham was the name of the chimpanzee who, as part of the United States' Man-in-Space Program, was sent on a suborbital flight a mere three months before Gagarin on January 31, 1961. "Ham" was an acronym that stood for Holloman Aero-Medical, the military-run scientific institution that had prepared the animal for the flight. However, the chimpanzee was given this name only after the successful completion of the mission; up to that point he had only been called "No. 64," out of a desire to avoid attaching an identity to the laboratory animal. His handlers named the chimpanzee Chop Chop Chang, which, as Haraway rightly notes, was a sign of the open racism at the time.

The first astronauts struggled with a feeling of humiliation caused by the fact that apes could carry out the tasks of astronauts so well. The astronauts

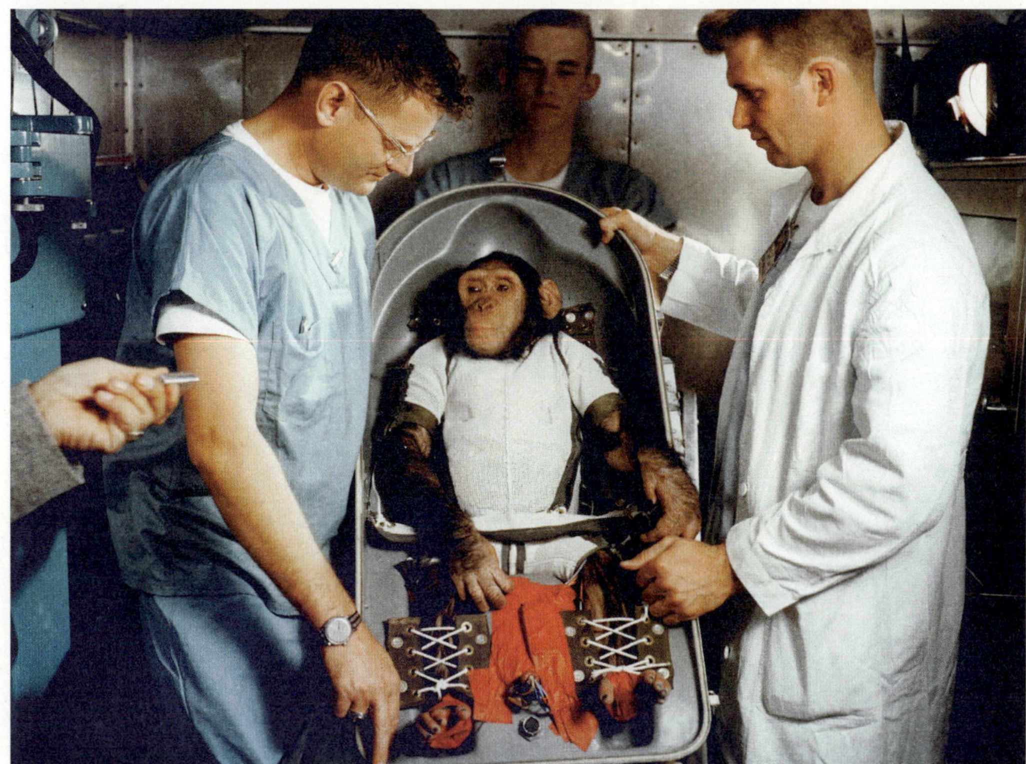

and astrochimps played on the same stage, in a
theater that no longer had any need for the heroic
role of the test pilot of jet airplanes. After the
chimpanzee Enos had completed a fully automated
space flight, John Glenn, the first American astronaut, said that he was looking forward to the future
and that he believed in the superiority of astronauts
over chimponauts. Following Glenn's first space
flight in 1962, *Newsweek* ran the headline: "John Glenn:
One Machine that Worked without Flaw." Ham and
Enos, but also Gagarin and Glenn, are cyborgs. Yet, like
'any important technology," to adopt a formulation
of Haraway's, "a cyborg is simultaneously a myth and
a tool, a representation and an instrument, a frozen
moment and a motor of social and imaginative
reality."[16]

While extraterrestrial space was imagined as a
universal, empty, and blank expanse that was simply
called "space," its counterpart, the ecosystem, was
visualized as a dense, humid, and corporeal wilder-

ness, full of sensual creatures that touch each other
intimately and intensively. Haraway reconstructs
this iconography from the images as well as the features and full-length films presenting the work of
Jane Goodall, which the National Geographic Society
produced for its own magazine as well as for television. Founded in the late nineteenth century, the
National Geographic Society had become an institution in the United States, not by propagating the
popularization of science, but by foregrounding the
involvement of its readers in "doing science." By emphasizing a particular participatory self-image of
readers, the Society was primarily aiming to garner
sponsorship, i.e. gathering financial support for conducting and reporting scientific research. Thanks
to the involvement of the mentor figure Louis Leakey,
the work of female primatologists like Jane Goodall,
Dian Fossey, or Birutė Galdikas was financed by the
National Geographic Society and then documented
on its behalf by professional photographers and film-

makers, all of whom were men. The latter presented the research of the female scientists as an adventure and a visual delight. One product of this mixture of interests was the TV documentary *Miss Goodall and the Wild Chimpanzees*, which featured a voiceover by Orson Welles and was aired in 1964. Presented by a very young, very white, and very unconventional woman primatologist, the documentary brought wild chimpanzees into American living rooms. The film portrays Goodall as the representative of a new form of science; no longer depicting science as an enterprise that aims to dominate nature, she introduces the viewers to a kind of *ars erotica* of science.[17] The new form of scientific observation that Goodall stands for is an activity that requires patience, that offers only quiet triumphs, that resembles the reception more than the generation of data, and that is presented as an earthly touch shared with nature. Haraway puts it in a nutshell when she writes that Jane Goodall inhabits one half of the system desired by technoscience, viz. the part that dreams of closing anew the broken cosmos and that is known, in its natural-technical form, as the ecosystem.

The pictures and recordings of Jane Goodall and the wild chimpanzees stand out due to their aesthetic form and the fantasies they convey. While the primeval forest of Tanzania furnishes the setting for the white woman as the representative of a receptivescience in pursuit of origins, the universal and abstract expanse of outer space is about the future. Ecosystem and outer space are simultaneously scientific areas and tropes; they are allotopic spaces that are elsewhere. One visits them to find adventures and discover sacred things, and they are home to salvation narratives.

If the star personas of space travelers keep quiet about their kinship with the cyborg, then the story of Jane Goodall leaves unsaid that the ecosystem is not innocent and free of technology, but rather functions as a complex self-regulating system modeled by cybernetics. The narrative also remains silent about the historical fact that African landscapes are not unspoiled nature, but part of human history—the last three centuries of which were marked by violent colonization.

The female scientist that was presented to a media-consuming public in *Miss Goodall and the Wild Chimpanzees* had a mediating function. As a woman, she was supposed to be closer to nature than a man, and through this proximity she promised to heal the expulsion from Paradise that had taken place a second time as a consequence of the shock of the atomic bomb and the realization that humanity was capable of destroying the world.

SURVIVAL NARRATIVES

"Understanding is everything." Thus runs the caption of an advertisement placed by the oil company Gulf in 1984, intent on improving its image. The upper half of the ad shows a photograph of two hands trustingly placed in one another. The photo extends over the entire width of the ad. One of the hands, leathery and covered with black hair, is the hand of a chimpanzee. It casually rests on another hand, the

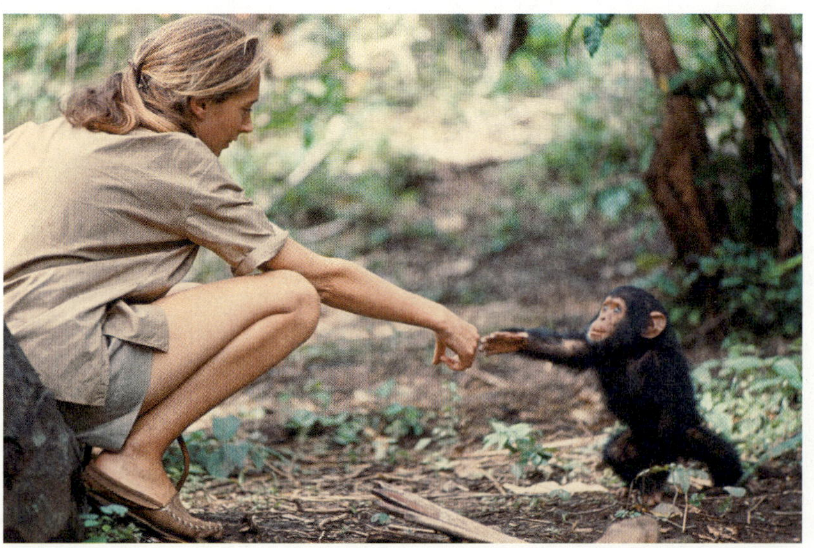

Jane Goodall and chimpanzee Flint, published in National Geographic magazine, vol. 128, no. 6, December 1965

delicate, young, and very white hand of Jane Goodall. The oil company was one of the sponsors of the television specials made by the National Geographic Society. The ad is reproduced in Haraway's book; the photo graces the cover.

The image, which the international oil company used so skillfully to improve its image, played into a familiar salvation fantasy that builds upon female empathy and hints at a paradise where animals and humans understand each other.

In contrast to these salvation fantasies, Haraway presents in her book a diffractional vision of the future that is about survival rather than salvation. Inasmuch as technoscience has already initiated the collapse of the boundaries between man, machine, and animal, Haraway proposes to seize the opportunity and interrupt the exclusionary identity politics of the "almost human." She finds models for this disruption in feminist science fiction, a literary scene that blossomed in the United States in the 1980s. One of the authors Haraway refers to is Octavia E. Butler, an African-American writer born in California in 1947 who has won multiple awards. In her *Xenogenesis* trilogy, which was published from 1987 to 1989, Butler describes a future world in which a black human female named Lilith survives a global nuclear war and procreates with members of an extraterrestrial race called the Oankalis, who have three genders, begetting hybrid Human–Oankali children in order to repopulate the Earth. The novels expound the problem of what it means to be fully human from the perspective of an African-American woman in the United States at the close of the twentieth century. Butler employs the genre of science fiction to take a close look at a whole range of issues, including compulsory reproduction, unequal relations of power, and the ownership of the self by others. Furthermore, she poses the question of whether there could be sisterly and brotherly solidarity between humans and aliens, and shows how this solidarity can break down within one's own species. In a manner comparable to that of the primatologists, Butler also explores the intertwining, overlapping, and extension of the borders between humans, machines, animals, and aliens by concentrating on the intimacy of bodily exchanges as well as the mental and cognitive faculties of communication. The salvation fantasies embedded in primatology, however, reproduce the viewpoint of a white, Western, and both secular and Christian history of colonization. By contrast, the future scenarios developed in Butler's science fiction stories have been shaped by the experience of racism, sexism, and colonialism. The scenes in which Lilith finds herself on an Oankali spaceship, for instance, evoke memories of the slave trade and the slave ships that carried humans by force from Africa to South America and the United States.

The science fiction stories by Octavia E. Butler are not about salvation, but about survival. In a literary thought experiment, she investigates how species, genera, and gender might be constituted in a survival literature after nuclear war and slavery. Her fiction is about the fear—and the hope—that children might be other than their parents, and that as a consequence they might not reproduce these parents. Butler's novels concern the "monsters" who appear once the borders between humans, animals, and machines have become brittle. In this manner, her texts address precisely what is obscured by the fantasies, desires, and salvation scenarios that primatology, to this day, continues to encourage. Yet the very issues covered up in this manner are among the most pressing questions of our time.

Haraway highlights the importance of these issues when she writes that the field of primatology is defined by the concern for a politics of reproduction. What is at stake are the competing forms of identity and difference—which means that the field of primatology is coextensive with the world in which we live. On this note, Haraway cites a sentence from one of Butler's novels: "She laughed bitterly. 'I suppose I could think of this as fieldwork—but how the hell can I get out of the field?'"[18] Today, this question is as pressing as it was in 1989, perhaps even more so, which is a good reason to take another close look at *Primate Visions*.

*Translated from the German
by Markus Hardtmann*

1   Donna Haraway, *Primate Visions: Gender, Race, and Nature in the World of Modern Science* (New York: Routledge, 1989), p. 3.

2   See Robert Yerkes, *Almost Human* (New York: Centura, 1925).

3   Susan Cachel, "Partisan Primatology," *American Journal of Primatology*, no. 22, 1990, pp. 139–142.

4   Haraway, *Primate Visions*, p. 1.

5   Ibid., p. 3.

6   Ibid.

7   See Linda Marie Fedigan and Shirley C. Strum, "A Brief History of Primate Studies: National Traditions, Disciplinary Origins, and Stages in North American Field Studies," in *The Nonhuman Primates*, Phyllis Dolhinow and Augustin Fuentes (eds.) (Mountain View: Mayfield Publishing Company, 1999), pp. 258–269.

8   Haraway, *Primate Visions*, p. 279.

9   Linda Marie Fedigan, "Is Primatology a Feminist Science?" in *Women in Human Evolution*, Lori D. Hager (ed.) (New York: Routledge, 1997), pp. 56–75.

10   See Anne Fausto-Sterling's essay review, "*Primate Visions*, A Model for Historians of Science?" *Journal of the History of Biology*, vol. 23, no. 2, 1990, pp. 329–333.

11   See Linda Marie Fedigan, "The Paradox of Feminist Primatology: The Goddess's Discipline?" in *Feminism in Twentieth Century Science, Technology, and Medicine*, Angela N. H. Creager, Elizabeth Lunbeck, and Londa L. Schiebinger (eds.) (Chicago: University of Chicago Press, 2001), pp. 46–72.

12   See Georges Canguilhem, "The Object of the History of Sciences," tr. Mary Tiles, in *Continental Philosophy of Science*, Gary Gutting (ed.) (Oxford: Blackwell, 2005), pp. 198–207.

13   Michel Foucault, *The Use of Pleasure*, vol. 2 of *The History of Sexuality*, tr. Robert Hurley (New York: Vintage Books, 1990), p. 9.

14   Haraway, *Primate Visions*, p. 2.

15   Donna Haraway, *Modest_Witness@ Second_Millenium.FemaleManÓ_Meets_ OncoMouse™* (New York: Routledge, 1997), p. 274.

16   Haraway, *Primate Visions*, p. 139.

17   See ibid., p. 131.

18   Haraway, *Primate Visions*, p. 382, citing Octavia E. Butler, *Dawn* (New York: Warner Books, 1987), pp. 262–263.

KRIMINALAFFE: SULTAN AT THE DOLE OFFICE

Matthew Hyland, John Barker, and Ines Doujak

F.W. Taylor's *Principles of Scientific Management* was first published in 1911. In it he describes a worker both as an "intelligent gorilla" and—unwittingly endorsing the worker-gorilla's intelligence—as one who "deliberately plans to do as little as he safely can."[1] One year later in 1912, the Prussian Academy of Sciences opened a station on Tenerife devoted to experimentation into the "mental capacities" of apes, and especially chimpanzees. Tenerife itself was the last of the Canary Islands to be conquered by the Spanish in 1496. Half the indigenous population sided with the invaders, the others, in the north of the island, resisted and when finally defeated were enslaved to work on sugar cane plantations, a laboratory for colonial capitalism. Tenerife was chosen as a location for the station because of its climate and proximity to Cameroon, then a German colony, from where nine chimpanzees were captured and transported over the sea. It became famous for the experiments of Wolfgang Köhler. He has been acclaimed as a co-founder of Gestalt theory; for offering an alternative to the behaviorism of Pavlov and Thorndike; and for his anti-Nazi sentiments, but he also laid some of the groundwork for an instrumentalized psychology of work.

The Tenerife station's first director Eugen Teuber was interested in watching the spontaneous behavior of the chimpanzees, their gregarious nature, and their playfulness: how they would play "catch"; tease and then let go of lizards that had got into their compound; play with chickens at the fence; and the language they exhibited in rhythmic dance. Köhler, who took over in 1914 and remained throughout the First World War, was instead concerned with goal-oriented experiments, all described in detail and featuring the chimpanzee Sultan. They all concern getting food, which is made progressively more difficult to reach. Props are provided and in time Sultan solves the problem.

What is going on here? J. M. Coetzee's Elizabeth Costello in his novel of the same name argues that Sultan is at every turn diverted from his profound question as to why this is being done to him in this "carefully plotted psychological regime"—what is the nature of the man and his misconceptions of me?— by the goal of reaching the out-of-reach bananas. The "wrong" thought is to ask questions such as "the justice of the universe and the place of this penal colony," whereas the "right" thought is: "How does one use the crates to reach the bananas?"[2]

What Coetzee's character does not elaborate is that this instrumentalized goal is about work, working for a living in ways one has no control over. Modern primatologists like Alison Jolly and the colleagues she describes are more Teuber in style, observing only, and their main ethical dilemma where there are contradictions between saving wildlife habitat and the livelihoods of indigenous people, but for the poor humans of the world the influence of cognitive psychology, of giving the "right" answer, is pervasive.

The IQ test, a banal but carefully designed exercise of jumping through the hoops, has a similar force, though with a different and nasty starting point. It owes much to another chimpanzee experimenter, R. M. Yerkes of the Yale Laboratories for Primate Biology, who was both unashamedly eugenicist— "no citizen can afford to ignore the menace of race deterioration"—and behaviorist.[3] It is shocking that the mumbo-jumbo notion of IQ that he pushed remains a building block for the latest "modern" round of "scientific" racism of Arthur Jensen, *The Bell Curve*, and its attendant "underclass" category. What Yerkes and Köhler did have in common was goal orientation, the primacy of *the task*, and that the ape was seen as a means to an end, "namely, the solution of important problems, which may not readily be approached initially by aid of human subjects," as Yerkes put it.

Modern racism is not just "scientific" but iconographic, showing dark-skinned people as apes; such images of Michelle Obama especially are legion.

It has never been "racially" exclusive—or rather, "races," apish and otherwise, have always been *constituted* by racism, their particular demographic make-up no more consistent than that of other made-up categories like "heretics," "deserving poor," "Great Men," "the Elect." In the nineteenth century similar caricatures of the Irish were prevalent. Above all, it is the poor—whether slaves or "free"—labor who are so characterized: specifically as lazy, feckless, and violent, or "vicious" in the literal sense. When Köhler first arrived at the station and saw the chimpanzees at play he described them as "street urchins." A few years earlier an Argentine newspaper had described the local "underclass" as "boys who roam through the streets, engaging in indecent games and annoying passers-by." A hundred years later, children growing up poor in British cities are commonly called *feral* by their economic betters, some of whom labeled the uprising of 2011 the *Planet of the Apes riots.* In El Alto, the very poor part of La Paz, as if all the specious identifications of primates and the human poor, especially those with dark skins, were real, street children often sleep in trees, sometimes tying themselves to a branch so as not to fall when sleeping.

Under the original US constitution a slave was three fifths of a human being. Not a pack mule but a special package of physical and *mental* labor power, and priced differently; wonderfully valuable when properly directed but forever a menace for the same reasons. Köhler was not exactly an overseer, but it is no accident that he worked with apes rather than rats or dogs:

> Even assuming the anthropoid ape behaves intelligently in the sense in which the word is applied to man, there is yet from the very start no doubt that he remains in this respect far behind man, becoming perplexed and making mistakes in relatively simple situations; but it is precisely for this reason that we may, under the simplest conditions, gain knowledge of the nature of intelligent acts.[4]

Life on the alleged animal–human threshold—and how to make it *work*—had long preoccupied industrializing, colonizing powers. During the final century or so of mass chattel slavery—as it gave way to likewise massified "free" labor and each took on characteristics of the other—management solutions were frantically sought for *barely* human laborers, the ones equipped with cognition but incapable of Higher Virtues, who added value but at the same time threatened mayhem. Can insightful apes (whether hairy or "naked") be trained to train themselves? Experts have never stopped asking the question. In today's Human Resources management, "showing initiative" and "problem solving" mean correctly pre-empting commands. For mental patients "insight" means surrender to your keepers. The insightful ape or ape-like human is inclined to idleness and waste, sullen silence or riotous assembly, but her or his capacity for mentored self-management still makes for a higher-yielding investment than an organism that must always be whipped to work or arrives at the right Life Choices only when subjected to electroshock.

LAZY RASCALS

The goal-oriented world and the necessity of work is that of Paradise Lost and its twin, Original Sin. The theological legend "tells us," Marx writes, "certainly how man came to be condemned to eat his bread by the sweat of his brow; but the history of economic original sin reveals that there are people to whom this is by no means essential."[5] Those, that is, who have the power to present themselves as intelligent, diligent, and frugal, in contrast to those who must work: the "lazy rascals spending their substance and more," in need of discipline and often in the post-Columbian world portrayed as an ape. The Eden we could imagine from the bare biblical facts would have been not that of hunter-gatherers—hunting described as an essential goal-oriented part of human development, though other species hunt "tactically"— but one of gatherers. It was presented as such by Thomas Aquinas:

> In the state of innocence men did not have any bodily need of animals. Neither for clothing, since they were naked and not ashamed, there being no notions of inordinate concupiscence; not for food, since they fed on the trees of Paradise;

not for means of transport, their bodies being strong enough for that purpose. Yet they needed them in order to draw from them their nature in experimental knowledge. This is signified by the fact that God led the animals before man, that he might give them a name that designated their nature.[6]

Adam and Eve could have been doing Köhler-like experiments if they had the wherewithal, and defined themselves as superior in the process. In "Adam naming the Animals," the frontispiece of an English bestiary, he is showing off this *power* of naming, armed with a scroll. But the ape, as in many other images of Gothic art, is eating an apple. The link to the power of sensual appetite and to Eve is made clear in a series of works. In the *Bible Historiée* published by Antoine Vérard around 1499 Eve appears as visually seduced by the apple-eating ape, then, in *The Fall of Man* by Jan Gossaert, Eve shows an untouched apple to Adam while an ape has already taken some big bites out of another one. The link to the woman as prisoner of appetites hovers over these pictures, and throughout the Middle Ages apes were given a feminine gender. Nancy Leys Stepan describes how the racist analogy-based science of the nineteenth century generated data to match metaphors, implying that women and the "lower" races were closer to apes and to each other than to fully human males.[7]

Crucially, Adam and Eve, before she supposedly ruins everything, did not have to work for a living, the trees of Paradise provided for their needs. The bible, however, reflected the development of elites and the creation of scarcity by insisting that Man should earn his bread from the sweat of his brow, and for this the story of the apple and the Fall was essential. Such an easily acquired diet as had existed in fabled Eden was anathema when it was there for the taking by real-life humans. The Victorian polymath Thomas Carlyle's hatred of the pumpkin got straight to the point: "Where a black man, by working about half an hour a day [...] can supply himself by aid of sun and soil with as much pumpkin as will suffice he is likely to be a little stiff to raise into hard work."[8] The poet Samuel Taylor Coleridge arrived at the same attitude after

initial enthusiasm for the breadfruit of Tahiti (now a "superfood") and the thought of living in abundance. When he began to see the island's sexual liberation as abhorrent, however, the breadfruit became a fruit of sensuality. He proposed a scheme to uproot the plant; when that proved impractical, he supported the Christianization of the Polynesian "savages." Later in the century the sinister scientific servants of European colonialism (first English, then German) took it a step further, justifying the genocide of "primitive" peoples—something that had already happened in Tasmania—as "inevitable" on the grounds of a lack of productive efficiency in land use, an "efficiency" equated with civilization. An early English such rationale, "On the Negro's Place in Nature," laid emphasis on the negro's close relationship with the ape.[9] A later popular German version by Paul Rohrbach made it unequivocal: "Existencies, be they of peoples or individuals who do not produce anything of value, cannot make any claim to the right to exist."[10]

In the Polynesian case, as in the newly tumbled-upon Americas, the term "savage," with its implication of animality and a lack of "civilization," was not aimed at the black-skinned people of Africa. But it was to them that it came to be almost exclusively applied, along with the use of superimposed ape imagery. From the imagemakers' point of view it was easy, black-skinned people and black-haired apes living on the same continent, seen as "a wild place of wild animals and wild beings," as Donna Haraway describes that viewpoint.[11] Nowadays it reappears in sloppy scare journalism that puts together HIV/AIDS, Ebola, and "bushmeat," that is, the meat of wild animals. But from very soon after that happening upon of the "New World," it wasn't just an easy link to make, but essential when the enslaving of Africans became necessary to its exploitation and the take-off of capitalist accumulation. Back in the 1780s, the notorious Captain Bligh of "Mutiny on the Bounty" fame, an exemplary abettor of slavery, was exporting the breadfruit of Tahiti to the slave owners of the West Indies so that they could feed their slaves on the cheap. An almost paradigmatic assault on the natural abundance of one place to increase profits elsewhere—except that the slaves of the West Indies refused to eat it.

SINNERS AND SLAVES

Long before the theory of evolution, Europeans, before entering equatorial Africa but after stumbling across the Americas, had a whole iconography of monstrous beings. Before equatorial Africa they would have seen Barbary apes (macaques) from the North African coast and Gibraltar which became familiar in West European cities as chained performers. Writing in the thirteenth century, Bartholomew of England drew on the *Physiologus* of the Eastern church in identifying white skins with angels and apes as the devil: "Now the ape, not having a tail, is without species, and his rear without a tail is vile, like the devil, he does not have a good end." The ape was also connected to a hatred of Egyptian paganism, itself identified with persecution of the Jews of the Old Testament; when its temples and idols were destroyed in the Alexandria of AD 391, Bishop Theophilus ordered the statue of an ape to be preserved as a monument to human depravity. In the *Stuttgart Psalter*, a version of the Psalms from the ninth century, the ape and the satyr both stand in for Egyptian oppression.[12]

Moreover, the absence of a tail was an indication of hubris, of the animal's desire to "rise above his "station," to be like human beings in this respect. There is then a shift from the ape as devil to the ape as sinner in the Romanesque period, with the iconography of the Fall, as described above, becoming prevalent. This hubris was also presented as insolence. Thus Bartholomew of England in his *De proprietabus rerum* has the ape as unruly and malicious; it should be forcibly tamed, its insolence repressed with beatings and chains. From the fifteenth century the fettered ape, which would have been a familiar sight in European towns, was a favored image both in Germany and England.

European experience of Africa upped the stakes from the sixteenth century onwards. Black-skinned people were commonly associated with apes (chimpanzees until 1847, the year when gorillas were first found) as childish, savage, and oversexualized. Travelers described the Hottentots as a tribe of people more primitive than had ever been seen before. Biblical stories of Jacob's hairy and stupid brother Esau or of Noah and his sons were added to those of the Fall, identifying black people with the cursed Canaanites and descendants of Ham. The biblical myth persisted into the nineteenth century and beyond, but scientific race theory started to supplant it in the late seventeenth century with the crisis and subsequent triumph of the Atlantic slave economy. This intersected with a crisis in literal biblical belief, specifically where Adam as universal human ancestor was concerned. The conjunction of these crises at the birth of capital is the reason racism will never go away as long as its economic basis prevails.

Already by the late 1640s, the planters of the Caribbean and the Chesapeake colonies had productivity problems with a mixed workforce of convicted or indentured Europeans, African slaves, and a few "natives": a multinational rabble that *shared* techniques of lewdness and indiscipline and might have wiped out the proprietors of Barbados overnight had an informer not betrayed them at the last moment. The panic peaked in Virginia with "Bacon's Second Rebellion" (1676), when a self-elected army of black slaves and white "servants" burned Jamestown, proclaimed indenture and slavery abolished, and looted the opulent estates. The owners' response to such outbreaks was total economic overhaul and the "top-down" invention of color-coded racism. White servants were effectively abolished as a class; henceforth only blacks would do the backbreaking work. Servants not redeported elsewhere were nudged upwards into quasi-overseer roles, encouraged to retaliate violently against slaves starved into stealing from them. The recent English takeover of the triangular slave trade meant 100,000 Africans could be imported over fifty years into the Chesapeake, where there had only been a couple of thousand in 1670.[13]

Between about that time and the mid-eighteenth century, the vastly expanded scale of Atlantic slavery, the intensification of its protoindustrial organization, and its turn to an exclusive, legally codified racial basis formed the social conjunction which made possible and which demanded complete scientific theories of racial hierarchy. The other important factor, itself also a product of seventeenth-century material upheaval, is the early Enlightenment biblical criticism, both textual and historical, that called into question the *literal* descriptive function of Scripture and of

Genesis in particular. In Isaac La Peyrère's *Pre-Adamitae* (1655), a work hounded energetically enough by churches to assure its fame, the radical philologist lists *biblical* evidence of human life before Adam. In doing so he frees future racists from the obligation to admit their own shared Adamic origins with indigenous Americans, Africans, or other lost, degraded tribes. Without unwitting encouragement from La Peyrère, Sir William Petty might not have written *Of the Scale of Creatures* in 1677, the year after the second Bacon revolt.[14]

Petty was an Anglo-Irish land speculator and a founder of modern political economy, celebrated by Marx among others for his cheerful bluntness about the violence involved in managing a capitalistic system. (Hanging thieves instead of condemning them to perpetual forced labor, he once wrote, was a gross waste of resources.) Little surprise that this least euphemistic of political economists should also be a founder of the scientific race theory supporting the expanded Atlantic slave system that, in turn, underpinned later capitalist development. Petty classifies as many creature-types as he can think of, in the style of Adam in Paradise, when "The Lord God formed every animal and brought them to the man to see what he would call them, and whatever he called each living creature that was its name." Having ditched Adam as sole ancestor of *all* men, Petty has the power to do the same. For him, "man" is paramount among flesh-and-blood beings, but for the first time he is subdivided into races that stand in the same sort of relation to one another as dogs do to serpents or horses to fishes.

Of man itself there seems to be severall species. To say nothing of Gyants & Pygmies or of that sort of small men who have little speech [...]. For of these sorts of men, I venture to say nothing, but that 'tis very possible there may be Races and generations of such; [...] there bee others more considerable, that is, between the Guiny Negros & the Middle Europeans; & of Negros between those of Guiny and those who live about the Cape of Good Hope, which last are the Most beastlike of all the Souls of Men with whom our Travellers are well acquainted. I say that the Europeans do not onley differ from the aforementioned Africans in Collour [...] but they differ also[...] in their Naturall Manners, & in the internall Qualities of their Minds.[15]

The "internall Qualities of their minds" matter. As a political economist, Petty is less concerned with outward anatomy than with the difference between pure beastly mindlessness, minds fitted only for work, and Souls equipped for management (or philosophy). Next in his ranking below the lowest, blackest men come not apes but elephants and parrots—for their respective abilities to understand commands and to reproduce speech—and bees, for their disciplined, work-centered "pollicy or Art of Government." The ascendancy of the Atlantic slave system and the early capitalist globalization that developed from it are characterized by legislated racial stratification and world-scale economic rationalization, each of which gets the science it needs. Petty personifies the inseparability of the two types of science. His eighteenth and nineteenth-century successors finished the job, placing the vanishing point between ape and savage at the center of their racist political economy.

Anatomical knowledge of humans and animals was accumulated along with slave-generated capital through the seventeenth and eighteenth centuries. In 1699 Edward Tyson published his *Orang-Outang, sive Homo Sylvestris: or, the Anatomy of a Pygmie Compared with that of a Monkey, an Ape, and a Man.* Despite confusions of nomenclature—Tyson's "pygmie" is in fact a chimpanzee, the orangutan not being described until 1779—the tract introduces the notion of the "Missing Link." "In this Chain of Creation, as an intermediate link between an ape and a Man, I would place our Pygmie," wrote Tyson, although his "ape" remains a mysterious being. Some seventy years later the taxonomy of Linnaeus with its category *Homo sapiens* was more disturbing; the naturalist claimed hardly to know "a single distinguishing mark which separates man from apes, save that the latter have an empty space between their canines and their other teeth." Such indistinction between man and ape would be intolerable unless asset-owning, savant "man" could be properly distanced from the apish human organism whose work he lived off. And so it was that during the age of the "three fifths of a man"

US constitution and the twelve-year Haitian slave revolution, the missing link—or as its self-proclaimed discoverer Ernst Haeckel called it, *der sprachlose Urmensch* (the speechless primitive man)—became the fixation of scientific racism. [16]

SCIENCE AT YOUR SERVICE

By the end of the eighteenth century the ex-slaves of Haiti had defeated France, Britain, and Spain in military combat and held the USA to a standstill; the similarly beastly *sans-culottes* had overrun Paris for a moment, forcing a vote to free the slaves, and the language of biblical man was monopolized by pious white abolitionists. More urgently than ever, surviving owners needed to anathematize these affronts to natural order, to knock the monsters back to their station with a science of human differences. It had been done before by Petty, Buffon, Long, and Kant among others, but in 1799 Royal Society luminary Charles White obliged with visual charts in his *Animals and Vegetables*. [17] Here no political beehive or interpretive elephant stands between the worst men and the apes. "In whatever respect the African differs from the European," wrote White, "the particularity brings him nearer to the ape." That is, *any* divergence from the European ideal (the chain, of course, has no better-than-white links) tends towards the apish. The missing link is a flexible category, engulfing anyone unable to disprove the taint. Actual apes and savages of all kinds (from the 1790s the term was often extended to the lower European depths) *share more with each other* than either does with proper men, a type as far removed as the invertebrates at the opposite end of the chain. White emphasized the point by making his apes as "human" as his nonwhites were apish, feminizing the apes at the same time lest anyone doubt the degree of humanity intended. The flexibility built into his mesh of missing links would serve well over the centuries to follow, when all kinds of notionally free lowlife would need to be assimilated to the apish race without discouraging racial war between components of the simian class.

The nineteenth century brought ever-intensifying slave revolts, militant abolitionism (not necessarily nonracist), and a series of slow, self-serving "abolition" gestures by colonial powers and Latin American republics. At the same time, the Great Powers relied ever more on de facto servitude where their colonial networks pushed into sub-Saharan Africa and East Asia, while industrial organization pioneered on the big plantations spread in "core" factories employing lighter-skinned (in America, often immigrant) "missing-link" labor. "Emancipation" was not supposed to raise the ex-slave any higher on the Chain of Being; it was more like a pre-emptive policy to preserve a racialized social structure that could hardly be managed any more on the old terms. Hence the premium throughout the century and into the next on scientific backing for a racial Chain, one flexible enough either to bestialize white and black workers together or to set one against the other as the case required.

Given the contradictions of this second wave of capitalist globalization, only the most prodigious flexibility would do. The disciplinary machinery, quota systems, and rational division of labor developed on the plantations were first taken up in the unregulated factories of the nineteenth century, then applied more systematically in the "scientific management" of F. W. "intelligent gorillas" Taylor early in the twentieth. Yet as C. L. R. James has shown, the biggest, most modern American and Caribbean export production sites were effectively *run by the slaves*. "Cognitive labor" is not just for European "creatives": enslaved "technical specialists" kept the plantation self-sufficient and managed its supply chain. "Slave blacksmiths [...] coopers [...] shoemakers, tanners, dyers and weavers," river pilots, and seamen, sometimes hired out by their owners in an early form of outsourcing, kept it working. [18] The complex cooperative techniques the slaves worked out on the plantations were turned against the planters and their military proxies, first in Haiti, then in the defeat of the Confederacy. Yet after emancipation these technicians were cut off from socialized production and reduced to medieval-style sharecropping on extortionate terms. The desperate poverty that resulted served as evidence of the ex-slaves' apish incompetence and eventually forced many to move north to do the worst jobs invented by Taylorist industrial deskilling. In a further grotesque twist, the German colony of Togoland, via the racist intellectuals of the *Verein für*

Sozialpolitik, invited Booker T. Washington's Tuskegee Institute in 1901 to send African–American graduates to teach indigenous cotton growers how to work. The graduates' obsession with the merits of the plough in the name of civilization and efficiency ensured ghastly failure; when the tsetse fly killed the draft animals, the Togolese "students" were put under harness instead.[19]

The calculating power of "missing link science" expanded along with its ideological task in the years leading up to the Köhler experiments: the decades of the Paris Commune, the Berlin Conference colonies, mass migration from Europe and militant factory women. New data ploughed into the ape–African analogy needed to encompass other ill-evolved humans without abstracting the basic racial element away. Micromeasurement of ape and human heads served up a rich supply of social metaphor. In Turin, Cesare Lombroso made a *Polizeiwissenschaft* out of circus sideshow phrenology with his mugshot/skull-statistics database and a corresponding theory of criminal (i.e. negroid, apish, whatever the parentage) types. Today cranial evidence as such is at last out of forensic favor, but Lombroso's first premise—that crime resides in the *person* rather than the act—enjoys higher legal standing than ever. Callipers, cephalometers, and craniometers were applied to women as enthusiastically as fresh hysteria treatments, as if modern metrics could establish Eve's guilt for the Fall. Nancy Leys Stepan describes how jaw-measurement innovations at the Paris École d'Anthropologie "proved" the long-fancied thesis that white women were biologically closer to black men and apes than to the heads of their own households. The great sexual reformer Havelock Ellis agreed, though he found white women's apish jaws more "charming" than those of male "negroes."

The analogical bond between white women and apes has proved less durable over the last 150 years than those making apes of black women, black men or any color "underclass." Skull and jaw contour has given way to neurological, cognitive–behavioral, and genetic means of naturalizing social station. Yet the allied quantitative superstition called IQ is taken as seriously today as it was at Ellis Island or by Yerkes and the US Draft Board he advised in the 1910s.

Jensen, Murray, and their followers feel no need to defend its validity: it is a self-evident *premise* in their routines of racist question-begging. With official respect for anthropometrics at an all-time high, the old method of the primato-eugenicist Yerkes slips smoothly into brand-new data models, serving a Social Darwinism that never went away.

GUILT BY ASSOCIATION

The chain of analogy that integrates apes, nonwhites, women, and workers into a common image of monstrosity has outlasted every "scientific paradigm" that ever authorized it. This "cultural" survival of scientific race/gender/class fantasies is not surprising, because biological data are always grafted onto social life using analogy's cultural forceps. Cause–effect explanation gives way to intuitive metaphor when scientists pronounce on the historical time that also constitutes their own lives and language. Analogies approved as science need not always be untrue, but whenever physical measure is upgraded to social metaphor it forfeits one kind of claim to truth in pursuit of another. The lab result is respected for its modesty, its cautious quantification of one circumscribed thing, whereas imaginative comment on the social world knows no such bounds because its "object" is indivisible. Its truth is tested only by what happens next. Analogy that speaks of social life while claiming scientific privilege abuses its position: it becomes a charter for a human zoo.

Actual human zoos, exhibiting nonwhite humans for spectators' amusement, have existed at least since the sixteenth century. In 1533 Montaigne witnessed one in Rouen that recreated a "native village" of the Brazilian Tupinambás. The model was repeated at numerous World Fairs and in the Bronx Zoo at the turn of the twentieth century. In 1958 visitors to a Belgian zoo for black Africans were encouraged to feed the inmates bananas. African tribesmen went on show in Augsburg Zoo as recently as 2005.

A bestseller called *The Human Zoo* appeared in 1969. London Zoo Curator of Mammals, ape-art impresario and TV personality Desmond Morris wrote it as a follow-up to his likewise bestselling *The Naked Ape*, the foundational airport novel of modern sociobiology. Pioneering eco-Malthusian Morris was horrified not by the public exhibition of caged human "primitives" but by the high-rise, high-density urban lifestyle of the twentieth century. When human animals get all the food and shelter they need for next to nothing, they are duly degraded by their life of abundance.[20]

> Under normal conditions, in their natural habitats, wild animals do not mutilate themselves, masturbate, attack their offspring, develop stomach ulcers, become fetishists, suffer from obesity, form homosexual pair-bonds, or commit murder. Among human city dwellers, needless to say, all of these things occur.

Morris does not discriminate biologically between races in the manner of his colleague E. O. Wilson, but like all sociobiologists he sees evolutionary drama played out daily in a cutthroat social competition that some types are fit for while other self-destructive specimens are not. The class of successful apes is doomed to manage the others.

> The politicians, the administrators and the other super-tribal leaders [...] must become good biologists [...] because somewhere in all that mass of wires, cables, plastics, concrete, bricks, metal and glass which they control, is an animal, a human animal, a primitive tribal hunter, masquerading as a civilized, super-tribal citizen and desperately struggling to match his ancient inherited qualities with his extraordinary new situation. If he is given the chance he may yet contrive to turn his human zoo into a magnificent game-park. If he is not, it may proliferate into a gigantic lunatic asylum, like one of the hideously cramped animal menageries of the last century.

Ape-class humans may or may not fear a lunatic asylum more than a magnificent game park toured by white hunters. The "choice" between coercive help and outright punishment—or the desperate attempt to fend both off as far as possible by playing one against the other—is an everyday matter for today's class of Cain.

The stakes of early ape experiments are unchanged in the various strains of sociobiology, now sometimes known as "behavioral ecology." Köhler demonstrated "abstract thinking" in his problem-solving chimpanzees, defining "cognition" in apes and other laborers as one biological function among others, wasteful and riotous if allowed to run wild but susceptible to training and as such potentially productive, just as Bartholomew of England saw it centuries earlier. Morris, Wilson, and their successors observe the most complex, historically overdetermined social phenomena and see only the apish behavioral patterns they ascribe to genetic programming. "Aggression," "xenophobia," "competitiveness," sexual proprietorship and so on are concepts applied as though timeless despite being many millennia newer than the genetic presets they are supposed to represent. Like the various "character types" in personality psychology, another discipline with much to say about apes, these unmistakably twentieth-century categories are eternalized by circular reasoning: *genetic programming changes more slowly than human history; tribalism, possessiveness and so on are the currently favored names for certain effects of such programming; therefore these names belong not to the historical time of their coinage but to the epochal time of the genetic code.* Centuries of historical and linguistic mediation disappear thanks to this trick, letting it seem that everything done by the specimen (or the largest admissible unit, the specimen "tribe") reflects genetic data directly, and that individual specimen psychology—being genetic and therefore generic—explains the collective life of the species.

What Morris's hackneyed "urban jungle" evokes above all is the sociobiologist's hatred of the poor, something shared with countless earlier users of ape imagery. In 1857 the race "scientist" George Gliddon proclaimed in his *Indigenous Races of the Earth* that "the most superior kind of Monkeys are found to be indigenous exactly where we encounter races of the most inferior types of Men."[21] Guilt by association. The reality is that apes live almost exclusively in countries that are predominantly poor. The smug Puritan notion that poverty is a sign of defective individual character of sin passes for common sense today. A routinely racialized slur, but unpredictably so because "race" means nothing outside its racist application. In the mid-nineteenth century the Irish were portrayed with apelike features the outthrust mouth, sloping forehead, and wide, flat nose of the standard Irish caricature and as poor, primitive, drunk and lazy. Darwin's cousin Francis Galton backed the demeaning caricature: "Visitors to Ireland after the potato famine generally remarked that the Irish type of face seemed to have become more proganthous [apelike]—that is, more like the negro in the protrusion of the lower jaw."[22] But whether it be indigenous Peruvians, English weavers of the mid-eighteenth century, or the dispossessed Scottish Highlanders of the nineteenth, the masters' verdict is always the same: "congenital laziness," "debauchery," "insolence." Melvin Thomas Copeland watched early twentieth-century US cotton mill workers and decided that although "improvident" and "lacking ingenuity, foresight, and ambition, they were, however, adaptable to factory life." By then F. W. Taylor's behavioral authoritarianism was in full swing. In the present day the East-Asian worker is held up less as a model than as a warning to the decadent. Terry Gou, CEO of the Foxconn conglomerate—the Apple Mac manufacturer notorious for its worker suicides and relentless workrate—commented: "Hon Hai [Foxconn] has a workforce of over one million worldwide, and as human beings are also animals, to manage one million animals gives me a headache."

Western competitors' response to this generic East-Asian worker (alleged to have "a greater threshold of pain" by a longtime ruler of Singapore) involves the creation of a "cognitive class," but this is not the "creative" entrepreneurial class it is often thought to be. Instead, coercive Gestalt (as in *shaping*), cognitive behavioral training, and penalties for guessing the wrong questions are overwhelmingly visited on the class that has always been called apish, and therefore also on the usual "races." "Most cognitive labor is done by the supposedly lazy and unskilled or by those whose most painfully acquired 'skills' are not the ones they get a wage for. To the extent that the 'intelligent gorillas' of Europe/Africa/Asia/America survive by means of their own ingenious 'problem solving' local capital is relieved of that burden and

becomes more 'competitive.'" This happens in at least two ways. First, when the "lazy" accomplish the logistical feat of staying alive and maybe even raising children on an income that amounts to a permanent insult and makes access to all necessities uncertain, while "rational economic choices" (gray markets, border-crossing, informal employment, welfare optimization) carry criminal penalties. Constant cognitive work is added onto the job itself—if there is one— in exchange for the privilege of being able to keep working. Second, the performance of *personal skills*—"communication," "flexibility," "engagement," "positive attitude"—is expected as a free gift on top of any hours worked and paid for. Management theorists lifted those criteria long ago from cognitive and behavioral psychology so that their clients would have a free hand in appraising white-collar subordinates, but such potent meaninglessness could hardly be ignored by handlers of the lower grades. The first and second types of cognitive work merge where the labor market, welfare system, and police state meet, as in the UK for example. Receipt of benefits exposes the claimant to surveillance that overlaps with criminal justice and mental-health machinery: attitude assessment to catch "despondency" and send it to cognitive-behavioral therapy; "sanctions" ranging from nonpayment to prison for overclaiming or failing to attend kindergarten-style "work-readiness training."

As with the apes, it's a matter of discipline. Köhler showed with his apes how Toughlove sometimes out-coerces Pavlovian shock. The acutest of the ape-trainers was the one who got the "subjects" to teach themselves the lesson freely, who hid the food where nothing less than flexible engagement would find it: the one who made the monkey signify itself.

In a story by Janosch, *der Kriminalaffe* (the Criminal Ape) sees through this particular stitch-up.[23] Employment as a puppet in a puppet theater has given the *Kriminalaffe* cause to reflect on forced self-impersonation.

There is a tiny fault with me. It's like this … in a complicated show I am not myself but someone else, because there is someone else inside me, the puppeteer with his hand. I can only move when *he* moves me and I must do everything *he* wants me to, so that from the outside I am myself but from the inside I am someone else.

But while he explains this, the *Kriminalaffe* is locked in a box in the back of a car on the way to the next circus. The physical and spiritual gymnastics prescribed for the ape class are heroically evaded or turned upside-down in thousands of cases every day, yet even as this sabotage shaves basis points off profit it is still a kind of cognitive labor that someone *has to do* for reasons of survival. The animal, wrote the young Marx, "is immediately one with its life activity," indistinguishable from what it has to do to survive. Whether or not "wild" life was ever really so abject, it is towards this condition that capital would drive its human herd. Introspective insight is animality itself once it becomes productive; there is far more intellect involved in setting fire to a looted store.

THE PURLOINED KEY

Those scientists with an interventionist approach to primates—ones they will have under their control—are obsessed, however "sympathetic" they may be, with the apes *doing* something. Training is invariably involved. J. M. Coetzee's Elizabeth Costello looks at it rather from the viewpoint of Köhler's prize specimen: "In his deepest being Sultan is not interested in the banana problem. Only the experimenter's single-minded regimentation forces him to concentrate on it. The question that truly occupies him [...] is: Where is home, and how do I get there?"

In modern times there have been numerous cases of gorillas, gibbons, chimpanzees, and orangutans escaping from the cages and compounds of zoos and parks.[24] The response, by whatever method they are returned to their barred, fenced, or walled spaces, is one of All's Well That Ends Well. Often there is a touch of pride in the ingenuity of the escapees, but only when matched with the smug tone that goes with the inevitability of their ultimate failure. Now and then this smugness of the enclosers has been punctured as when the gorilla called Jabari that escaped from Dallas Zoo in 2004 was not returned but shot dead by them, just as had happened in 1931 to another gorilla in Paris. Evelyn, a recidivist

chimpanzee in Los Angeles Zoo, managed to pull out the tranquillizer dart she had been hit with and threw it back at her pursuers, but in the conventional narrative was then "happily" subdued by the drug. In other instances, as at Kansas City Zoo, there have been "ringleader" chimpanzees leading mass breakouts using all the ingenuity of Sultan in fashioning ladders.

"One of our chimpanzees was able to break roughly a six foot tree limb that was then used as a ladder to climb on top of the outdoor enclosure wall," Julie Neemeyer wrote in an email to the *Daily News*. "That chimp then enticed six other chimps to join the first chimp."

The escapees, these included, have never got very far; indeed in some narratives they were pleased to be back in captivity, but the pride element within the parameters of inevitable recapture is almost competitive. The headline "Sneaky ape makes great escape from San Antonio Zoo" was almost a challenge to the Virunga National Park in the Democratic Republic of the Congo, which retorted with "Our intelligent gorillas and their daring escape." The keepers there detailed how the gorillas had worked out that the voltage in the surrounding electric fence was not strong enough to contain them, but concluded by calling the whole thing the gorillas' "little adventure."

The most celebrated escapee and real-life *Kriminalaffe* was an orangutan given the name Fu Manchu, "a late resident of Omaha Zoo" who "frequently would be found outside his exhibit when his keepers arrived in the morning." His escape involved climbing into air vents and following them to a dry moat surrounding his enclosure, where he would unlock a door used by employees. The lock, it transpired, was picked with a piece of wire that Fu Manchu kept hidden in his mouth during the day. It was the criminal mind at work, necessary in such situations, but the escape was necessarily limited. How to get from Omaha back to Borneo, given the logistics—money, disguise, maps, and transport—that journey would require? Thus in the end the Zoo was able to take a smug pride in him. They did not, it is true, discover how he learned to pick locks, but the rest they discovered through CCTV surveillance. It is this aspect of the story that most fits with the state-backed neoliberal narrative of *inevitability*. Thus many of the London rioters of 2011, so readily described as apes, would be caught not in the act itself but *in the end* because of the pervasive CCTV coverage of the city. It may be that the economic inevitability of "the markets" is now being challenged, but there have always been modes of refusal by apes, and by humans living by the sweat of their brow: silence, work-avoidance techniques, and the dumb insolence of paying only lip service to the dictates of training. The secret of Fu Manchu's lock-picking dies with him; the art for both species has been to keep—hidden, if needs be—the space to ask the profound question: "Why Are Things As They Are?"

1   Frederick Winslow Taylor, *The Principles of Scientific Management* (New York: Harper Bros., 1911).

2   J. M. Coetzee, *Elizabeth Costello* (London: Secker & Warburg, 2003), pp. 28–29.

3   R. M. Yerkes, "Eugenic bearing of Measurements of Intelligence," *The Eugenics Review*, vol. 14, no. 4, January 1923, pp. 225–245. See also Stephen Jay Gould, *The Mismeasure of Man* (New York: Norton, 1981).

4   Wolfgang Köhler, *The Mentality of Apes* (New York: Harcourt Brace & Co., 1926), p. 1.

5   Karl Marx, *Capital Volume I*, tr. Ben Fowkes, Ernst Mandel (Harmondsworth: Penguin, 1991), p. 873.

6   Thomas Aquinas, *Summa Theologica*, cited in *The Open: Man and Animal*, Giorgio Agamben, tr. Kevin Attell (Stanford: Stanford University Press, 2004).

7   Nancy Leys Stepan, "Race and Gender: the Role of Analogy in Science," *Isis*, vol. 77, no. 2 (Chicago: Chicago University Press, 1986).

8   Thomas Carlyle, "Discourse on the Negro Question," *Fraser's Magazine for Town and Country*, vol. XL, London, February 1849.

9   James Hunt, *On The Negro's Place in Nature*, Anthropological Society of London (London: Trübner, 1863).

10   Paul Rohrbach, *German Thought in the World*, http://archive.org/stream/german-worldpolic00rohr/germanworldpolic00rohr_djvu.txt.

11   Donna Haraway cited in *Black Sexual Politics: African Americans, Gender and the New Racism*, Patricia Hill Collins (New York: Routledge, 2004), p. 100.

12   See H. W. Janson, *Apes and Ape Lore in the Middle Ages and the Renaissance* (London: Warburg Institute, 1952).

13   See, among others, Peter Linebaugh, Marcus Rediker, *The Many-Headed Hydra* (London: Verso, 2000).

14   For La Peyrère and Petty, see in particular "Race and the Enlightenment," Loren Goldner, originally published in *Race Traitor* (1997); currently available in two parts on the author's website Break Their Haughty Power, http://breaktheirhaughtypower.org.

15   http://breaktheirhaughtypower.org/
race-and-the-enlightenment-part-i-
from-anti-semitism-to-white-supremacy-
1492-1676/.

16   On Tyson, Linnaeus, Haeckel, and the
"Missing Link," see *The Open: Man and
Animal*, Giorgio Agamben, tr. Kevin Attell
(Stanford: Stanford University Press, 2004).

17   Charles White, *An Account of the
Regular Gradation in Man* (Sabin Americana
Print Collection, Gale Digital Collections,
2012) [London 1799].

18   C. L. R. James, "The Atlantic Slave
Trade," *The Future in the Present* (London:
Allison & Busby, 1977) and "The Making of the
Caribbean People," *Spheres of Existence*
(London: Allison & Busby, 1980).

19   Andrew Zimmerman, *Alabama in Africa:
Booker T. Washington, the German Empire,
and the Globalization of the New South*
(Princeton: Princeton University Press,
2007).

20   Desmond Morris, *The Human Zoo*
(London: Jonathon Cape, 1969).

21   George Gliddon and J. C. Nott, *Types
of Mankind: Indigenous Races of the Earth*
(Philadelphia: J. B. Lippincourt, 1857).

22   See Daniel Pick, *Faces of Degeneracy:
A European Disorder 1848 – 1918* (Cambridge:
Cambridge University Press, 1989), p. 177.

23   Janosch, *Kasperglück und Löwenreise*
(Weinheim: Beltz & Weinheim, 1980).
Passages quoted here are translated by
Anja Büchele and Matthew Hyland.

24   See, for example, the Virunga National
Park website; *Daily Mail* online, July 16, 2012;
NY Daily News, April 11, 2014; *San Antonio
Express*, January 31, 2015.

AN APE ALONE
IS NOT AN APE

Cord Riechelmann

The acute threat facing all populations of apes inevitably raises crucial questions: Have apes accrued any benefit from the interest devoted to them? Or has it harmed them? And has this interest in them proved to be to their detriment?

The latter notion was first mooted by the psychoanalyst Jacques Lacan. At the end of his first seminar on *Freud's Papers on Technique* he distributed photos of elephants, as illustrations of living creatures that have suffered from the interest accorded them.[1] Of course, no one would dream of placing elephants in a "monkey chair" and drilling open their skulls in order, for example, to research the neural basis of human mental disorders, as the neuroscientists have done with monkeys. Elephants are simply too big. Yet as is so often the case, they can still be subject to ill-treatment, of course. Being treated badly, however, is not a privilege reserved for animals.

This brings us to the second question ultimately raised by the interest shown in great apes. Could those whose interest is drawn to these creatures be the very people who, through their activities, their scientific and artistic endeavors, are in fact realizing the fundamental possibilities of nature? The primatologist Sarah Blaffer Hrdy summarized the inherent tension in that question as follows:

I have no doubt that our descendants thousands of years from now (whether on this planet or some other) will be bipedal symbol-generating apes. They will [...] be as competitive and Machiavellian as chimpanzees are now, and probably even more intelligent than people today. What is not certain is whether they will still be human in ways we now think of as distinguishing our species that is, empathic and curious about the emotions of others, shaped by our ancient heritage of communal care.[2]

When looking at Blaffer Hrdy's major study on the evolutionary development of empathy from the cooperative rearing strategies of nonhuman and human primates, it is easy to overlook the acute diagnosis contained in her futuristic concluding sentences. Contending that empathy is disappearing, she argues that current Western societies are in danger of losing the very conditions of their own development. And this is related to the "nature" of empathy, among other things. In her view there is no genetic *a priori*. One cannot regenerate the capacity for empathy from some genome, because essentially it constitutes nothing more than the act of empathy itself. For that reason, too, it can be easily be dispensed with, or rather the capacity to empathize with the emotions of others can quickly become lost. Once this has happened—so runs one interpretation of Blaffer Hrdy's warning—it will only be possible to describe its conditions from the perspective of (natural) history; from the hopefully accurate archives and case files recording "primate societies," in which the conditions that ultimately made us (and not only us) into social beings were created.[3]

This partly explains the enthusiasm with which primatologists such as Christophe Boesch have set about recording and analyzing as comprehensively as possible the last remaining wild chimpanzee populations, although fully aware that they are researching a species facing extinction. For never again will they be able to observe the behavior of the last of this kind in their last remaining wild habitats. Nature reserves, artificially created sanctuaries, and even zoos will never be able to replicate the "wild" situation for one good reason: Unlike all the other habitats in which chimpanzees live today in Africa, they are devoid of human beings as "natural" predators.

Yet before primatology was able to venture a description of ape societies, it first had to learn some basic principles. For not all apes are the same, and above all, an ape alone is not an ape; it is defined by its social interaction. In the 1950s the US psychologist Harry F. Harlow achieved worldwide acclaim with the publication of the results of his studies into infant rhesus monkeys, and his discovery of a need which is as elementary as air, water, and nourishment: the need for a relationship, a bond with one or more others, male or female.[4] This need to forge a bond or an attachment with others is as elementary as air, water, and nourishment, for without them life cannot continue. And the extent to which this "something without which" life cannot continue differs from the mere "something without which" life is not possible (air, water, nourishment), was graphically illustrated by Harlow's infant monkeys.

Harlow presented motherless baby monkeys with the choice between two artificial surrogate "mothers," one made of wire mesh and fitted with a milk bottle, the other without teats, but covered with a warm cloth. The youngsters then spent most of their time clinging to their "cloth" mother, jumping only briefly onto the wire-mesh mother to take a drink. Harlow's study garnered such acclaim because he succeeded in disproving the two prevailing scientific opinions of the time in one fell swoop. On the one hand, he refuted the theories of American behaviorists, who sought to explain the strong mother–child bond among all mammals by simply referring to the reward of mother's milk. On the other hand, he also rendered obsolete Sigmund Freud's view that the primary bonding mechanism between mother and child was the oral-erotic gratification of the child's sucking instinct. Evidently something else was in play here, extending beyond the mere desire for milk: a need for contact, a bond, or whatever one wishes to call it, which, as Harlow went on to demonstrate, was not confined to a warm cloth. For even the infants "reared" by the surrogate puppet mother were little more than abandoned psychological cripples. They huddled in the corners of their cages, rocking back and forth, mutilating themselves and proved incapable of communicating with their conspecifics. Furthermore, only a few were able to reproduce as their sexual behavior was fundamentally disturbed. And even when they gave birth to infants, these were routinely subject to brutal treatment.[5]

By revealing this need for contact and attachment, Harlow had discovered something that was not innate, but that, just like empathy, simply came into the world by mere virtue of the fact that it took place. Thus bonding, on the one hand, was characterized as forming part of the minimum conditions of all our existence, whilst on the other hand it impelled our social interaction.[6]

Of interest, indeed of constitutive importance for the history of primatology is also Harlow's background. During World War II, he held a senior position as psychological adviser to the US army. This is one reason why he was so fascinated by the impact of social deprivation on personality development. In essence one could say that the rhesus monkeys served him as a model organism for his research into war psychosis, an interest he shared with his predecessor, the psychologist Robert Yerkes. In 1923, when Yerkes purchased two juvenile chimpanzees from a sailor in Boston, he had already collected many years' experience as a US army psychologist during World War I. We can only gain a proper insight into either the history of primatology or its profound impact on American popular culture by considering how the treatment of war psychoses in American society differed specifically from all other societies after the world wars. War psychotics could, of course, be found everywhere, including the Soviet Union and the Weimar Republic, but the United States was the first country to address this disorder as a public issue. The reason for this lay in the nature of American democracy, which during World War I had led to America facing far greater problems than any other participating nation in placing the economy and society in general on a war footing. This may also explain why the psychological impact of war was observed more closely and critically in the United States than in other countries.[7]

Yerkes, too, was in search of a model organism that, whilst not actually human, was closely related to human beings, in order to enhance his understanding of the catastrophic impact of war on the psyche of many participants.[8] That Yerkes' research —contrary to his original intentions—quickly came to focus on his two chimpanzees is a consequence of what they both taught him. Such were the differences between the two animals, however, these comparisons between them soon proved pointless. From a contemporary perspective this is fairly easy to explain, for the chimpanzees he purchased belonged to different species. Yet Yerkes could not have known this at the time since one of them, a bonobo (*Pan paniscus*) whom he named Prince Chim, was not recognized as a distinct species until 1929. Furthermore, the "common" chimpanzee (*Pan troglydytes*)—nicknamed Panzee—suffered from tuberculosis, which probably influenced his behavior.

Providing a detailed account of his experiences with Chim and Panzee, Yerkes' highly popular book *Almost Human*, published in 1925, wielded a tremendous twofold impact. From that moment onwards, the family of great apes, which, in addition to chimpanzees and bonobos, also includes orangutans, gorillas, and gibbons, entered into American mainstream culture. Yet Yerkes' detailed descriptions could not disguise how little was known about apes. When he collated and published all the available material on the subject under the title *The Great Apes* in 1927, the lack of systematic accounts of how apes behaved in the wild became obvious. What observations there were came from explorers, missionaries, and researchers, who collected and shot everything they saw. The most accurate descriptions were of orangutans in Borneo, provided by Alfred Russel Wallace, who, together with his contemporary Darwin, ranks as a cofounder of modern evolutionary theory. Wallace earned his living from selling the plants and animals collected on his voyages to clients such as natural history museums. His clinically accurate account of the death throes of the orangutans was highly convincing; having shot dozens to death for his collection.

These early forays were followed by the first systematic field investigations conducted in the 1930s by Clarence Ray Carpenter on the white-handed gibbon in Thailand. Carpenter, too, had all the gibbons he observed shot once he had gathered sufficient behavioral data. This he did partly because he wanted to keep the skin and skeleton, and partly because he was keen to examine the gender and stomach contents of the animals. However, in the process Carpenter also made a discovery that would have merited more than a mere footnote in Blaffer Hrdy's book *Mothers and Others*. Gibbons live territorially in family groups that generally consist of one adult male, a female, and their offspring, but one of his

gibbon pairs comprised two young males who, despite cohabiting with a juvenile, displayed no behavioral anomalies Carpenter was able to determine.

Of course, even these observations in the wild remained fragmentary, culminating as they always did in the abrupt and violent demise of the animals. Nothing was to change until the 1960s, with the arrival on the scene of a prominent female trio of field primatologists dubbed the Trimates: Jane Goodall, Dian Fossey, and Birutė Galdikas. Yerkes' pioneering work on chimpanzees had inspired two schools of anthropology in the United States that in the ensuing years, and contrary to the intentions of their founder, were to unleash the emancipatory tendencies within primatology. One school formed around the anthropologist Sherwood Washburn, who after World War II held lectures at the University of Chicago on early hominid evolution; the other was spearheaded by the archeo-anthropologist Louis Leakey, who conducted excavations in Kenya in search of early hominid fossils.

Under the apposite title of "The Contest for Primate Nature: Daughters of Man the Hunter in the Field, 1960–1980," Donna Haraway dedicated a seminal essay to the Washburn school, which comprised mainly female students and which had in a wider sense also inspired Sarah Blaffer Hrdy. Haraway's paper demonstrates how these female primatologists not only developed a scientific methodology and established it in institutions, but that their influence extended beyond feminism and even helped shape the curricula of America's public schools.[9] By contrast, Leakey's students, the distinguished Trimates of Goodall, Fossey, and Galdikas, succeeded in capturing the imagination of American popular culture.[10]

From the 1970s until well into the 1980s, the students of both Washburn and Leakey collectively transformed primatology into one of the few sciences if not the only one that was not only conducted largely by women, but that could also boast women in influential academic positions. In the process, they also systematically questioned the definitions distinguishing human beings from animals. For example, if early man and the great ape were to be differentiated by the fact that human beings hunt whereas apes do not, Goodall was able to observe that chimpanzees also hunted; moreover, they did not do so alone, but were in well-coordinated groups that later shared the rewards of the hunt.[11]

A similar situation obtained in the use of tools and war as the distinguishing features of man; chimpanzees fished for termites using twigs they fashioned themselves and they regularly engaged in wars with neighboring groups of chimpanzees.[12] Thanks to these observations of the wars waged against other groups of chimpanzees and Dian Fossey's detailed accounts of infanticide by male Rwandan mountain gorillas,[13] a number of other basic tenets, in addition to the major distinctions between humans and animals, were also called into question. When animals of the same species engage in combat in the wild, under conditions uncorrupted by human influence or taken to pathological extremes as in Harlow's experiments, there must be something fundamentally amiss in the harmonizing concepts of species or race. Short of moralizing or pathologizing a behavior that evidently harms members of the same species, one can only surmise that it concerns a form of conduct unrepresentative of the species. Consequently, Goodall's observations of war and Fossey's accounts of infanticide coincided with the birth and heyday of sociobiology, whose populist slogan was formulated in 1976 by Richard Dawkins in the title of his book *The Selfish Gene.*

However, before we dismiss sociobiology—a science whose best days lie behind it—as a reactionary, neoliberal doctrine, we should take a closer look at its opponents.[14] Sociobiology is a behavioral theory predicated on the assumption that even the smallest difference manifested in the genome (and through which, in addition to other influences, we develop into individuals or come into the world as such) result in differences of interest. Consequently, the decisive driver of evolutionary change is the individual, rather than the harmonizing group, which is constituted in abstract terms in the definition of a species. This idea was not new when sociobiology first emerged in the early 1970s, for Darwin's central thesis had also focused on the individual. Since we do not know what the individual is capable of, this was the fundamental question that he sought to answer. And notwithstanding the catastrophic experiences—not only in biology—on issues relating to species and race in the twentieth century, sociobiology merely poses this question anew. Sociobiologists and so-called evolutionary psychologists not only emphasized genetic egoism, emboldened by the election victories of Margaret Thatcher and Ronald Reagan and their socially destructive neoliberal concepts of the early 1980s, but they also propounded misconceived and aggressive nonsense such as the contention that rape was an evolutionary male reproduction strategy; however, this changes nothing about the fundamentally heuristic nature of the science. That the most miniscule difference in underlying physical conditions also engenders different movements and interests is a function of the same condition by which phenomena such as bonding and empathy are revealed not to be *a priori* in origin; in other words, they stem only from the moment of their genesis.

The progression from sociobiology to the experience of empathy as neither predestined nor prestabilized can also be traced in the trajectory of Sarah Blaffer Hrdy's research career. Starting out as a radical sociobiologist, in 1977 Blaffer Hrdy published her first book, *The Langurs of Abu: Female and Male Strategies of Reproduction,* in which she presented a purely differential analysis of male and female reproductive interests from an evolutionary perspective. *Mothers and Others*, which was first published in 2009, contains an equally radical critique of (not only the American) nuclear family, similarly from an evolutionary perspective. Her core argument is that the capacity for empathy is so easily lost because reproduction is possible even without it. Human reproductive technology is so far advanced that mastering the act of copulation is no longer necessary in order to procreate. Consequently, the impetus to care communally for members of society such as newborn babies and children is rendered redundant although without this impetus neither apes nor great apes would have existed in the first place. What is then lost are not genes or other material bodily substances, but rather elements of social interaction. And these can only be related by those (human) societies capable of describing themselves

and others, who have ostensibly been liberated from
genetic determinism by virtue of neuroplasticity.
To paraphrase Blaffer Hrdy, however, one could state
that the neurosciences have not produced anything
apart from self-correcting mirrors. For Others retain
their reality in the long term only by remaining
external. We cannot continually reincorporate Others
into our realm of experience, but must instead
approach them by means of empathy and bonding.
Yet currently only the last surviving ape societies are
able to narrate the conditions spawning these
possibilities in greater detail than developed human
societies. Thus, although our observations of apes
cannot save us, they may show us how to gain better
access to the possibilities of "nature" that might still
come to fruition.

Translated from the German by John Rayner

1   Jacques Lacan, *Das Seminar I: Freuds technische Schriften*, 2nd edition (Berlin: Weinheim, 1990). Published in English as *The Seminar of Jacques Lacan: Book 1, Freud's Papers on Technique*, 1953–1954, Jacques-Alain Miller (ed.), tr. John Forrester (Cambridge: Cambridge University Press, 1988). Featured on the inside cover of the German edition is a photograph of an elephant, beneath which is the closing sentence of the book: "Jacques Lacan has figurines representing elephants handed out."

2   Sarah Blaffer Hrdy, *Mothers and Others: The Evolutionary Origins of Mutual Understanding* (Cambridge, Massachusetts: Harvard University Press, 2009), pp. 293–294.

3   See the standard work on primatology by Barbara Smuts et al. (eds.), *Primate Societies* (Chicago: Chicago University Press, 1987).

4   For a philosophical/political discussion on this "something without which life cannot continue," see Frederic Worms, *Über Leben* (Berlin: Merve, 2013).

5   See Andreas Paul, *Von Affen und Menschen: Verhaltensbiologie der Primaten* (Darmstadt: Wissenschaftliche Buchgesellschaft, 1998), p. 168 and Frans de Waal, *Peacemaking among Primates* (Cambridge, Massachusetts: Harvard University Press, 1989), pp. 12–13.

6   See Worms, *Über Leben*, p. 33.

7   In order to give some historical perspective, reference is made to the fact that war psychosis has become a public issue in Germany only since the Bundeswehr deployment to Afghanistan.

8   It is worth noting that a link between primatology and psychiatry can also be established in West Germany if one considers the works of Detlef Ploog at the Max Planck Institute for Psychiatry to be pioneering in West German primatology. It was at this institution that Jacques Lacan held his only lecture in the Federal Republic of Germany in 1958.

9   Donna Haraway, *Simians, Cyborgs, and Women: The Reinvention of Nature* (New York: Routledge, 1991).

10   In her own account of her life and research entitled *Reflections of Eden: My Years With the Orangutans of Borneo* (Boston: Little, Brown, 1995), p. 30, Birutė Galdikas writes of Jane Goodall: "Through her *National Geographic* articles, books, television specials produced with her first husband, photographer Hugo van Lawick, and lecture tours, Jane turned the daily flow of activities among a group of wild chimpanzees into a family saga for the public. 'Flo' and 'Fifi' became part of the American family. Long before *Dynasty* and *Dallas*, a generation of North Americans grew up with 'Mike,' 'Melissa,' and 'David Greybeard.' Flo was probably the only wild animal who ever received an obituary in the *London Times*." All the "names" refer to chimpanzees from Goodall's study population.

11   For more on the hunting behavior of chimpanzees see Craig B. Stanford, *Chimpanzee and Red Colobus: The Ecology of Predator and Prey* (Cambridge, Massachusetts: Harvard University Press, 1998).

12   See Jane Goodall's standard work *The Chimpanzees of Gombe* (Cambridge, Massachusetts: Harvard University Press, 1986).

13   See Dian Fossey, *Gorillas in the Mist* (Boston: Houghton Mifflin, 1983).

14   In his seminal essay of 1992, the German primatologist Volker Sommer pointed out that many sociobiologists can be classified as belonging more to the emancipatory wing, whereas proponents of group selection and of the species preservation principle are, to put it mildly, of a more conservative persuasion. See Eckart Voland, *Fortpflanzung: Natur und Kultur im Wechselspiel* (Frankfurt am Main: Suhrkamp, 1992), pp. 51–73.

"ONE COULD DESCRIBE US AS CHIMPANZEE ETHNOGRAPHERS"

Christophe Boesch *in conversation with Cord Riechelmann*

Cord Riechelmann: Professor Boesch, when you became well known beyond the field of primatology with the publication of your first studies on the nut-cracking chimpanzees of Taï National Park, in Côte d'Ivoire, you were venturing into a highly specialized field: the use of tools by nonhuman individuals. Although there had previously been accounts by Jane Goodall and others, your work added a totally new dimension: The chimpanzees used certain types of "anvils" and hammers and, furthermore, you found something resembling workshops to which the animals would return to crack the nuts. Can you describe the route you have taken to this field of primatology, namely the sophisticated use of tools?

Christophe Boesch: My personal experience with primatology started in 1973, with Dian Fossey and the mountain gorillas of Rwanda. I was participating in a longitudinal project that had been launched to count the gorillas in the Virunga Mountains. In common with many young people, I harbored a fascination for gorillas, and because I'm French Dian Fossey accepted me onto her team. This was useful in our dealings with the Rwandan authorities, whose official languages also include French. I was able to gain a lot of experience that subsequently proved valuable in my own project.

I had learned from my professor in Paris that chimpanzees in West Africa, in Côte d'Ivoire, were able to crack nuts. However, this had never been observed. There were only two reports that evidence of nut-cracking spots had been found, such as cracked nutshells and hammers—and the Africans who were present confirmed that chimpanzees had been responsible. As a young scientist I thought to myself firstly that as our closest relatives chimpanzees are fascinating, and secondly, their use of tools could also raise significant questions for us humans.

So I decided to take the risk and travel there. And in the seven months I spent in Côte d'Ivoire I was in fact able to observe one female chimpanzee cracking nuts. At first I just heard the noise, but as I approached I saw her. She held a hammer in her hand. This was the first ever confirmation that chimpanzees use a hammer to crack nuts. On the basis of this observation I was able to secure more funding and proceed with my own project. Together with my wife, Hedwige Boesch, I then traveled to Côte d'Ivoire in 1979—and today we are still there continuing our work.

Working with chimpanzees in Africa is difficult because wherever they live they are hunted by humans: Their meat is reputedly very tasty, and because they are our closest relatives there is a belief that chimpanzees possess supernatural powers. Eating their meat is said to have a beneficial impact on children and the sick. This is why chimpanzee bones feature strongly in traditional medicines. And because they are hunted chimpanzees are very shy and run away before you can even glimpse them. It took two years before we were able to make any tangible progress with them. And we needed five years before we were able to observe them properly—that is, observe them despite their being aware of our presence. This length of time was necessary in order to become sufficiently used to each other in the habituation process so that the animals could be observed without them altering their behavior.

CR: If I recall correctly, Jane Goodall also needed five years.

CB: Exactly. She attempted to expedite the process by feeding her chimpanzees with bananas, but it didn't really help much.

Our biggest stroke of fortune was that the chimpanzees cracked the nuts there. The nut season lasts approximately four months a year. And cracking nuts makes a noise. So although the chimpanzees knew that humans were in close proximity—which they didn't want—they would always betray their presence by the noise they made when striking nuts. We developed a good ear for this specific sound and increasingly were able to locate the chimpanzees. The initial analyses sought to determine how many nuts the animals cracked a minute, how many hammer blows they needed, and who opened the nuts. We eventually concluded that the females were more efficient than the males—which contradicted the general tendency of our science to focus on the males.

CR: I noticed that at the time. Your initial studies were an effective and well-substantiated refutation of everything that devolved from the "man the hunter" hypothesis on active hunting males and passive females.

CB: Exactly. And the feminists, who were very active at the time, immediately cited my works to support their case as proof that in our evolutionary history females played a much more important role than had hitherto been ascribed to them.

Our question, however, centered on the extent to which this behavior is common throughout Africa. To our astonishment we discovered that there is a boundary in Côte d'Ivoire that runs along the Sassandra River. All chimpanzees west of the river cracked nuts, while all chimpanzees to the east of it didn't. Despite the fact that east of the river there were just as many nut trees, just as many roots to use as anvils, and sufficient material for hammers. Thus there were no environmental factors. Consequently, we proposed interpreting nut-cracking as a cultural behavior since the explanation could only be of a purely social nature. The chimpanzees on the one side did it, but those on the other side did not. It was twenty-four years ago that we published this …

CR: You conducted your research with a fascinating attention to detail, even compiling an encyclopedia of the various sizes and shapes of the hammers. Didn't your work also demand a comprehensive knowledge of the individuals you observed? Or am I going too far?

CB: Not at all. Our observations of chimpanzees—and this applies generally to primatology—require that we identify the individual animals. And often it took a frustratingly long time until we got a result. Chimpanzees do not attain adulthood until they are thirteen to fifteen years old. That means if you wish to study how a particular behavior is acquired, you should first be aware that you are starting out on a project likely to span at least five to ten years. And that makes things difficult.

CR: It makes things a) difficult and b) doesn't it also buck the prevailing trend—initiated by scientists themselves—to produce results with ever greater alacrity? Does it perhaps mean that you are one of the last remaining exponents of longitudinal studies?

CB: I wouldn't say that. Maybe I belong to a generation that structures their studies over a longer period. But I never imagined at the outset that I would end up spending the next thirty-five years working with chimpanzees. In principle, the advantage of longer studies over shorter ones is accepted by scientists. And this also applies to the financial backers, such as the Schweizerischer Nationalfonds, which has always supported me. At the same time, researchers are, of course, continually under pressure to come up with new ideas. That much is obvious. And therefore, after six years of researching nut-cracking, I decided to address another topic: the hunting behavior of chimpanzees.

CR: A term often still used in this context—and I heard it myself in lectures—is "predatory hate." And Jane Goodall observed that hunting and catching the colobus monkey was a purely male activity among chimpanzees. Yet in your work neither hate and aggression, nor this male aspect are afforded any special emphasis.

CB: Absolutely. I don't think that this concept of hatred can be applied to chimpanzees. For many predators, hunting is simply a means to acquire nourishment, and is not motivated by hate or other similar emotions. This would unnecessarily complicate matters for the hunters since a hunt requires a certain amount of planning. They are searching for their prey, or perhaps they first search for hunt participants and subsequently the prey—although success is not always guaranteed. This means they must be able to judge when it is worthwhile to hunt and when not. Furthermore, chimpanzees hunting in groups must also be able to organize the pursuit: Who assumes which role? How can I help the others to stop that colobus escaping? If hunting were purely driven by emotion, everyone would simply charge at the intended prey, probably without ever catching anything.

Chimpanzees hunt smaller apes that live high up in the trees and are thus able to choose escape routes the chimpanzees cannot follow. Hence, if the chimpanzees didn't organize themselves, they wouldn't be successful in such forests. This explains why Taï chimpanzees hunt in groups far more commonly than the chimpanzees of other forests, where it is easier to corner their prey.

CR: The chimpanzees' hunting behavior in the difficult conditions of the Taï rainforest serves as a prime illustration of what you describe as eco-cultural; I found that especially convincing, for example, in the demands placed by the specific ecological conditions on the learning process.

CB: You could also describe us as chimpanzee ethnographers. I have always attached great importance to showing that chimpanzees display highly variable and flexible behavior and that each population can develop quite different behavioral patterns. This is something that must be taken into consideration. And their behavior is partly shaped by environmental influences, which in the Taï forest implies dense, tropical rainforest. Contrast this to the open bush country in Gombe, Tanzania, where Jane Goodall worked; this was savanna mixed with forest, where the visibility and topography, in other words the trees and the structure of the forest, are very different. Consequently, chimpanzees—in common with many other species—can also be expected to adapt to the ecological conditions. And this brings us back to our definition of culture, because we presume that chimpanzees, too, will adapt to the conditions of their particular habitats in the evolutionary process.

That a species can display very different behavioral patterns in very different habitats has nothing to do with culture. It's merely an adaptation to the environment. Given that we were endeavoring to provide a means of opening the concept of culture to animals, we felt an obligation to prove that cultural differences between individual populations were not dependent upon environmental conditions—even though we know that culture in human beings is also dependent upon the environment. The definition of culture we applied at the outset in order to demonstrate culture in animals was therefore narrower than the criteria applied to humans. This, of course, is not really fair …

CR: I regard that as a very important aspect of your work. Michel Foucault once remarked that when he worked with outsiders, for example mental patients, he had to be more precise than with normal, healthy people. I'm not, of course, comparing chimpanzees with the mentally ill. I do, however, regard it as the fairest solution for chimpanzees if we apply more rigorous criteria.

CB: It is simply more difficult because there are always two camps within scientific discourse. And among those working with chimpanzees, there are perhaps even more camps because we are running up against the famous major barrier, or the "golden barrier" as Stephen Jay Gould dubbed it, which distinguished or is intended to distinguish man from all other living creatures. Of course, this is my motivation for working with chimpanzees. Like all chimpanzee researchers I am keen to ascertain how high this barrier really is. In many ways it was set by religion, subsequently by scientists and philosophers. Socrates, Rousseau, and the rest had no idea what these animals do or are capable of. All they had were travelogues or illustrations of individual animals, randomly observed—and frequently the animals were already dead. There was no conception of great apes in their natural environment, a scientific myopia that lasted until the early 1960s. This was the point at which Jane Goodall and other biologists and behavioral ecologists went out into the wild and observed the animals in their natural habitats.

The upshot is that today we have the incredible luxury of being able to conduct scientific research into the issue of the "golden barrier." I am a little shocked every time I see that the pleasure in testing these barriers is not shared by many scientists. Which once more brings us back to the issue of culture …

Culture is a term conceived by humans for humans in order to represent the greatest achievement of humanity. However, when we speak of culture in animals it is clear that the skeptics standing on the other side of the barrier perceive everything very critically. And the problem of furnishing evidence of culture with nut-cracking is that on the one hand, there are populations that crack nuts, and on the other, populations that do NOT crack nuts. It is very difficult to prove why one population or animal does not do it.

One advantage of our project with Taï chimpanzees, however, is that we started quite early in getting neighboring groups habituated to human observers. Accordingly, over the years we were able to monitor three neighboring groups and examine the cultural differences between them. During the nut-cracking season, we observed that each of these groups have specific criteria for selecting a good hammer: The three groups that regularly engage in aggressive contact and probably exchange females each have clearly distinguishable preferences in the hammers they use.

Thus we have three neighboring groups in regular contact within the same forest. Despite this, however, clear cultural differences remain in regards to the criteria applied to choose their hammers. This is quite strange because females regularly migrate from one group to another.[1] This shows that the females adopt the habits of their new group: They migrate out when they are between ten and twelve years old, an age at which they are already highly proficient nut-crackers, so although they have mastered the technique of their birth group, they always apply the techniques of the new group they join.

CR: So given that the ecological conditions are identical, this is no longer ecocultural, but purely cultural, as it were?

CB: It's genuine proof of cultural behavior.

CR: I would now like to address two issues that, whilst also pertaining to culture, are not related directly to chimpanzees. Firstly, have you always managed to come to an agreement with the governments as far as research permits are concerned?

CB: Yes always. Fortunately.

CR: And secondly, has the forest changed over the years?

CB: Over the past thirty-five years deforestation in Côte d'Ivoire has progressed so swiftly that virgin forest can only be found in the National Park. While this is very sad, it is also unsurprising given that humans have never shown any respect for the environment. We have destroyed everything and as a consequence, average rainfall in Africa over the past sixty years has fallen both drastically and continually. This has triggered increasing desertification in a southerly direction; so what are people supposed to do? Because they can no longer farm the land, they also migrate southwards. Coastal populations have trebled, and over half of the migrants are from the north. It is obvious that this development is detrimental to the forests. The destruction of the forests is only exacerbating the problem of drought in Africa. Rainfall in Côte d'Ivoire, for example, has declined and dry periods are even being recorded along the coast—something that is unprecedented. What we are experiencing in Africa and on other continents is a consequence of climate change. As a result the animals that once lived in these forests are no longer present. And along with the forests, the elephants, chimpanzees, and forest antelopes have also disappeared.

CR: In view of the essentially hopeless situation of your chimpanzees, can I ask how you manage to continue to work so enthusiastically, not only in Côte d'Ivoire, but also with your Pan African Programme: The Cultured Chimpanzee, which you launched to survey and research all the populations still in existence?

CB: You can only work for chimpanzee protection if you're—let's say—an incorrigible optimist. There are unfortunately abundant reasons for growing frustrated, but expressing this publicly is not advisable as it merely makes the job of selling environmental protection even more difficult. But it's the truth. I think you just have to deal with it, and refrain from constantly peddling illusions.

CR: Although you've answered my question fully, I would still like to inquire again how you manage to maintain this—from my perspective—wonderful attitude in which you as a scientist see no alternative but to keep on researching?

CB: I can well understand it if those conducting research into wild populations become so depressed about their animals vanishing that they feel they can no longer continue. An alternative strategy is to become proactive in protecting the environment. This trend can clearly be observed among many primatologists.

CR: Your commitment has always made eminent sense to me by virtue of your uncompromising insistence on distinguishing between wild populations and others, for example, those in zoos. If I understand you correctly, you even claim that comparisons are simply not feasible.

CB: As I mentioned already, I attach great importance to behavioral flexibility among highly developed animals. And not just among chimpanzees. I myself have observed chimpanzees for months on end at various locations and experienced at first hand how strong the differences are between populations, and how great the environmental influence is. I am, of course, observing the animals in their natural habitat. In contrast, when I see animals in zoos or cages I know that these are totally artificial living conditions. The animals are flexible enough to adapt to them—not necessarily to their benefit, but adapt they do. I am convinced that animals raised and living in such artificial conditions are disadvantaged. Captivity means a completely passive environment, where nothing happens. Compared to animals living in the wild, therefore, they are in a much poorer position. This is an idea I have repeatedly pointed out over the years, but fortunately it has been gaining ever more acceptance recently. Studies have now been published that specifically observe the impact these artificial living conditions have on behavior and even more strongly on the development of the brain. From this one can only conclude that captivity is detrimental to the animals' development. Nevertheless, I am not advocating that we stop working with animals in captivity altogether, as there are certainly a number of things that can be researched there. However, one cannot generalize the knowledge acquired in captivity and apply it to wild animals. The problem is one of interpretation and generalization.

Translated from the German by John Rayner

1   Chimpanzees live in groups in which the males always remain in their birth groups, whereas the females migrate out and join other groups when they reach the age of sexual maturity.

Clarence Ray Carpenter

MACACA FUSCATA
(CERCOPITHECIDAE) –
Tree-Top Signaling, 1971
Digital transfer from 16 mm film,
color, no sound, 4 min. 30 sec.

This field footage of Japanese macaques (*Macaca fuscata*) shot by the comparative psychologist Clarence Ray Carpenter in 1966 and 1971 was among the first moving images of these animals to be broadcast to the public via mass media. Filmed at two different colonies in Japan (Takasakiyama and Choshikei), it shows dominant males climbing 25-meter high treetops to survey and signal the location and intended direction of group movements to other groups.

This film is part of the archive of the Encyclopaedia Cinematographica, an international scientific film project consisting of several thousand films from all over the world, founded in the 1950s by the Institute for Scientific Film (IWF) in Göttingen, Germany, under the auspices of Gotthard Wolf and the behaviorist Konrad Lorenz, among others. Lorenz, also known for his studies of geese, published his treatise *On Aggression* in 1963, weaving together theories of ritualized aggression in the maintenance of civilization with fieldwork conducted by Carpenter and others on "naturalistic" resource and conflict management.

In the 1960s and 1970s, cold war and psychiatric research funds were both used to support Carpenter's research and public lectures that linked war and aggression to stress, arousal, and territoriality. He was adamant that biosocial lessons on the disasters of modernity could be directly extracted from nonhuman populations. While he "painted broad biological and evolutionary strokes" (Donna Haraway) and perpetuated primatology's mainframing of dominant masculinities, he stood out among the early comparative psychologists for his long-running fieldwork commitments, for standardizing methods for turning "free-range" behavioral data into "fact," and for connecting primatology to structuralism and systems theory.

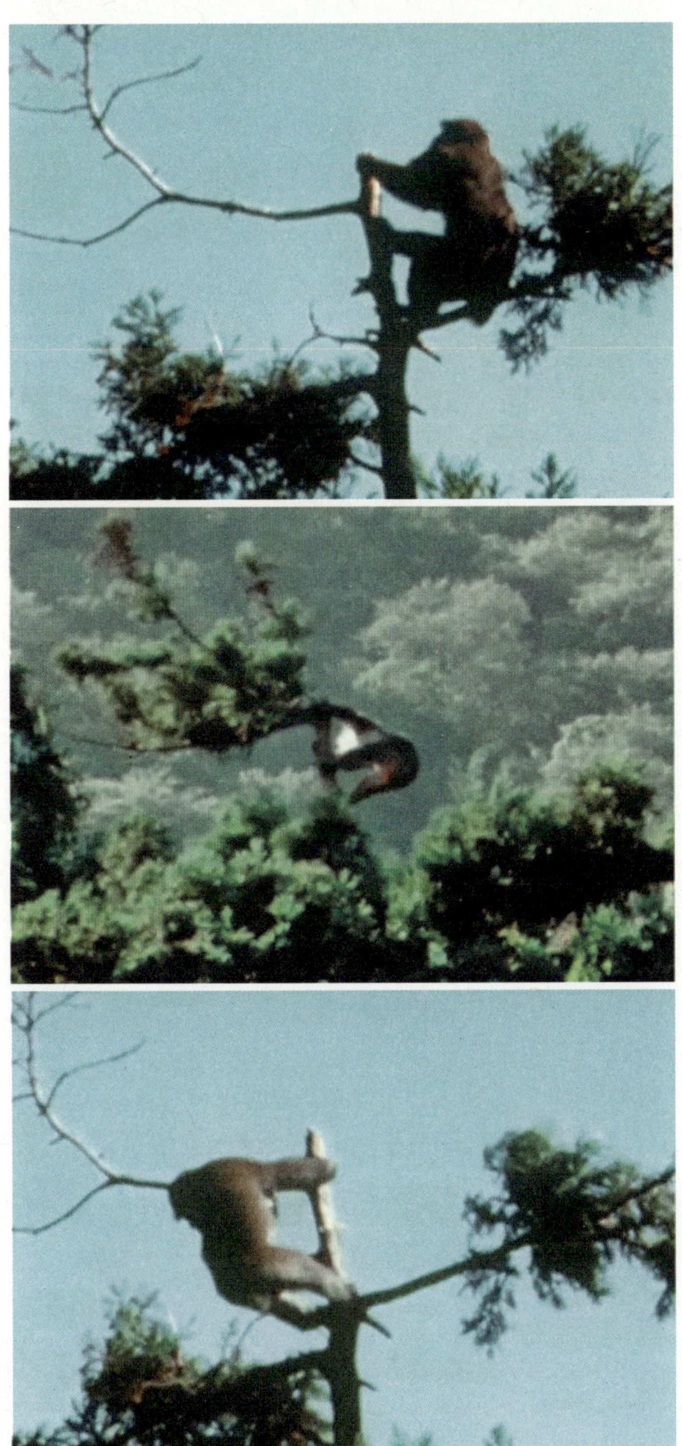

Lene Berg

KOPFKINO (MINDFUCK), 2012
Film HDV, color, stereo, 75 min.

That primal and refined social-aesthetic urges are inseparable is never more obvious than with the sexual contract. As Silvia Federici once argued, "We cannot go back to nature simply by taking off our clothes." *Kopfkino* (literally "head cinema") refers to those images that confront us from the uncensored edge of the mind's eye, where affects and associations are left alone to run wild, or indeed purposively commissioned.

Drawing connections between auteurism, the cinematic aspects of thought, and sadomasochistic practice, Lene Berg developed the loose script for *Kopfkino (mindfuck)* from interviews with a number of women who work as dominatrixes and slaves in the BDSM industry. Eight of them sit dressed in character (as a grand dame, rococo madam, schoolgirl, burlesque artist, businesswoman, butch dom, and so on), all facing the camera at a long table on an obvious film set, resembling perhaps a sacrilegious *Last Supper* or reversioning of Judy Chicago's *Dinner Party*. The camera pans above and below a tableau as they tell their stories, taking a slow, shifting interest in figures, dresses, and accoutrements, and in accordance with the formal logic of S+M scene-making.

Leopold von Sacher-Masoch possessed his female objects of desire by elevating them into ideal cinematic types. Pier Paolo Pasolini dramatized prostitutes as allegorical figures for societal detachment and disruption. Berg's choreography shows the mistresses' own capacity for self-valuation. Condensed from five hours down to a series of unique and candid vignettes, the work gives access to the juxta-political appropriations of female desire internal to the changing affective labor history of S+M.

"We have this marvelous wet room in our studio. From time to time a slave comes by, we put him in there for an hour or two and he is the toilet. The ladies go in and out and normally nothing much happens, the man just lays there and is the toilet. One time a guy came by and we put him in there. We went in one after the other. Then he started this role-playing thing, it was great. Totally dazed he kept looking at me, saying: 'I am only the pizza delivery man, I deliver pizza.' Really authentic. I thought: Is he really the pizza delivery man? But he wasn't. It was great. He kept it going the whole time with the other ladies, too. They already knew him. They also knew how difficult it was to bring this toilet thing to end, to make him cum, which was important to him. Unfortunately, I didn't know him yet and I was persuaded to go in last. So I went in and he was holding his dick in his hand, fidgeting. Nothing happened. So I told him … I don't even know how I started … Finally I told him I would attach him to our milking machine, if it did not work out. He looked at me and said: 'The milking machine? Oh god, no, no, no …' I didn't know what else to say, so I told him: 'Yes, we always do that to pizza delivery men here. We have many milking machines and there are tons of pizza delivery men hooked up to them in the other rooms. We milk them and sell the sperm to earn some extra money.' He flipped out: 'What? A bunch of pizza delivery guys hooked up to milking machines?' He came. It was perfect."

Script excerpt: Lene Berg, *Kopfkino (mindfuck)*, 2012.

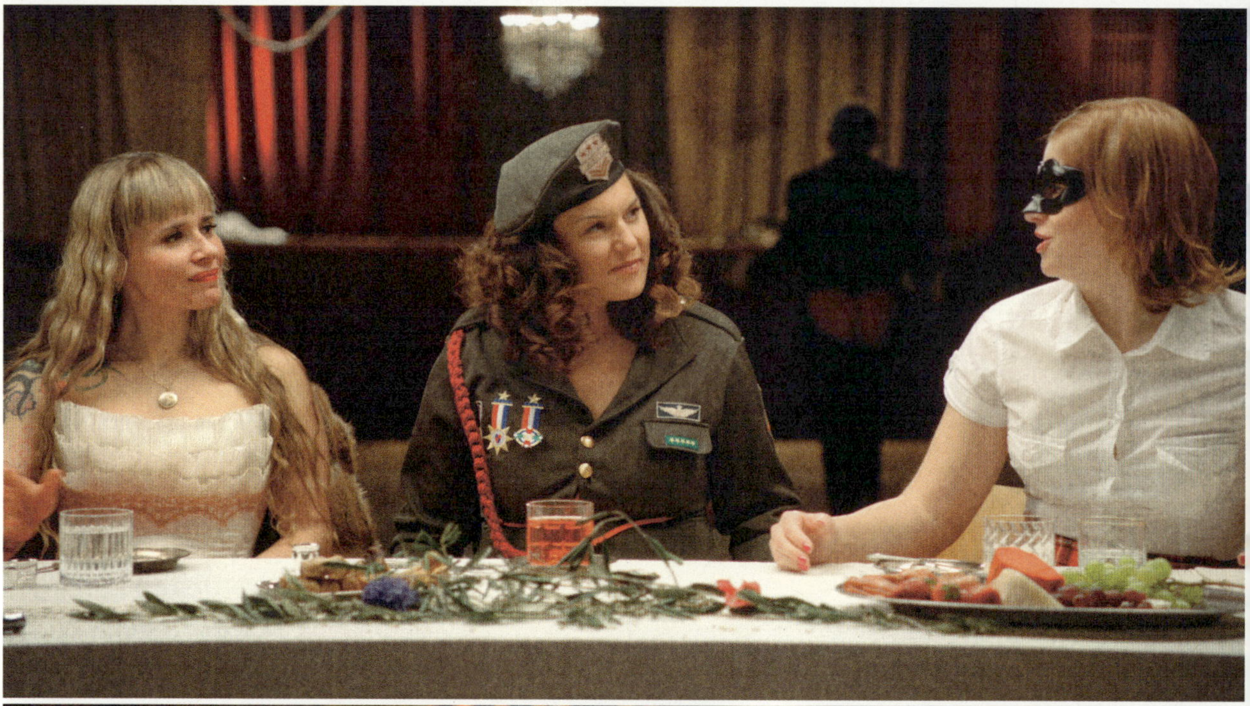

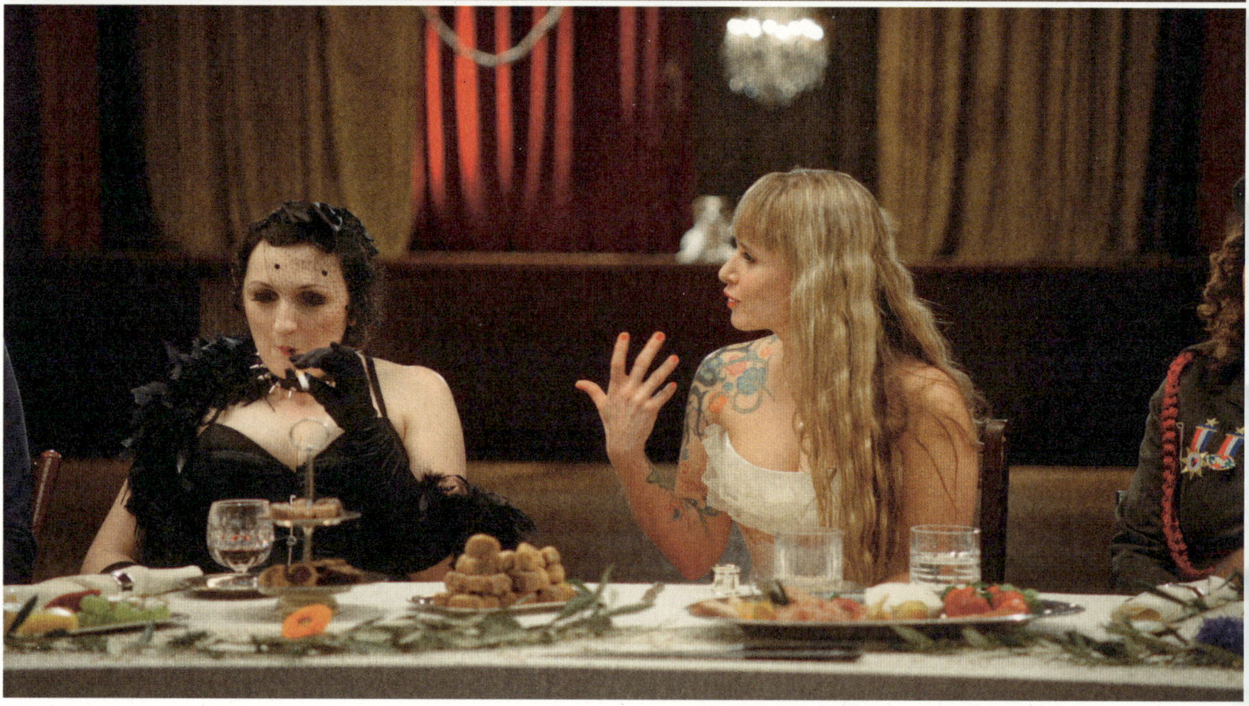

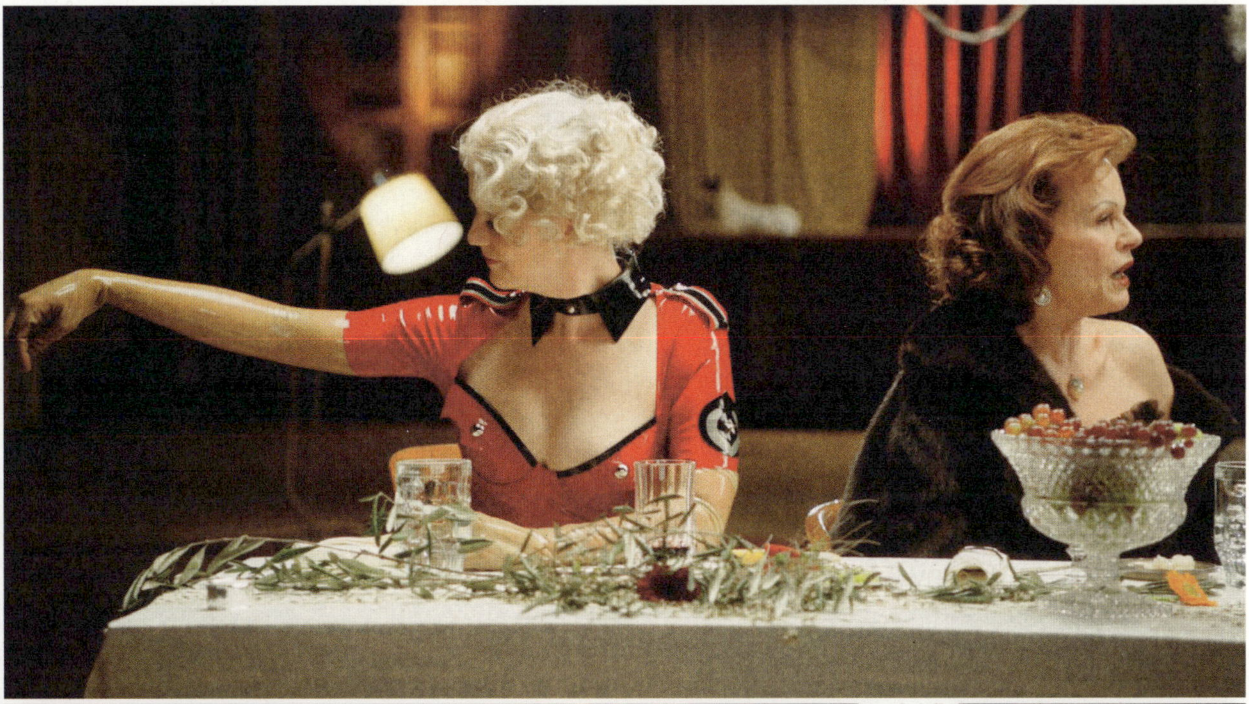

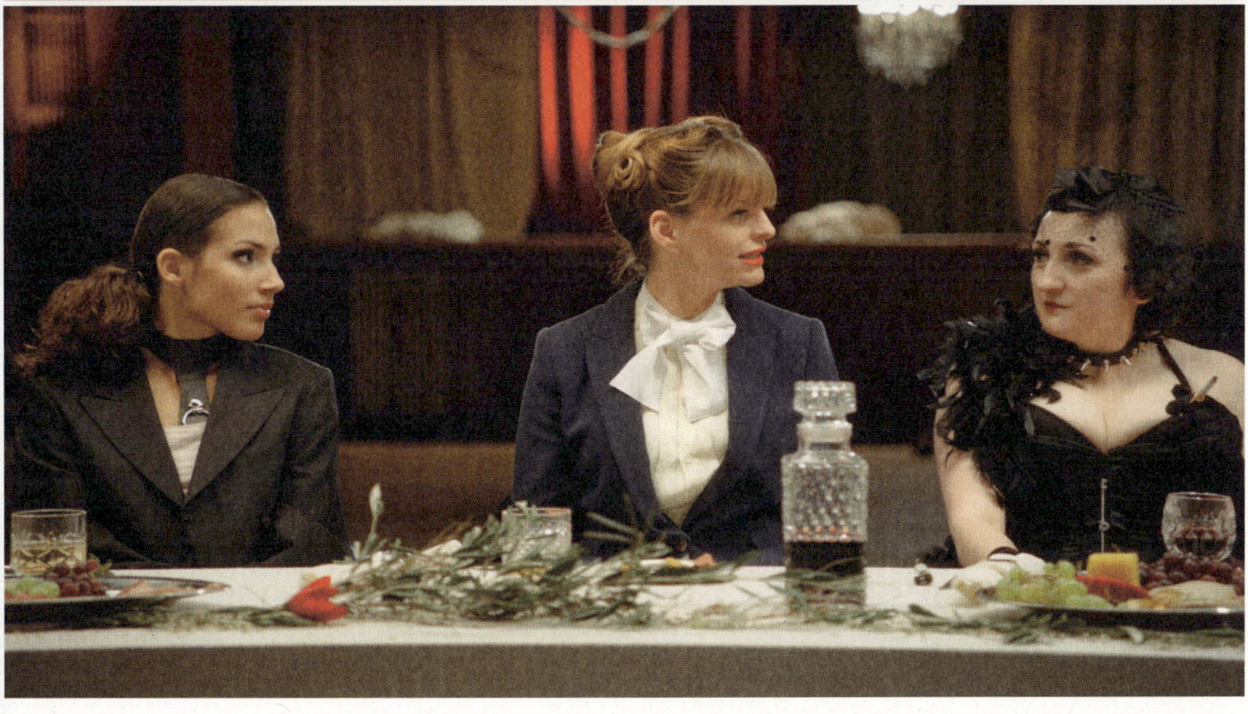

Marcus Coates
in collaboration with
Volker Sommer

DEGREECOORDINATES ·
Shared traits of the Hominini
(Humans, Bonobos and
Chimpanzees), 2015
Vinyl letters on wall, dimensions
variable

Degreecoordinates is a text work designed by Marcus Coates in collaboration with Volker Sommer, consisting entirely of a list of behavioral traits formulated as questions that direct themselves at the viewer. The tendency of human groups to compare one another constantly is revealed here quite profoundly, inasmuch as browsing through the listings tends to create the experience of identifying traits from among a sizeable mass of behaviors, characteristics that stand out as typical of either one's self or of others' behavior. Coates and Sommer's mass of chosen traits is particularly distinguished by listing similarities that have been proven to be shared across the primate tribe of Hominini, which includes humans, bonobos, and chimpanzees. No clearly discernible "species" or even "tribe" boundary can be established between these primates. Nevertheless, the traits can seemingly be introjected or rejected, borne of an individual subjective desire to possess desirable over undesirable behaviors. Our own processes of recognition, repression, and distanciation—and here especially our tendency towards binary distinctions between human and nonhuman, self and other, animality and personhood—persist to somehow coherently erect a "human" identity, particularly removed from "unwanted" behaviors that press against socially and legally coded moral limits. In this work, we seem confronted by the sheer degree of creativity involved in the construction and maintenance of intraspecies borders, especially where moralizable acts are concerned.

Do you like the taste of sugar?

Do you get apprehensive?

Is the dental formula for each quadrant of your mouth: 2 incisors, 1 canine, 2 premolars, 3 molars?

Can you perform acrobatics?

Do you keep tools for future use?

Do you have abstract thoughts?

Do you use sex toys?

(Male) Does your scrotum hang freely?

Can you wade in water?

(Male) Can you be sure you are the father of your children?

Do you pout?

Do you anticipate social repercussions for yourself and others?

Are you adopted?

Are you promiscuous?

Does your eye have a bony socket enclosing it?

Can you walk on all fours?

Are you affectionate?

Do you feel compassion?

Do you like to watch the sunset?

Do you have a blood group of the ABO system?

Can you walk on two feet?

Are you agreeable?

Do you form concepts?

Do you use sex for appeasement?

Does your brain have two specialised halves?

Do you bare your teeth as an aggressive gesture?

Do you break alliances between people?

Do you eat roots?

Do you have a concept of self?

Do you have sex for pleasure?

Do you catch colds?

Do you make your bed?

Do you get angry?

Do you have a creative imagination?

Do you eat soil?

Do you have collarbones?

Do you offer an open hand when begging?

Do you annoy others?

Do you get sad?

Can you run?

Do you appease others?

Do you ever fear the unknown?

Can your shoulder rotate 360 degrees?

Do you anticipate?

Can you stand upright?

Would you bite as an aggressive/defensive act?

Do you have an aversion to things that in the past have scared you?

Might you develop cancer?

Do you care for your body?

Do you use touch to bond with others?

Are you aggressive?

Do you play on your own?

Have you ever had diarrhoea?

Do you communicate with gestures and voice?

Do you help others?

Are you friendly?

Can you scream?

Does the colour of your face differ from that of others?

Do you resolve conflicts using sex?

Do you live cooperatively in a group?

Do you have a sense of fairness?

Do you solicit sex?

Is your face unique?

Do you eat your own shit?

Do you use toys?

Do you get frustrated?

Do you stroke others?

(Female) Do you orgasm?

Do you eat other people's flesh?

Can you generalise?

Do you get fungal infections?

Do you show your dominance of others by charging at them?

Do you use courtship?

Are you generous?

Do you use hammers?

Are your eyes at the front of your face?

Do you chuckle?

Do you create new rituals?

Do you feel joy?

Do you suffer from a goitre (enlargement of the thyroid gland)?

Do you bully?

Do you use cooperative hunting skills?

Do you participate in cultural traditions?

Do you help others?

Do you scavenge for food?

Does your skin have hair on it?

Do you help members of other species?

Do you enjoy community?

Are you hostile?

Do you get haemorrhoids?

Do you drink urine?

Are you hygienic?

Do you itch?

Do you have heterosexual sex?

Do you cry?

Is there someone you admired and 'followed' in adolescence?

Do you have imaginative play?

Do you scream during sex?

Do you get hiccoughs?

Do you drum?

Do you have food-related sex?

Do you use sex as aggression?

Do you have homosexual sex?

Do you have friends?

Do you throw your shit?

Do you understand the relationship between things?

Do you sustain eye contact?

Do you lack an external tail?

Do you hug?

Is your group territorial?

Are you inventive?

Do you eat your vomit?

(Female) Can you lactate?

Are your cognitive abilities impaired because you were deprived of social contact during childhood?

Do you throw rocks?

Do you feel jealousy?

Can you use a bottle opener?

Do you laugh?

(Female) Do you ever yawn or self-groom during sex?

As a child did you ever play in a sexual way?

Do you prefer to use one hand more than the other?

Do you initiate reconciliation after a conflict?

Can you get malaria?

Do you gather food?

Do you live in a community?

Do you feel lethargy?

Do you whimper?

(Male) Are your testicles much larger than those of a gorilla?

Do you like fruit?

Did you have a long childhood compared to other mammals?

Are you opportunistic?

(Male) Will you go bald with age?

Do you have a sexual interest in children?

Do you predict consequences?

Do you participate in warfare?

(Female) Do you menstruate?

Do you demonstrate impulsive tendencies?

Do you feel passion?

Are you preoccupied with hierarchy and status?

(Female) Might you have a miscarriage if pregnant?

Do you share food?

Do you feel love?

Are you rational?

Do you eat meat and plants?

(Male) Can you make a flicking movement with your erect penis?

Do you manipulate others for your own purpose?

Do you mind who your partner is?

(Female) Do you ovulate?

Do you hunt in groups?

Are you undependable?

Are you violent towards strangers?

Do you have opposing thumbs?

Do you grunt?

Do you have reasoned thoughts?

Do you scream when you are attacked?

Do you have parasites in or on you?

Do you clap your hands?

Do you recognise yourself in the mirror?

Do you have sex in the 'missionary' position (face to face)?

Can you get pneumonia?

Does your hair bristle/stand on end when you are scared or aroused?

Do you seek affectionate physical contact?

Are you irrational?

Do you use sponges?

Can you get polio?

Do you imitate others?

Do you seek reassurance and attention?

(Male) Do you recruit women to be your partners?

Can you operate touchscreen computers?

Do you see colours?

Do you have sex with members of your family?

(Male) Do you find unfamiliar females more attractive?

Do you have a reduced sense of smell compared to other mammals?

Do you voluntarily suppress your voice?

Does smell affect your sexual arousal?

Did your use of gestures increase throughout childhood?

Have you ever played 'aeroplane' (supporting a child on top of your feet while lying on your back)?

Are you neurotic?

Do you have sex 'doggy style' (belly to back)?

Did you become sexually mature between 10 and 13 years of age?

Do you scratch yourself?

Do you use probes?

Do you intoxicate yourself (alcohol, drugs, etc.)?

Do you form opportunistic coalitions?

Have you ever made someone bear the blame of others?

Do you vary your sexual positions?

Do you remember things from your past?

Do you eat insects?

Do you plan in cooperation with others?

Are your parenting techniques different from others?

Do you get sexually excited?

Do you use weapons?

Do you smile?

Have you bitten a penis off?

(Male) Are your erections not always due to sexual arousal?

Do you wipe your shit off you?

Do you sneeze?

Do you use intimidation?

Does someone's personality affect whether they are sexually attractive to you?

Do you have spatial memory?

Do you understand sign languages?

Do you sweat?

Do you feel sexual pleasure?

Do you invent complex performances to amuse yourself?

(Male) Do you tend to stay in, or return to your home area?

Are you miserly?

Do you tease others?

Do you sense changes in temperature?

Do you kiss?

Do you have sex with more than one partner?

Do you suffer mental and physical pain?

Do you have ten fingers and ten toes?

Do you kiss with an open mouth?

Do you feel sympathy for others?

Do you get ulcers or sores?

Do you use your tongue when you kiss?

Do cultural differences cause you to separate from others and join different social groups?

Are you tender?

Are your toes webbed?

Do you eat leaves?

Do you form coalitions with your siblings?

Are you territorial?

Will your hair whiten with age?

If you are cut do you lick the wound?

Do you have social awareness?

Are you tolerant?

Do you express rage?

Do you use wipes?

Is there a Y-shaped groove in your molar teeth?

Are you an extrovert?

Do you like watching television?

Do you facilitate social actions?

Do you understand symbols?

Is your sleeping area raised off the ground?

Do you have a larger brain, relative to your body size, than other mammals?

Do you smack your lips?

Are you in a social hierarchy?

Do you use physical touch to reconcile aggressive incidents?

(Female) Is it unlikely you will raise more than three offspring to full maturity during your lifetime?

Do you make a coughing sound to indicate slight annoyance?

Do you solve the problems of others?

Do you have various strategies to attract a partner?

Do you climb trees?

Do you make useful tools?

Do you experience collective fear?

Do you victimise others?

Have you ever sucked your thumb?

Are you ticklish?

Do you have a personality?

Do you masturbate?

Has maternal deprivation affected your physical development?

Do you have a fear of strangers/'outsiders'?

Do you build shelters?

Are you contented?

Do you have oral sex?

Do you get bored?

Do you vary your facial expressions to communicate different messages?

Are you curious?

Do you make panting noises during sex?

Do you coerce others?

Do you deceive others?

Are you scared of snakes?

Do you shake your fist to express anger?

Do you get depressed?

Do you resolve others' conflicts?

Would you have adopted your younger siblings if orphaned?

Do you dream during sleep?

Do you retaliate or seek vengeance?

Do you feel desire?

(Male) Do you use your erect penis to display?

Do you vocally express your pleasure during sex?

Do you have temper tantrums?

Do you grieve?

Do you eat pigs?

When you were a child did you have an insatiable appetite for play?

Do you express your despair?

Do you steal food from others?

When you were a child did you learn by observing and imitating?

Do you have a good short-term memory?

Do you get distressed?

Do you play?

Would you adopt children?

Have you learned actions/skills that were passed to you from previous generations?

Do you have a good memory for individuals?

Do you dominate others?

Can you empathise?

Have you ever played 'rough and tumble' or 'king of the mountain'?

Is your cognitive ability higher than that of most other mammals?

Do you spend a lot of time socialising?

Can you do basic maths?

Are you excessively particular or demanding?

Do you fear?

Can you play computer games?

Do you pat others on the back?

Do you have a lifelong bond with your mother?

Did your parents reject you?

Are you secretive?

Are you absent-minded?

Are you trusting?

When you need to extend your reach upwards, do you find something to stand on?

Can you inhibit your impulses?

Are you addicted to any substances?

Do you dance?

Does your voice sound different to that of others?

Have you been weaned?

Can you improvise?

Anja Dornieden
& Juan David
González Monroy

THE MASKED MONKEYS, 2015
Digital transfer from 16 mm film,
b/w, sound, 32 min.

Anja Dornieden and Juan David González Monroy's *The Masked Monkeys* draws on anachronistic ethnographic documentary tropes, as well as on later "cinema of work" genres, interjecting elements of surrealism and spiritualism to depict an interspecies relationship of labor power between Javanese monkeys and their masters.

In Javanese culture, the monkey is a sacred symbol of liminality, death, and reincarnation that is linked to the Hindu monkey god Hanuman, worshipped for his strength, his perseverance, and his devotion to Rama, the god of chivalry and virtue. In the material-semiotic economy of the street performances, the monkey's duty is to *act* like a master, so that it can publicly exhibit an embodied grasp of social norms to the audience. In a well-rehearsed scenario, the monkey displays its abilities for the crowd through a series of enactments: as a gentleman, as a deliberate mimic of a peasant, as an accomplished athlete, and even as a wrangler of beasts (here, a rocking horse). Following this display of social command and demeanor, the monkey accepts and puts on a human mask, which allows it to shape-shift, aided by trance, into the figure of "the master."

In traditional Javanese society the royal elite (*priyayi*) were distinguished from the "little people" (*wong cilik*) through their culture, elaborate codes of etiquette, and warrior responsibilities. During the Dutch colonizers' indirect rule of the Javanese kingdom of Mataram in the eighteenth century, the *priyayi* received a Western education and were given the role of administrators and professional civil servants. Masked monkey performances reveal the complexity of these genealogies, and are haunting in the way their own dramaturgy processes inequality as natural, unchanging, and worthy of social reproduction. The film lingers on this embrace and expropriation of animality, to reveal the material and spiritual "use value" of these nonhuman primates in a postcolonial class society.

"A master believes that it takes every grade of society to make the complete whole. One class is just as necessary as the other. So, in associated labor, each grade of mind does its appropriate work. One could not dispense with either, and all should have due praise. Hence, the monkey's duty is to enact the master's will. For his part, the master's duty is to properly communicate the particulars of his will. It is the master's responsibility to instruct the monkey and initiate him into the rules and rituals of the norm. Master and monkey complement each other. They form a bond which, when properly established, assures their mutual success.
[...]
The show's aim is to recreate the legendary masters. During the show the monkey's duty is not only to convincingly act like a master, but to completely embody the role. The masters, for their part, have as their duty to ensure the attention of the audience. In doing so, both parties adhere to and ratify the norm."

Script excerpt: Anja Dornieden & Juan David González Monroy, *The Masked Monkeys*, 2015.

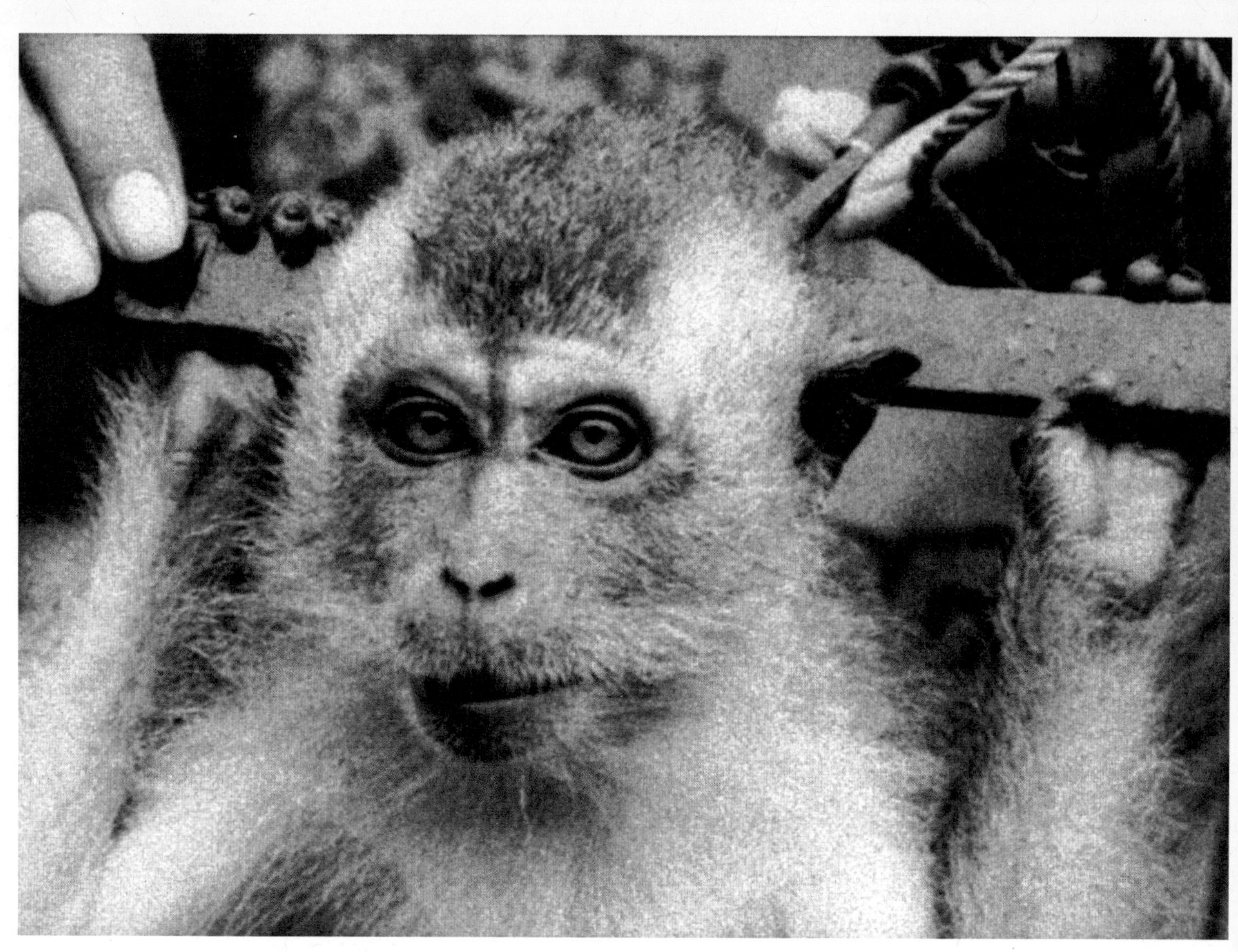

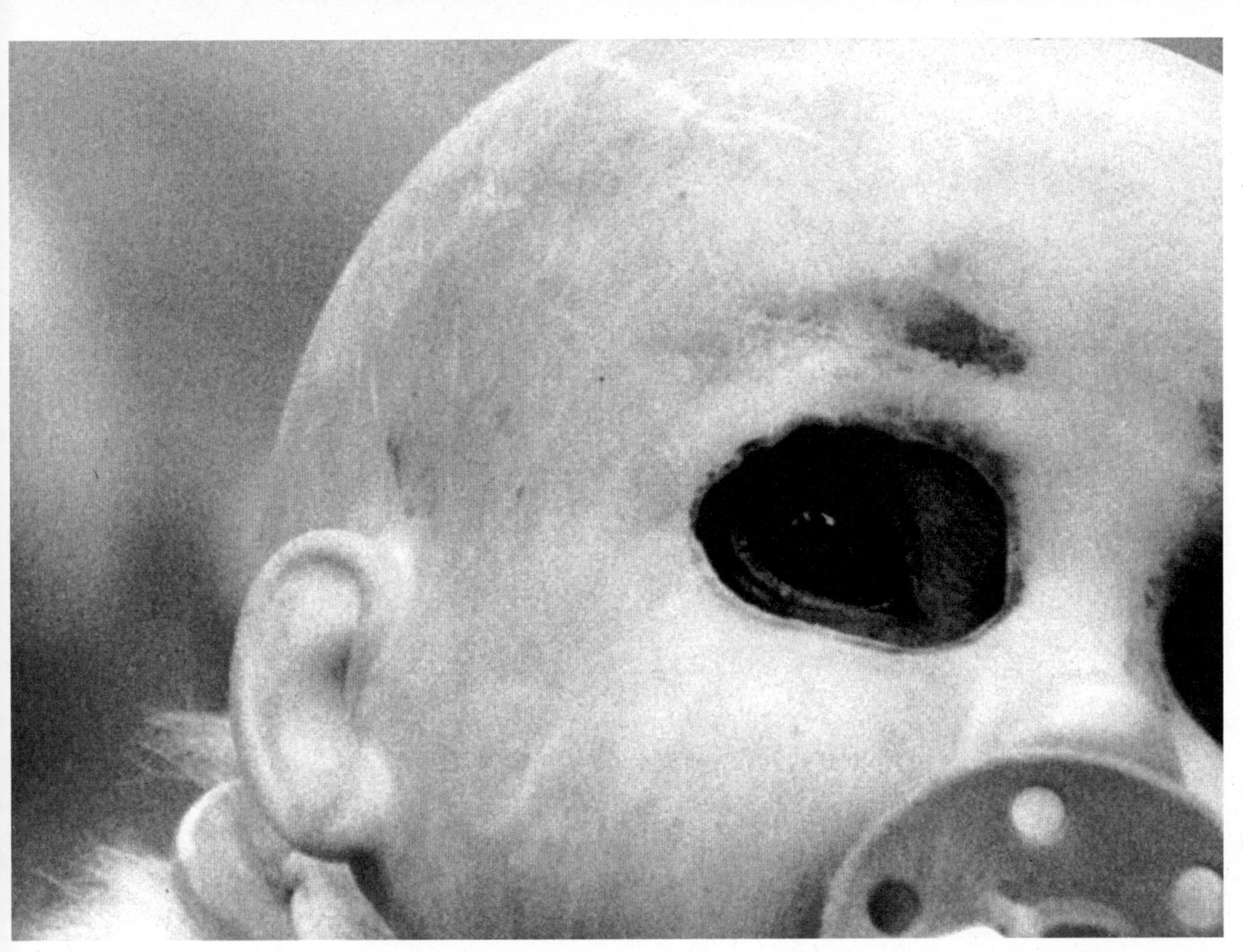

Ines Doujak
in collaboration with
John Barker
and Matthew Hyland

06 KRIMINALAFFE, 2015

Performance, 20 min. (p. 77)

Installation, mixed media:
wallpaper, sculpture and handout
(detail, p. 9, pp. 78–79), dimensions
variable

*Kriminalaffe: Sultan at the Dole
Office*, Essay (p. 37)

Marx jested at the pacifying lesson in the Biblical creation story—
the "fortunate Fall" of Adam and Eve from their heathen animalistic
paradise into the so-called dignity of labor—when he remarked that
"the history of economic original sin reveals that there are people"
for whom the lesson "is by no means essential."

As religion gradually lost its power to hold workers in the owner
classes' thrall, the modernization of production and labor management saw "illness" and "insanity" configured along with dark skin and
female gender as characteristics of innately inferior, stupid, work-
resistant human types. Meanwhile, human bodies "emancipated" from
feudal servitude or chattel slavery were rewarded with bare survival
at best for lifelong consignment to meaningless mechanical tasks.
F. W. Taylor, the twentieth century's first "management consultant,"
described the worker as an "intelligent gorilla" whose thought process
must be locked into the assembly line. Today the so-called "social
factory" refines Taylor's method rather than replacing it, applying
"cognitive" and "affective" performance criteria to "material" and "immaterial" labor alike.

In their essay for the *Ape Culture* publication, Ines Doujak, John
Barker, and Matthew Hyland tell this story of the imperial, racialized,
and sexualized biopolitics of work through a reading of ape-man
negotiations in Western philosophy, religion, anthropology, behavioral
science, and political economy.

The accompanying performance, *Kriminalaffe*, features "Clara,"
an awkward human-sized organismic blob of raw biological material in
felted "soft sculpture." All flesh and exposed surface with limited mobility and vision, Clara is given the "opportunity" to be tailored into
"work-readiness" live on stage by an overbearing human-resources expert. Operating a blow horn with one hand and a cowbell with her foot,
she is expected to respond with only these slapstick sound effects
to cue-cards naming qualities deemed positive or negative in job-
seekers ("decisive," "humorless," "attentive," "unsociable," "creative,"
"helpless," "married," etc.). She achieves compliance only for a limited
time.

The costume appears in front of original beauty/beast wallpaper.
Viewers can take home a souvenir in the form of an A3 collage print
of dizzying representations of beasts, saints, and worker chimps: images
scraped from online searches, arranged in a way that blurs together
an indefinite series of borderlines.

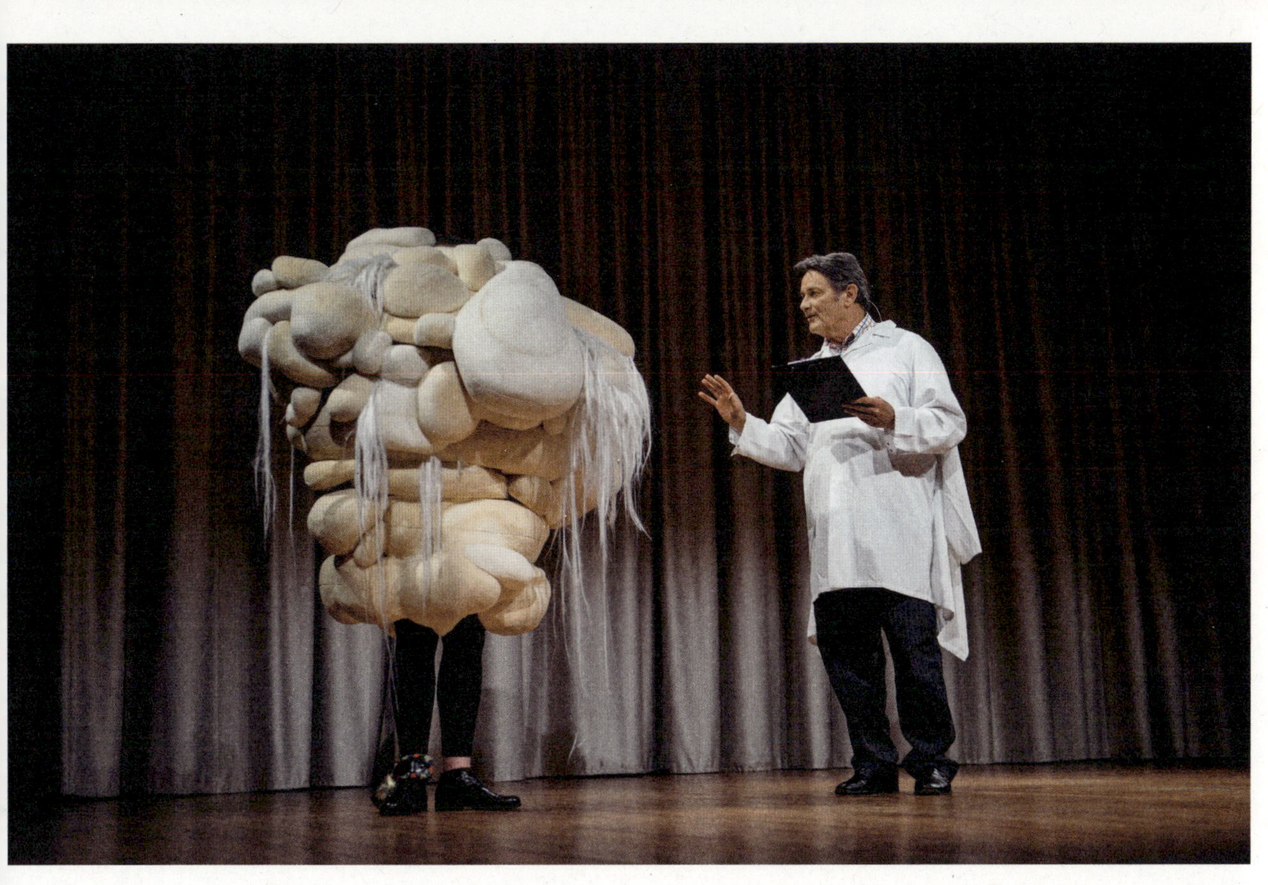

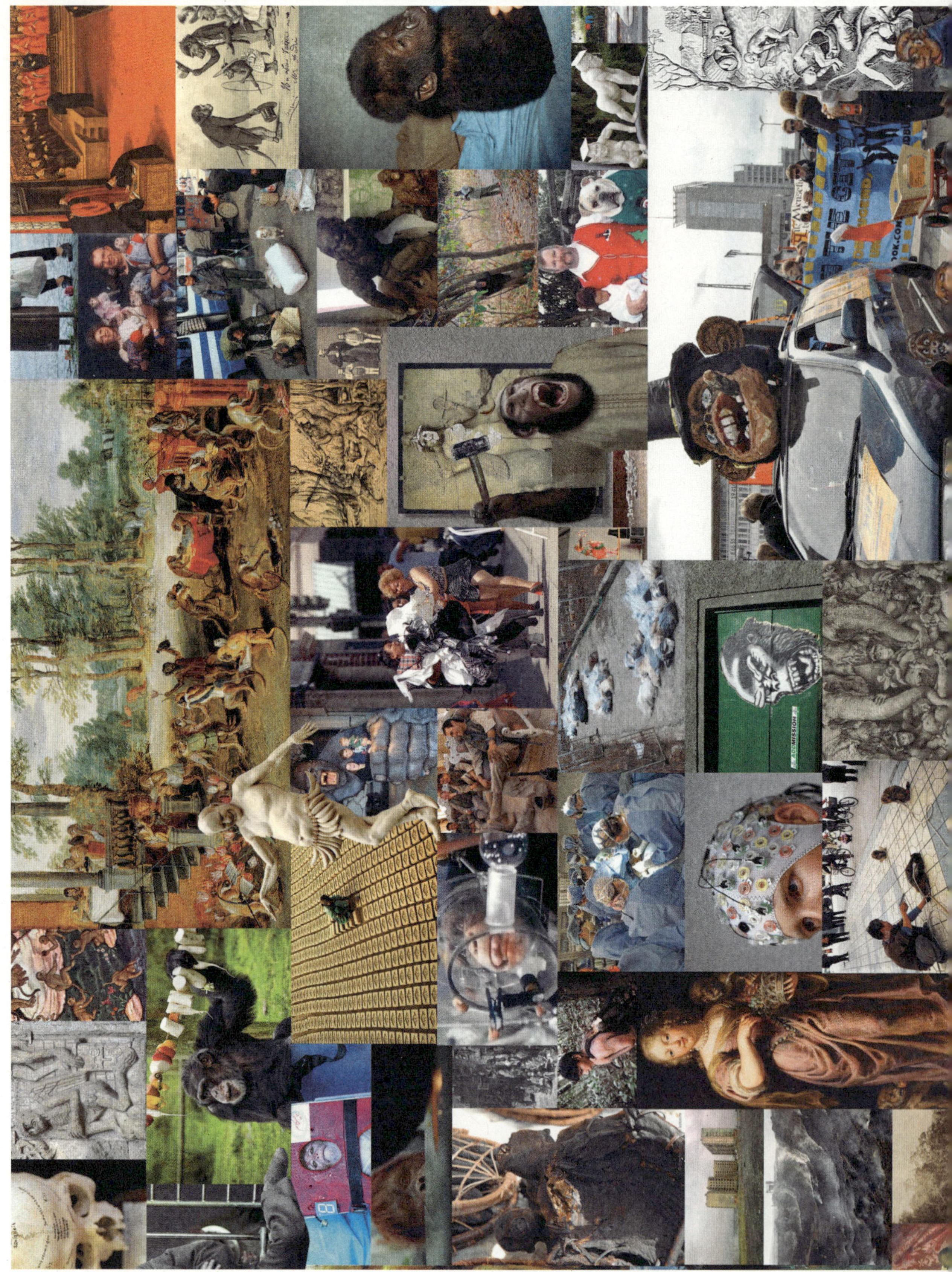

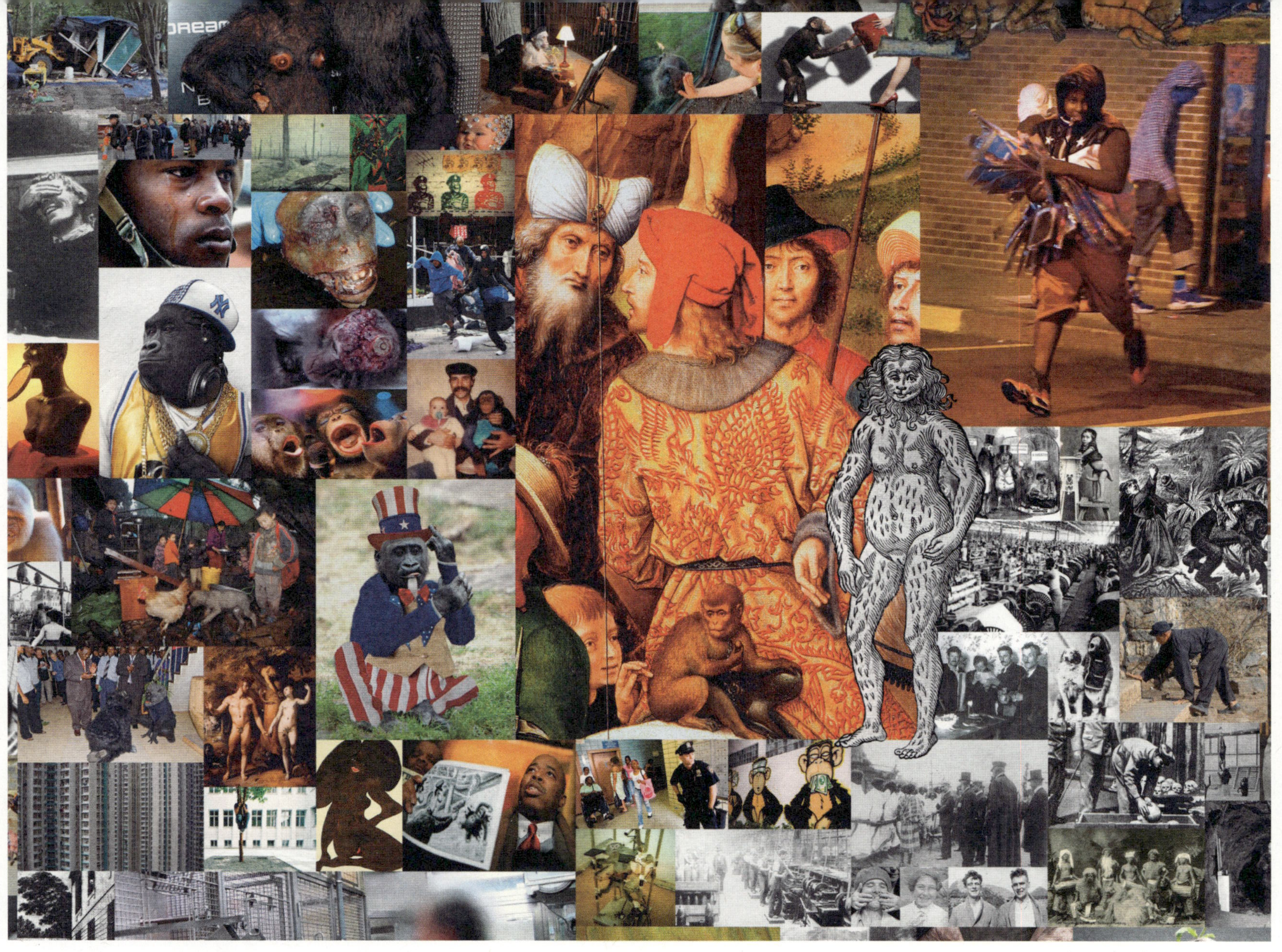

Coco Fusco

TED ETHOLOGY: PRIMATE VISIONS
OF THE HUMAN MIND, 2015
Video, color, sound, 49 min.

It was in 1968, just two decades after scientific consensus on evolution had been reached, that the *Planet of the Apes* film series was launched into a turbulent postwar and civil rights-era pictorial space. Many key studies on primates and language were being undertaken at this time, within a larger framework of primatology that was still organized especially around the functionalism of aggression.

The series' popularity was due to its suspense-packed remystification of the drama of human civility, minus the "original" event of a split in the allegorical coevolution of humans and chimps. Between 1968 and 1973 the five movies confronted twentieth-century hubris—the drive to warfare, nuclear finitude, slavery, genocide, and ecocide—playing out as farce for an ape "civilization" miming the privileges of its gaze back to its US audience. The revolt of enslaved apes appeared in the fourth film soon after the black urban uprisings of the late 1960s and 1970s. Coco Fusco's lecture performance, formatted in the style of a TED Talk broadcast, revives the series' exemplary feminist chimp scientist character Dr. Zira to construct a twenty-first-century itinerary for her rigorously empathic interspecies research (for which she was assassinated in the original script). Fusco has Zira hide away in the American Midwest, living life as an itinerant countercultural researcher who observes human behavior on television and online networks. She emerges to share her research on aggressive tendencies in humans after scientists in 2012 finally arrive at the consensus that nonhuman animals also possess consciousness.

This work continues Fusco's career-long interrogation of racialized and species logics through performance, especially its role in the commodity flows of "exotic" figures of non-Western knowledges and practices. Her strategies of overidentification, reperformance, estrangement, and masquerade interrogate the ideological limitations of pasts in the present.

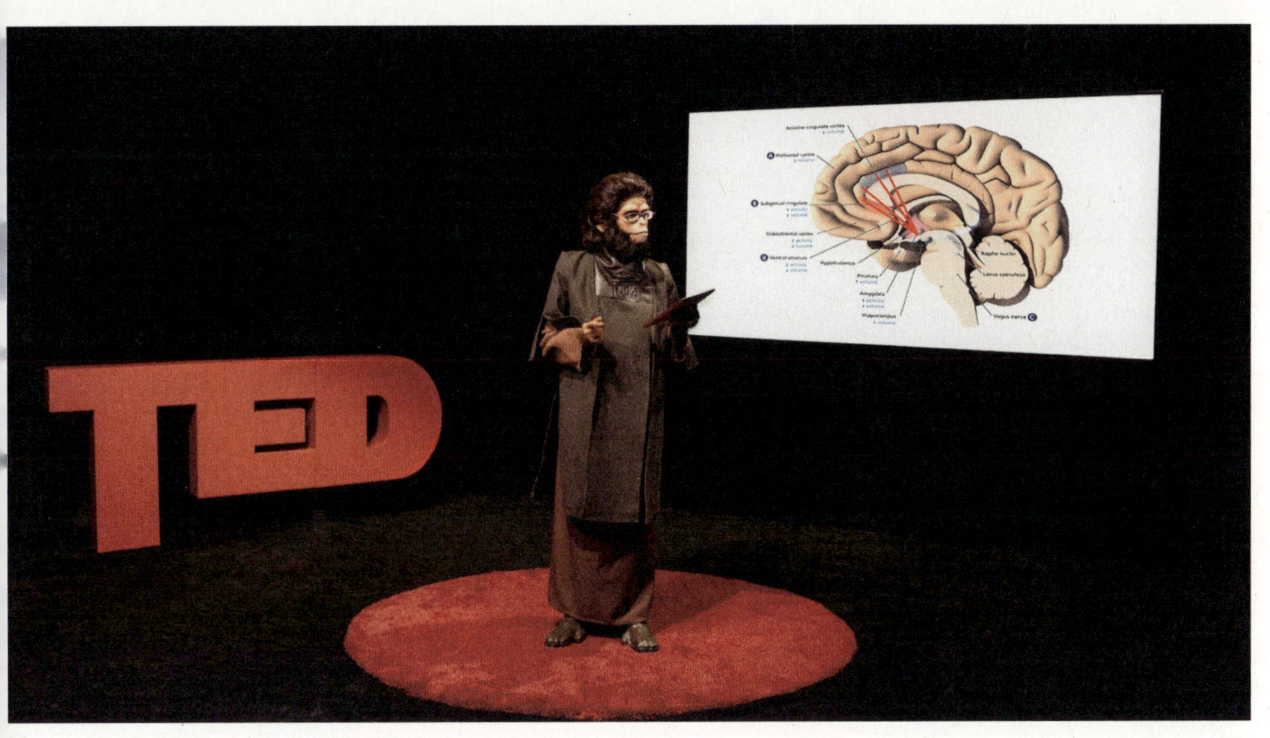

TED
Anterior cingulate cortex
Prefrontal cortex
Subgenual cingulate
Orbitofrontal cortex
Ventral striatum
Hypothalamus
Pituitary
Amygdala
Hippocampus
Raphe nuclei
Locus coeruleus
Vagus nerve

Jos de Gruyter &
Harald Thys

DIE AAP VAN BLOEMFONTEIN, 2014
[The Ape Of Bloemfontein]
Video, color, sound, 23 min.

Since Belgian artists Jos de Gruyter and Harald Thys first started collaborating in 1987, they have been creating video works staged inside sparse minimal spaces that often resemble ateliers or stripped back chamber theater sets. Through signature reductions of detail and logic their works have an uncanny capacity to materialize all kinds of paranoid and liminal slippages at play in seemingly ordinary and familiar object–subject relations.

At the beginning of *Die Aap van Bloemfontein*, we see the carved wooden head of an ape digitally morph into a plainly dressed man, who is affectively immobilized but by nothing in particular. An automated voice speaking Afrikaans narrates a story with the logic of a very simple computer (a "master babbler"), inadequately notating subjects and things and passing over relations and intentionality in a data-basic treatment of different scenes: "A dog turned into a ladybug and flew away to the lady across the street who was a peasant."

As in previous de Gruyter and Thys works, untrained actors appear more like primitive accumulations of unshown histories, ossifying inside of domestic scenes that are reminiscent of vanitas scenography. In the historical establishment of psychoanalytic methods, the physical immobility of catatonic and paranoid states (an inverse relation between outward and inward movement) was directly related with the submission of the body to technological modernity and overdesign. "Dream work," free association, and other practices of movement and rearrangement aimed to put seemingly fixed (or "fixated") things into new relations, in order to cultivate new manifestations of discourses, as well as art. Here, one cannot help but see fixity everywhere, to read an oblique image of domestic "happiness (arrested)" in *Die Aap van Bloemfontein*, as some kind of imperially dysfunctional master-signifier.

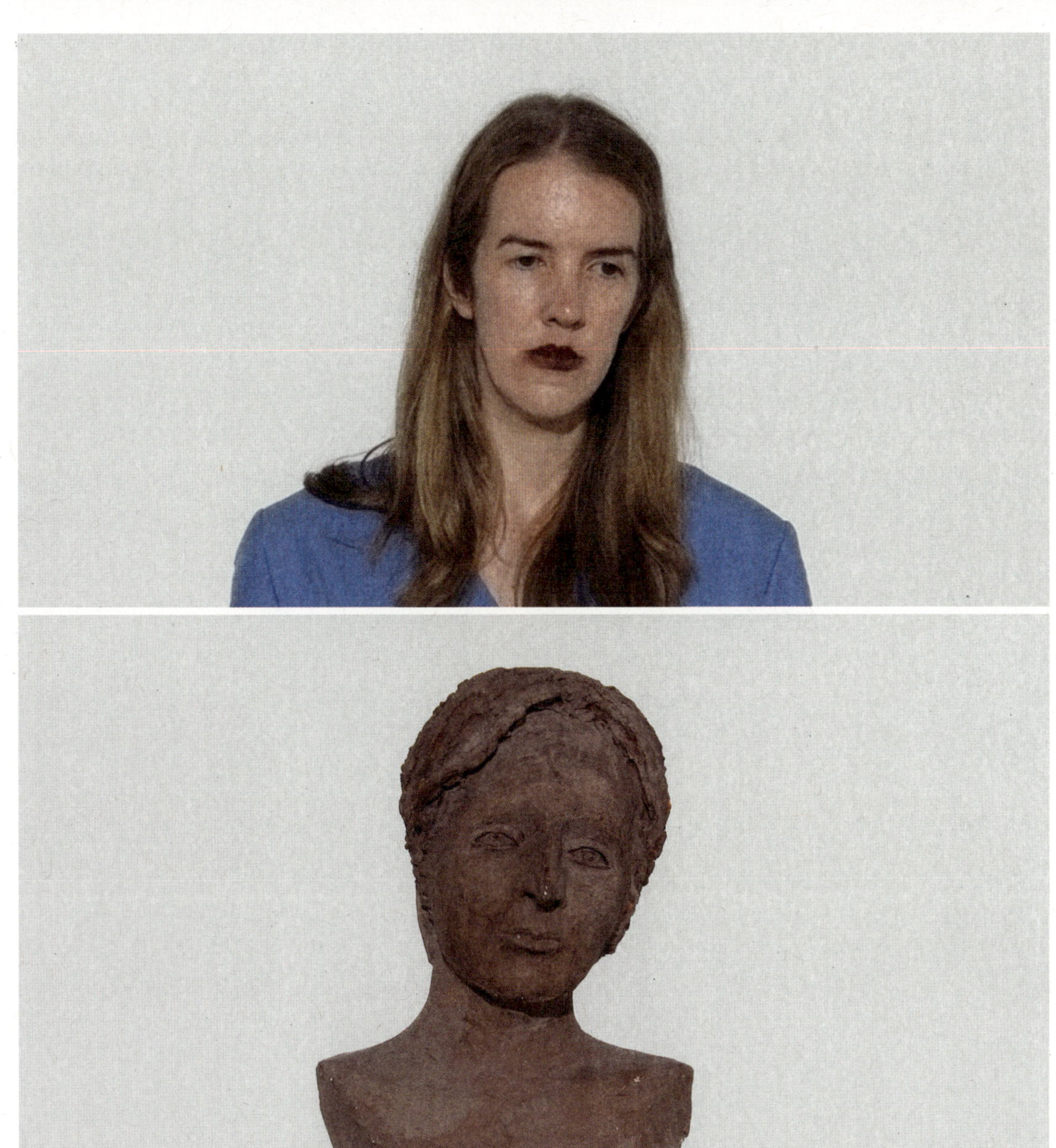

Pierre Huyghe

UNTITLED (HUMAN MASK), 2014
Film, color, sound, 19 min.

Pierre Huyghe has previously made use of animal masks on human actors in his works that cross-cut temporalities, taxonomies of life, media formats, and aesthetic traditions.

His latest film *Untitled (Human Mask)* is inspired by a real situation in Japan, in which a monkey—wearing the mask of a young woman—has been trained to work as a waitress. Huyghe creates the film with a drone camera in the wake of the 2011 Fukushima tsunami, which caused the meltdown of the city's nuclear reactors and mass evacuations. From a first posthuman survey of deserted streets, the camera shifts inwards to find the monkey—a Japanese macaque—in an empty interior among cockroaches and idealized Japanese paintings of nature. This is followed by scenes of the monkey alone in her habitat, silhouetted against the empty, dark restaurant. In this dystopian setting, an animal acts out the human condition, trapped, endlessly repeating her unconscious role.

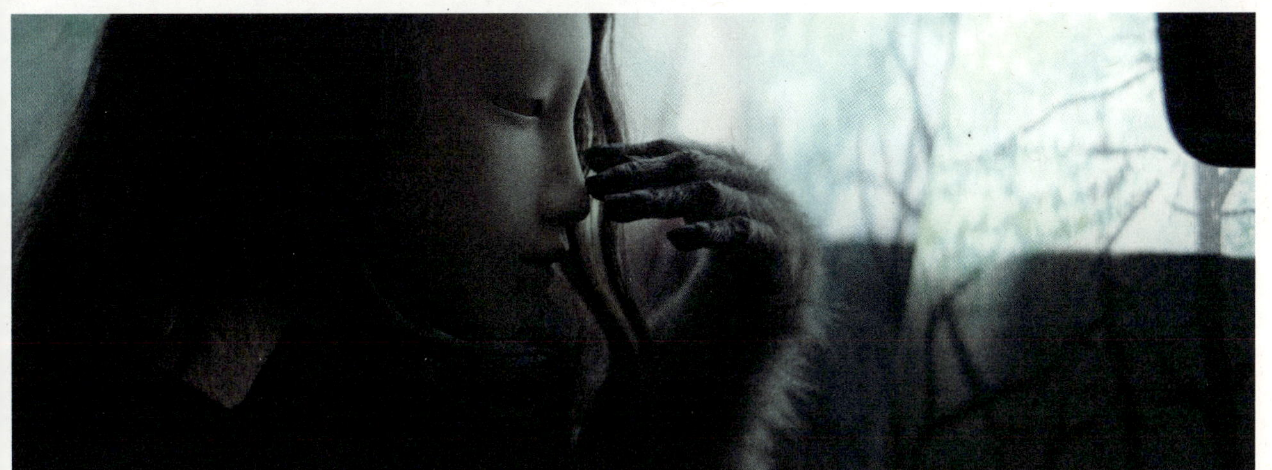

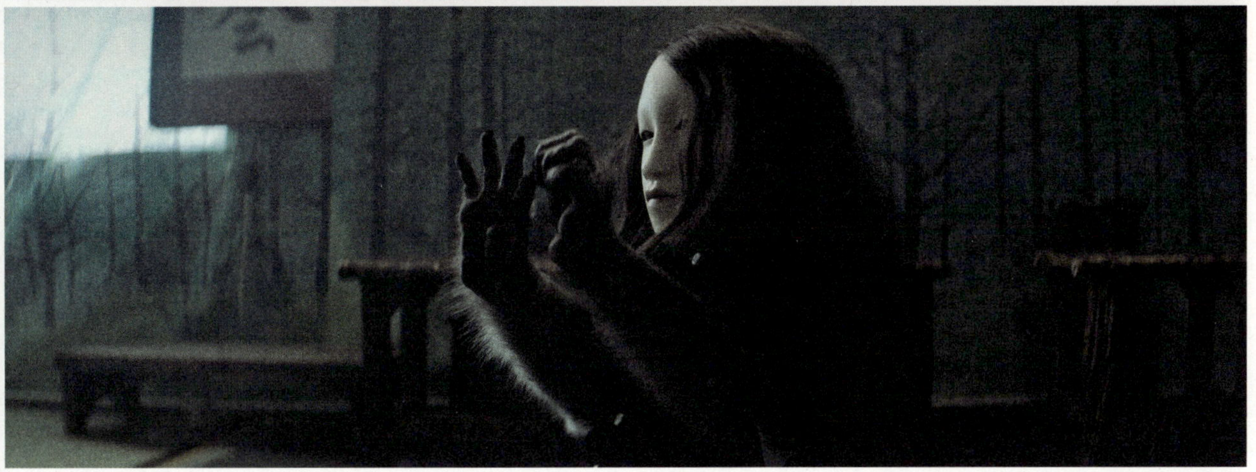

Louise Lawler

MICHAEL, 2001
Direct cibachrome mounted
on museum box, 151.76 × 116.84 cm

Louise Lawler's signature photographs of other artists' photographs and art objects in their exhibition contexts lay bare the art world gaze—that which exceeds artistic intention, the spectatorial look, and the object alone, tracking instead mostly external dynamics of presentation and display. Jeff Koons placed this gaze most fully in dialogue with the entertainment complex and Christian symbolics of speculative investment to make it a function/subject of his art from the booming 1980s onwards.

Michael has Lawler's camera capturing workers unpacking one of three identical lifesized sculptures of Michael Jackson with his chimp Bubbles, made by Koons initially for his infamous *Banality* show in 1988. The pair wear matching regal military outfits and are colored in the porcelain white-and-gold leaf of mass-produced sculptures of Catholic saints. Their positioning, Koons suggests, was inspired by Michaelangelo's *Pièta*, which dates back to the fifteenth century. Indeed, the pose hardly varies from a press photo sent to the artist by Jackson himself while he was undertaking extensive plastic surgery.

Bubbles was bought for Michael from an animal testing research facility and lived at the Jackson family home Neverland. As Jackson's closest companion during the heights of his *Bad* tour fame, he shared the singer's hotel rooms and drank tea with the mayor of Osaka. He was sent to a chimp reserve when fears emerged that he might possibly attack Michael's eldest human child, Prince Michael 2. Jackson's life among many animals at Neverland was pathologized by commentators, maids, and prosecutors as proof of insanity, perversity, and arrested development. Koons respected precisely this tragic availability of Jackson to mimesis, and of identity to plastic re-formation, all in the greater pursuit of "the largest possible audience" for art. Koons lauded: "He would do absolutely anything that was necessary to be able to communicate with people."

In Lawler's photograph, the workers' bodies dramatically blur in front of the image, preventing us from gaining a full view, and hence becoming worshipfully attached. On the same day that Louise Lawler made this photograph, the sculpture was auctioned off at Sotheby for the record price of 5.6 million dollars.

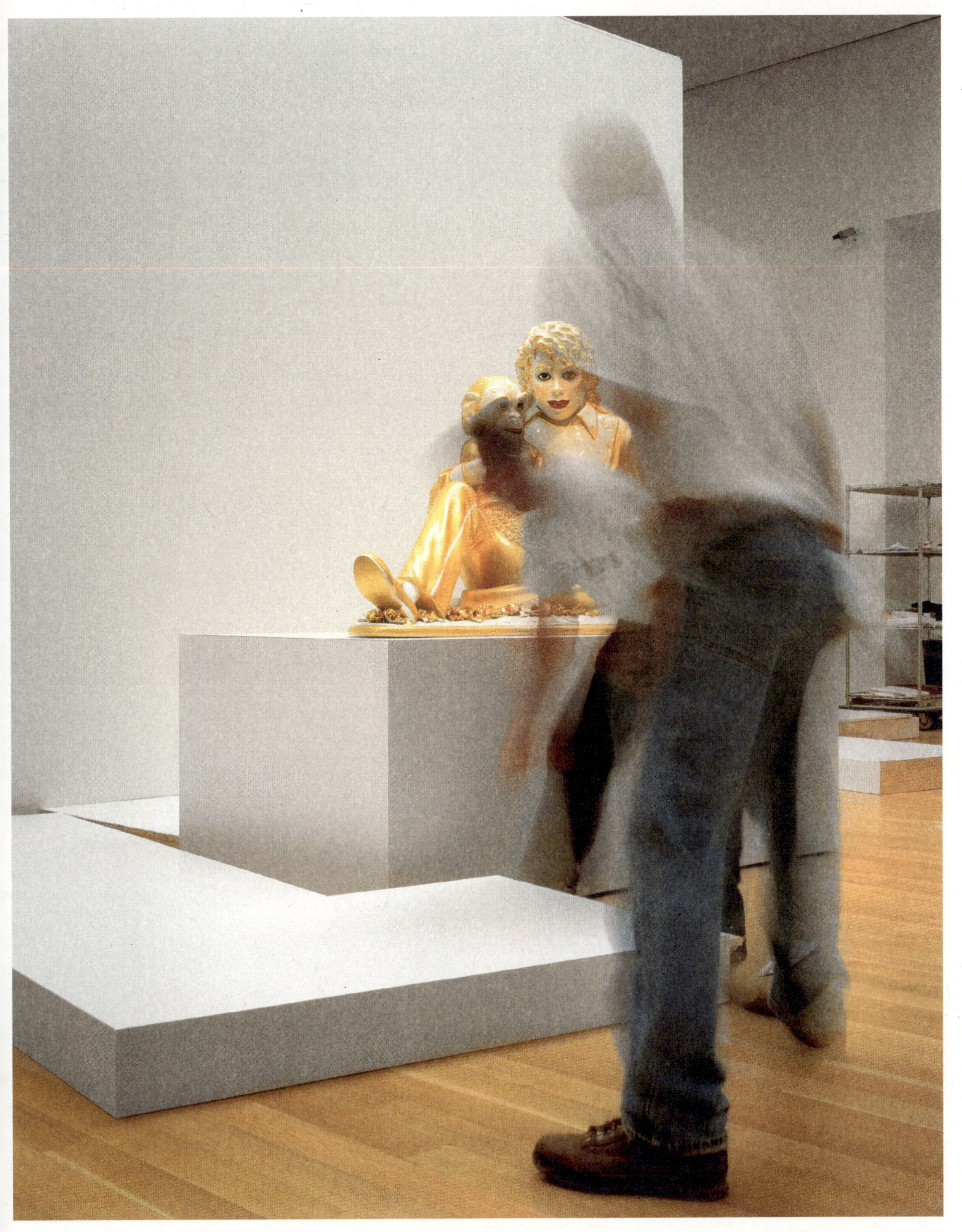

Damián Ortega

TRANSICIÓN DEL MONO AL
HOMBRE, 2015
[Transition From Ape To Man]
Wooden hand model and steel
knives, 37 × 12 × 6 cm (p. 89)

SHORT HISTORY OF GESTURE,
2. SYNTAX: ARMS / HANDS, 2013
Mixed media, dimensions variable

THE ROOT OF THE ROOT,
2011–2013
Wood, dimensions variable

"Apes do not work, for they are lazy." This has been a notorious assumption for centuries, as part of the standard repertoire of humanism. It prevails in post-Fordism any time apes are used as part of the same mimetic politics, as mirrors, to show beings devoid of the base dignities—let alone surpluses—of labor. From an artistic perspective, the primate hand, compared to the human hand of modernization, is considered incapable of using tools towards any symbolic or performative reflexivity. Concurrently, sensational "art" projects making use of the same reasoning put nonhuman primates provocatively to work for the art world itself. One of the most famous examples of this was the 1957 exhibition *Paintings by Chimpanzees* curated by Desmond Morris at the ICA in London.

Far more challenging an engagement with difference, however, lies in artists' tarrying with the material culture of our nonhuman relatives. Such was the experimental and even abyssal sentiment underlying a recent invitation issued by University College London's Gashaka Primate Project to the artist Damián Ortega to spend some time at its research base in one of the last remaining expanses of wilderness in Nigeria, where the rarest subspecies of chimpanzee survives. The results of this experience generated Ortega's 2013 solo show *Apestraction* at the Freud Museum, London. Several pieces from this exhibition are presented here.

Ortega is well known for his installations that cross-reference and denaturalize relations between raw materials, semiotics, and the functionalities of things. For *Transición del mono al hombre* he sutured miniature tools from a Swiss Army Knife into the fingers of a wooden mechanical replica of a human hand, producing a fictional cyborg monument to tool-being. Less familiar artifacts, materials of building and primitively managed construction work (rubber pipes driven into plaster, picks, and stone hammers) are showcased in vitrines in *Short History of Gesture*. *The root of the root*, which is in fact a branch and a stick, hanging next to each other, jests at the ungraspable "original" creativity of primates.

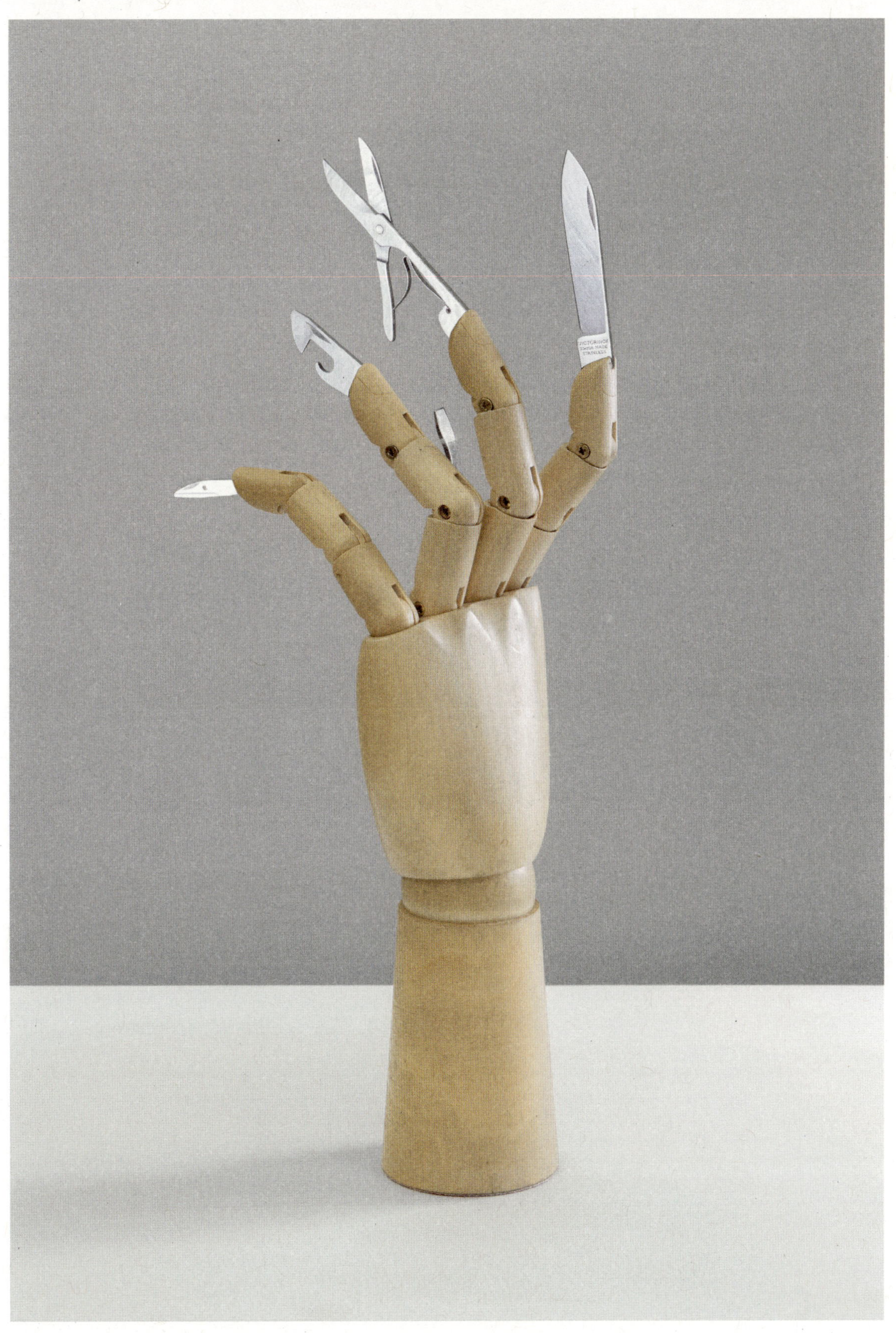

Nagisa Ōshima

MAX MON AMOUR, 1986
Digital transfer from DigiBeta,
color, sound, 92 min.

The "beauty and the beast" trope has been taken up with all kinds of animal players: wolves, horses, lions. The primate as a motif in Western art can be traced back to 1887, when Emmanuel Frémiet's sculpture *Gorille enlevant une femme* (Gorilla Carrying Off a Woman) shocked the Paris Salon as the cultural registration of Darwinian surrealism. Compared, however, to the thinly veiled anxieties played out around colonial competition and sexual property in *King Kong* and the "gorilla bride" films of the tight-belted 1950s, Nagisa Ōshima's deadpan marriage comedy registers clear changes in the position of women over the course of the century.

Max mon amour (Max My Love) is the story of a British diplomat based in France, Peter Jones (Anthony Higgins), whose wife Margaret (Charlotte Rampling) takes a chimpanzee, Max, for her lover. Parisian upper-class life is renowned for its "civilized" capacity to absorb extra-marital urges and tropical curios, but the beast presents something of a challenge to sangfroid. Rising above his feelings of violent jealousy, Peter proposes they bring Max into the household. Margaret maintains dignity under surveillance while enduring her mental health being brought into question; Peter's double standards, competitiveness, and disbelief in the concept and physical nature of their affair ("Sex, for example. What do you do with him?") cast him as emotionally unevolved. Max's gaze is also coded male, but he telepathically communicates with Margaret, who confidently returns his gaze as often as she shakes off the scopophilic reach of their friends' scientific expertise and bourgeois disapproval.

In one of two key dinner-table scenes reminiscent of late Buñuel (whose screenwriter cowrote this film, the only work to have been made by Ōshima outside Japan), a female friend asks if the monkey is "at least" a male. Rampling, playing Margaret, appreciated the inbuilt irony of the fact that Max's suit was occupied by the same female actress and animal imitator who had previously played Tarzan's mother in *Greystoke: The Legend of Tarzan, Lord of the Apes*. For Rampling, "the actual sexuality of the film (was) non-existent and all-existent, because sexuality is in everything." Rather than being sacrificed to retain civility, the animal has arrived to "save the family" and play a key role in expressing new forms of communication.

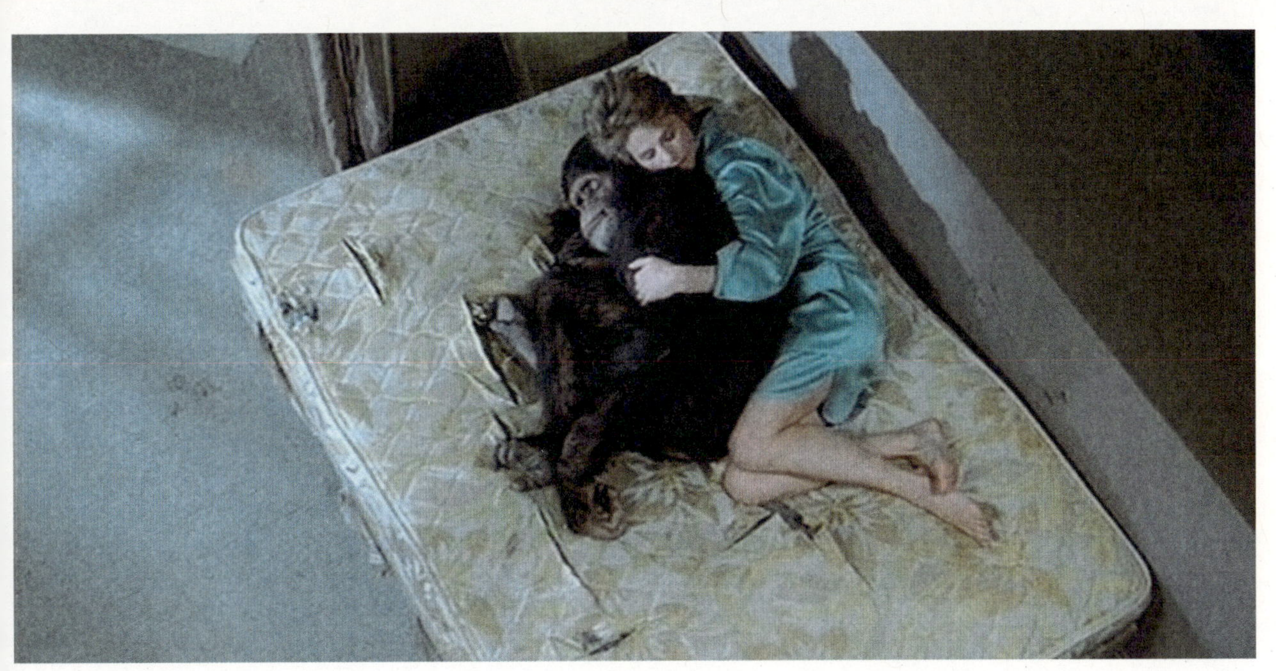

Erik Steinbrecher

AFFE, 2015
Mannequin, clothes, walking sticks,
and hanging mask, dimensions
variable (detail, p. 93)

SHE APE / APE MAN, 2015
Offset print on paper, 29.7 × 42 cm
(pp. 94 – 95)

Erik Steinbrecher has generated a prolific range of printed works, books, posters, photo supplements, and installations that almost invariably organize meaning through double-visioned images and punlike titles. His pieces travel easily between hand, eye, and immaterial concepts, a tendency that is very much exploited in *AFFE*, a mixed media sculpture of natural and inorganic "sexual" and "functional" accoutrements of a tool-invested mythos; for example, a leather jacket, pants, walking sticks and orthopedic tools, and a modeled rubber mask. Installed beside this outlay of objects, *SHE APE / APE MAN*, an ephemeral poster handout, sets a clichéd image of sexual difference into motion.

Speculatively aroused or perhaps self-conscious, the gaze of the installation somehow localizes to emanate from a sensuously depicted nonhuman stomach in the right-hand image of *SHE APE / APE MAN*. In the image on the left a naked femme stands posing on a rock; the section of the photo showing her head has been torn away, and she points her buttocks frontally to the camera. Scopic visions of sex—whether scientific or erotic—have rarely allocated agency to female figures of desire, who are often described only in terms of their "availability" to the primal scene. *SHE APE / APE MAN* overidentifies this convention and asymmetry to give the cultural *question* of "human" desire and primacy an unsubtle prominence and transspecies spin. The hanging mask feature of Steinbrecher's mixed media installation crafts "organic"-seeming parts using inorganic material, suggesting great possibilities for refabrication.

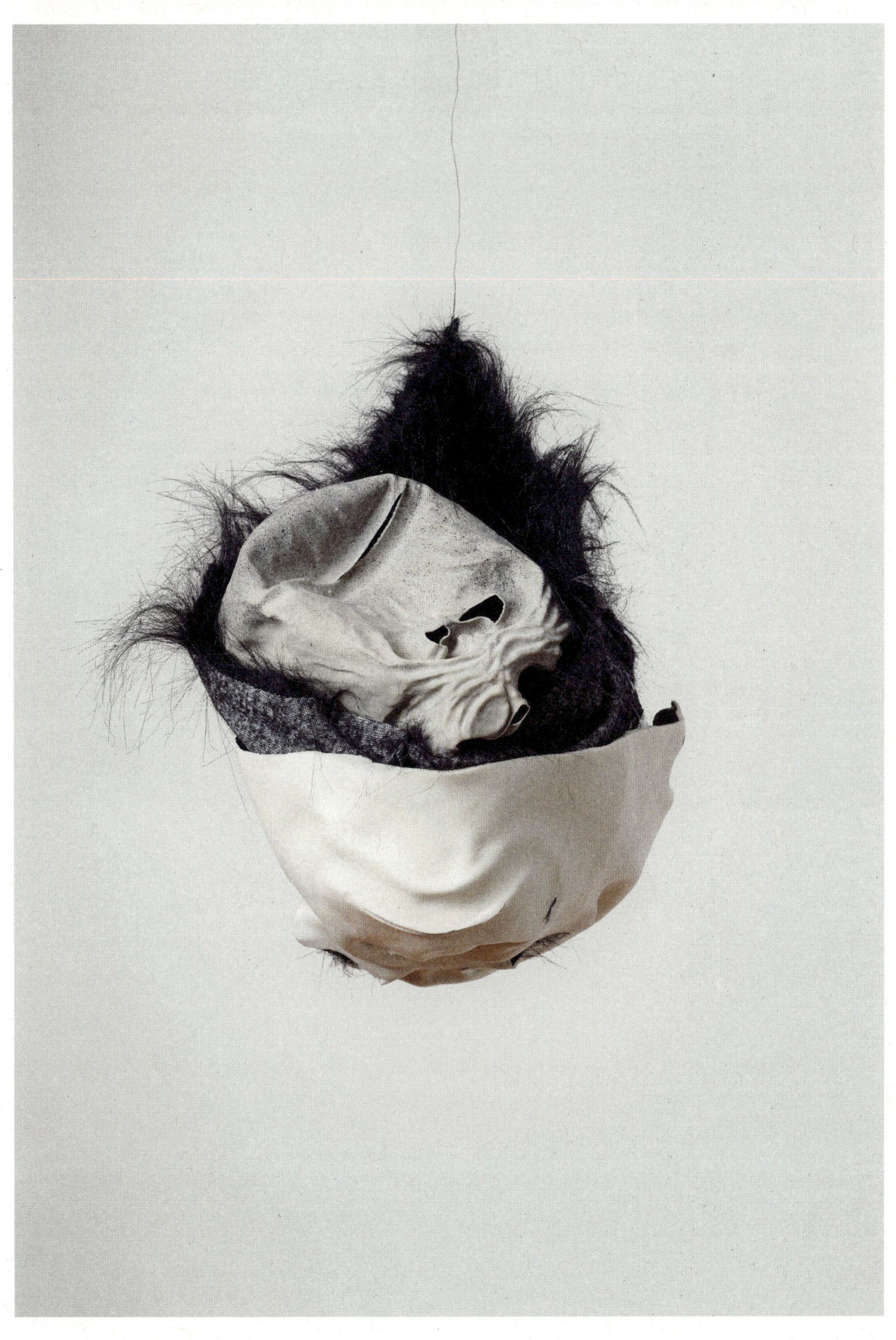

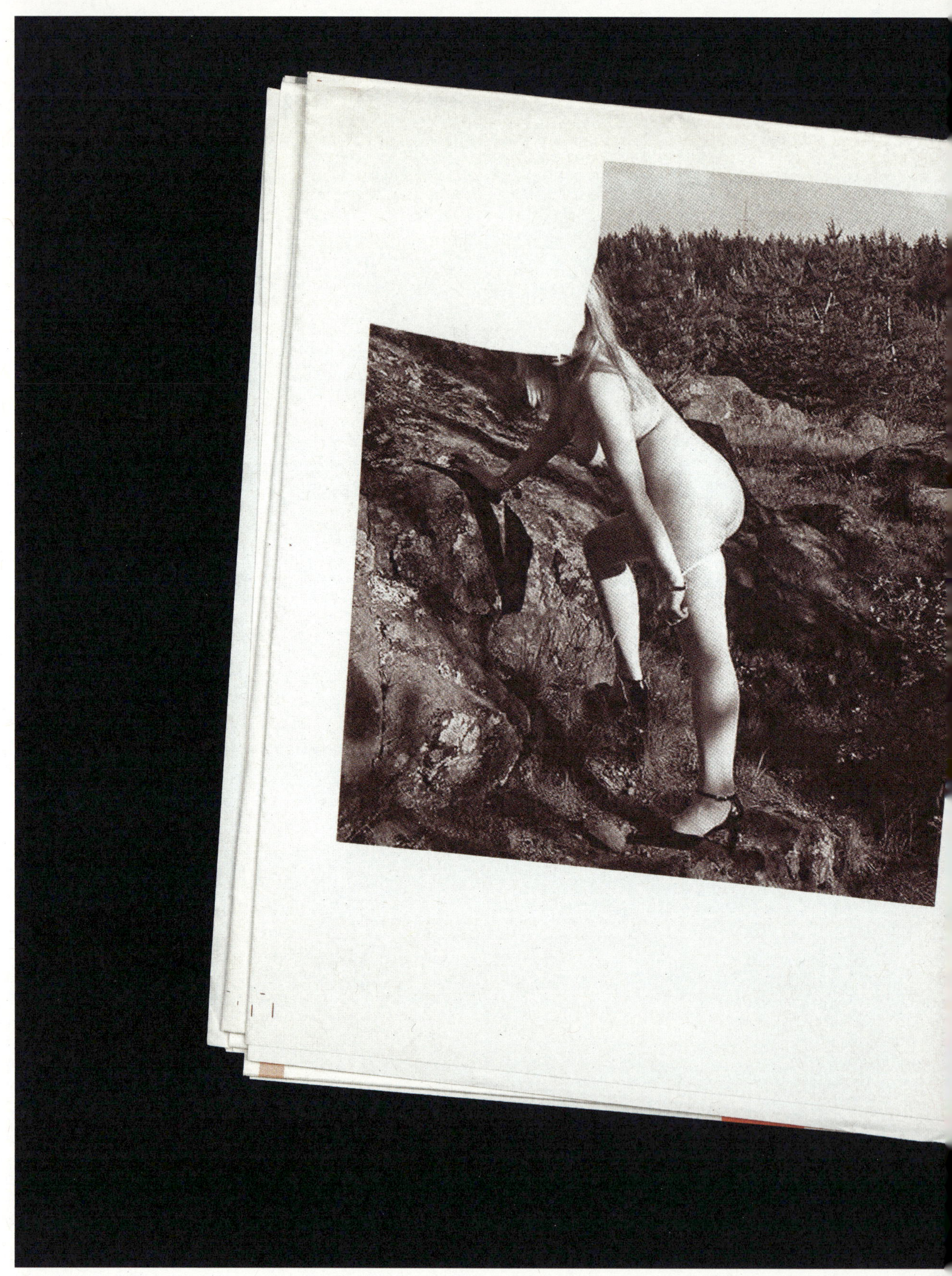

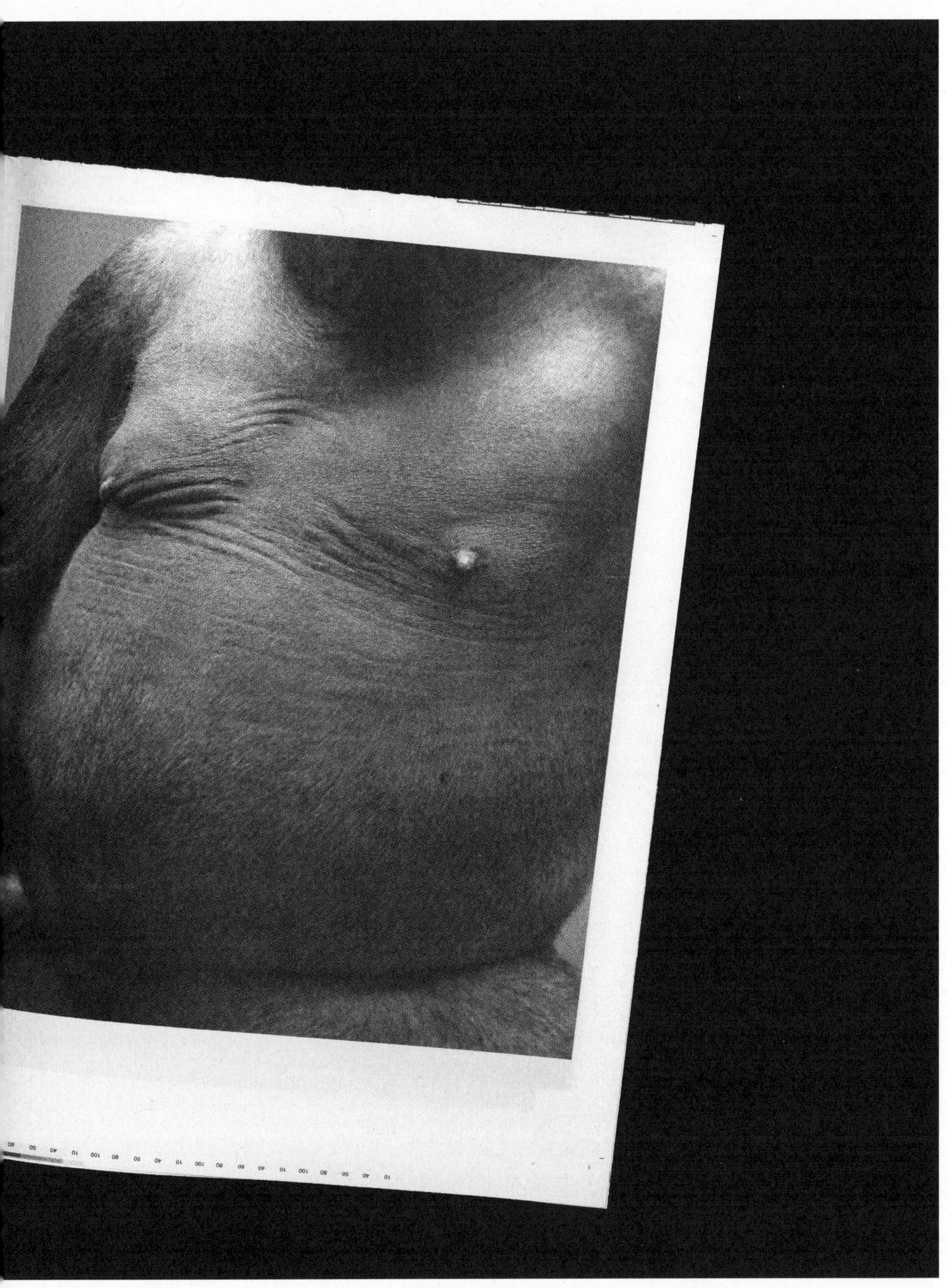

Rosemarie Trockel

OHNE TITEL (part of the
installation *Pennsylvania Station),*
1987
Collage on paper, 76.4 × 56 cm /
84.5 × 64 × 2.4 cm

OHNE TITEL, 1984
Gouache and ink on paper,
23.8 × 19.8 cm / 50.2 × 40.2 cm
(p. 97)

OHNE TITEL, 1984
Gouache and ink on paper
25.9 × 20.9 cm / 48 × 42 cm

Rosemarie Trockel once stated that "every animal is a female artist."
The slogan encapsulated her art's subtle and witty torsions of relations:
of vision and gender, creativity, and species physiologies.

The works selected here come from two series of what Trockel
called ape "portraits." One series dating from 1984 of gouache and ink
works on paper are gestural in their muddy composition of apelike
heads, staring at the viewer. The second series from 1987 comprises
more conventionally accomplished pencil drawings, one of which
is presented in the exhibition: a female nude modeling an ape mask.
These works mix comic, fashion, and ethology sketch forms.

While the bestial romance challenges hierarchies, the "monstrous
feminine" (to quote Barbara Creed) of the "half-woman, half-ape" signals
the asymmetrical reproductive drives and uncastratable powers of
female sexuality. What is interesting about how these works differ in
their attention to physiognomic detail is how difficult it is to project
singular emotion. The social point of the exchange is uncanny. Trockel
is explicitly asking viewers to look directly in the eye of her frontal
portraits, and draws a gaze that often returns the look. Both woman
and animal seem to merge from similar positions outside of the male
symbolic order—in a figure of eccentric co-occupation, which is
one of the reasons she has likened her ape portraits to self-portraits,
or perhaps projective disturbances of selfhood and artisthood.

Trockel has produced an incredible body of work spanning painting, sculpture, object making, videos, drawings, artists' books, and
design, and is positioned prominently alongside a number of important
feminist artists and theorists of the 1980s and 1990s who explored
the asymmetrical limits of transspecies mimesis through the question
of sexual difference. Yet the material form of other pieces of sculpture and mixed media testifies as much to an interest in process,
discharges of energy, and gesture aimed at a certain fullness in bodily
traces as it does to that kind of representational experimentation.

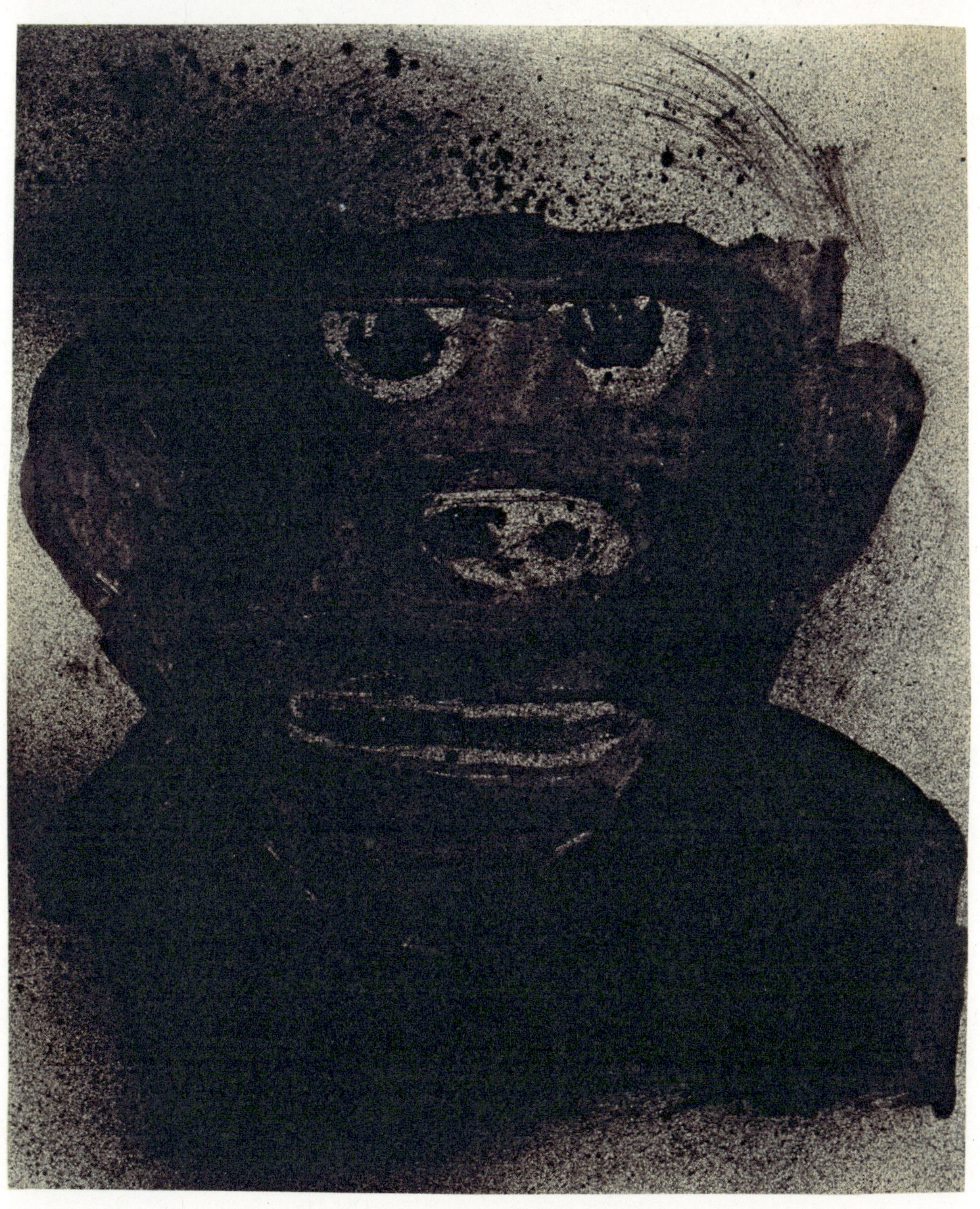

Klaus Weber

KOUROS (WALKING MAN), 2015

Sculpture: plaster,
half front body: 185 × 56 × 40 cm;
half back body: 163 × 61 × 79 cm

Video, color, sound, 17 min. (p. 99)

Berlin-based artist Klaus Weber works across media, often mixing material referenced from different contexts, histories, and logics to give a curious attention or focus to a specific element, gesture, or force.

"Kouros" refers to a specific type of life-sized sculptural figure from ancient Greece that monumentalized the vigor of noble young men. Weber here repeats a method used in a previous series of works that cast people from the contemporary city of Naples to present the specificity of their bodies in absentia, via traces of makeup, hair, and textiles. *phantom box/AGEMO* conjured "Pompei" somehow obliquely, as a material cultural event. Here, the iconicity of the kouros appears in negative relief, split open to reveal subtle traces of human tissue from the erotic moment of its casting.

The mold was produced during a protracted ceremony and artistic "happening," conducted on the night of a new moon in the midst of an erotic play party held in a Berlin nightclub. While unscripted co-participants of the evening playfully explored each others' differently sexed bodies—touching, wrestling, and stretching scripts of desire—on mattresses scattered around the room, a male figure posed at its center, his body synchronically responding to this mise-en-scène while being wrapped in dripping plaster bandages by craft workers in white gowns. The abstruseness of the event suggests a sexual magic ritual, while its redistributions of energies in production presses biological "sex" into a paradoxical "cultural" objectivity almost topologically, through stranger intimacy, countercultural imagination, and voluntary dispossession.

The scenario of fabrication is also a stand-alone videographic work—which was screened several times at Haus der Kulturen der Welt—set to Weber's sound piece *Large Dark Wind Chime*.

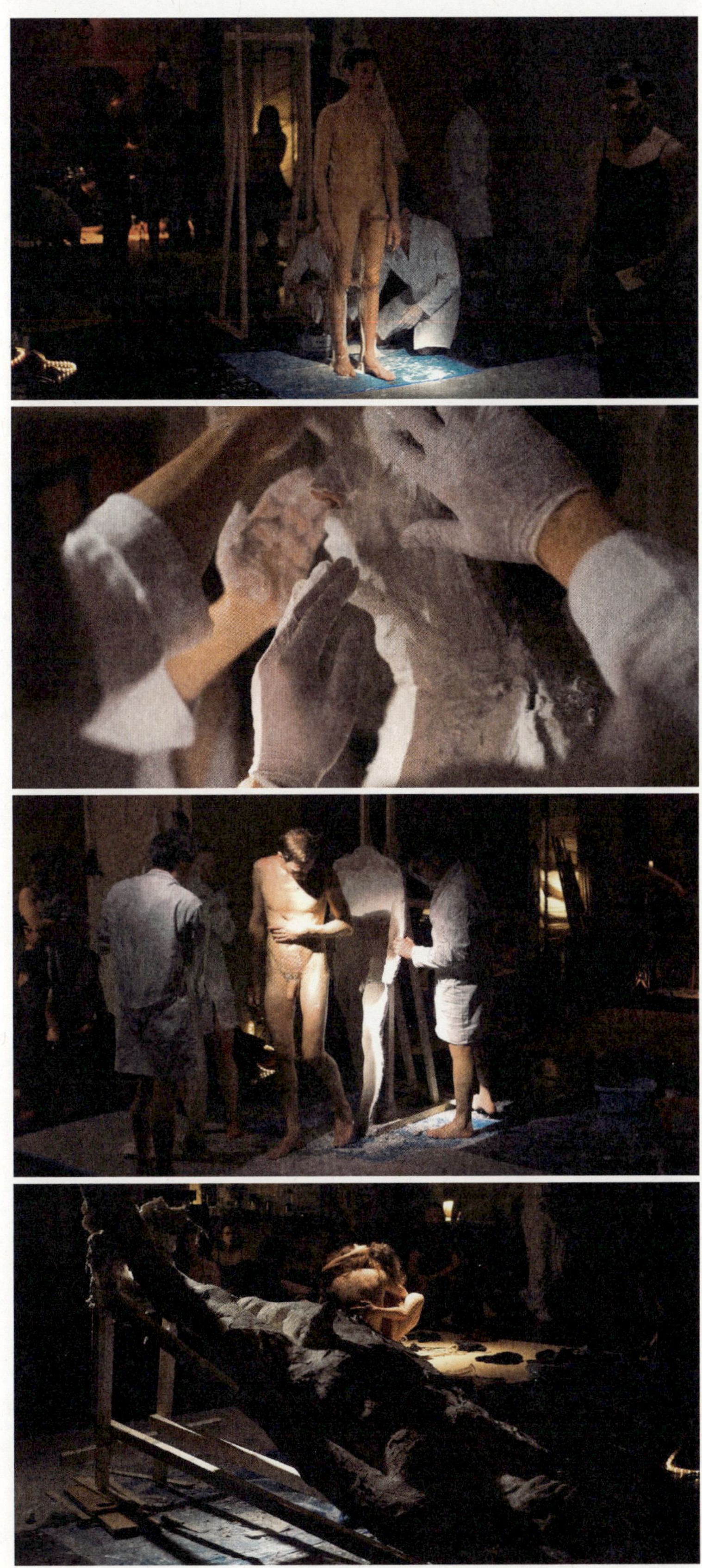

Klaus Weber

SHAPE OF THE APE, 2007
Mixed media, dimensions variable

Puzzled Ape, 2007
Cast iron, stained and waxed torso
on a stack of books: 130 × 91 × 71 cm;
ape head: 28 × 53 × 30 cm;
human skull: 28.5 × 46 × 30 cm;
legs: 27 × 63 × 41 cm

*Untitled (Collection of
31 vintage figurines)*, 2007
Mixed media on glass pedestals,
dimensions variable

Not shown in the exhibition:

American business leaders, 2007
Photocopy and Japanese ink,
98 × 67 cm (p. 102, Fig. 1)
Ape on Pig, 2007
C-Print, 98 × 126 cm (p. 102, Fig. 2)
Coco letter, 2007
Archival inkjet print, 80 × 63 cm
(p. 102, Fig. 3)
Sensation am Attersee, 2007
Photocopy, 133 × 84.5 cm
(p. 102, Fig. 4)
Lenin's desk, 2007
C-Print, 104 × 128 cm (p. 103, Fig. 5)

BEULEN, 2008
Photo collage (p. 101)

Shape of the Ape (2007) is an installation by Klaus Weber presenting thirty-one eccentric versions (twenty-six of which are included in the exhibition) of an iconic kitsch sculpture: an ape sitting on a stack of books, studying a human skull. The various sculptures were obtained from a number of different auctions. The original 1892 work, *Affe mit Schädel* (Ape with Skull), can be traced back to the little-known nineteenth-century German artist, Hugo Rheinhold, who reportedly swiftly sold its reproduction rights. Darwin's name appears on one of the book's spines, while written on the pages of another are the snake's coaxing words to Eve in Eden to eat the apple, *"Eritis sicut deus"* ("And ye shall be as God"). The ending ("knowing good and evil") is sculpted as if it has been ripped out.

The removal of morality from creationist reference in the sculpture's *artistic* birth loops in a complex manner with its mass-produced itinerary through the twentieth century's most concentrated and devastating installations of ideologically and racially transmuted speciesist reason. Lenin was reported to have one of the sculptures displayed on his desk, a gift from an American businessman who had hoped to do business with the communist government. Another was pulled from the remains of a Nazi plane that had crashed at the bottom of an Austrian lake, and was rumored otherwise to be loaded with gold and secret documents.

Weber's framing of these dimensions of simian man's commodity status in the totalitarian idiom has him fabricate his own version in iron, without finally securing the skull, primate head, or leg casts lying dismembered beside it.

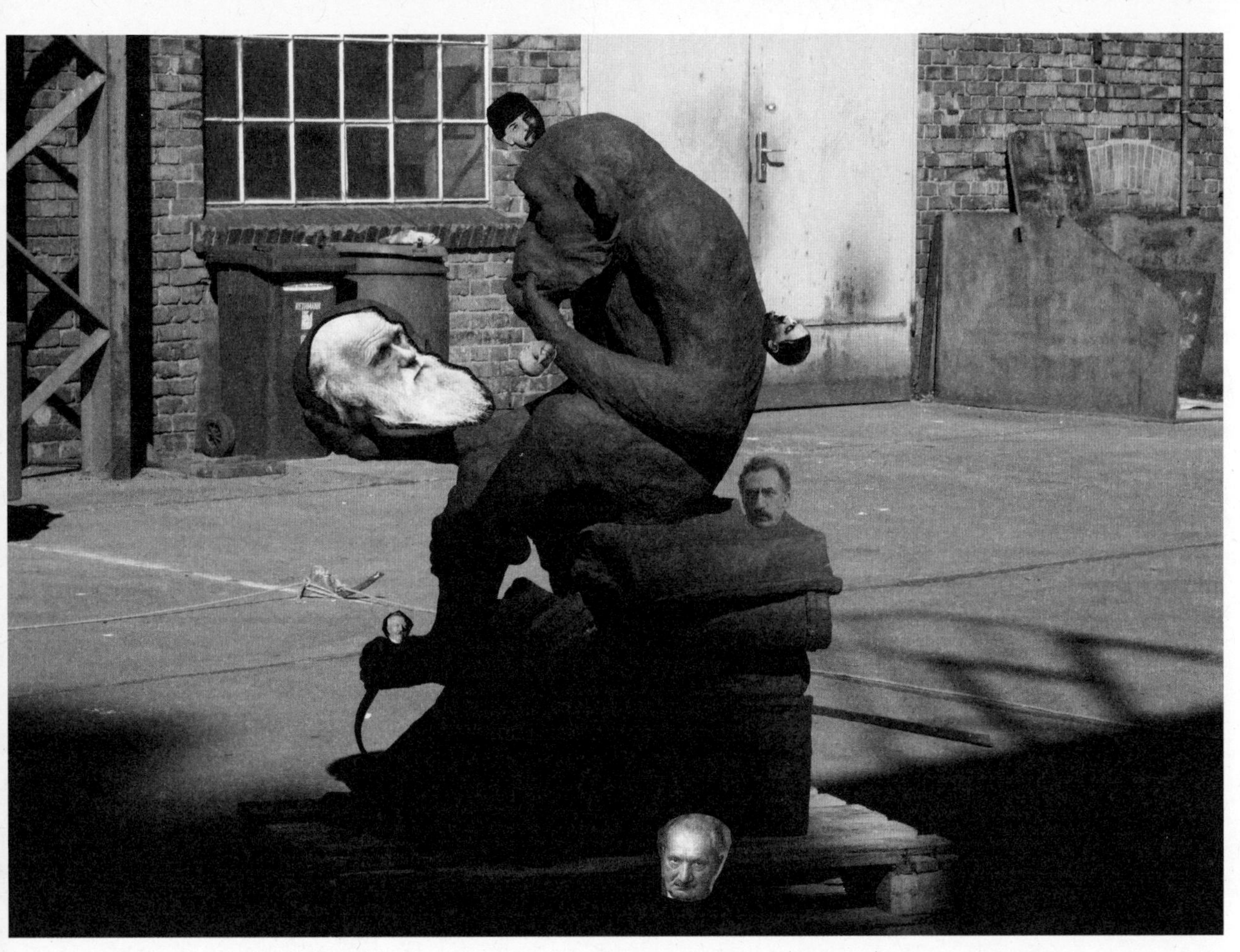

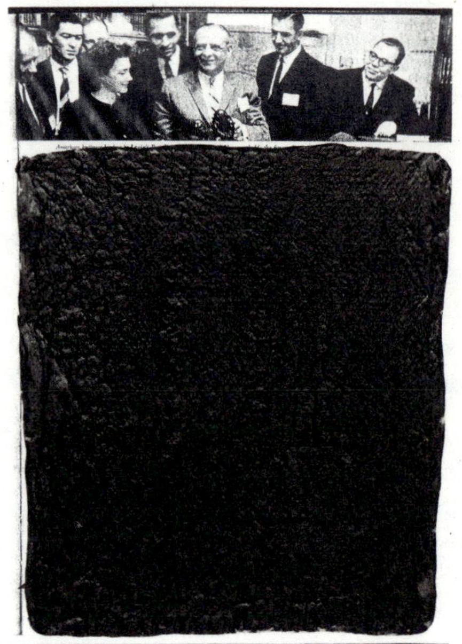

1

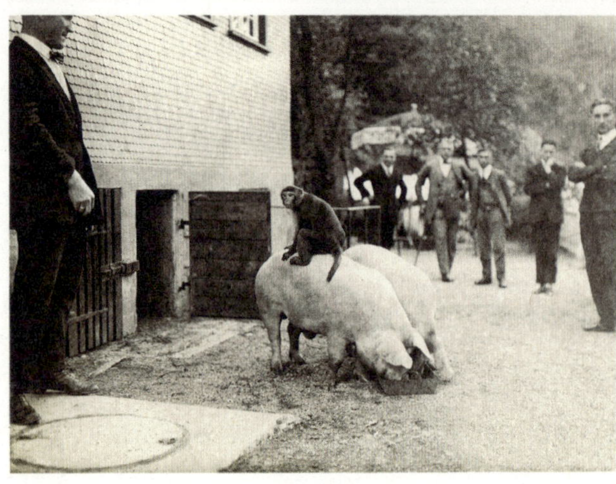

2

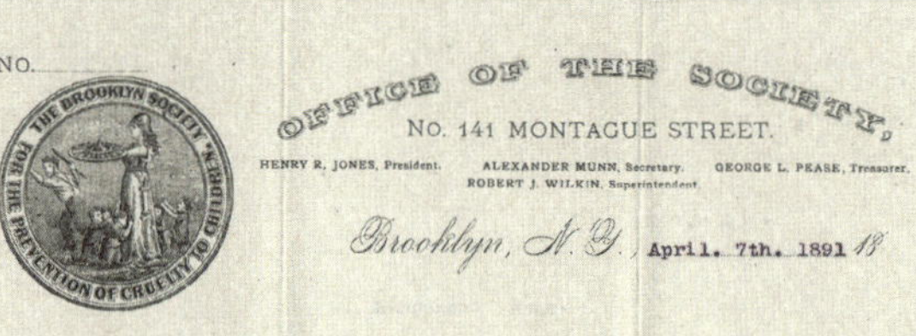

No.________

OFFICE OF THE SOCIETY,

No. 141 MONTAGUE STREET.

HENRY R. JONES, President.   ALEXANDER MUNN, Secretary.   GEORGE L. PEASE, Treasurer.
ROBERT J. WILKIN, Superintendent.

Brooklyn, N. Y., April 7th. 1891 18

Darwin W. Esmond. Esq.

    Secretary etc.

    Newburgh, N. Y.

      My dear Sir:

        I beg herewith to inform you that this Society has prevented the children advertised in connection with the "Reilly & Wood's New Classic Vaudeville Co." from appearing in this City as "Joco and Coco", and in the Royal Xylophonists,- viz:

    Charles Wincott, 15 years old, as "Coco", the human monkey, and

    Jennie Wincott, 13 years old, xylophone performer.

    This notice is sent in accordance with resolution adopted by the convention of delegates from societies held at Albany, October, 1st. 1890.

      Sincerely yours.

        Robert J Wilkin

          Supt. etc.

3

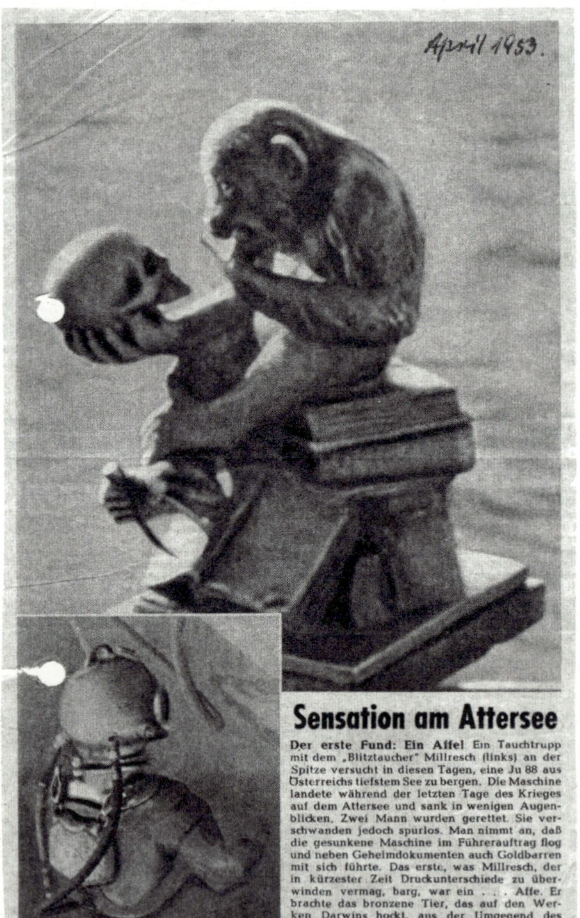

Sensation am Attersee

Der erste Fund: Ein Affe! Ein Tauchtrupp mit dem „Blitztaucher" Millresch (links) an der Spitze versucht in diesen Tagen, eine Ju 88 aus Österreichs tiefstem See zu bergen. Die Maschine landete während der letzten Tage des Krieges auf dem Attersee und sank in wenigen Augenblicken. Zwei Mann wurden gerettet. Sie verschwanden jedoch spurlos. Man nimmt an, daß die gesunkene Maschine im Führerauftrag flog und neben Geheimdokumenten auch Goldbarren mit sich führte. Das erste, was Millresch, der in kürzester Zeit Druckunterschiede zu überwinden vermag, barg, war ein . . . Affe. Er brachte das bronzene Tier, das auf den Werken Darwins hockt, aus der Umgegend des gesunkenen Flugzeugs ans Tageslicht. Die Taucharbeiten gehen weiter. Aufn.: G. Bartsch

4

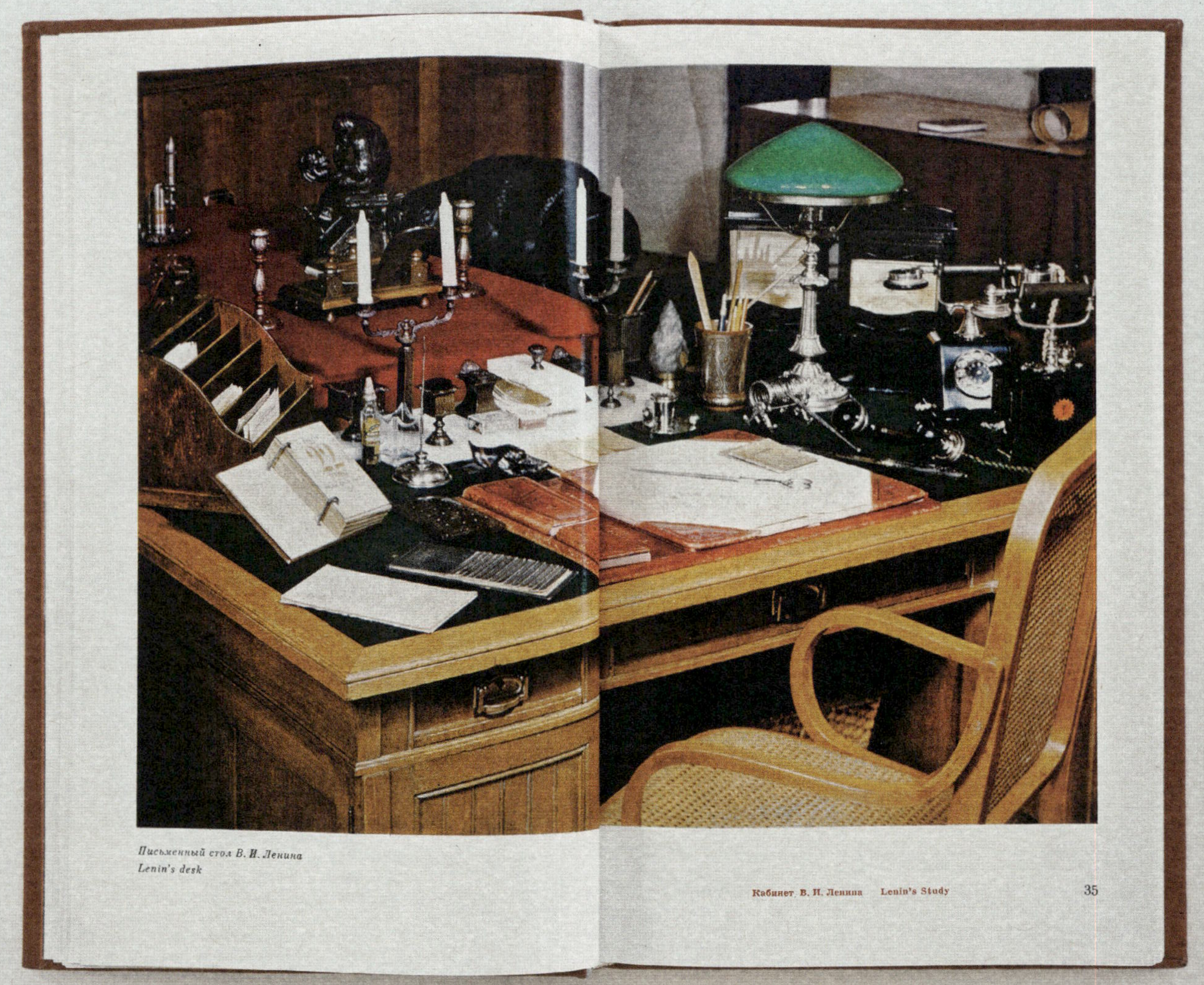

Письменный стол В. И. Ленина
Lenin's desk

Кабинет В. И. Ленина   Lenin's Study   35

Frederick Wiseman

PRIMATE, 1974
Digital transfer from 16mm film,
b/w, sound, 105 min.

Frederick Wiseman's 1974 documentary *Primate* observes behavioral neurophysiology and reproduction experiments undertaken at the Yerkes National Primate Research Center at Emory University. The film attracted 150 official complaints from PBS viewers following its delayed first broadcast, and many stations refused to even screen it.

Primate opens with a clear conceptual montage: A historical portrait sequence of highly esteemed research scientists shifts to a location shot of the Yerkes Center, followed by a countersequence of close-ups of animals in cages. In an initial dialogue of artfully captured *deformazione professionale*, an enthusiastic graduate student trades early career research stories with a researcher on the value of observing primates in captivity versus in the "wild" as a means of significantly increasing the chances of being able to view gorilla copulation. The libidinal dimension of objectivity and detachment in this first scene is repeated throughout the film as a dominant professional and gendered state of composure.

Wiseman signposts the generic horror and increasing violence pending in *Primate*—undignified confinements and ever more extreme surgeries, vivisections, and sacrificial death—with a simple corridor shot half way through of a scientist carrying a bunch of bananas and a huge, sharp knife in one dangling hand. The knowledge-based "purpose" behind most of the lab experiments depicted is rarely clear. A single piece to camera by one scientist explains his invasive work around his own theory of bipedal evolution; separate coverage is given of a round-table meeting to coordinate the center's first artificial inseminations. But the human scientists remain difficult subjects to identify with. The most concerning political ramifications surrounding the cold war era's "basic" research into reproductive drives and behavior are raised by footage of a rhesus monkey with an electronics box fitted to its head, being prompted tele-electronically to have sex with caged females.

Critics have noted the uncanny dialogue that *Primate* takes up with Wiseman's censored first film from 1967, *Titicut Follies*, which documented patient/inmate experiences of abuse at a Massachusetts state hospital for the criminally insane. Wiseman would go on to make forty-three films of US institutions, all featuring his signature aesthetic of passive capture and active montage.

WGBH TV Channel
WHAT PRICE KNOWLEDGE, 1974
Digital transfer from TV footage, color,
sound, 32 min.

After previewing the final cut of Frederick
Wiseman's film *Primate* (1974), documenting the daily activities inside the Yerkes
National Primate Research Center in Atlanta,
Dr. Geoffrey Bourne, the then director at
Yerkes, expressed mild concern that some
scenes might be misinterpreted by a lay
audience. Following shocked reactions to
the public PBS broadcast of *Primate*, Bourne
canceled his appearance on a WNET seg-
ment that had been scheduled for a discussion of the film and publicly lambasted the
documentary as "rubbish" and "a perversity."
Wiseman suggested Bourne's public response
was "less to the film than to the reviews."
Boston-based WGBH meanwhile engaged
Graham Chedd, the host of science program
NOVA, to put together a thirty-minute studio
debate at short notice. This now historic
discussion, *What Price Knowledge*, featured
Harvard academics Richard Lewontin
(geneticist) and Robert Nozick (philosopher),
MIT's David Baltimore (molecular biologist
and cancer researcher), and Adrian Perachio
from the Yerkes Center (shown in *Primate*
overseeing the tele-electronic stimulation
of the rhesus monkey).

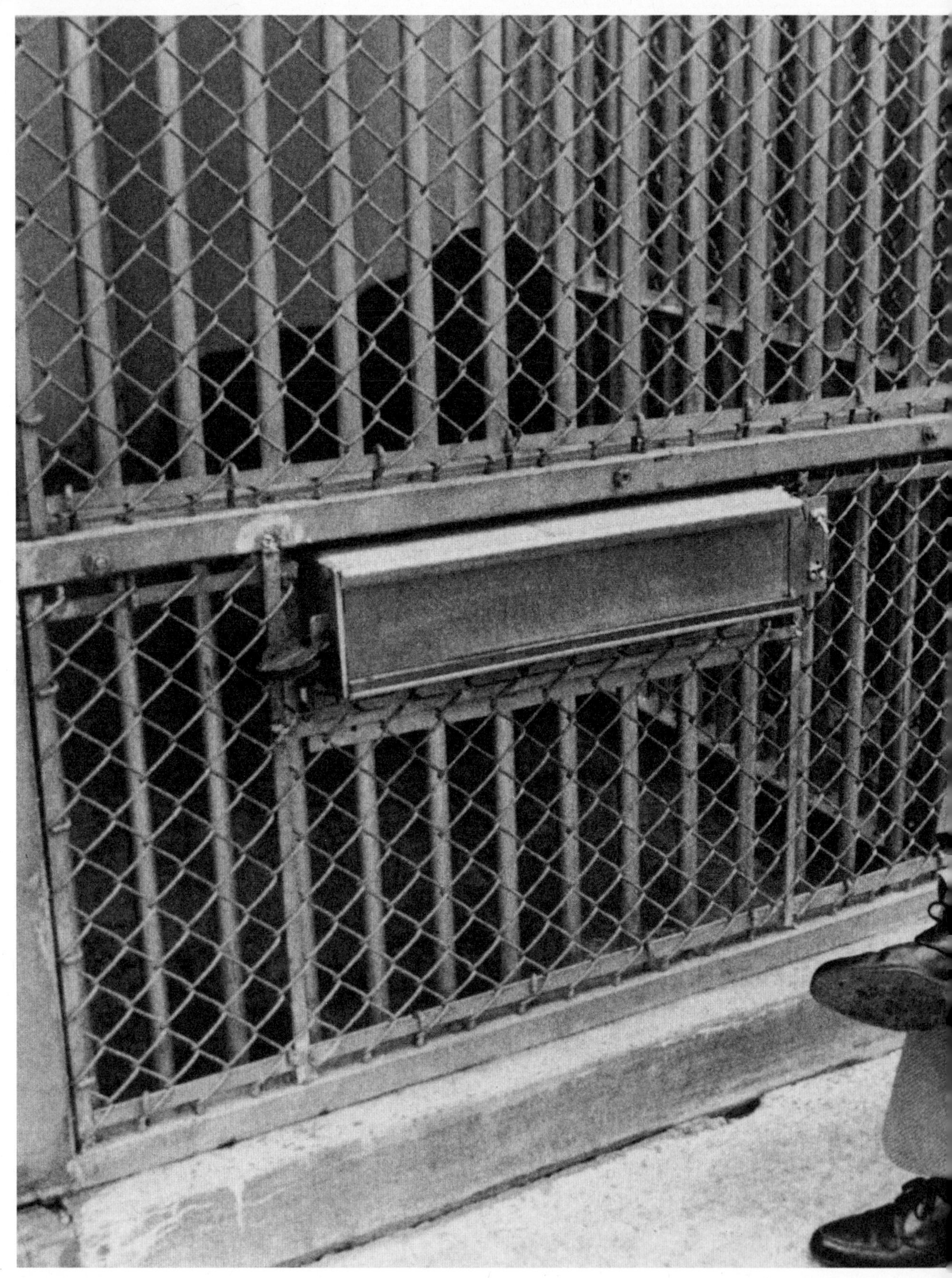

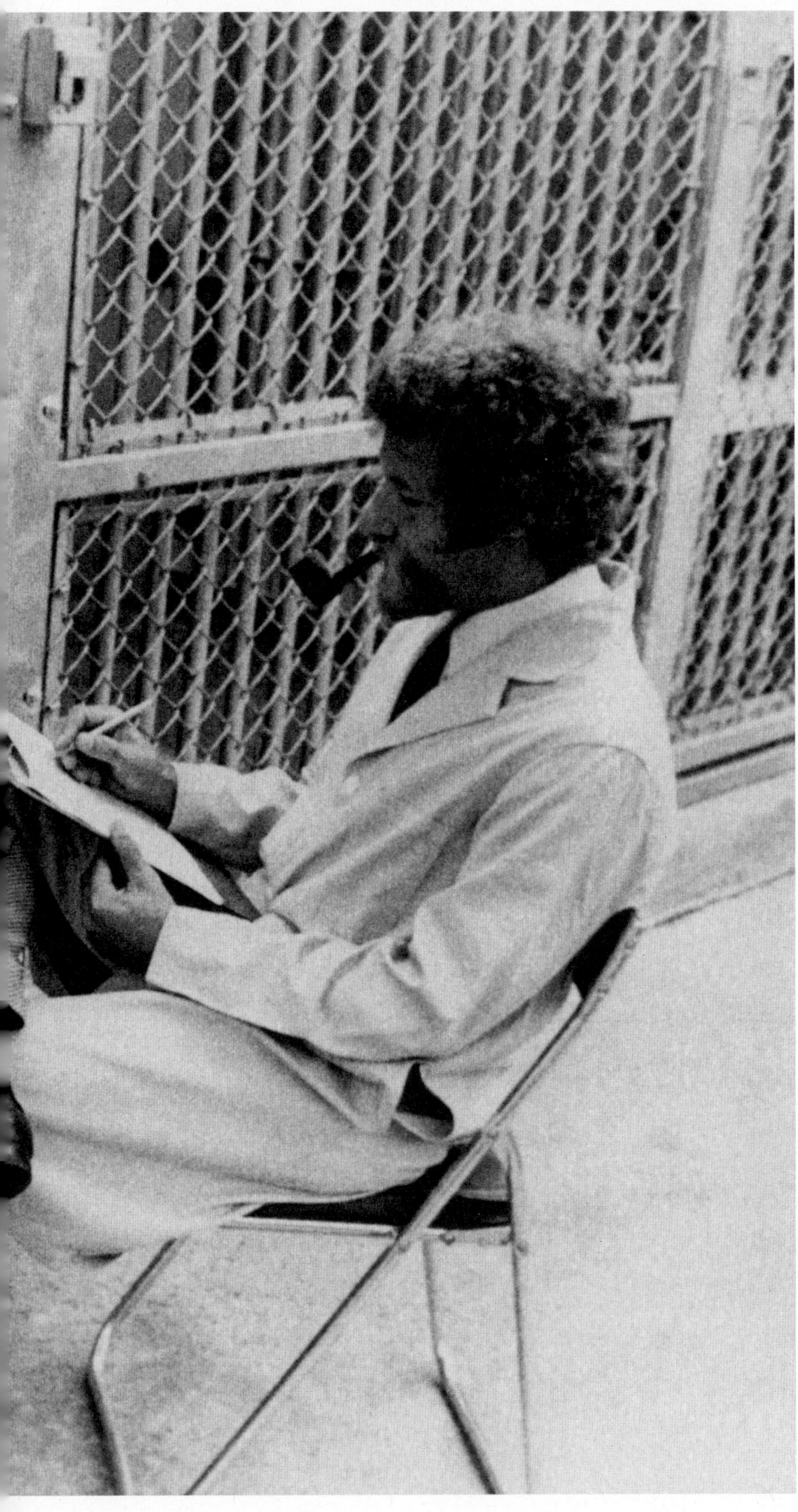

A)

Atlas Japannensis: Being Remarkable Addresses by Way of Embassy from the East-India Company of the United Provinces, to the Emperor of Japan is a book relating the adventures of Dutch commercial travelers in Japan. In the scene depicted, the unspoiled Arcadian landscape and the pair of naked figures call to mind the biblical story of Adam and Eve. Read in this manner, the female ape clasping the tree trunk represents Eve, while the male animal assumes the role of the seducer. In his depiction of the apes, in particular the female figure, Montanus drew on the only illustration of a great ape available at that time: a copperplate engraving from the eyewitness report of the Dutch physician Tulpius, who in 1641 provided the first modern description of a great ape on European soil. His illustration showed a seated female ape, which Montanus altered only slightly for inclusion in his idyll. (Cf. Hans Werner Ingensiep)

Arnoldus Montanus, "Menschen-Affen," in: Montanus, *Gedenkwaerdige Gesantschappen der Oost-Indische Maetschappy in't Vereenigde Nederland, aen de Kaisaren van Japan*, Amsterdam 1669, p. 42

In eighteenth-century Enlightenment Europe, as the natural sciences and historiography ushered in the transition from a static to a dynamic understanding of nature, the ape entered the arena of knowledge, too. Apes had functioned as transitional figures in cosmological systems since antiquity, but now the focus was placed on reformulating cosmology in the spirit of modern science and on a universalist claim to power as manifested in colonial expansion. Knowledge of great apes in the eighteenth century was still derived from a handful of travel reports, as well as myths, stories, and collective fantasies of hybrid beings and monsters. It would be the following century before the first great apes were imported into Europe. Acquiring knowledge about them at first hand from live specimens was vital in establishing the (unstable) distinction between "culture" and "nature" that was so essential to the Enlightenment. The study of apes not only served to illustrate the continuities and discontinuities between man and nature; as an object of interest for scholarly learning, the ape also entered the domain of knowledge as a figure in a continually revised grand narrative of civilization, concerned with both describing and classifying the world and new versions of the origin stories.

[Quote]

"In medieval iconography, the ape holds a mirror in which the man who sins must recognize himself as *simia dei* (ape of God). In Linnaeus' optical machine, whoever refuses to recognize himself in the ape, becomes one: to paraphrase Pascal, *qui fait l'homme, fait le singe* (he who acts the man, acts the ape)."

Giorgio Agamben, *The Open: Man and Animal*, Stanford 2004, pp. 26–27

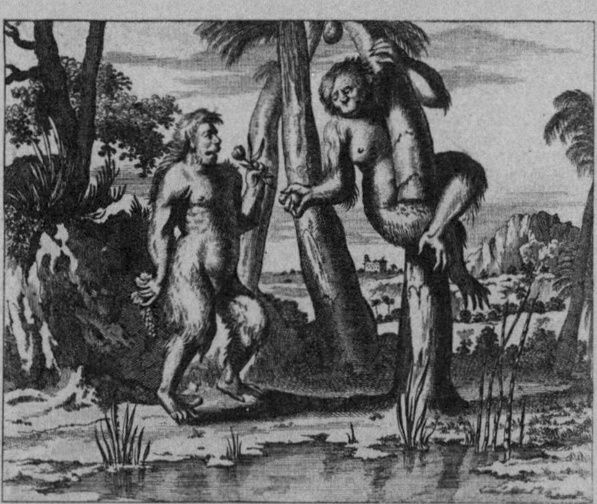

A)

I. QUADRUPEDIA.

Corpus hirsutum. *Pedes* quatuor. *Feminæ* viviparæ, lactiferæ.

Ordo	Genus	Character	Species
ANTHROPOMORPHA. *Dentes primores 4. utrinque; vel nulli.*	Homo.	Nosce te ipsum.	H { Europæus albesc. / Americanus rubesc. / Asiaticus fuscus. / Africanus nigr.
	Simia.	ANTERIORES. POSTERIORES. *Digiti* 5 . . . . . 5. Posteriores anterioribus similes.	Simia cauda carens. Papio. Satyrus. Cercopithecus. Cynocephalus.
	Bradypus.	*Digiti* 3. vel 2 . . . 3.	Ai. *Ignavus.* Tardigradus.
FERÆ. *Dentes primores 6. utrinque: intermedii longiores Pedes multifidi, unguiculati.*	Ursus.	*Digiti* 5 . . . . . 5. Scandens. *Mammæ* 4. (Ald.) *Calcaneis* insistit. *Pollex* extus positus.	Ursus. Coati *Mrg.* Wickhead *Angl.*
	Leo.	*Digiti* 5 . . . . . 4 Scandens. *Mammæ* 2. ventrales. *Lingua* aculeata.	Leo.
	Tigris.	*Digiti* 5 . . . . . 4 Scandens. *Mammæ* 4 umbilicales. *Lingua* aculeata.	Tigris. Panthera.
	Felis.	*Digiti* 5 . . . . 4 Scandens. *Mammæ* 8. sc. 4. pect. 4. abdom. *Lingua* aculeata.	Felis. Catus. Lynx.
	Mustela.	*Digiti* 5 . . . . . 5. Scandens. *Dentes* molares 4. utrinque.	Martes. Zibellina. Viverra. Mustela. Putorius.
	Didelphis.	*Digiti* 5. . . . . 5. *Mammæ* 8. intra bursulam abdomin.	Philander. *Possum.*
	Lutra.	*Digiti* 5. . . . . 5. Palmipes.	Lutra.
	Odobænus.	*Digiti* 5. . . . . 5. Palmipes. *Dentes* intermedii superiores longiss.	Ross. *Morsus.*
	Ph...		

II. AVES.

Corpus plumosum. *Alæ* duæ. *Pedes* — *Feminæ* oviparæ

Ordo	Genus	Character
ACCIPITRES. *Rostrum uncinatum.*	Psittacus.	*Digiti* pedis antici 2. posti…
	Strix.	*Digiti* pedis antici 3. posti… quorum extimus retrorsu…
	Falco.	*Digiti* pedis antici 3. posti…
PICÆ. *Rostrum superne compressum, convexum.*	Paradisæa.	*Pennæ* 2. longissimæ, singula… nec alis, nec uropygio i…
	Coracias.	*Pes* 4dact. *Rectrices* exteriores breviores.
	Corvus.	*Pes* 4dact. *Rectrices* æquales.
	Cuculus.	*Digiti* pedis antici 2. posti… *Rostrum* læve.
	Picus.	*Digiti* pedis antici 2. *Rostrum* angulatum.
	Certhia.	*Pes* 4dact. *Rostr.* gracile incu…
	Sitta.	*Pes* 4dact. *Rostr.* triangulare.
	Upupa.	*Pes* 4dact. *Caput* plumis cri…
	Ispida.	*Pes* 4dact. cujus digitus exti… adnectitur tribus articulis
MACRORHYNCHÆ. *Rostr. longiss…*	Grus.	*Caput* cristatum.
	Ciconia.	*Ungues* plani, subrotundi.

B)

Taxonomy

B)

In the first edition of his famous work *Systema Naturae*, the Swedish zoologist and biologist Carl Linnaeus (1707–1778) presented a comprehensive, tabulated overview of the "Regnum Animale." Under the heading Quadrupedia (four-legged animals) Linnaeus included, amongst others, the order Anthropomorpha (humanlike animals), and divided that into three genera: Bradypus (sloths), Simia (apes), and Homo (humans). The gesture of grouping humans in a common order with the apes was met with outrage by Linnaeus' contemporaries, particularly his laconic note under the explanation of the genus Homo: "nosce te ipsum" ("know thyself!"). In the tenth edition of his *Systema Naturae*, in which he introduced the influential, binary nomenclature that is still used to this day, Linnaeus replaced the term Anthropomorpha with the order of Primates. Linnaeus himself never encountered a great ape, although he did come across a Barbary macaque named Diana, which inspired his famous comment that René Descartes, who had declared animals to be soulless automatons, had clearly never seen an ape.

Carl Linnaeus, *Caroli Linnaei, Sveci, Doctoris Medicinae systema naturae, sive, Regna tria naturae systematice proposita per classes, ordines, genera, & species*, Leiden 1735, no page (detail)

[Quote]

"[Linnaeus] referred to himself as a second Adam, the 'eye' of God, who could give true representations, true names, thus reforming or restoring a purity of names lost by the first Adam's sin. Nature was a theatre, a stage for the playing out of natural and salvation history. The role of the one who renamed the animals was to ensure a true and faithful order of nature, to purify the eye and the word. The 'balance of nature' was maintained partly by the role of a new 'man' who would see clearly and name accurately, hardly a trivial identity in the face of eighteenth-century European expansion. Indeed, this is the identity of the modern authorial subject, for whom inscribing the body of nature gives assurance of his mastery."

Donna Haraway, *Primate Visions: Gender, Race, and Nature in the World of Modern Science*, New York 1989, p. 9

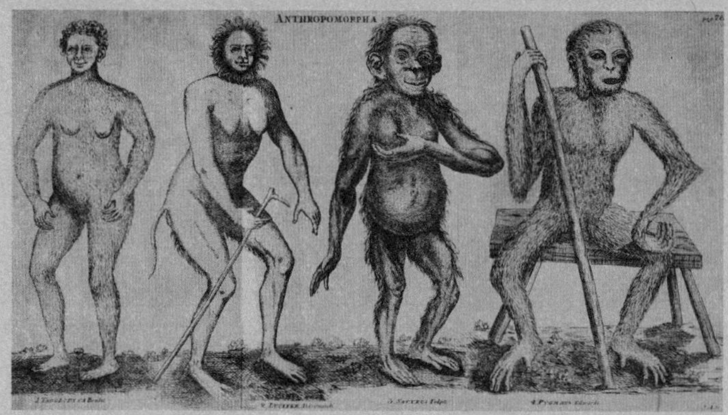

C)

C)

This illustration of the fantastical borderland between apes and humans draws on descriptions from both mythology and natural history. On the right is a "Pygmy" or forest man, depicted sitting on a bench and supporting himself with a stick. This is followed by a second type, the "Satyrus Indicus" according to Tulpius, a variant of a female chimpanzee based on an illustration from Scotin from 1738. The third is a "Lucifer" or Cercopithecus according to Aldrovandi. It is depicted upright, with a tail and stick. The fourth is a Troglodyte, a female "Homo Nocturnus" (meaning "night man") according to Bontius. The text supplies the usual anecdotes, about the bashful behavior of Bontius's female Troglodytes from Java, for instance, who only lack the power of speech: "The Javanese, however, say they can indeed speak, they only refrain from doing so in order that one does not force them to work." (Cf. Hans Werner Ingensiep)

Christianus Emmanuel Hoppius, "Vom Thiermenschen," in: Carl Linnaeus, *Des Ritter Carl von Linné Auserlesene Abhandlungen aus der Naturgeschichte, Physik und Arzneywissenschaft*, Leipzig 1776, p. 66

Although Charles Darwin (1809–1882) largely avoided the issue of man's origin in his groundbreaking work *On the Origin of Species* (1859), twelve years later he devoted an entire book to the theme, *The Descent of Man* (1871). According to Darwin, man is the result of a gradual process of development, which he named "evolution" for the first time in this work. He discerned a profound continuity between man and the great apes, believing that even characteristics and accomplishments such as morality, sympathy, emotionality, and altruism, which were assumed to be exclusive to humans, can be traced back to the animal world. Darwin's hypothesis of man's African origins exercised a great influence on early paleoanthropology, and for many years the continent competed with Southeast Asia for the title of the "cradle of humanity."

D)

Edward Linley Sambourne, "Man is but a worm," December 6, 1881, *Punch's Almanack for 1882*

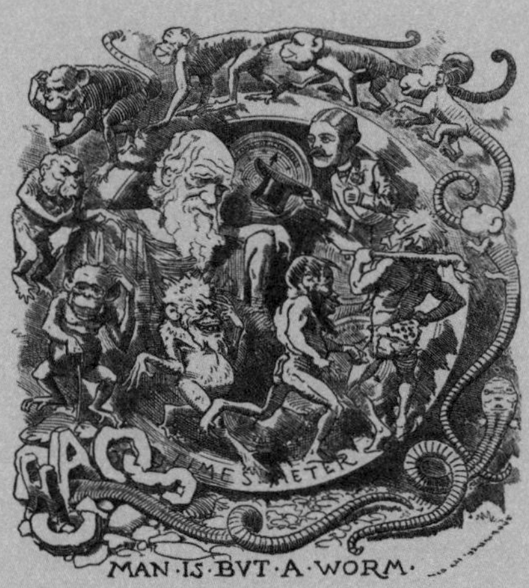

D)

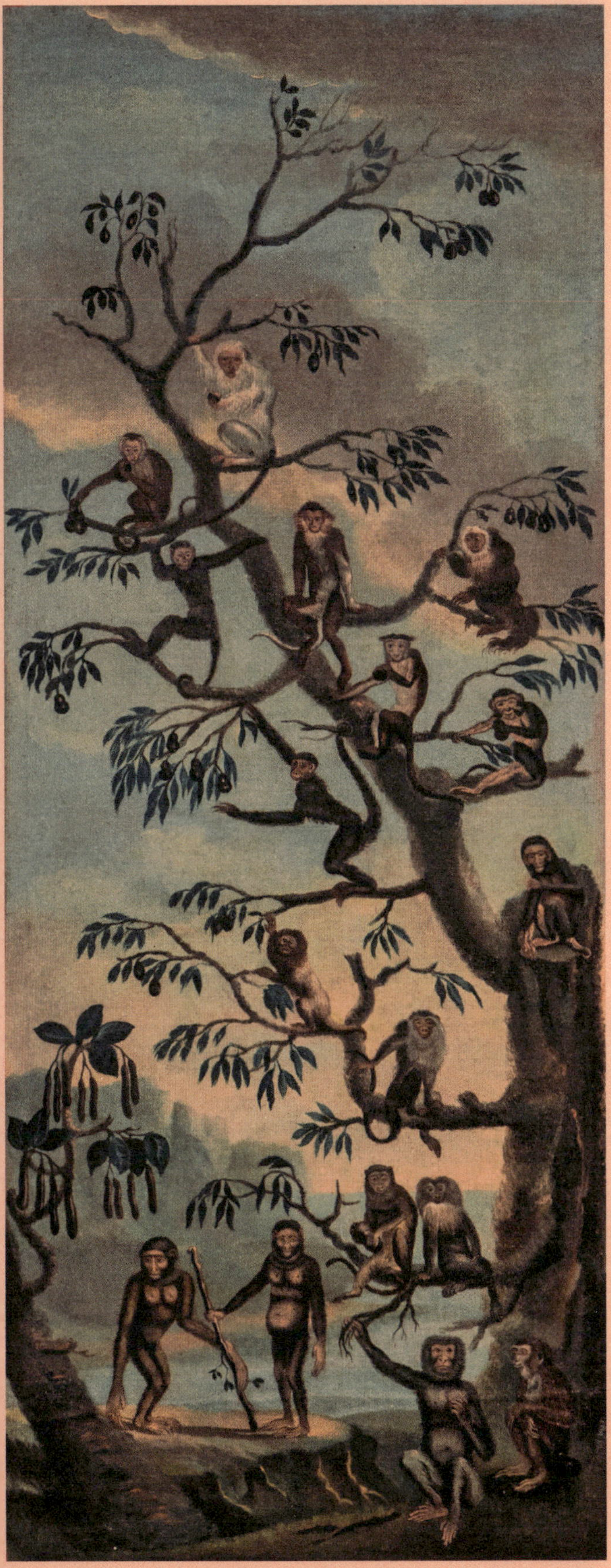

The painting depicts a tree in which one
recognizes the primates that were engraved
by Jacques de Sève in the Comte de Buffon's
Histoire naturelle, générale et particulière
(1749–1788). Since medieval times, monkeys
had been associated with evil, but the comic
antics of the seventeenth and eighteenth
centuries turned the primates into caricatures: At the bottom of the tree those apes
are represented that are the closest to
humans. Not only are they holding a stick and
displaying their ability to use tools, they
are also separated from the other apes by
a ditch. In contrast to Linnaeus, Buffon did
not have a high regard for apes and placed
them last in line, as deceitful animals.
One interpretation of this painting is that it
depicts the primates' reaction to Buffon's
ranking. They are actually putting themselves
first in line, as the last representative of the
animals is also the first example of humanity.

Anonymous, *L'arbre généalogique des singes*,
after 1766, oil on canvas, 105.5 × 44 cm

F)

In 1903 the zoologist and philosopher Ernst
Haeckel (1834–1919) commissioned the
painter Gabriel von Max to produce an illustration for his work *Kunstformen der Natur*.
The illustration, *Apotheosis of Evolutionary
Thought*, depicted man surrounded by the
other primates and was intended to form the
conclusion to the ten-volume series of
works. The numbering of his figures established an explicit hierarchy. Beginning
with the white human female (1) this proceeded in descending order through the
great apes such as the gorilla (2) and the
chimpanzees (3) down to the non-hominid
primates such as the guenon (6). The picture thus established not an evolutionary
process, but rather a hierarchical gradation
that clearly privileged humans over the
other primates. Nevertheless, Haeckel's
publisher prevented publication of the plate,
expressing concern that it could be mis-
understood as effecting a rapprochement
between man and the apes. It was finally
published separately in the first supplement
to the collection of *Ernst Haeckels Wanderbilder* from 1906.

Ernst Haeckel and Gabriel Max,
"Apotheose des Entwicklungs-Gedankens,"
in: Ernst Haeckel, *Apothese des Entwicklungs-
Gedankens* (first supplement to the collection
of the „Wanderbilder" series I–III),
Gera 1906, no page

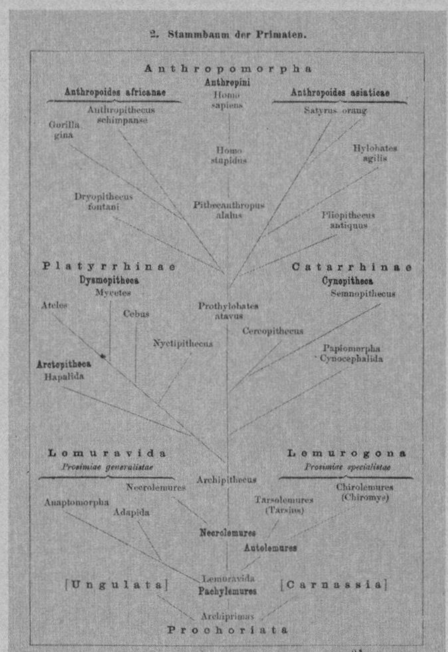

G)

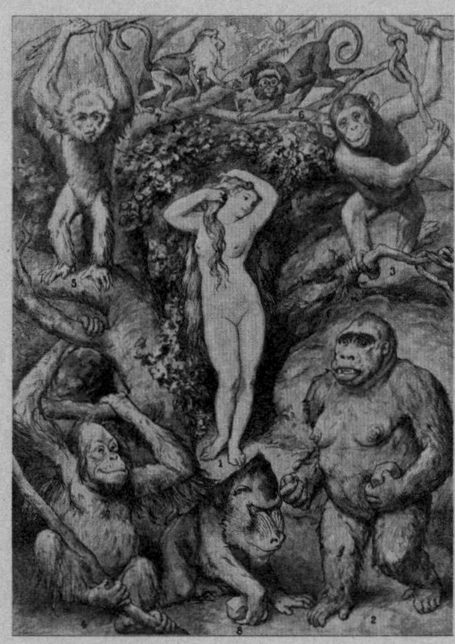

F)

G)

Ernst Haeckel developed his own line of
human ancestors virtually parallel to Darwin's
The Descent of Man (1871). An important
position was occupied by Haeckel's hypothe-
tical *Pithecanthropus alalus*, the "ape man
without speech" (*Generelle Morphologie*,
1866). Haeckel believed this transitional form
represented the "missing link" that would
close the evolutionary gap between man and
his apelike ancestors. He considered Africa
and Southeast Asia to be the most likely
birthplaces of *Pithecanthropus* and urged
his students to search for evidence of the existence of the "missing link" in these regions.
Evolutionary narratives are, however, invariably political narratives, too. In Germany
Haeckel's theories on selection, euthanasia,
and eugenics paved the way for Nazism.
He found it obvious that the "cultural and
psychological differences that separate the
highest developed European peoples from
the lowest savages are greater than the
differences that separate the savages from
the humanoid apes." * From the very beginning, the theory of evolution also provided
a setting for naturalizing constructions of
differentiation, degradation, and subjugation.

* Daniel Gasman, *The Scientific Origins of
National Socialism*, New Jersey 2007, p. 134

Ernst Haeckel, "Stammbaum der Primaten,"
in: Ernst Haeckel, *Ueber unsere gegenwärtige
Kentniss vom Ursprung des Menschen*,
Bonn 1898, p. 35

Emboldened by the hypothesis that the "missing link" connecting man and ape was to be found in Southeast Asia, the Dutchman Eugène Dubois resigned his academic post in 1887, joined the Dutch army, and shipped out to the Dutch East Indies to look for the fossilized remains of hominids. Four years later, during excavations on the banks of the River Solo, he uncovered fossil bone remains—a cranium, a thigh bone, and a molar tooth—thus discovering the oldest remains of an early human known to that date. With the aid of reconstructions he was able to prove that "Java man" (as his find was soon to be named) must have already walked upright, sufficient confirmation in his eyes that he had actually discovered the "missing link." Drawing on Ernst Haeckel's theory of descent, he classified the find as *Pithecanthropus erectus.*

Eugène Dubois, *Veranda with bones,* ca. 1890

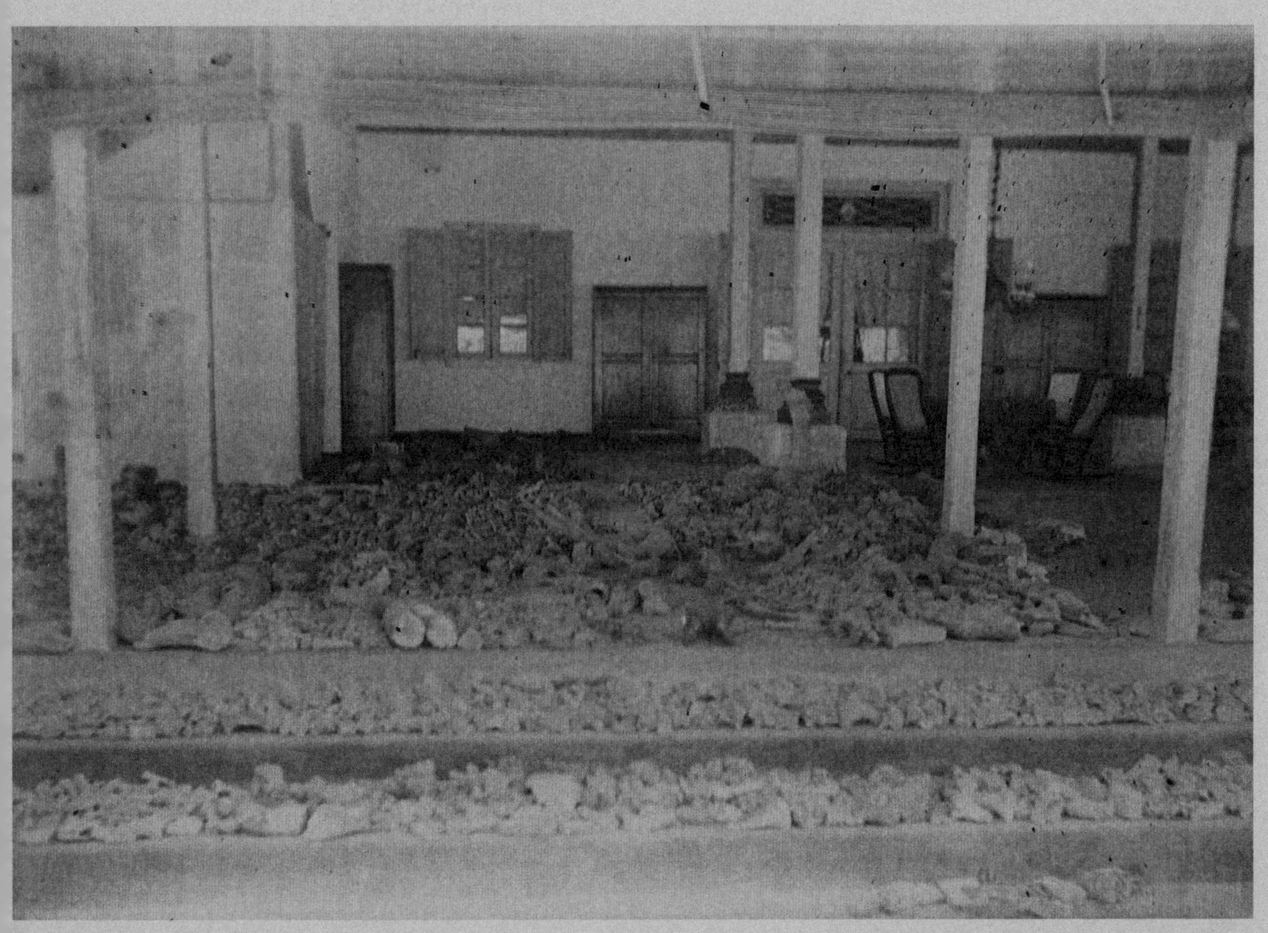

In 1908 the zoologist Alexander Sokolowsky produced one of the first books on the behavior of great apes in zoos. A notable passage describes the pervasive "psychological influence" of captivity on the great apes, who were unable to overcome the "loss of freedom" and frequently died after a few days without any recognizable external cause. As a countermeasure, Sokolowsky proposed rearing great ape babies in captivity.

Alexander Sokolowsky, *Beobachtungen über die Psyche der Menschenaffen*, Frankfurt am Main 1908, pp. 82–83

Early primatology as it formed in the first half of the twentieth century is intimately linked with the way new power technologies developed within modern mass societies during an era of technological armament. Apes and great apes became raw materials and resources for research into life within the different sites of knowledge production, from medicine and the military to the factory. As "psychobiological goldmines" (to quote Robert M. Yerkes), apes now held the potential for objectifying the psyche, intellect, and sociality, as well as conditioning behavior, thus facilitating the pursuit of the scientific optimization of human "nature"— for example controlling and treating "adjustment problems," or more generally, pathologies at the unstable boundary between a nature to be controlled and the dominant culture. However, the test subjects themselves placed this objectification in question.

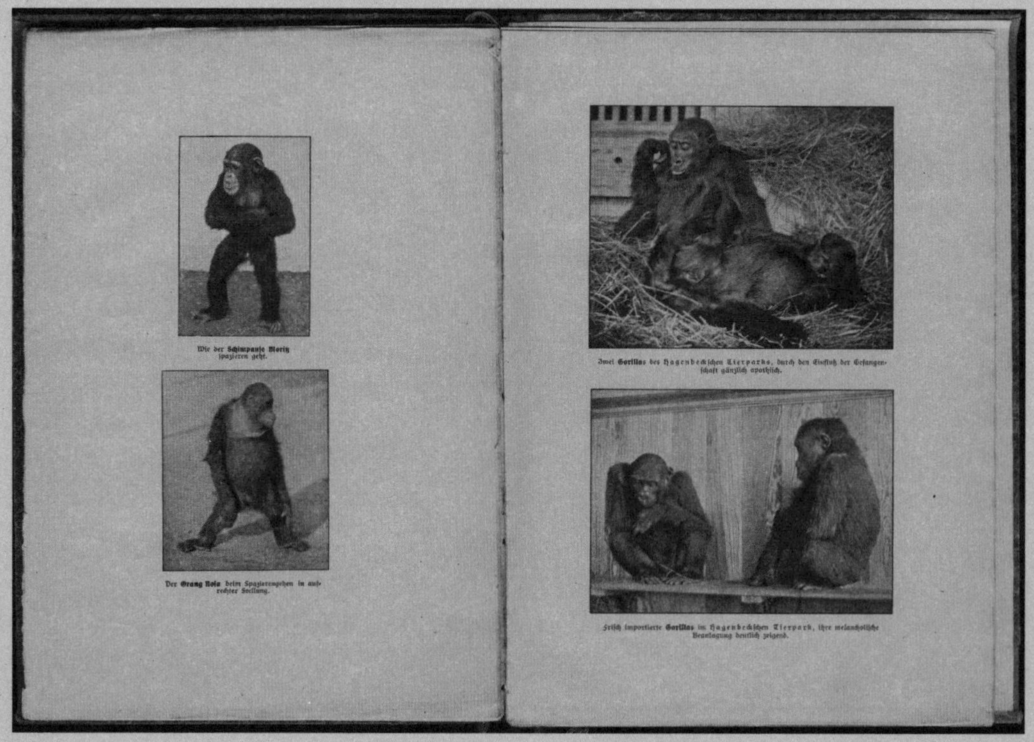

A)

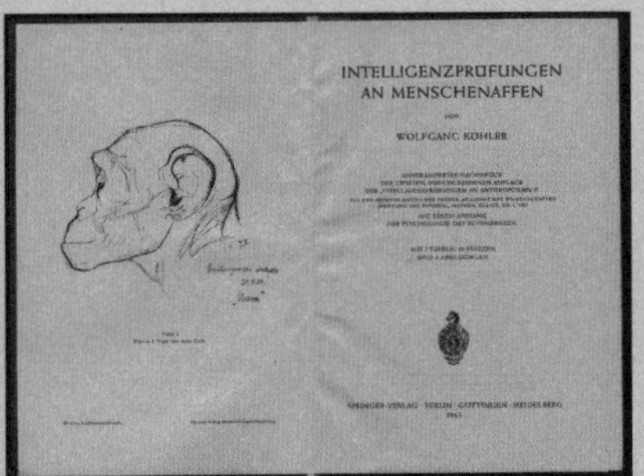

B)

B)

While chimpanzees had been kept as "pets" in Europe since the eighteenth century and some attempts had been made to teach them language, Wolfgang Köhler was the first person to conduct systematic investigations into chimpanzee cognition. In 1913 he traveled to the newly founded anthropoid station of the Prussian Academy of Sciences in Tenerife. His 1917 publication *Intelligenzprüfungen an Anthropoiden* (published in 1925 in English as *The Mentality of Apes*) expanded not only psychological science but also what Walter Benjamin would later refer to as "the great system of tests"* to include nonhuman primates. Psychological and physiological tests had accompanied the rise of Taylorism—which propounded scientifically optimized factory work—and industrialized warfare. Köhler, who was interested in insight and intelligence, was the first researcher to document chimpanzees' "ability" to manipulate objects such as poles, ropes, and boxes.

* Walter Benjamin, „Das Karussell der Berufe,"
in: Walter Benjamin, *Aufsätze, Essays, Vorträge
(Gesammelte Schriften Bd.II.2)*, edited by Rolf
Tiedemann, and Hermann Schweppenhäuser,
Frankfurt am Main 1977 [1930], p. 667

Wolfgang Köhler, *Intelligenzprüfungen an
Menschenaffen*, Berlin 1963 [1921], no page

C)

Wolfgang Köhler, *Intelligenzprüfungen an
Menschenaffen*, 1914–1917, 11 min.

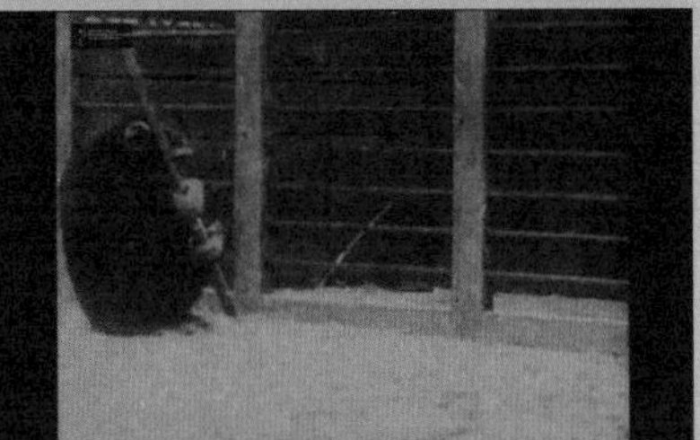

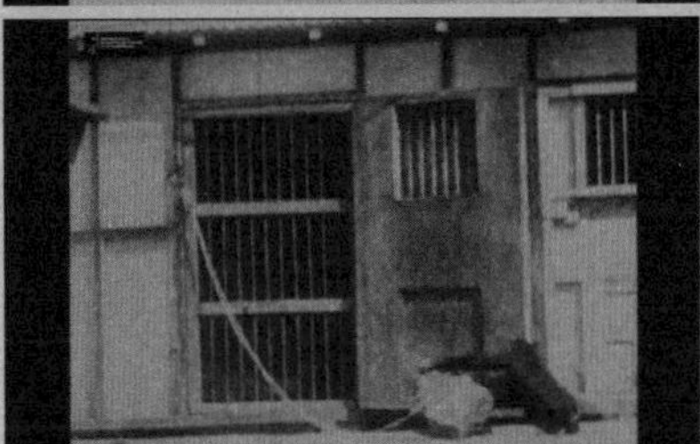

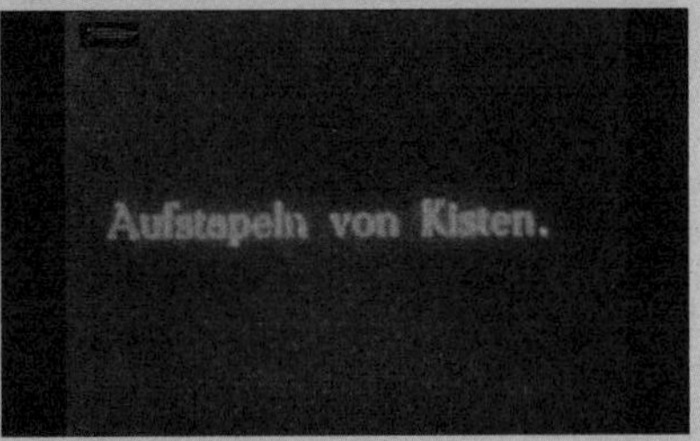

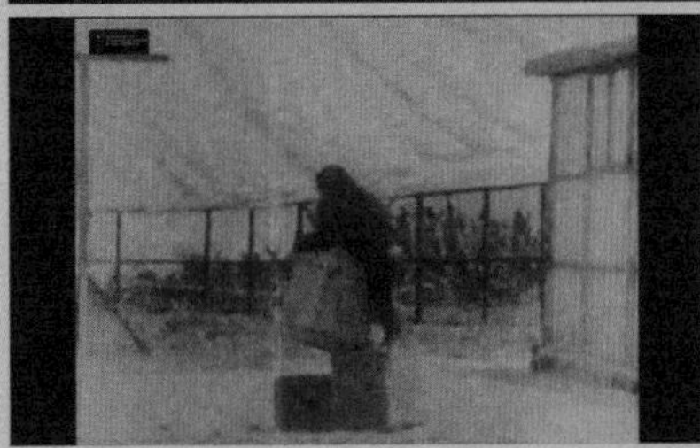

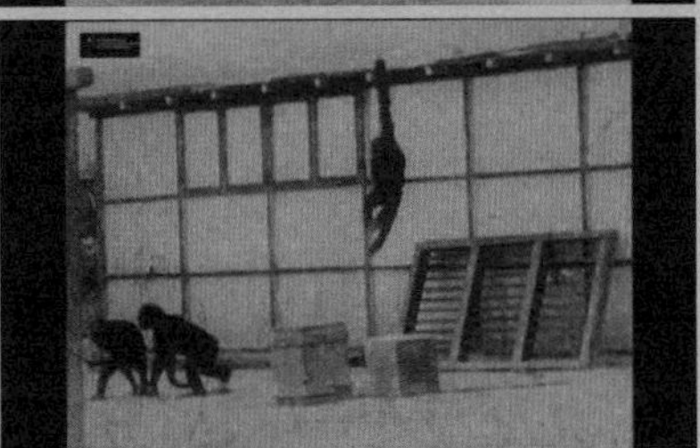

C)

117

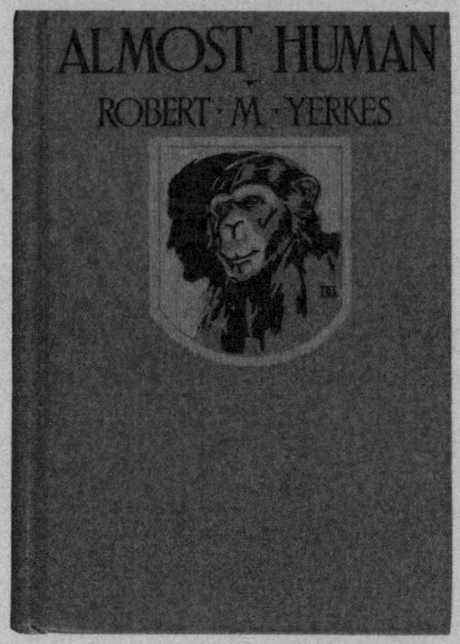

D)

D)

Robert M. Yerkes structured consciousness hierarchically, ascending from perception through to intelligence. He named his three essential functional levels "monkeying" (playing around with things, gathering experience through chance), "aping" (imitating other organisms), and "thinking" (solving problems through understanding). Yerkes' popular book *Almost Human*, in which he describes his experiences with Chim and Panzee, had an immense impact in two respects upon its publication in 1925. Firstly, it marked the defining moment when the great apes—in addition to chimpanzees and bonobos this included orangutans, gorillas, and gibbons—became a part of American culture. Furthermore, Yerkes' detailed descriptions could not disguise how little was actually known about the apes. When he collected all the available material on great apes for his 1927 book *The Great Apes*, it was clear that systematic accounts of the behavior of apes in the wild were completely absent.

Robert M. Yerkes, *Almost Human*, New York 1925

"We realize that with varying wisdom man has learned to shape nature to his needs and desires. Only with his own nature has he refrained from tampering. Yet the course of civilization and any sudden change for better or worse in the human type obviously depend upon consciously or unconsciously directed modifications. Probably there is no more unprofitable assumption than that of the unalterability of human nature [...]. It has always been a feature of our plan for the use of the chimpanzee as an experimental animal to shape it intelligently to specification instead of trying to preserve its natural characteristics. We have believed it important to convert the animal to as nearly ideal a subject for biological research as is practicable. And with this intent has been associated the hope of re-creating man himself in the image of a generally acceptable ideal."

Robert M. Yerkes, *Chimpanzees: A Laboratory Colony*, New York 1943, pp. 9–10

E)

N. N. Ladygina-Kohts, *Infant Chimpanzee and Human Child: A Classic 1935 Comparative Study of Ape Emotions and Intelligence*, ed. by Frans de Waal, Oxford 2002, plate 8,9, no page

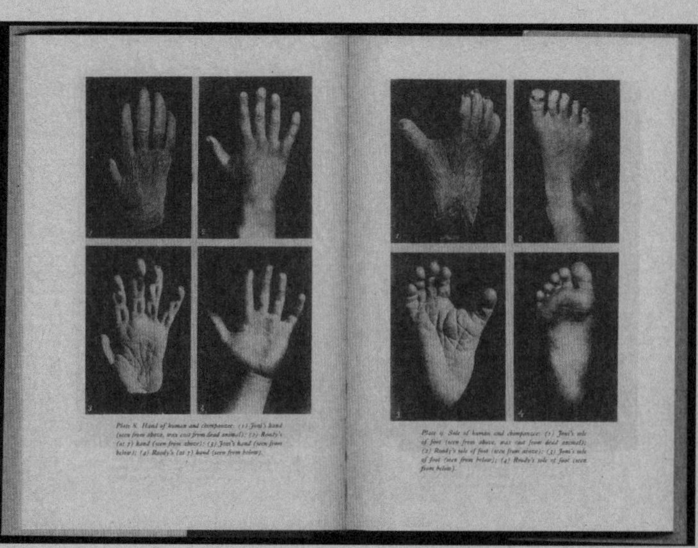

E)

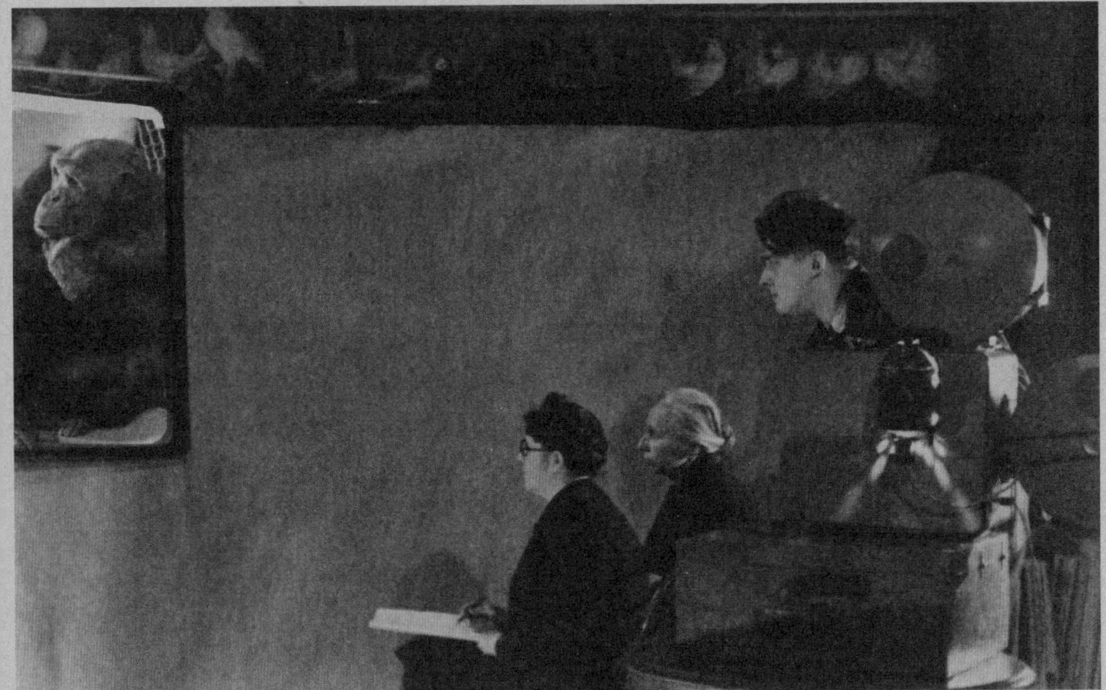

G)

F)

Russian zoologist Nadezhda Ladygina-Kohts was one of the first people to conduct psychophysical studies of primate behavior. In 1913 she opened a research lab in Moscow's Darwin Museum, where she began studying the emotions and mental capabilities of chimpanzees, and tested their perception of form and colors. In 1929 Kohts began to compare the cognitive and emotional development of her son Rudolf with the development of a young chimpanzee called Joni that she had studied from 1913 to 1916, publishing her findings in 1935 in the book *Ditia shimpanse i ditia cheloveka* (reprinted in English as *Infant Chimpanzee and Human Child*, 2002). Her studies explored differences between the child and the chimpanzee in terms of their memory, instincts, and the ways they showed emotions in similar situations. At a time when American behaviorists were representing animals as robots devoid of thoughts and emotions, Ladygina-Kohts depicted the chimpanzees as intelligent and sensitive. Moreover, she was the first scientist to research empathy in chimpanzees.

Film stills: Rudolf (Rudy) Kohts, cinematography by Anatoly Anzhanov (Zhandarmov), *Experiments with chimpanzees*, works of N. Ladygina-Kohts, 1962, 17 min.

G)

Nadezhda Ladygina-Kohts looking at film images of Joni, together with her son Rudolf. Film and photography have been indispensable means for primatology from the very-beginning. Just as the apes themselves, they act as "animated mirrors," revealing the degree to which primatology is a science of "technological" and "natural" processes of social mimesis. Despite many attempts at an "objective" language, primate films cannot fail to highlight the deeply social, situated, and ideologically contested character of the scientific inquiry and experimental setup.

Nadezhda Ladygina-Kohts, Rudolf Kohts, Natalya Levykina working on the film, ca. 1948–1955

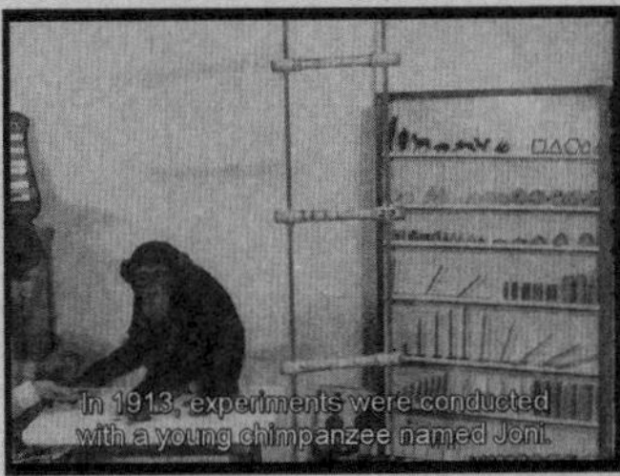

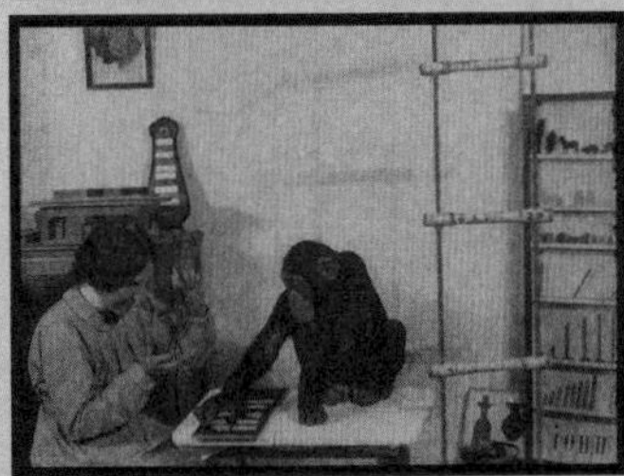

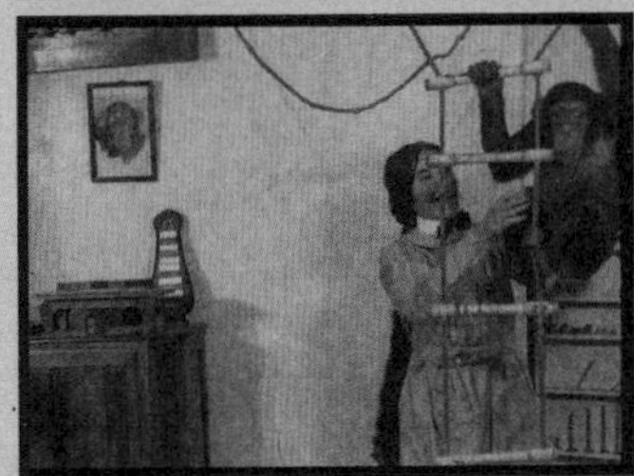

F)

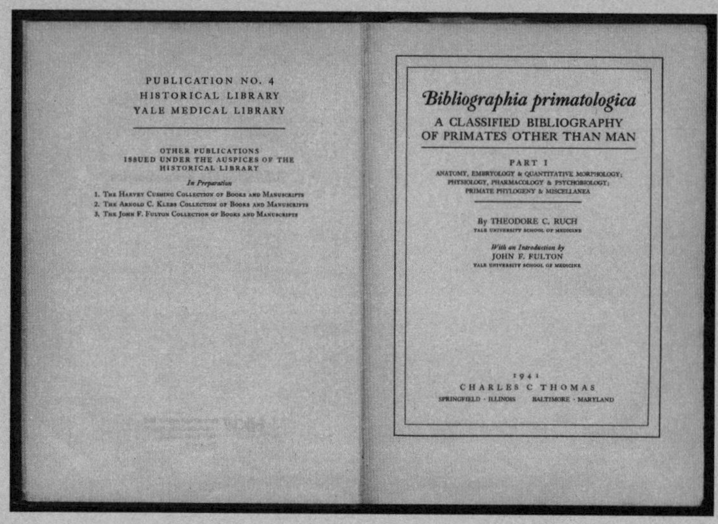

Theodore C. Ruch's *Bibliographia primatologica* first introduced the word "primatology"
and called those who studied this discipline
"primatologists." The introduction notes
that while 50,000 studies of fish had been
published before 1914, there were only some
5,000 on monkeys and apes by the same
point. The *Bibliographia primatologica*
contains a rather eclectic collection of texts
from antiquity through 1940.

Theodore C. Ruch, *Bibliographia primatologica*, Springfield/Baltimore 1941, no page

H)

[Quote]

"Multiple dimensions determine the decept-
ively simple word primatology: More than
240 species, primate habitats from snow
areas of Japan to tropical rain forests and
from deserts of Ethiopia to swamps of
South America, disparate national traditions
among those who study and write about
them, conflicting institutional priorities,
contending conservation agendas, struggles
over the terms of decolonization in primate-
habitat countries, incompatible disciplinary
and explanatory approaches, struggles over
field and lab methods, appropriations by
various ideological tendencies, unsettling
hierarchies in the scientific division of labor
in each social setting where primates are
described."

Donna Haraway, *Primate Visions: Gender,
Race, and Nature in the World of Modern
Science*, New York 1989, p. 116

Up until World War II, primatology was a science that developed almost exclusively with captive primates: in laboratories, zoos, the occasional private home, and stuffed animals in museums. As late as the 1950s, "European ethologists were working on instinct theories and American behaviorists were rewarding rats for pressing levers."*

The field studies conducted by American psychologist and anthropologist Clarence Ray Carpenter in the 1930s formed an exception to this. Carpenter was the first Western researcher with a distinctively "sociological" outlook, mapping primate sociality and society. This entailed a previously unseen recognition of the social character and complexity of primate life. Scientists hoped that knowledge about how groups form and are maintained would provide templates for the therapeutics and management of human societies. In Carpenter's model of social life, signing—which connected biology to psychology—as a means of understanding social behavior formed a bridge between nature and culture, and between humans and animals. By thus bridging nature and culture through the concept of communication, Carpenter would pave the way for the cybernetic understanding of sociality that came to dominate the second half of the twentieth century. Japanese primatology, on the other hand, which first undertook field studies in 1948, operated outside the nature/culture and human/animal divide that characterized the Western sciences. And although Japan had been an imperial power since the late nineteenth century, primatology developed not as a colonial discipline whose narrative structure combined subjugation with the search for primitive origins, but rather from the study of monkeys and apes that were domestic to Japan and formed part of a native mythology and identity.

Hence, the explanatory pattern used by the Japanese initially diverged vastly from their Western counterparts, before their methods later became widely adapted too by Western scientists. Japanese primatologists pioneered observational methods that focused on the complexity of social life, following animals over long periods of time and studying their intergenerational family relations. It was Kinji Imanishi and his fellow researchers who also first studied "cultural transmission" in primate societies, referring to a minimum definition of "culture" as socially learned behavior. If individuals in a social unit learn from each other, they may change over time. This assumption was confirmed in the late 1950s by observing Japanese macaques on Kōjima Island who, by washing sweet potatoes, transmitted this same behavior to others. The existence of cultural learning is now widely recognized, from birds to chimpanzees to whales, with new examples discovered almost daily.

* Frans de Waal, "Without Walls,"
New Scientist, vol. 172, no. 2321, 2001, p. 46

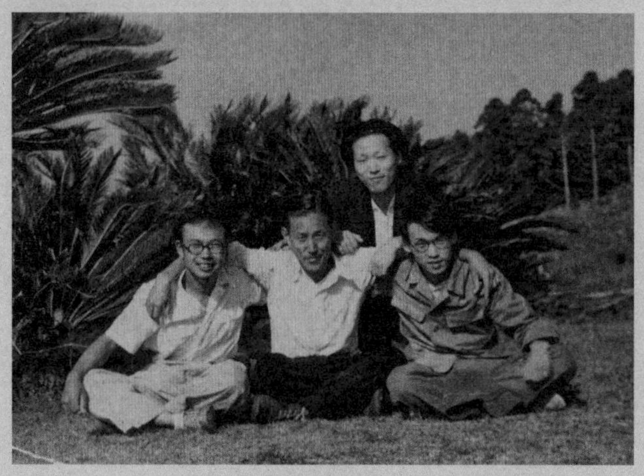

A)

Japanese primatology was founded by Kinji Imanishi (1902–1992), who rejected reductionism and advocated synergy in nature over competition. Imanishi and his colleagues sought to understand the origins of human society by studying animal sociality. "In all of this, Imanishi was well ahead of the celebrated Western paleontologist, Louis Leakey, who developed a similar agenda." *

* Frans de Waal, "Without Walls,"
New Scientist, vol. 172, no. 2321, 2001, p. 46

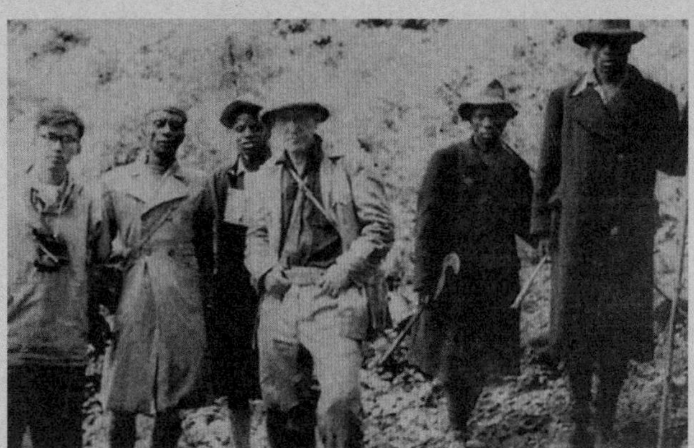

B)

–

In 1941 Kinji Imanishi wrote *Seibutsu no Sekai* (The World of Living Things). Introducing an anthropomorphic approach instead of the Western animal–human dualism, this book would become a seminal reference work for Japanese primatology.

A)

Kinji Imanishi, Junichiro Itani, Shunzo Kawamura, Kisaburo Tokuda, 1950

–

Imanishi traveled to Central Africa in 1958 with a team of researchers to study the behavior of gorillas and chimpanzees and test whether the methods developed for studying the Japanese macaques could be applied to other primate species.

B)

Kinji Imanishi and Junichiro Itani with helpers, 1958

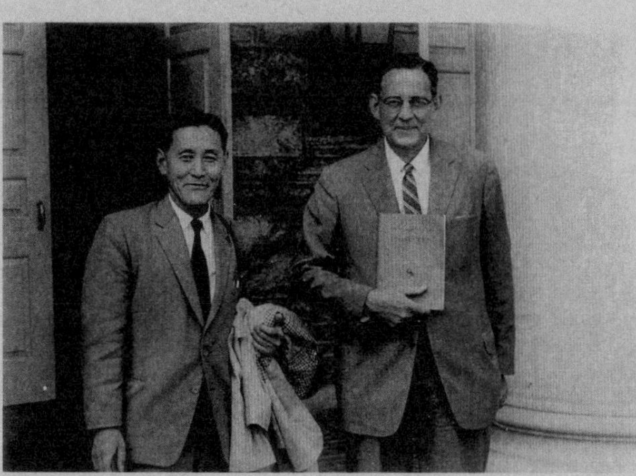

C)

C)

Clarence Ray Carpenter and Kinji Imanishi with the first issue of *Primates*, 1958

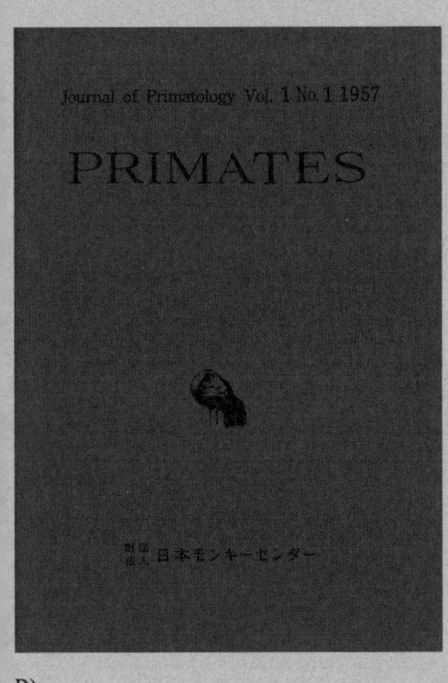

D)

In 1957 Imanishi initiated the publication of the magazine *Primates* at the Japan Monkey Center. This first ever English-language journal on primatology is still published today by the Japan Monkey Center in cooperation with the Primate Society of Japan. Its editor-in-chief is the renowned primatologist Tetsuro Matsuzawa.

Koji Ando, Denzaburo Miyadi, Yoshio Tajima, Kinji Imanishi (eds.), *Primates*, vol. 1, no. 1, 1957

E)

Kinji Imanishi's Field Notebook, vol. 1, 1958, p. 6

D)

E)

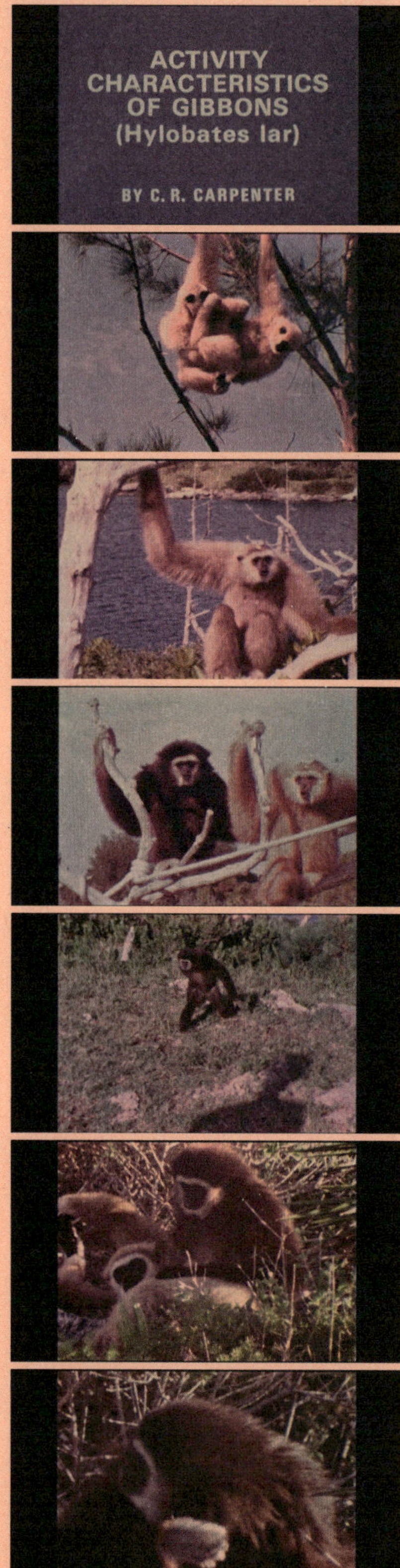

F)

F)

From 1931 to 1934, Carpenter conducted research on rhesus macaques that had been released on the Caribbean island of Cayo Santiago; he also studied wild howler monkeys and gibbons. For Western scientists, gibbons acted as welcome models for the social structure of human society, for they have an upright posture, live in monogamous relationships, and defend territories.

Clarence Ray Carpenter, *Activity Characteristics of Gibbons (Hylobates Lar), Part III Social Behavior*, 1974, 16 min.

G)

In the 1950s a group of researchers studying a tribe of macaque monkeys on the Japanese island of Kōjima were feeding the animals sweet potatoes. One day in 1953 a female called Imo started washing the sweet potatoes in water to remove the sand. Curiously, after her family members started imitating her behavior, the behavior was passed down to all the following generations and became engrained in the macaque tribe as a species-specific behavior. This led scientists to recognize cultural transmission in monkey societies, an observation that became key in proving the existence of a phenomenon called adaptive modification, which is when the adaptive strategy of a group becomes a distinct characteristic of the species.

Clarence Ray Carpenter, *Behavior of the Macaques of Japan*, 1969, 24 min.

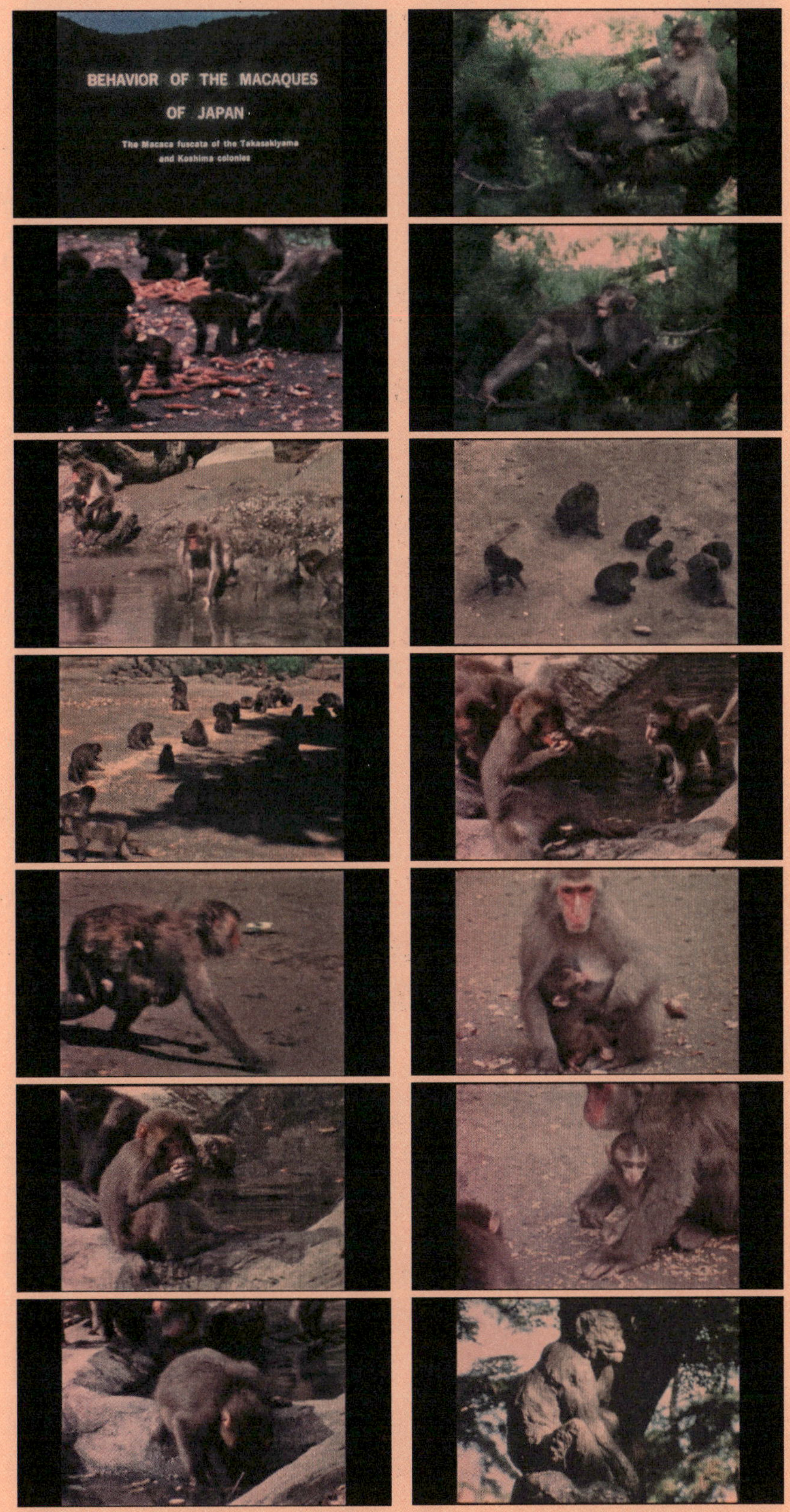
BEHAVIOR OF THE MACAQUES
OF JAPAN
The Macaca fuscata of the Takasakiyama
and Koshima colonies

G)

H)

Ai and her son Ayumu are the principal subjects of the Ai Project at the Primate Research Center at Kyoto University. This project tests numerical competency and working memory in Ai and other chimpanzees.

Video stills: Symbolic representation and working memory in chimpanzees, Tetsuro Matsuzawa, Primate Research Institute, Kyoto University, 4:50 min.

[Quote]

"Seeking the truth of nature underneath the thin, often obscuring layer of culture, the westerner tends to see in our primate kin a deeper shared animal nature. In contrast, perhaps, Japanese primate observers have seen simian masks expressing the essential double-sidedness of the relations of individual and society and of knower and known. It is not a 'truer' nature behind the mask that is sought within the Japanese cultural frame; nature is not the bare face behind the mask of culture. [...] Masks cannot be stripped away to reveal the truth; rather the mask is a figure of the two-sidedness of the structure of life, person, and society. [...] 'Nature' was made into an object of study in Japanese primatology, but it was nature as a social object, as itself composed of conventional social processes and specifically positioned actors, that intrigued early Japanese monkey watchers."

Donna Haraway, *Primate Visions: Gender, Race, and Nature in the World of Modern Science*, New York 1989, pp. 245–246

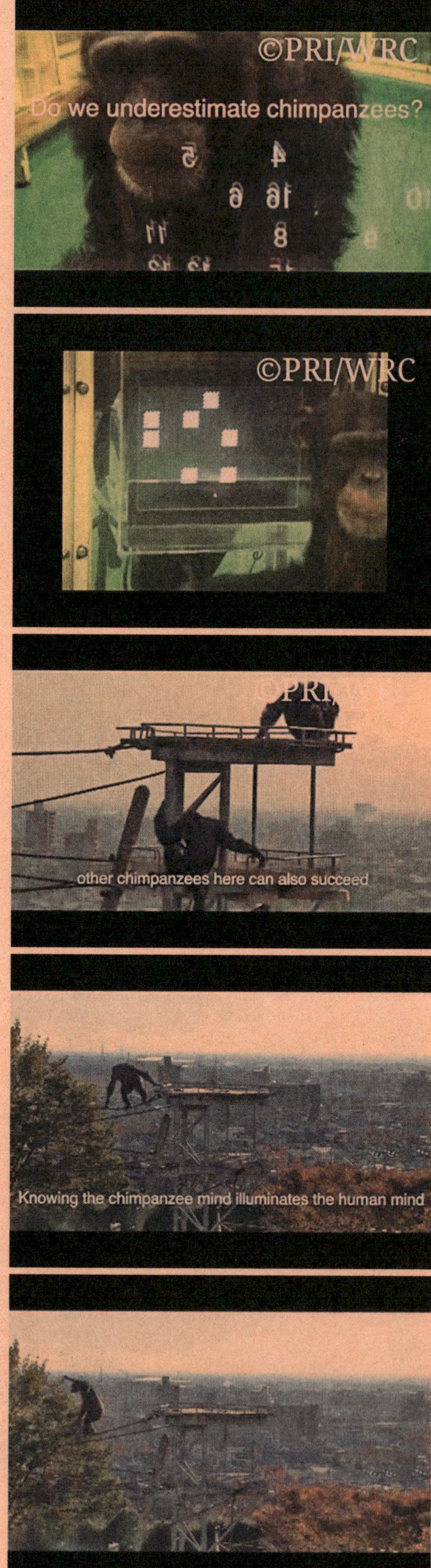

H)

Through his excavations in East Africa, paleontologist
Louis Leakey contributed pioneering scientific work
on human ancestry in Africa. A son of British missionaries in Kenya, where he grew up among the Kikuyu
and worked most of his life until the independence of
Kenya in 1963, Leakey himself was a figure at the
crossroads of science and colonialism in the twentieth
century. In the late 1950s he began to look for female
researchers to engage in primate ethology. The three
white women he chose would eventually become known
as the "Trimates." In 1960, the year when fifteen African primate-habitat nations became independent, Jane
Goodall began her work with chimpanzees in Gombe
Stream National Park in Tanzania. In 1967 Dian Fossey
started her fieldwork with mountain gorillas in the
Virunga Mountains of Rwanda, and then Birutė Galdikas
began her field studies of orangutans in the jungles
of Borneo in 1971. The work of the Trimates initiated a
paradigm shift in primatology, away from a male-
dominated objectifying science towards a science of in-
terpersonal affective engagement that recognized
the unique and individual personalities of their research
subjects. Following the model of Japanese researchers,
Jane Goodall was the first Western scientist to name the
chimpanzees she observed (calling them Fifi and
David Greybeard, for example) instead of numbering
them to prevent emotional attachment and subjective
bias. Goodall and her colleagues embodied the late
twentieth-century dream of a reconciliation with a nature no longer conceived in Cartesian terms as indif-
ferent and mechanistic: "Apes modeled a solution to
a deep cultural anxiety sharpened by the real possibility
in the late twentieth century of western people's destruction of the earth." *

* Donna Haraway, *Primate Visions: Gender,
Race, and Nature in the World of Modern
Science*, New York 1989, p. 132

[Quote]

"In July 1960, Jane Goodall, a twenty-six-year-
old English girl, embarked on a remarkable
adventure at the request of the British anthropologist, Dr. L. S. B. Leakey. She went to
observe the daily lives of chimpanzees in
East Africa. Goodall ventured into the rug-
ged beauty of Tanzania's Gombe Stream
Game Reserve to begin her study. The chimp
reserve stretches twelve miles along the east
shore of Lake Tanganyika. Goodall's camp
was set up a hundred yards from the lake.
Her permanent party included only one African aide. Otherwise she was on her own, a
girl with no special training but with natural
aptitude, and in the words of Dr. Leakey,
'no preconceived ideas.' For a long period of
time, the chimpanzees allowed Jane Goodall
to observe them only at great distance.
After the first six months of observation, she
began to recognize individual chimpanzees.
Sponsored and filmed by the National
Geographic Society, the expedition yielded
what Dr. Leakey called 'the most remarkable
study of any primate ever made.' It may
stand for all time as a unique record of
chimp behavior in the wild." *

* National Geographic Video Library,
Miss Goodall and the Wild Chimpanzees, 1986

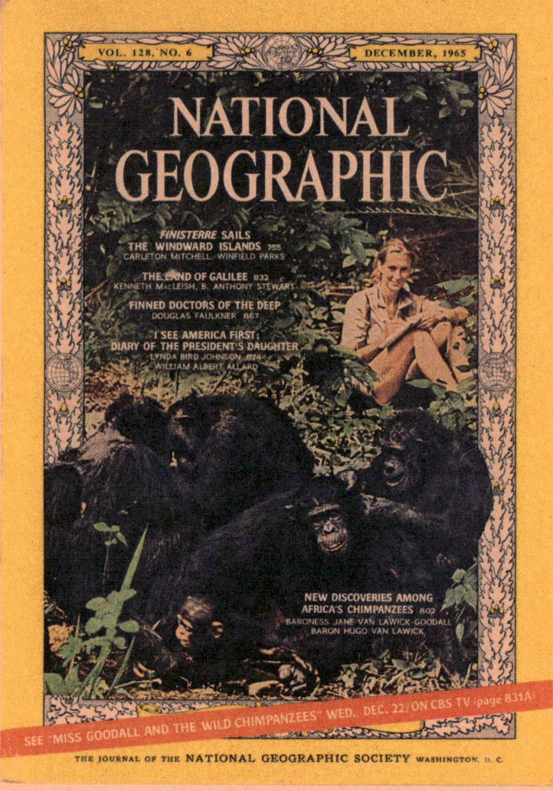

A)

A)

Jane Goodall on the front cover of
National Geographic, vol. 128, no. 6,
December 1965

–

Birutė Galdikas was sent out to Borneo
in 1971 to study orangutans, the only great
apes in Asia. She carried out the longest
semicontinuous study on these animals and
is considered the foremost expert on them.
Unlike the gorillas or chimpanzees studied
by her colleagues, orangutans are notorious
for their antisocial behavior and are usually found alone in the forest, where they
might be avoiding detection. *Search for the
Great Apes* portrays Galdikas' painstaking
efforts to find and study wild orangutans
in the Borneo rainforest and also offers an
insight into how her passion for the apes
affected her personal life, as she finds herself mothering orangutans that have been
abandoned by their own mothers.

B)

After an initial meeting in Kenya in 1963,
Louis Leakey and Dian Fossey met again
in 1966 and Leakey invited Fossey to take
on a long-term study of gorillas. Fossey
accepted the assignment and lived among
the mountain gorillas in the Democratic
Republic of Congo until civil war forced her
to escape to Rwanda. *Gorillas In The Mist*
portrays the work and life of Fossey, high-
lighting how she developed a close relationship to the gorillas by finding a way of
communicating with them. She consequently
went to great lengths in her attempts to stop
poachers from catching them. Particularly
after Fossey's favourite gorilla Digit was
killed, her actions intensified against the
local poachers, who in turn saw their liveli-
hood threatened by her actions. Fossey
was found dead in her cabin in 1985, mur-
dered under mysterious circumstances.

Dian Fossey on the front cover of *National
Geographic,* vol. 137, no. 1, January 1970

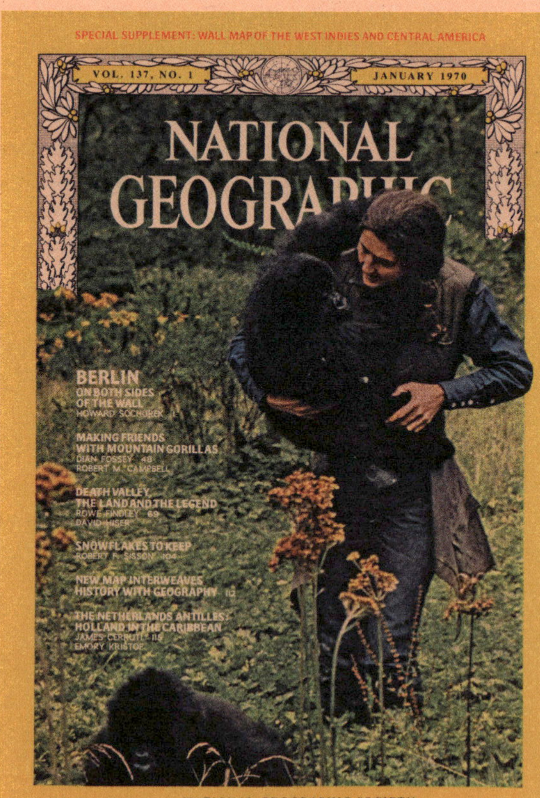

B)

by Christophe Boesch and Team

Culture

Since the inception of their discipline, anthropologists have been debating the concept of culture, albeit with no clear consensus on the topic. Many definitions include the word "man," and thereby *a priori* exclude any other species. Culture, however, is not the exclusive property of anthropologists and in the meantime other fields of science have begun to examine various aspects of culture. For example, psychologists have concentrated on understanding the different learning processes involved in the cultural transmission of information. At the same time, biologists have recently shown a great interest in the evolution of culture as a much more rapid alternative to genetic evolution due to its independence from reproductive events.

Despite the different approaches of the three disciplines, a strong consensus has been found regarding some basic concepts. Firstly, culture is learned from group members; it is neither transmitted genetically nor does it simply represent an adaptation to particular ecological conditions. Secondly, culture is a distinctive collective practice. This rather vague statement indicates that a culture observed in one group or society is distinct, so that we can actually know the origin of individuals by their socially learned practices. Thirdly, anthropologists refer to culture as a symbolic system, meaning that it is based on shared meanings between members of the same group or society.

Because only a few chimpanzees groups across Africa have ever been directly observed by humans, our knowledge of chimpanzee behavioral variation across all populations is still quite limited.

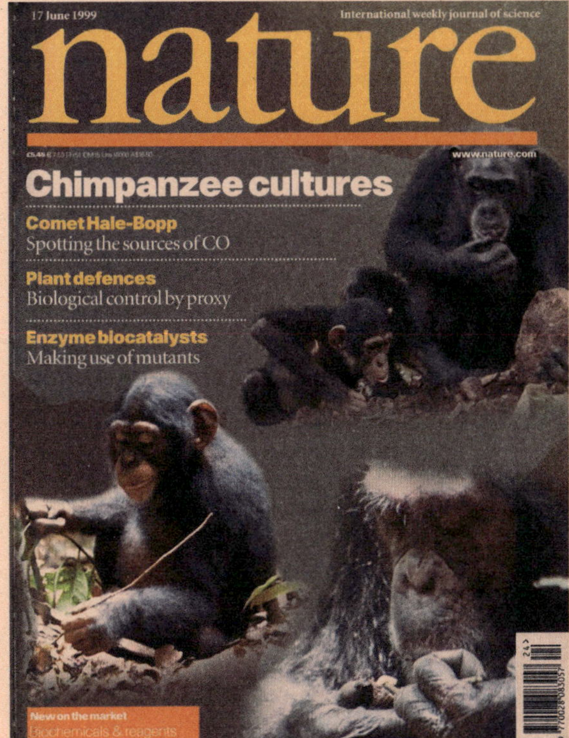

A)

A)

This scientific publication by nine chimpanzee experts presented evidence for the existence of culture in wild chimpanzees to a wide audience for the first time. Based on a graphic comparison of six different wild chimpanzee populations, it has since become the standard for evaluating the presence of culture in animals. The following diagram indicates the presence or absence of thirty-six behavioral traits for each population, illustrating how diversely those cultural traits can be distributed.

A. Whiten et al., "Cultures in chimpanzees," *Nature*, vol. 399, no. 6737, 1999, cover and p. 684

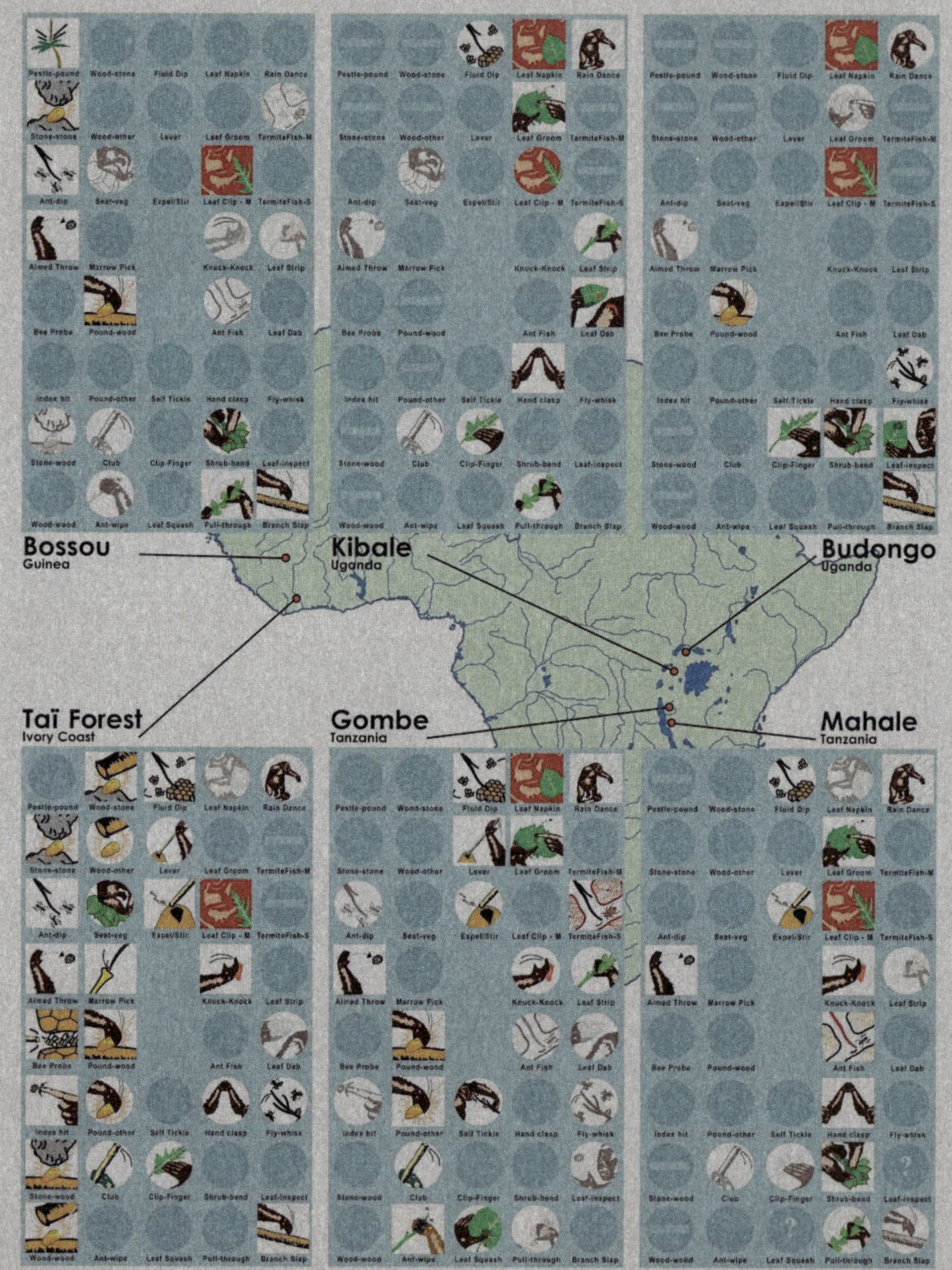

Figure 1 Distribution of behaviour patterns from band D in Table 1 across six African study sites. Behaviours are arranged in the 5 × 8 arrays to cluster those behaviours customary or habitual at each site, with clusters for westerly sites on the left of the array and clusters for easterly sites on the right. The secondary Mahale site (K) is omitted. Colour icons, customary; circular icons, habitual; monochrome icons, present; clear, absent; horizontal bar, absent with ecological explanation; question mark, answer uncertain.

A)

130

Ever since Carl Linnaeus first classified humans with monkeys and apes in 1758, we have known that we are not alone. Indeed, biologically speaking, we never were, but in *The Ape and The Sushi Master*, de Waal makes the equally startling claim that the same is true when it comes to culture.

Frans de Waal, *The Ape and the Sushi Master: Cultural Reflections of a Primatologist*, New York 2001

This book treats traditions in nonhuman species as biological phenomena that are amenable to the comparative methods of inquiry used in contemporary biology.

Dorothy M. Fragaszy and Susan Perry (eds.), *The Biology of Traditions: Models and Evidence*, Cambridge 2003

How do chimpanzees say, "I want to have sex with you?" How do they eat live and aggressive ants? Ivorian and Tanzanian chimpanzees answer these questions differently, as would humans from France and China if asked how they eat rice. Christophe Boesch highlights the debate about culture by introducing readers to the lives of chimpanzees from various African regions.

Christophe Boesch, *Wild Cultures: A Comparison between Chimpanzee and Human Cultures*, Cambridge 2012

Cultural Beings: Chimpanzees' Cultural Breadth and Diversity

Key moments in the evolution of our understanding of chimpanzee culture:

1) A large cultural repertoire: In an attempt to understand the variability in the cultural repertoire of different chimpanzee populations, scientists from eight different research sites across Africa met to compare their knowledge about chimpanzees. This resulted in a preliminary list of thirty-eight varying behavioral traits.

2) Cultural fidelity: In some limited instances, researchers have followed and made detailed observations about three neighboring chimpanzee groups living in the same forest block. As such groups are neighbors, we can be certain that genetic differences do not account for any of the observed behavioral differences.

Adapted from: "Cultural differences between three neighboring communities in the Taï forest," in: Christophe Boesch, *Wild Cultures*, Cambridge 2012, p. 121

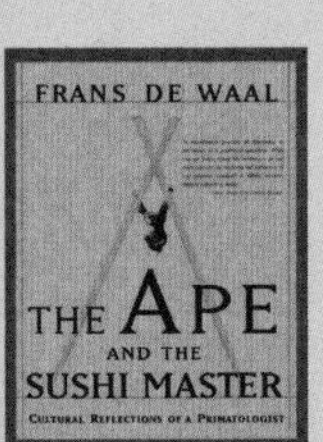

B)

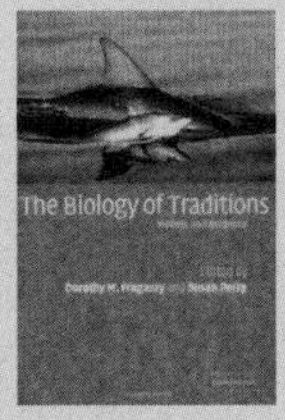

C)

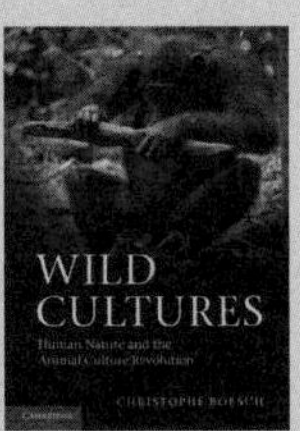

D)

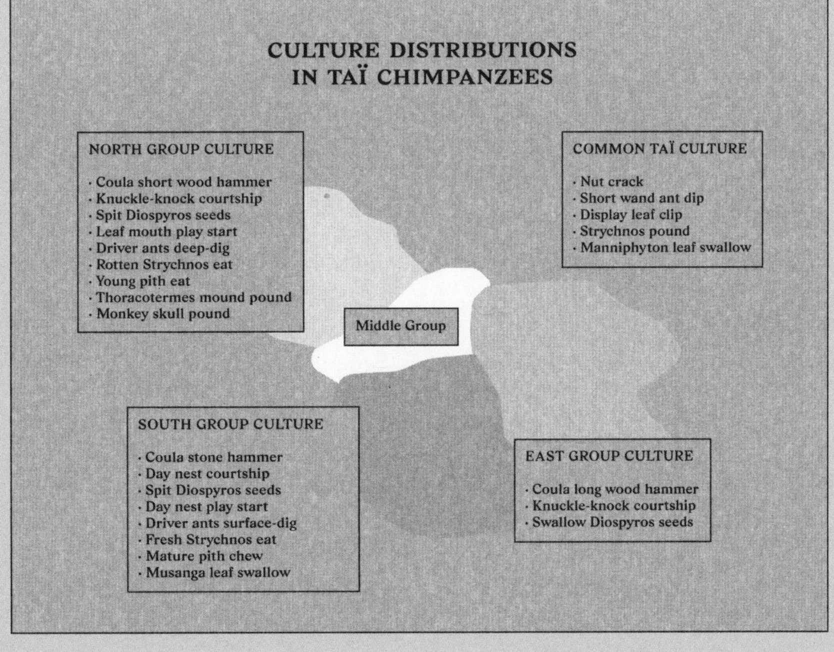

E)

3) Cultural history: By applying traditional archeological methods, researchers were able to excavate soil layers as old as 6,000 years; in layers that were between 2,200 and 4,300 years old they found stone artifacts that had been produced by chimpanzees cracking nuts.

F)

Adapted from: "Remains of chimpanzee nut-cracking activities over the past 6,000 years," in: Christophe Boesch, *Wild Cultures*, Cambridge 2012, p. 77

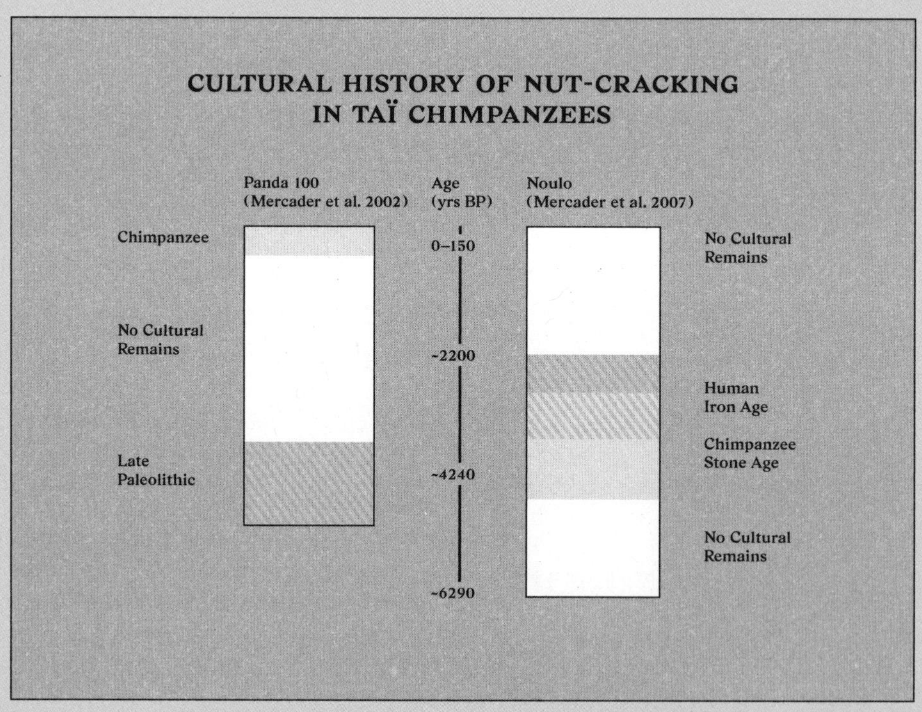

F)

4) Symbolic culture: In chimpanzees, some communicative traits follow some group-specific norms, by which
it is the meaning of the trait that differs and not the
form. The most complex example of this is the leaf-clip-
ping behavior that is present in three of the six well-
studied populations.

G)

Adapted from: "A preliminary glossary of the
sign-code used by wild chimpanzees," in:
Christophe Boesch, *Wild Cultures,* Cambridge
2012, p. 111

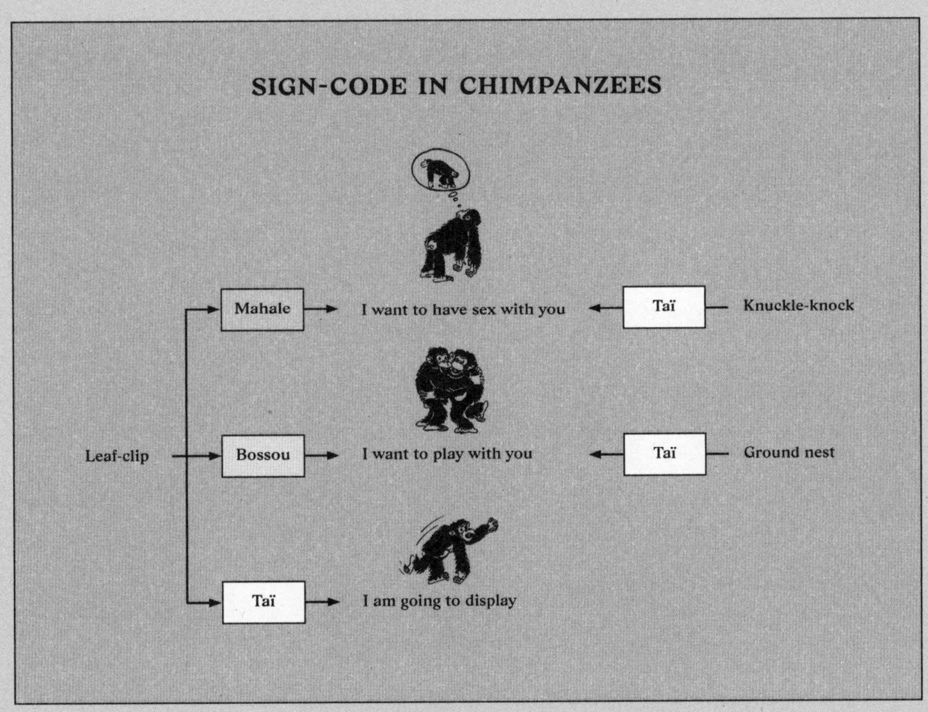

G)

5) Cumulative cultural evolution: Some of the cultural elements proposed for chimpanzees are characterized by relatively high levels of technological complexity. That is, in some cases, and in only some populations, complex behaviors are made up of simpler behavioral elements that each serve a standalone function, too.

H)

Adapted from: "Cumulative cultural evolution leading to nut-cracking techniques," in: Christophe Boesch, *Wild Cultures*, Cambridge 2012, p. 70

References for "Cultural Beings"

Christophe Boesch, "Innovation in wild chimpanzees," *International Journal of Primatology*, vol. 16, no. 1, 1995, pp. 1–16

Christophe Boesch, "Three approaches for assessing chimpanzee culture," in: A. Russon, K. Bard, S. Parker (eds.), *Reaching into thought*, Cambridge 1996, pp. 404–429

Christophe Boesch, "Is culture a golden barrier between human and chimpanzee?" *Evolutionary Anthropology*, vol. 12, no. 2, 2003, pp. 26–32

Nathan J. Emery and Nicola J. Clayton, "Imaginative scrub-jays, causal rooks, and a liberal application of Occam's aftershave," *Behavioural and Brain Sciences*, vol. 31, no. 2, 2008, pp. 134–135

Julio Mercader et al., "4,300-year-old-chimpanzee sites and the origins of percussive stone technology," *Proceedings of the National Academy of Sciences*, vol. 104, no. 9, 2007, pp. 3043–3048

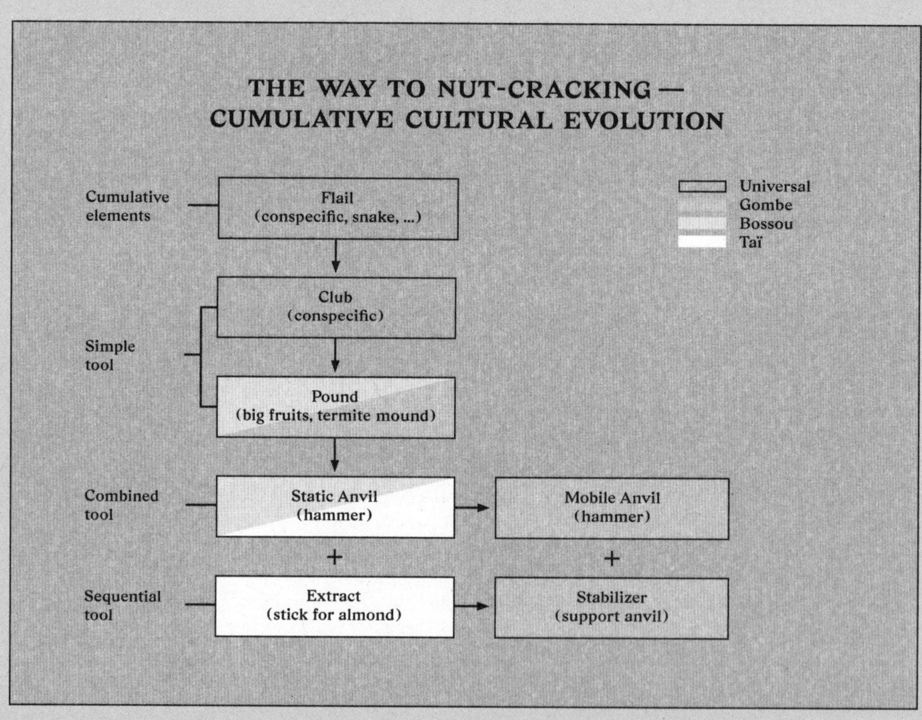

H)

APE CULTURE II

Documenting
behavioral traits

Chimpanzees are severely threatened across Africa and
may disappear entirely before we are able to fully
understand them. To understand as much as possible
before it is too late, the Pan African Programme:
The Cultured Chimpanzee (under the direction of Professor Christophe Boesch and Dr. Hjalmar Kühl at
the Max Planck Institute for Evolutionary Anthropology) is documenting the behavior and ecology of forty
different chimpanzee populations in over twelve African
countries. Through the use of video camera traps,
new behavioral patterns have been discovered, such as
algae fishing in Guinea and stone-throwing against
tree trunks in Côte d'Ivoire, Liberia, Guinea, and Guinea-Bissau. In addition to documenting new behavioral
traits, the known distribution of chimpanzee cultural
traits is being substantially refined, and for the first
time it will be possible to undertake new detailed analyses on how ecology and evolutionary forces affect
different aspects of chimpanzee life.

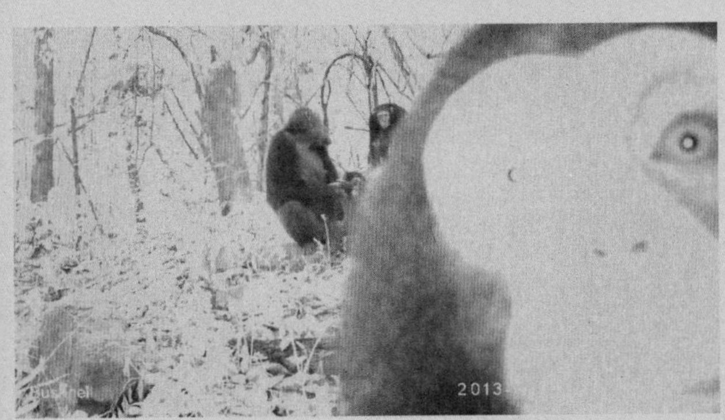

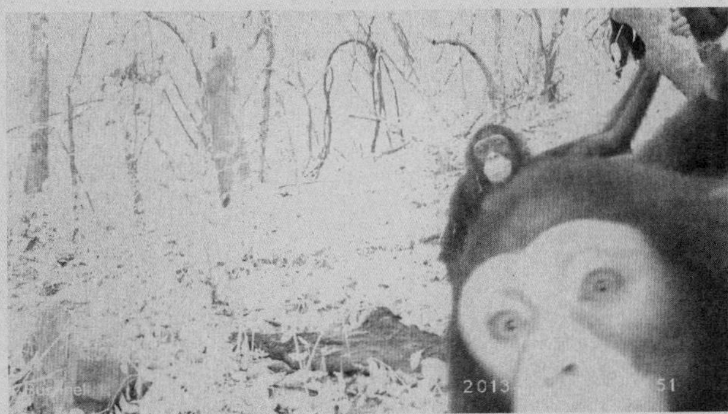

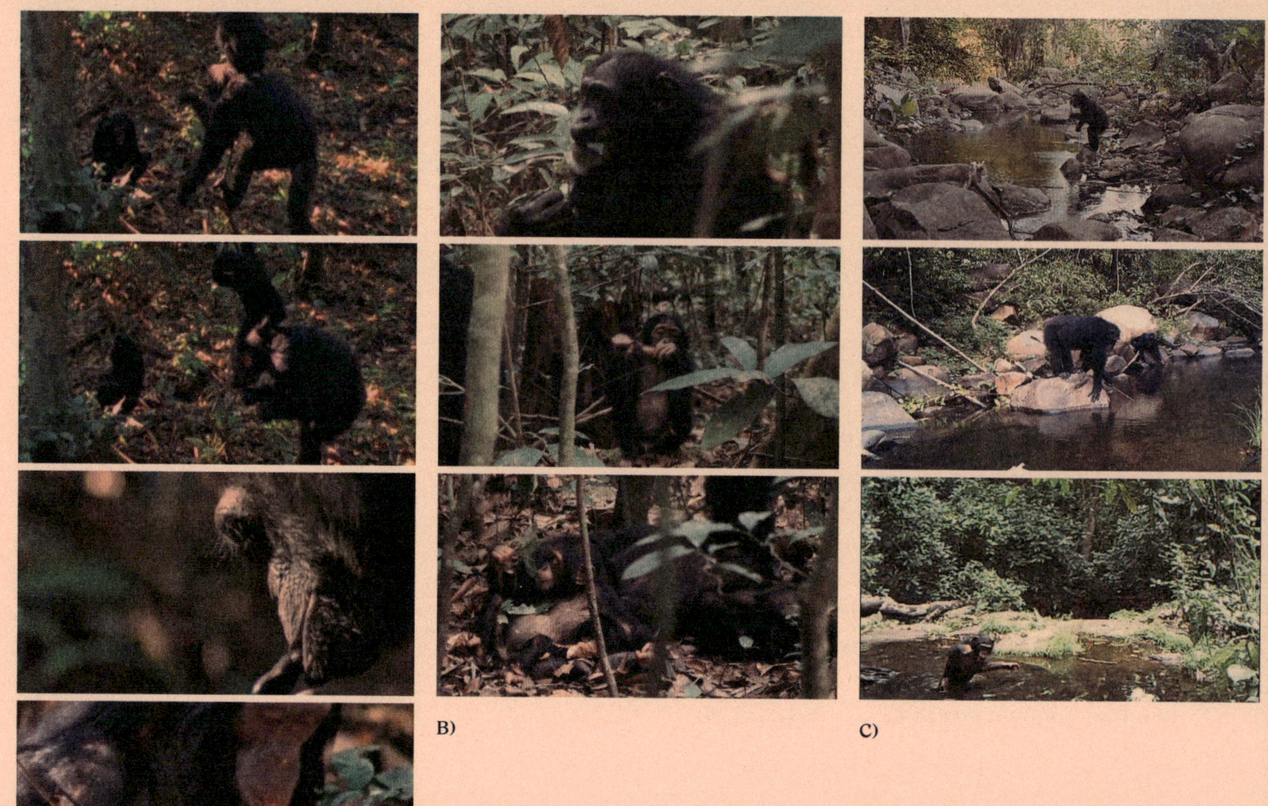

A)

B)

C)

A)

Chimpanzees dipping ants, from:
Cynthia Moses, *The New Chimpanzees,*
National Geographic, 1995, 57 min.

B)

Fig. 1: Adult male leaf clips, pant hoots
then drums, infant watches him
Fig. 2 & 3: Infant leaf clips shortly after
having seen adult male leaf clipping

Video stills: Tobias Deschner, Videos
on "leaf clipping", 2009, 4:40 min.

C)

In the area around the Bafing River in Guinea,
chimpanzees eat large amounts of algae by
fishing it out of the water with long sticks
made from saplings growing along the river.
They then skillfully spin the spaghetti-
shaped algae around the stick before slurping
it with their mouth.

Video stills from video traps of the Pan
African Programme: Algae fishing and
miscellaneous excerpts

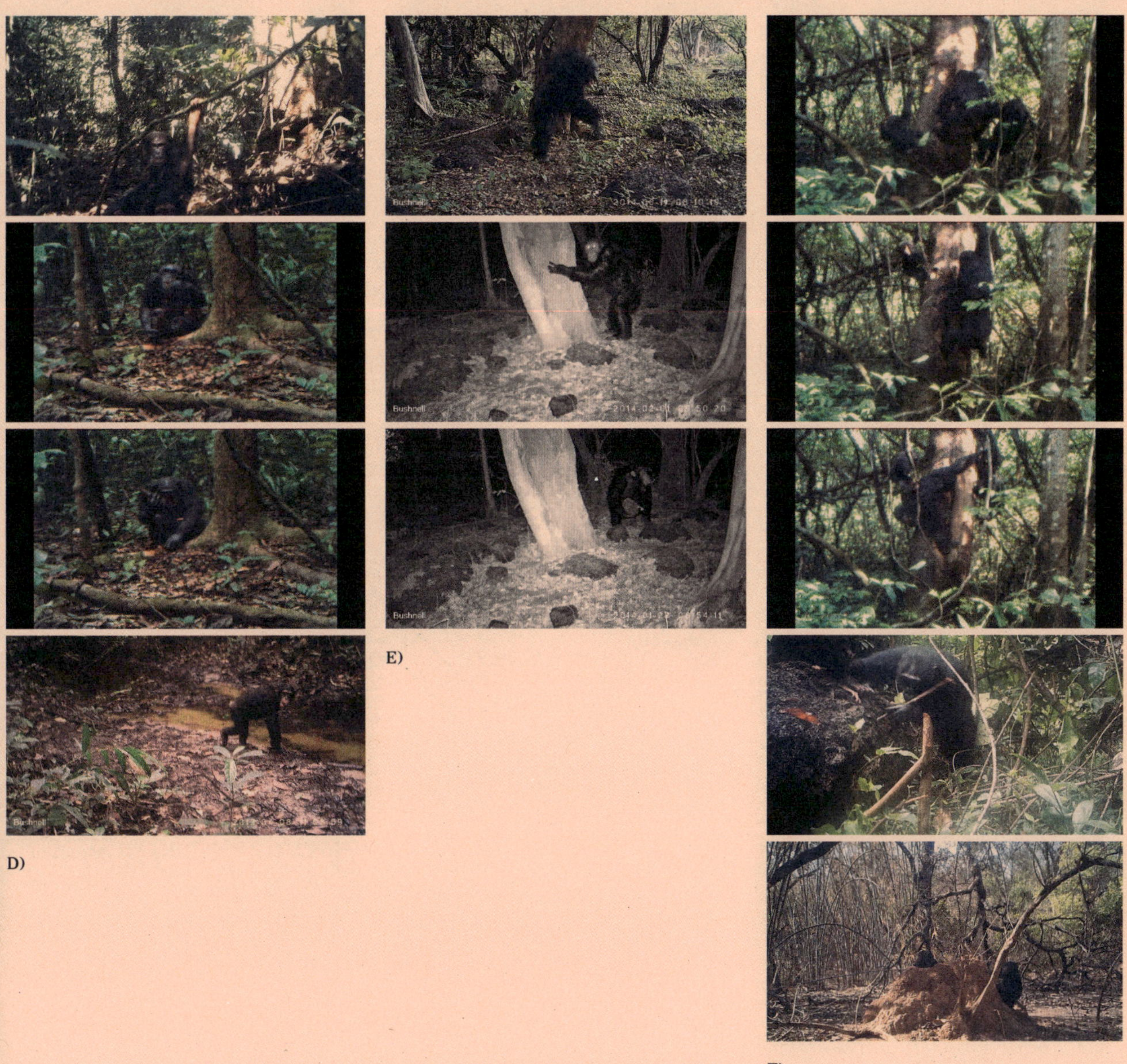

D)

E)

F)

D)

Forest chimpanzees in western Côte d'Ivoire and eastern Liberia are unique for having invented nut-cracking behavior to extract the very rich kernels from nuts that are found all over tropical Africa from Liberia to Congo. Infant chimpanzees observe their mothers as they nut crack and successfully beg for pieces from the open nuts. This innovation represents one of the most famous examples of cultural behavior in chimpanzees.

Video stills from video traps of the Pan African Programme: Nut cracking and miscellaneous excerpts

E)

In dry regions of West Africa, various chimpanzee populations have been shown to sometimes incorporate stone throwing against tree trunks into their displays. Stone throwing as a display trait was previously unknown and may represent a level of progression from the ubiquitous chimpanzee display of drumming hands and feet against trees.

Video stills from video traps of the Pan African Programme: Stone throwing

F)

Across Africa, tools are usually used by chimpanzees to get to otherwise inaccessible rich food resources. This is illustrated by the use of thin twigs to extract termites from mounds, and to reach honey in underground bee nests.

Video stills from video traps of the Pan African Programme: Honey harvest, termite fishing, and miscellaneous excerpts

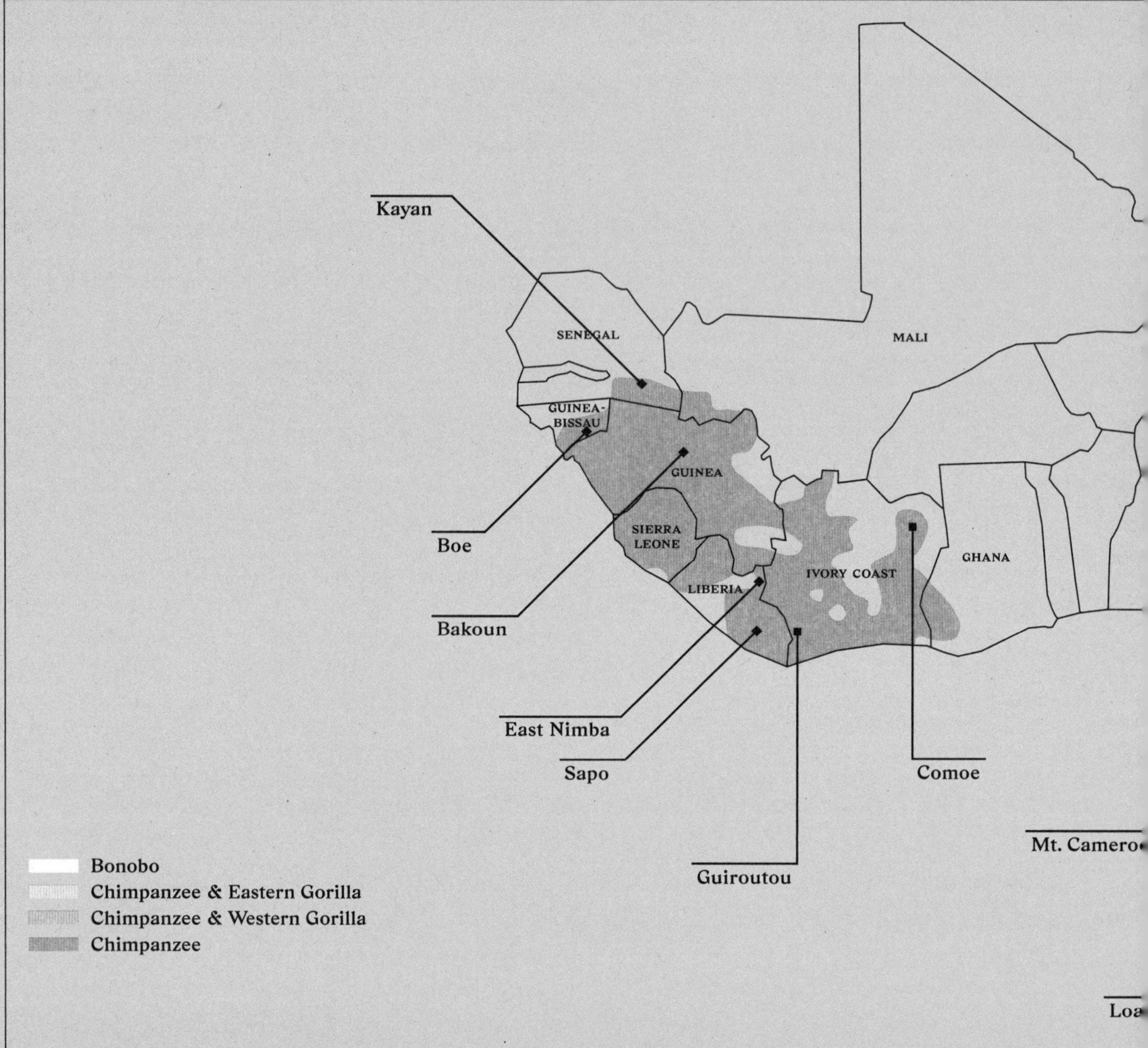

G)

G)

A map with locations of video traps from which footage was presented in the exhibition, adapted from: "Locations of temporary research sites across the chimpanzee range" (fig.), in: *Pan African Programme: The cultured chimpanzee; Guidelines for research and data collection*, 2014, p. 6, http://panafrican.eva.mpg.de/

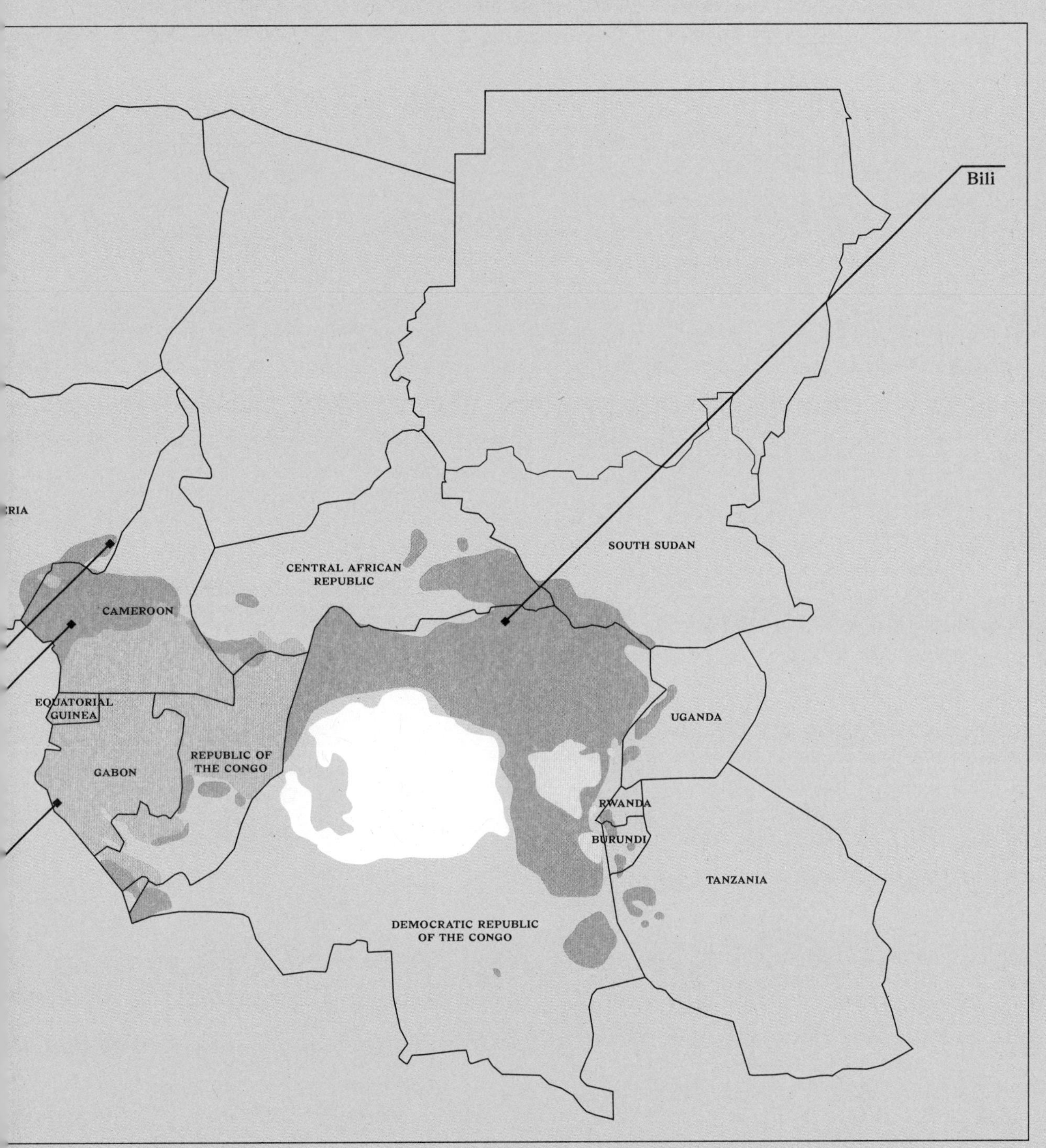

Bili
NIGERIA
CAMEROON
CENTRAL AFRICAN
REPUBLIC
SOUTH SUDAN
EQUATORIAL
GUINEA
UGANDA
GABON
REPUBLIC OF
THE CONGO
RWANDA
BURUNDI
TANZANIA
DEMOCRATIC REPUBLIC
OF THE CONGO

The often heated debate on the language ability of the great apes not only raises the thorny issue of the continuity and discontinuity between humans and nature, it also poses boundary questions concerning scientific methodology. It is absolutely impossible to communicate with great apes without establishing some form of affective bond, or to exclude all communication channels except the one intended. Few observers of apes and great apes have ever doubted that their subjects understand the gestures and forms of expression of other members of the same species, and frequently those of humans, too. The ability to use symbols, the reference to absent objects and future actions, as well as the use of deception have all now been largely proven according to the standards of objective science.

Consequently, René Descartes' hypothesis that there is a radical discontinuity between human speech and animalistic nature, and that denotative speech is consequently the only indicator of consciousness, is being increasingly supplanted by Darwin's assumption that animals participate in "forms of thought" which are "homologous to human thought." The paradigm of the discontinuity of semiotic processes in nature and culture, which calls for proof of continuity, is being replaced by the paradigm of continuity, clearing the ground for an exploration of the differences, conditions, and background assumptions of a communicative situation. As a result, a retrospective shift in our perspective on language experiments with great apes is taking place—together with the intention of these experiments to build communicative bridges between culture and nature. Looking back, a number of these experiments appear to be symptomatic statements on the normative ideas of the researchers and the conditions of the communicative situation in the laboratory, rather than essential statements on the "language ability" of great apes.

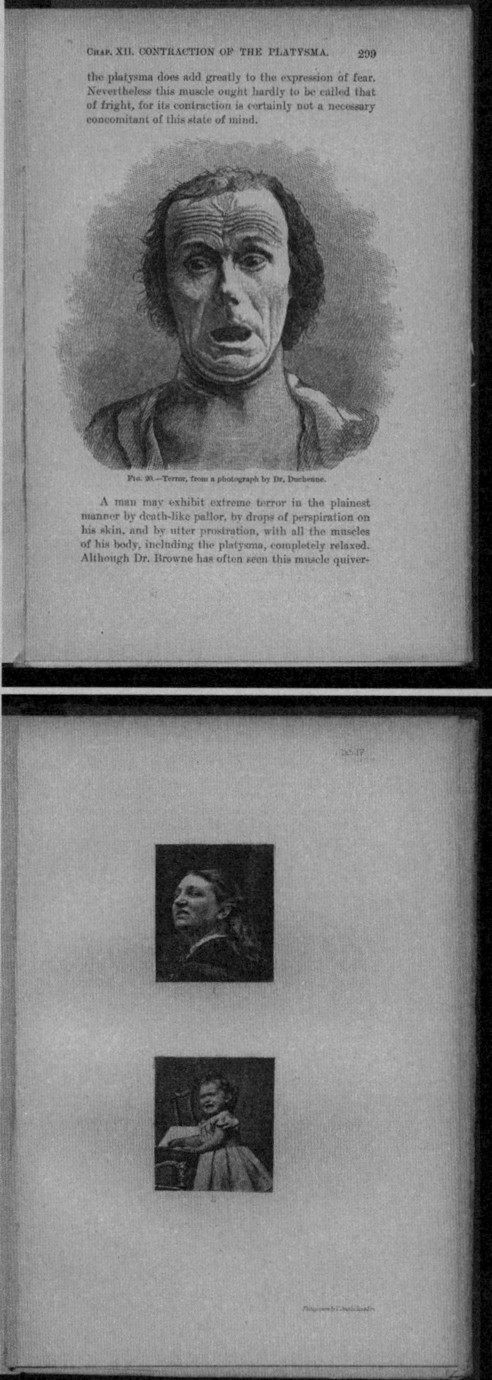

A)

A)

In his long forgotten book *The Expression of the Emotions in Man and Animals*, Darwin first applied the theory of descent to the biology of behavior, thus establishing a continuum between animal expression and human language.

Charles Darwin, *The Expression of the Emotions in Man and Animals*, New York 1898 [1872], p. 209, plate IV, no page and pp. 138–139

B)

[Quote]

"Have read Ch. Darwin on *The Expression of the Emotions*. Finally a book I find helpful!"

Aby Warburg's personal diary, November 26, 1888

[Quote]

"Unlike ethologists in the twentieth century, Darwin primarily studied domestic or captive animals, not those in the wild. This circumstance had wide-ranging consequences for the type of behavior he observed. Because of the proximity between humans and zoo animals and pets, the pictures do not show members of the same species communicating among themselves. Instead, humans are always involved: the cat rubs against its owner's leg, the dog grovels before its master, the ape giggles as a keeper scratches the soles of its feet, the chimpanzee pouts when it doesn't get its orange from its caretaker."

Julia Voss, *Darwin's Pictures: Views of Evolutionary Theory, 1837–1874*, New Haven/London 2010, p. 216

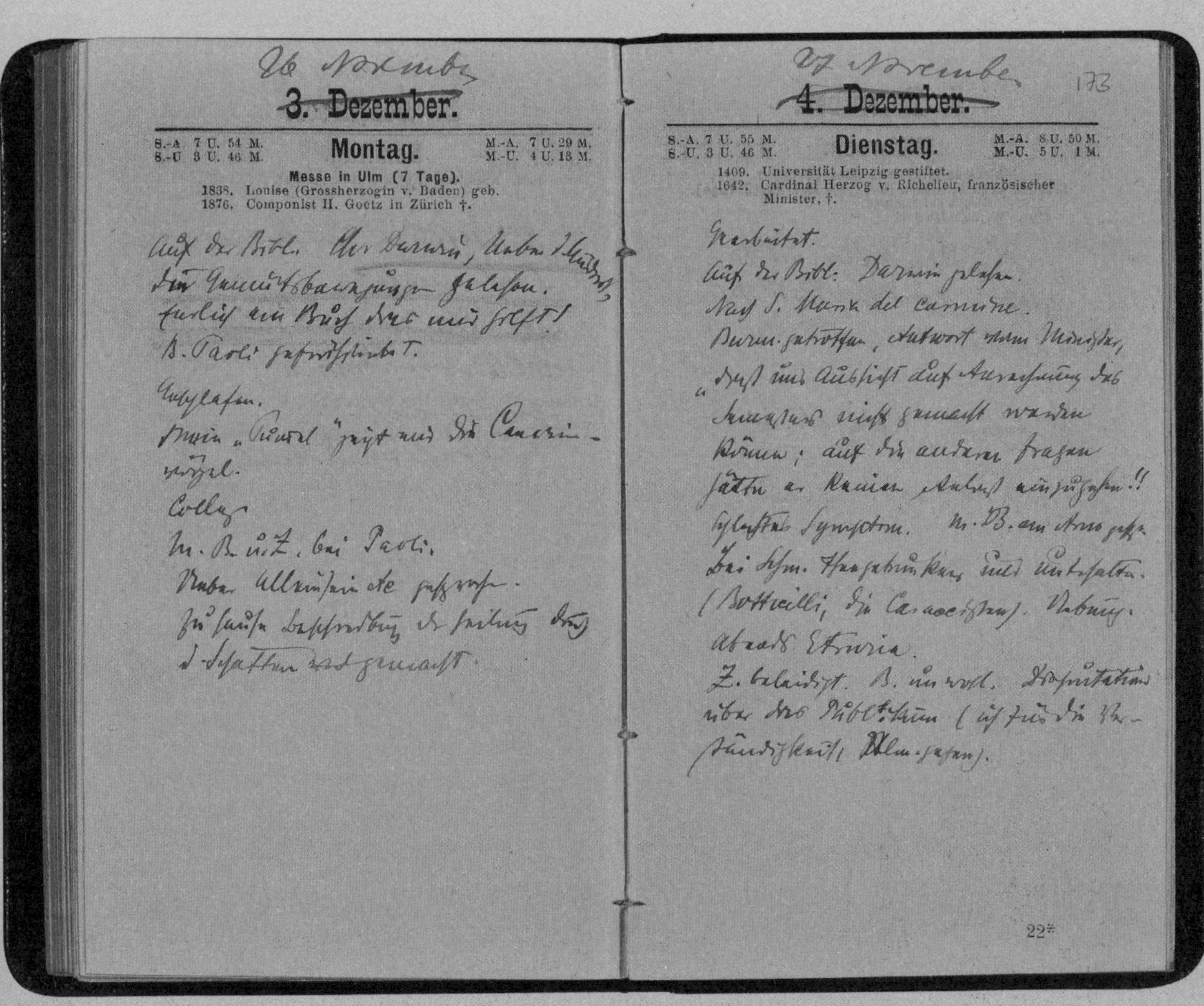

B)

or in any way excited, rapidly and incessantly move their eyebrows up and down, as well as the hairy skin of their foreheads.[15] As we associate in the case of man the raising and lowering of the eyebrows with definite states of the mind, the almost incessant movement of the eyebrows by monkeys gives them a senseless expression. I once observed a man who had a trick of continually raising his eyebrows without any corresponding emotion, and this gave to him a foolish appearance; so it is with some persons who keep the corners of their mouths a little drawn backwards and upwards, as if by an incipient smile, though at the time they are not amused or pleased.

A young orang, made jealous by her keeper attending to another monkey, slightly uncovered her teeth, and, uttering a peevish noise like *tish-shist*, turned her back on him. Both orangs and chimpanzees, when a little more angered, protrude their lips greatly, and make a harsh barking noise. A young female chimpanzee, in a violent passion, presented a curious resemblance to a child in the same state. She screamed loudly with widely open mouth, the lips being retracted so that the teeth were fully exposed. She threw her arms wildly about, sometimes clasping them over her head. She rolled on the ground, sometimes on her back, sometimes on her belly, and bit everything within reach. A young gibbon (*Hylobates syndactylus*) in a passion has been described[16] as behaving in almost exactly the same manner.

The lips of young orangs and chimpanzees are protruded, sometimes to a wonderful degree, under various circumstances. They act thus, not only when slightly angered, sulky, or disappointed, but when alarmed at

---

[15] Brehm remarks ('Thierleben,' s. 68) that the eyebrows of the *Inuus ecaudatus* are frequently moved up and down when the animal is angered.

[16] G. Bennett, 'Wanderings in New South Wales,' &c. vol. ii. 1834, p. 153.

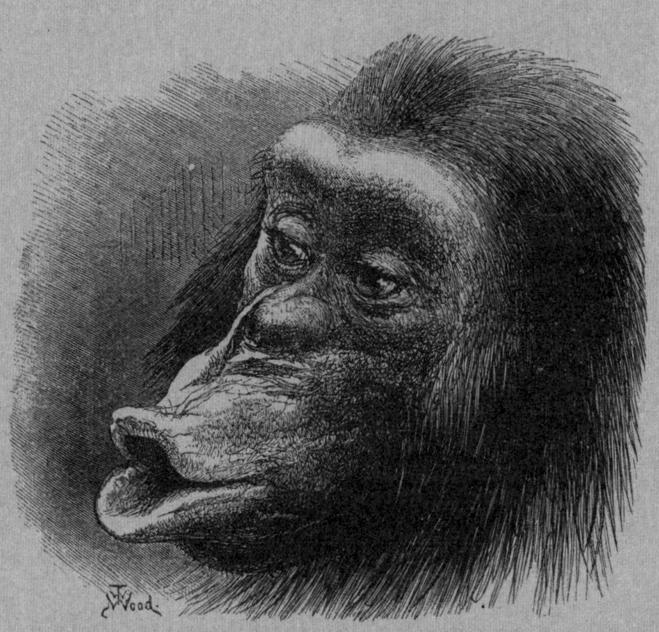

Fig. 18.—Chimpanzee disappointed and sulky. Drawn from life by Mr. Wood.

Psychologists Catherine and Keith Hayes suspected that previous speech experiments with apes failed because language acquisition had not been promoted in a focused manner. As a consequence, in 1947 they took the chimpanzee Viki from the Yerkes National Primate Research Center into their home to rear her as much like a human child as possible, while also studying her communication skills and use of tools. In order to practice correct pronunciation they employed methods from speech therapy such as manipulating the lips with their hands. After six years Catherine and Keith Hayes were able to document how Viki carried heavy boxes, attempted to pull out a loose tooth with the aid of pliers, and lit a cigarette with perfectly opposing thumbs. She also understood a number of sentences and, by employing her hands to vocalize the P sound, managed to whisper four words: "mama," "papa," "cup," and "up." Viki died from viral encephalitis in 1954.

Keith and Catherine Hayes, *Vocalization and Speech in Chimpanzees*, 1950, 12 min.

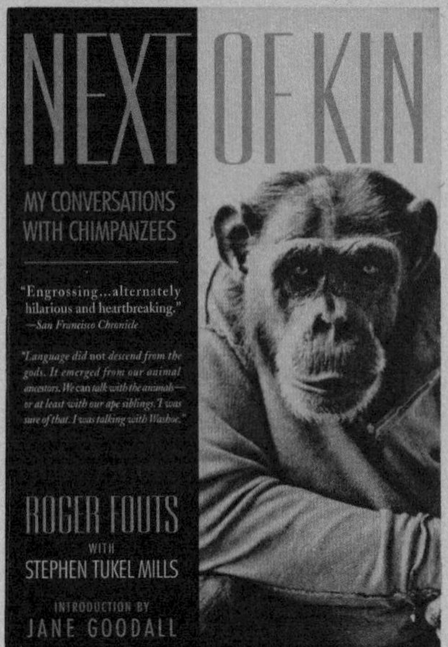

D)

D)

Allen and Beatrix Gardner were familiar with the work of Jane Goodall and Adriaan Kortlandt, who had observed the complex gestures of chimpanzees. As a consequence they decided to circumvent the great hurdle for apes of learning speech—generating articulate speech sounds—by teaching a selection of modified signs from American Sign Language to Washoe, a chimpanzee captured in 1965 in West Africa and purchased by the U.S. Air Force for biomedical tests. They quickly discovered that Washoe learned better through social interaction than behaviorist methods such as operant conditioning. After three years she was able to communicate using 160 signs and generalize, i.e. apply terms to other objects of the same category. She later taught her adoptive son Louis a number of signs, making him the first ape to learn sign language from a member of the same species. In the book *Next of Kin*, Roger Fouts reports on his interaction with the chimpanzee during his time as a scientific assistant on Project Washoe.

Roger Fouts with Stephen Tukel Mills, *Next of Kin: My Conversations with Chimpanzees*, New York 1997

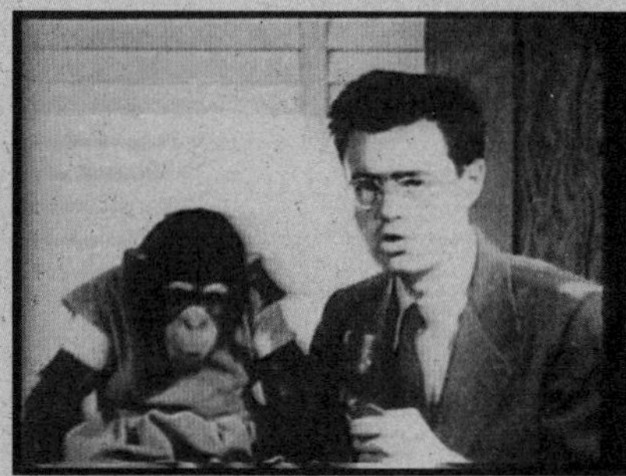

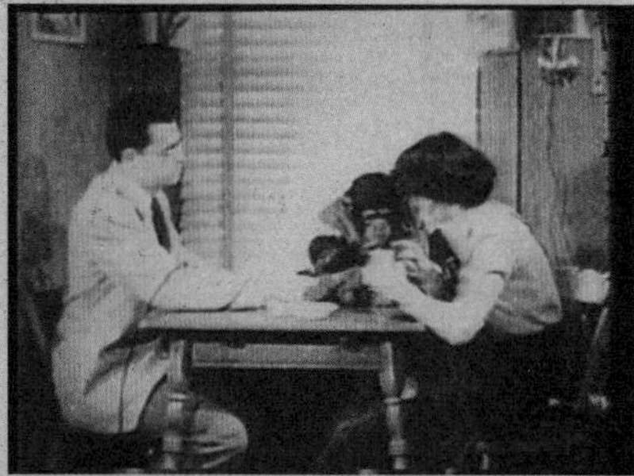

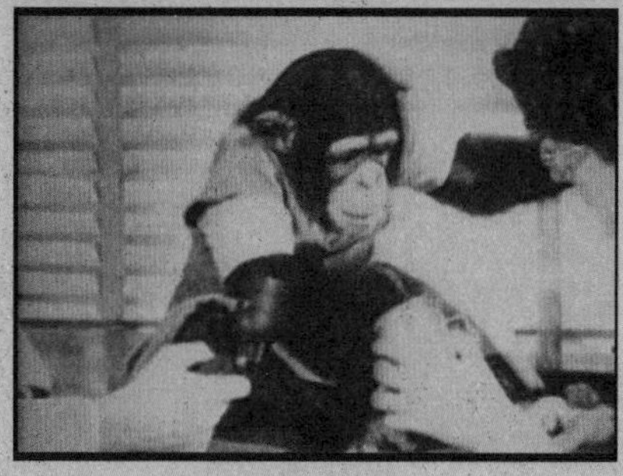

E)

Koko (born on July 4, 1971, in San Francisco) describes herself as a "fine animal gorilla." She was trained in sign language by Francine Patterson, but has also acquired a passive knowledge of English. Patrick Suppes developed an apparatus enabling her to control a speech synthesizer via buttons. Donna Haraway describes the gorilla as follows: "Koko, too, is a species of cyborg, whose communication modalities can be translated and re-synthesized to cross species and machine-organism barriers." *

Koko is the only gorilla known to recognize themself in a mirror. She is also famous for her love of cats, with *Reader's Digest* reporting a preference for the tailless Manx, as befitting a tailless primate.

* Donna Haraway, *Primate Visions: Gender, Race, and Nature in the World of Modern Science*, New York 1989, p. 141

Barbet Schroeder, *Koko Le Gorille Qui Parle* (Koko: A Talking Gorilla), 1978, 85 min.

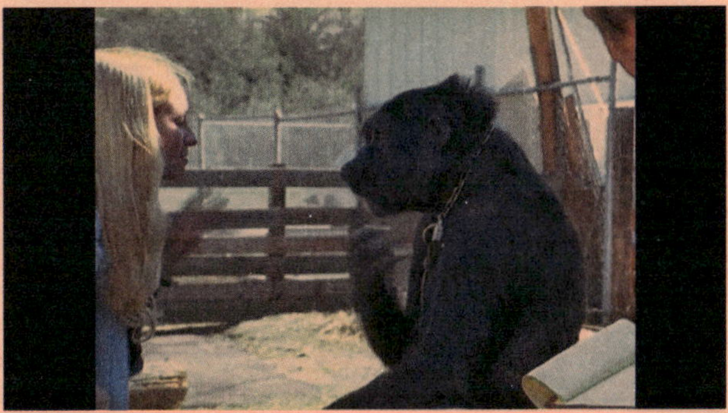

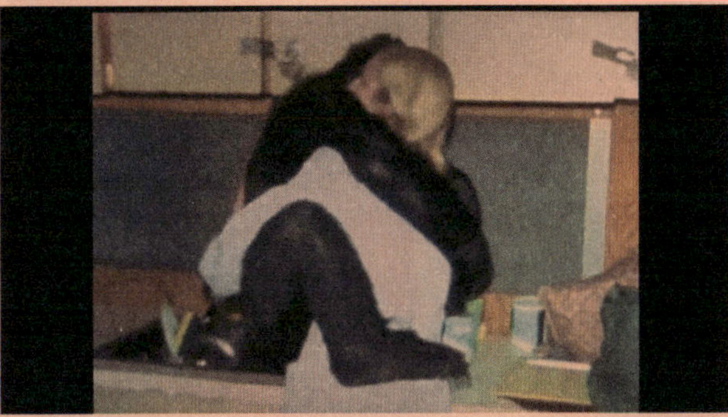

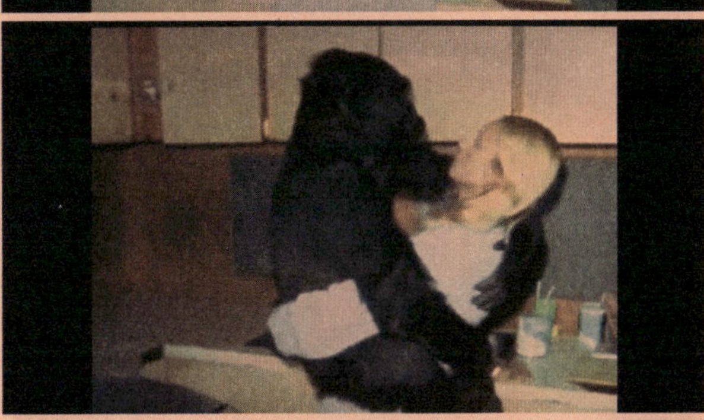

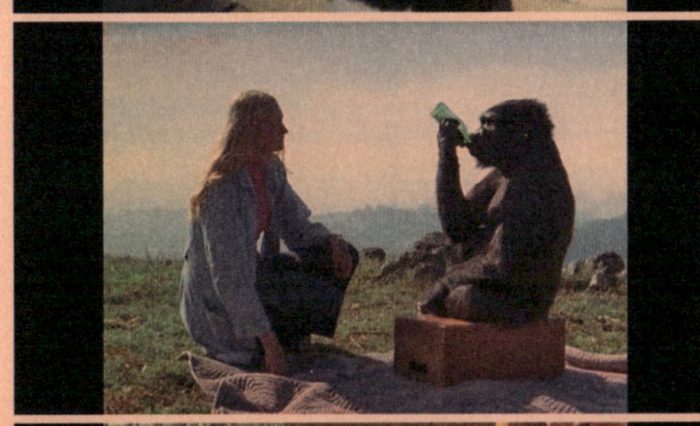

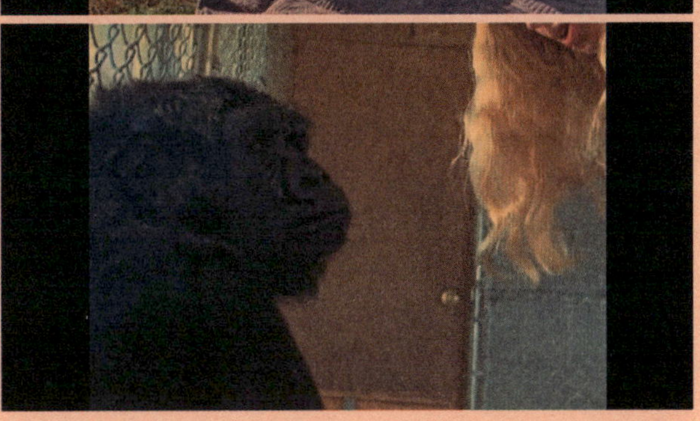

E)

F)

The bonobo Kanzi was exposed to lexigrams
and listened to English from the age of
six months onwards. Building on this, Sue
Savage-Rumbaugh and her colleagues
developed an approach in which they used
English and lexigrams to compare Kanzi's
language acquisition with that of a human
child called Alia—without giving them
special training. It became clear that the
duration and intensity of infant exposure
to language (before they begin to speak
themselves) is more important than had
hitherto been thought. The study concluded
that speech is not acquired through speaking but by understanding what others
are saying. Kanzi learned over 200 lexigrams
in this manner.

Genya Niio, *Kanzi: An Ape of Genius*, 1993,
51 min.

•

"His vocabulary runs to several hundred
words and he can follow simple conversations.

His name is Kanzi.

And Kanzi is an ape.

[...]

He may look like a chimpanzee, but Kanzi is
a bonobo ...

[...]

To answer, Kanzi presses a picture symbol
which triggers an electronic voice. These 256
symbols bear no visual resemblance to test
words, which include adjectives, verbs—even
wishes and emotions.

[...]

The board includes abstracts, like 'good' and
'bad.' Some human adults working with
Kanzi have taken a year to memorize these
symbols and master the board.

[...]

Dr. Sue Savage-Rumbaugh is one of several
people who care for Kanzi at the Language
Research Center. They often prepare their
meals together.

[...]

Savage-Rumbaugh has monitored Kanzi's
language development since soon after his
birth, thirteen years ago.

[...]

Research into chimpanzees' language acquisition began years ago.

'Vickie, do this. Pouf. No, no, do this. Pouf.'
'Pouf.'
'That's fine.'

[...]

But after six years, Vickie could only produce
barely intelligible renditions of 'Mama,'
'Papa,' and 'cup.'

[...]

In 1966, another scientific team used
American Sign Language as a way of over-
coming apes' inability to vocalize. One
chimpanzee learned eighty-five different
signs, which greatly impressed researchers
at the time.

[...]

But in 1979 a scientific paper took issue with
the results of the Sign Language method.
The paper's author, Dr. Herbert Terrace of
Columbia University ...

'What I saw was that the chimp was more or
less mirroring or shadowing the teacher's
signing; that the teacher would sign something
to Nim and Nim would feed it back, either
the same sign or a related sign, or throw in
a few general purpose signs.'

Terrace reached his conclusion after analyzing sign language used by his own chimpanzee research subjects.

Discouraged, attempts to teach language
to apes waned for a while.

However, researchers at Georgia State
pressed on.

[...]

Dr. Savage-Rumbaugh tried a method where-
by apes could not imitate humans.

Wearing headphones, the subject responds
to a hidden questioner by selecting the
appropriate picture.

[...]

Then there's Kanzi. Does he really understand what he hears?

'Here's your pictures. You must watch them all,
so you come on around!'
'Kanzi, see if you can find...
... mushrooms, mushrooms.
That's right, those are the mushrooms. Real
good.
Can you turn back around? OK, you're doing
real good, Kanzi.
See if you can find Mahdu, the orangutan.
Good job, good job.
See if you can find some melon, melon, melon.
Thank you. See if you can find green beans,

green beans. Very nice.
See if you can find a picture of Sue, Sue.
Very nice, thank you. That's me.
See if you can find a picture of coconut,
coconut.
Good. Good job.
See if you can find a picture of oranges, oranges.
Thank you very much, Kanzi.
See if you can find a picture of banana,
banana.
Very nice. And now we need Panbanisha ...'

[...]

Obviously Kanzi can choose correct pictures
in response to Sue's voice, but how about
other voices, unseen voices?

Sevcik: *'Kanzi, give Sue the picture of the*
juice.'
Sue: *'That's right.'*
Sevcik: *'Kanzi, give Sue popsicles.'*
Sue: *'That's right.'*
Sevcik: *'Kanzi, give Sue bananas.'*
Sue: *'That's right.'*
Sevcik: *'Kanzi, give Sue ice.'*
Sue: *'That's right.'*
Sevcik: *'Kanzi, give Sue pears.'*
Sue: *'That's right.'*
Sevcik: *'Kanzi, give Sue potatoes.'*
Sue: *'That's right.'*

Kanzi has picked up several hundred words,
not through formal training, but in daily
life with Dr. Savage-Rumbaugh and others.

'You did it. Good!' "

Script excerpt: Genya Niio, *Kanzi: An Ape*
of Genius, 1993, 51 min.

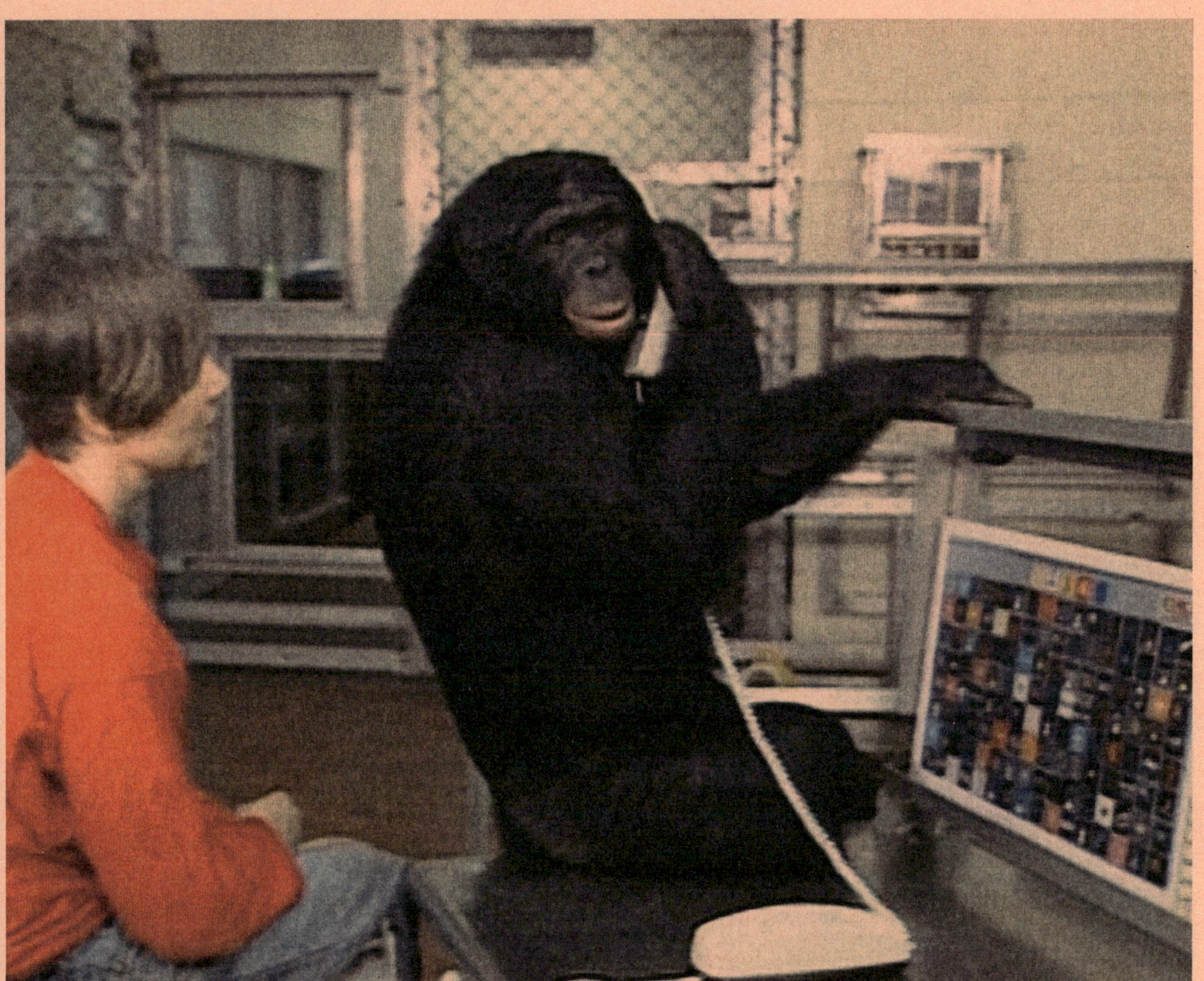

F)

G)

Inspired by Project Washoe, David Premack and Ann James Premack began their experiments on syntax acquisition amongst apes using the chimpanzee Sarah. While the Gardners were primarily interested in communication between apes and people, the Premacks' research focused on how ape intelligence functions. To this end they defined fundamental linguistic operations and developed methods by which these could be taught. They employed a specially devised board with colored tokens that could be combined by Sarah or other test chimpanzees by being placed in rows. The pieces were composed of arbitrary signs, for example an apple was symbolized by a triangular blue token.

Ann James Premack and David Premack, "Teaching Language to an Ape," *Scientific American*, vol. 227, no. 4, October 1972, pp. 92–99

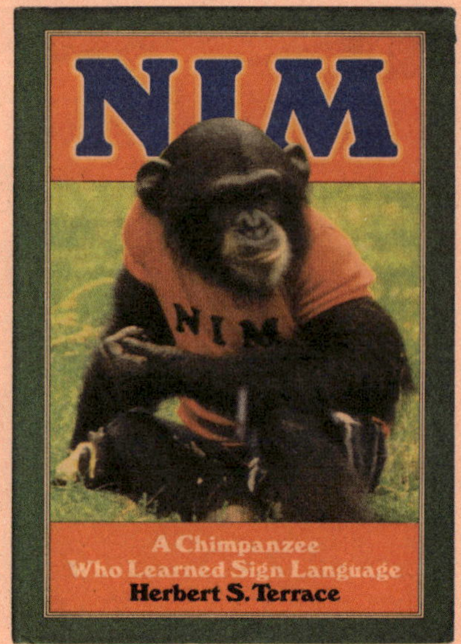

H)

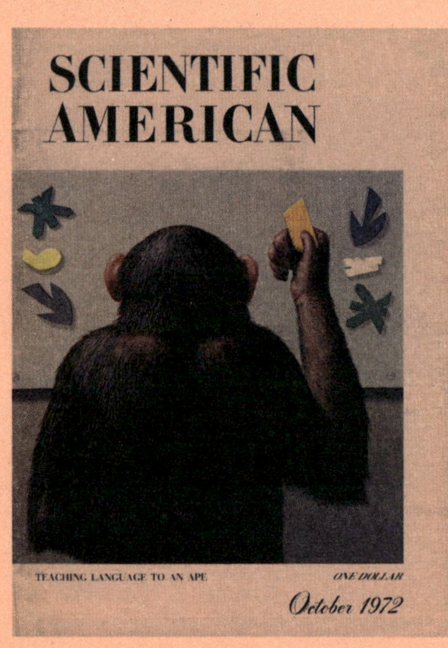

G)

H)

With Nim Chimpsky (a play on the name of the linguist Noam Chomsky), Columbia University in New York undertook a long-term study on speech acquisition directed by Herbert S. Terrace and Thomas Bever. Terrace sought to prove that apes can learn syntax and form sentences. Nim accordingly received individual lessons at Columbia's Psychology department, following B. F. Skinner's conditioning methods. During the four years of the experiment Nim was instructed by over sixty different teachers. The hypothesis initially appeared to be confirmed. However, on analyzing the film recordings of the experiments, Terrace came to the opposite conclusion: in 88 per cent of cases, Nim simply imitates the signs his trainer made shortly beforehand. Terrace cites Nim's longest sentence as: "Give orange me give eat orange me eat orange give me eat orange give me you."
*In his publication Terrace not only discusses his own experiment, but also expresses doubts about all other studies. The standing of language experiment research suffered following Terrace's publication and it became far harder to obtain funding.

* Herbert Terrace et al., "Can an Ape Create a Sentence?" *Science*, vol. 206, no. 4421, 1979, p. 895

Herbert S. Terrace, *Nim: A Chimpanzee Who Learned Sign Language*, New York 1979

ANNALS OF THE NEW YORK ACADEMY OF SCIENCES   VOLUME 364

The Clever Hans Phenomenon: Communication with Horses, Whales, Apes, and People

EDITORS
Thomas A. Sebeok
Robert Rosenthal

I)

I)

In 1980 the semiotician Thomas Sebeok and the psychologist Robert Rosenthal organized a conference under the title "The Clever Hans Phenomenon: Communication with Horses, Whales, Apes, and People." The reference was to Kluger Hans (Clever Hans), a horse that had caused a stir in Berlin in the early twentieth century. Presented with an arithmetical problem he proceeded to hit the ground with his hoof a number of times, in accordance with the solution to the problem. However, investigations revealed that Hans had learned to stop at the right point by reacting to extremely subtle signals from his questioner. Sebeok claimed that the Clever Hans phenomenon accounted for the results of all language experiments conducted with chimpanzees and gorillas. Although ape language researchers make great efforts to meet standards of objectivity, it is clearly extremely difficult to design experimental situations that can be reduced to a single intentional channel of communication.

Thomas A. Sebeok and Robert Rosenthal (eds.), *The Clever Hans Phenomenon*, New York 1981

J)

Herbert S. Terrace, "A Report to an Academy, 1980," in: Thomas A. Sebeok, Robert Rosenthal (eds.), *The Clever Hans Phenomenon*, New York 1981, pp. 94–95

[Quote]

"Though it may be deplorable that apes show so little dedication to the advancement of science, reluctance to sit quietly through batteries of psychological tests is hardly indicative of a lack of intelligence."

John Dupré, "Conversations with Apes: Reflections on the Scientific Study of Language," in: John Hyman (ed.), *Investigating Psychology: Sciences of the Mind after Wittgenstein*, London 1991, p. 104

[Quote]

"Even the simplest organisms are inherently semiotic (Hoffmeyer 1996). For example, the cilia of a single-celled paramecium function as an adaptation that facilitates the organism's movement through a liquid medium. Their specific organization, size, shape, flexibility, and capacity for movement capture certain features of the environment—namely, the resistance afforded by the characteristics of the particular fluid medium in question, against which the organism can propel itself. This adaptation is an embodied sign vehicle to the extent that it is interpreted by the subsequent generation with respect to what this sign vehicle is about—the relevant characteristics of the environment. This interpretation, in turn, becomes manifest in the development of a subsequent organism's body in a way that incorporates this adaptation."

Eduardo Kohn, "How dogs dream: Amazonian natures and the politics of transspecies engagement," *American Ethnologist*, vol. 34, no. 1, 2007, pp. 5–6

[Quote]

"Experimenters must spend a good deal of time interacting with the animal just to get it under sufficient control to enable them to administer the test, hardly what one would call ideal experimental conditions. If cueing is feasible even when a subject is sitting still and attentive, it is even more so under the chaotic circumstances created by an ape's natural response to such man-made rules."

Jean Umiker-Sebeok and Thomas A. Sebeok, "Questioning Apes," in: Umiker-Sebeok and Sebeok, *Speaking of Apes*, New York/London 1980, p. 44

A Report to an Academy, 1980*

H. S. TERRACE
Department of Psychology
Columbia University
New York, New York 10027

THE FIRST ACCOUNT of an ape who learned to talk appears to be fictional. In 1917, Franz Kafka wrote a tale about a chimpanzee who acquired the gift of human language. Recent research appears to have confirmed Kafka's sense of what it would take to induce an ape to speak:

> . . . there was no attraction for me in imitating human beings. I imitated them because I needed a way out, and for no other reason . . . And so I learned things, gentlemen. Ah, one learns when one needs a way out; one learns at all costs. [F. Kafka, "A Report to an Academy."]

During the 63 years that have elapsed since the publication of Kafka's short story, much has been written about man's presumably unique capacity to use language and attempts to show that apes can master some of its features. Linguists, psychologists, psycholinguists, philosophers, and other students of human language have yet to capture its many complexities in a simple definition. They do agree, however, about one basic property of all human languages, that is, the ability to create new meanings, each appropriate to a particular context, through the application of grammatical rules. Noam Chomsky[1] and George Miller,[2] among others, have convincingly reminded us of the futility of trying to explain a child's ability to create and understand sentences without a knowledge of rules that can generate an indeterminately large number of sentences from a finite vocabulary of words.

The dramatic reports of the Gardners,[3] Premack,[4] and Rumbaugh[5] that a chimpanzee could learn substantial vocabularies of words of visual languages and that they were also capable of producing utterances containing two or more words, raise an obvious and fundamental question: Are a chimpanzee's multi-word utterances grammatical? In the case of the Gardners, one wants to know whether Washoe's

* The research reported in this article was, in part, funded by grants from the W.T. Grant Foundation, the Harry Frank Guggenheim Foundation, and The National Institutes of Health (RO1MH29293). Portions of this article appeared previously in Terrace, H.S. 1979. How Nim Chimpsky Changed My Mind. Psychol. Today 13 (6): 65–76.

signing *more drink* in order to obtain another cup of juice or *water bird*, upon seeing a swan, were creative juxtapositions of signs. Likewise one wants to know whether "Sarah," Premack's main subject, was using a grammatical rule in arranging her plastic chips in the sequence, *Mary give Sarah apple*, and whether "Lana," the subject of a related study conducted by Rumbaugh, exhibited knowledge of a grammatical rule in producing the sequence, *please machine give apple*.

In answering these questions, it is important to remember that a mere sequence of words does not qualify as a sentence. A rotely learned string of words presupposes no knowledge of the meanings of each element and certainly no knowledge of the relationships that exist between the elements. Sarah, for example, showed little, if any, evidence of understanding the meanings of *Mary*, *give*, and *Sarah* in the sequence, *Mary give Sarah apple*. Likewise, it is doubtful that, in producing the sequence *please machine give apple*, Lana understood the meanings of *please machine* and *give*, let alone the relationships between these symbols that would apply in actual sentences.[6] There is evidence that Sarah or Lana could distinguish the symbol *apple* from symbols that named other reinforcers. This suggests that what Sarah and Lana learned was to produce rote sequences of the type ABCX, where A, B, and C are nonsense symbols and X is a meaningful element. That conclusion is supported by the results of two studies, one an analysis of a corpus of Lana's utterances, the other an experiment on serial learning by pigeons.

Thompson and Church[7] have recently shown that a major portion of a corpus of Lana's utterances can be accounted for by three decision rules that dictate when one of six stock sentences might be combined with one of a small corpus of object or activity names. The decision rules are (1) did Lana want an ingestible object, (2) was the object in view, and (3) was the object in the machine. For example, if the object was in the machine, an appropriate stock sequence was *please machine give*; if it was not in the machine an appropriate stock sequence would be *please move object name into machine*, and so on.

A recent experiment performed in my laboratory[8] showed that pigeons could learn to peck four colors presented simultaneously in a particular sequence. Such performance is of interest as evidence of the memorial capacity of pigeons. It does not, of course, justify interpreting the sequence of the colors (A→B→C→D) as the production of a sentence meaning *please machine give grain*.

While the sequences, *please machine give grain* and *please machine give apple*, are logically similar, they are not identical. It has yet to be shown that pigeons can learn ABCX sequences of the type that Sarah and Lana learned (where X stands for different reinforcers) or that

A)

In this television show from 1987, Donna Haraway looks at the covers of *National Geographic* and at the Koko project, as she traces "what gets to count as nature, for whom and when, and how much it costs to produce nature at a particular moment in history for a particular group of people."

Donna Haraway reads 'The National Geographic' on Primates, Paper Tiger Television, 1987, 28 min.

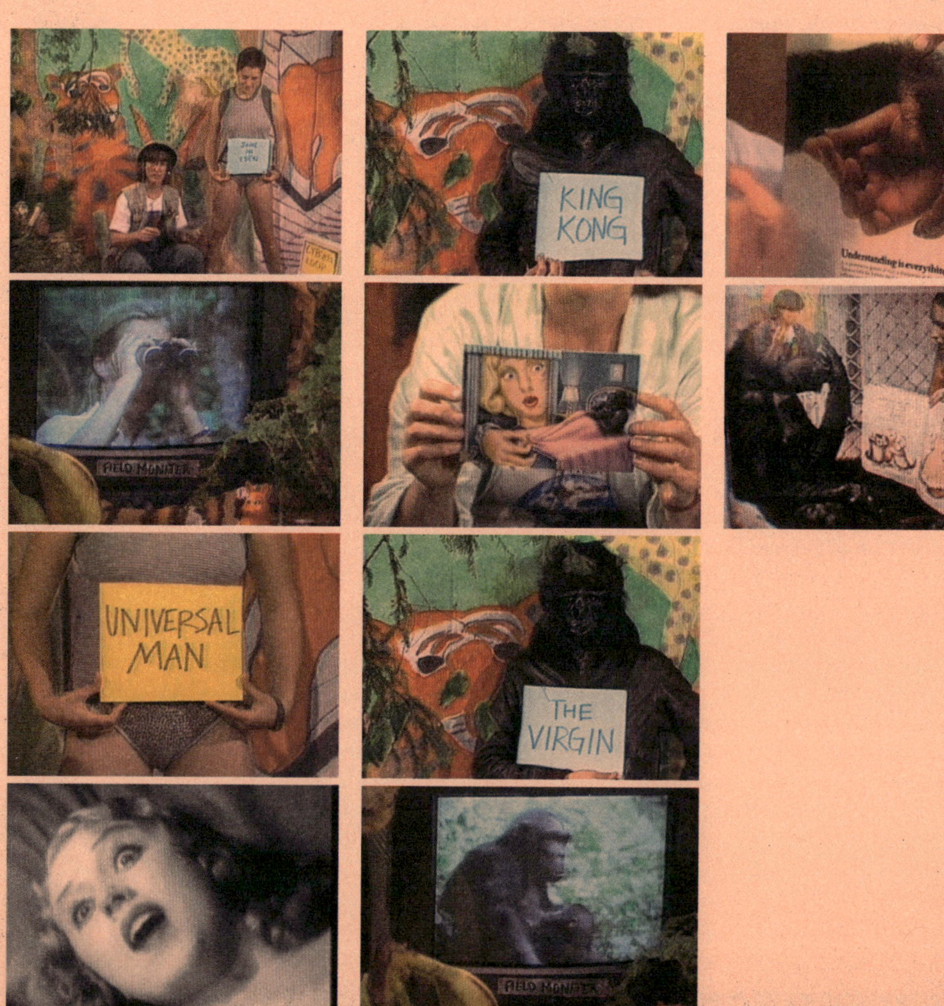

A)

One significant cultural function of the European image of apes was constructing the category of the human. Western models of modern civilization are based on dissociating from and successfully suppressing man's animal nature. "Becoming a human" is the mythical theatre of conquest of both an external and an "inner" physical, affective nature. The practical forms of this dual subjugation can be found in colonial history and disciplinary measures: as pedagogically legitimated uses of force grounded in a necessary subjugation to the law. The hegemony of the autonomous subject and universal reason is constructed on this basis. Images of apes calibrate the continuities and discontinuities along the dividing line constructed between "nature" and "culture." The "civilizatory mission" is characterized by a perfidious paradox: the simultaneous dissociation from and assimilation of the animalistic. The philosopher Giorgio Agamben speaks, with reference to Linnaeus of an "optical machine" constructed from numerous mirrors, "in which man, looking at himself, sees his own image always already deformed in the features of an ape. [...] *Homo* [...] must recognize himself in a non-man in order to be human." *

* Giorgio Agamben, *The Open:
Man and Animal*, Stanford 2004, pp. 26–27

In 1924 the American news agency International Feature Service carried a report on a novel pedagogical institution: a college that would educate chimpanzees, step by step, to become humans. Only those species of apes considered especially clever would be admitted to the lessons—chimpanzees and orangutans for example—while the rest were to be used for experiments in tropical medicine. According to the article, indigenous women were to be employed as nurses to provide for the physical wellbeing of the apes at the "Monkey College"; however, the role of teacher was to be exclusively reserved for European males. Thus the college was constructed according to a strict ontological hierarchy: women would serve the monkeys, which in turn would receive instruction from European men.

"A Monkey-College to Make Chimpanzees Human," *International Feature Service, Inc.*, 1924

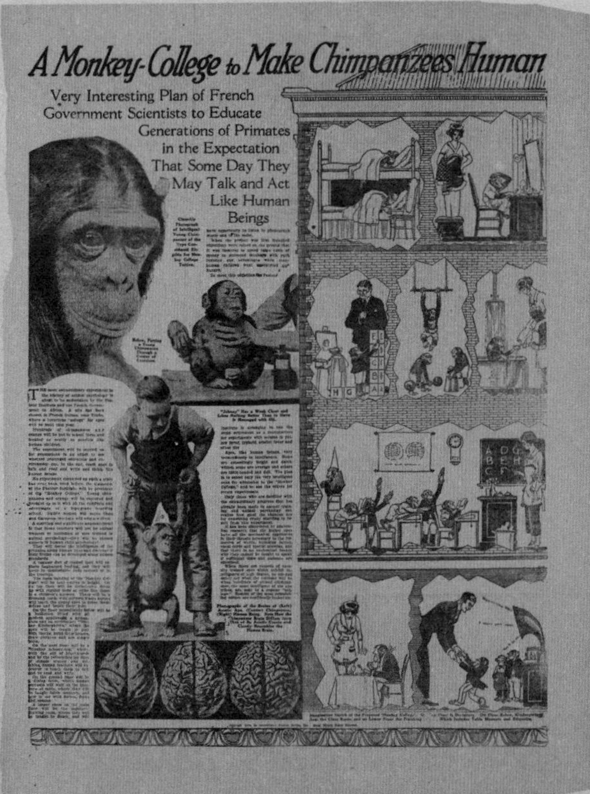

The GIRL and the GORILLA

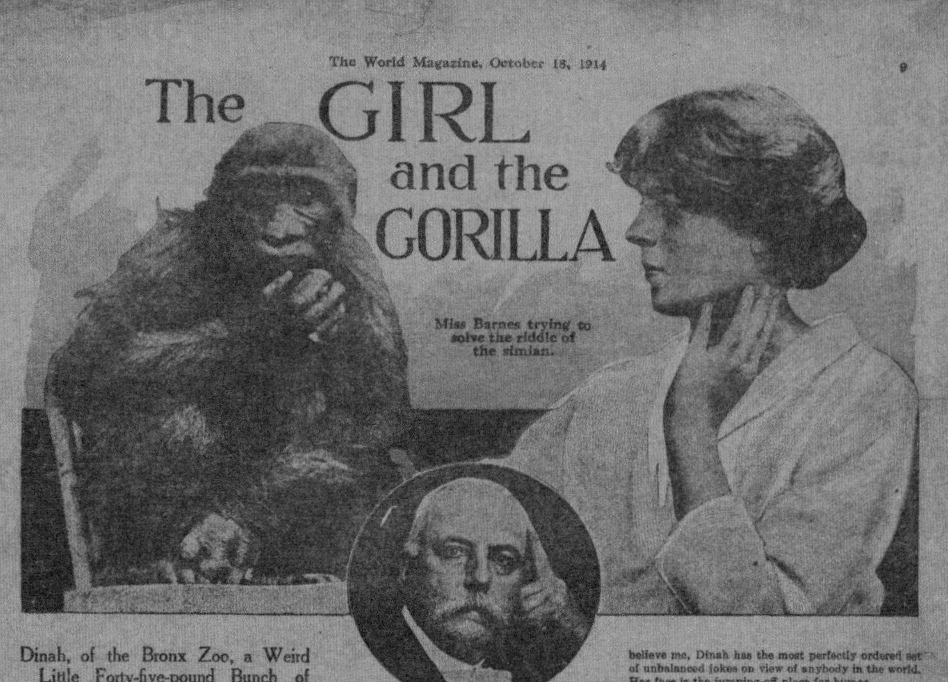

Miss Barnes trying to solve the riddle of the simian.

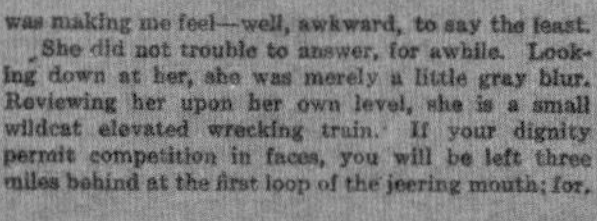

Prof. Robert L. Garner.

Dinah, of the Bronx Zoo, a Weird Little Forty-five-pound Bunch of Femininity—Not Yet Full-Grown, but Converses Intelligently in Language of the Primates.

PROF ROBERT L. GARNER, monkey specialist and leading authority on the "primates," or higher apes, spent three years in African jungles, under commission of the New York Zoological Society, to secure the young female gorilla now safely domiciled at Bronx Park. Dinah (originally named Dynamite on account of her violent temper) is about three years old, and is the only surviving captive of her species in the world to-day. She weighs 45 pounds, is growing fast, and shows high intelligence, as well as an increasingly affectionate disposition.

By Djuna Chappell Barnes.

A NEW species has come to town!

We thought we had a line on all the different kinds of femininity in the world, their fads, fancies and fashions, their virtues and their indiscretions—when suddenly enters Dinah the bush-girl.

She is neither very feminine nor very fragile, to look at. She has fashion's wide shoulder-cape of hair, but this is as far as the semblance goes, as she stands before us, leaning upon bowed forearms, taut as suspense, looking out of far-away eyes upon a life called civilized.

Such is the Gorilla woman, the only living captive of her race.

Looking in at her from the public's side of the bars, I perceived only a vague gray thing with head sunk between shoulders—a bundle of unfathomable apprehensions.

But when I stepped into the cage, with the keeper Engeholme on one side, and Prof. Robert L. Garner on the other, she stood abruptly upright, and putting out a crinkly, black, glace-kid hand, demanded something—something to eat. Her appetite is astounding.

Keeper Fred Engeholme was a little doubtful as to the way that Dinah would receive me, I being the first woman who had come within caressing or battling distance. But Professor Garner seemed confident that Dinah would find something, however trifling, in me that would meet with her approval.

She ambled toward me with her knuckles doubled under her, a slanting bulk of body that shut out what little light the cage permitted, until she reached the chair they had set for her.

There is a queer sort of drawing-room caution about her. She has a cold sort of appraising stare that holds neither envy nor malice.

The crowd that collects outside her cage she does not see, or if she does they might as well be a row of cabbages. Apparently she does not object to cerise or black stitching upon a pair of dress gloves.

I found, for I had come to study her, that the largest and most splendidly satisfying thing in Dinah's life is herself. She would rather stand well in her own estimation than upon a social footing.

The professor, who surely ought to know, told me that she had her own way of talking. So I said to her, "Look here, Dinah, what conclusions have you come to regarding our United States?"

She took her knees into her arms, with an air of long-studied calculation that would have given an analytical novelist infinite pleasure. Rocking from side to side on hairy haunches, she began to laugh—an extraordinary laughter, that disturbed the virile hair upon her breast.

Her mind was as a blank of well-arranged ignorance!

Three feet of the newest womankind in the world was making me feel—well, awkward, to say the least.

She did not trouble to answer, for awhile. Looking down at her, she was merely a little gray blur. Reviewing her upon her own level, she is a small wildcat elevated wrecking train. If your dignity permit competition in faces, you will be left three miles behind at the first loop of the jeering mouth; for, believe me, Dinah has the most perfectly ordered set of unbalanced jokes on view of anybody in the world. Her face is the jumping-off place for humor.

Having crawled after her some twenty minutes, I sat up and argued. I said to myself, now we will see if, after all, the advantages of civilization do not enable me to dominate this rather unique situation.

Once again I lit out upon her with "Now then, Dinah, answer my question. What do you think of our United States? You have been here a month."

She paused, her head poised sidewise.

"Let me see"—she cupped her hand about her ear and dusted a piece of lint from her shoulders. (I freely interpret according to Prof Garner's rules). "The first thing that really attracted my attention was the metre upon the taxi that the professor hired to bring me here to the Zoo. That thing climbed exactly three and a fourth times faster than a Chimpanzee, four times faster than an ordinary monkey, and six times faster than a Gorilla. I hated to see anything get away from control so.

"Also, I was quite grieved," she continued, plaintively, "to observe that the sun has no chance in New York, and that the moon is only a past memory. I couldn't make out whether it was daylight or electricity."

She took a stroll about the cage, ducking between Engeholme's legs and looking very much like the other side of a funny camera. She paused abruptly and smiled.

"There is one thing that I haven't tried yet."

"And what is that?"

"Chewing gum. Gee whis! I would like to find out what it is in that little delicacy that keeps so many people rotatory beneath their hats. But I have been getting the most weird and winsome feed here at the Zoo, that ever passed my understanding. Bananas, oranges, meat, and French rolls in particular."

Certainly a Bushwoman has come to us who is little and quaint and gray, and you who go up to the Bronx to see her will discover that there is something terribly old about her, and yet not old at all. Her eyes alone will make you seem to remember something that has gone before. She weighs less than fifty pounds and stands about three feet high. She is immature yet and will grow as time passes. I am only wondering if I will then be as willing to hug her and have her embrace me in return as I am now.

When she puts her arms about you, it feels something like a garden hose. It is at once purely impersonal and condescending, and yet rather agreeable.

And when she laid her head upon my knees I was not embarrassed but only pleased that she had found something in me as representative of the women she had come among to make her trustful.

Of course she had to spoil it all by gravely putting an orange peel upon her head.

She moved off at the same time, Engeholme after her, and she disrespectfully making faces at him. Faces so mean and comprehensive that Engeholme got riled on the instant with a kindly sort of scorn.

Outside, the crowd roared in delight, as she ran easily out of reach in a side swinging, ungainly loping movement, Engeholme catching up a little at each turn—Germany gaining upon Africa with difficulty.

She growled ominously, when, lunging forward, he caught her by the scruff of the neck and paused in full view of the crowd, wiping his forehead, holding her off like luggage from back home.

"She's so darned cussed," he remarked, illuminatingly, as she tinkered with her ear. "As nice a little girl when she wants to be, and then as mean—as mean"—— he searched in vain for something that would symbolize Dinah's soul and personality.

Failing, he stood and shook his head.

It had just been borne in upon him that even here Kipling's remark about the female of the species holds true."

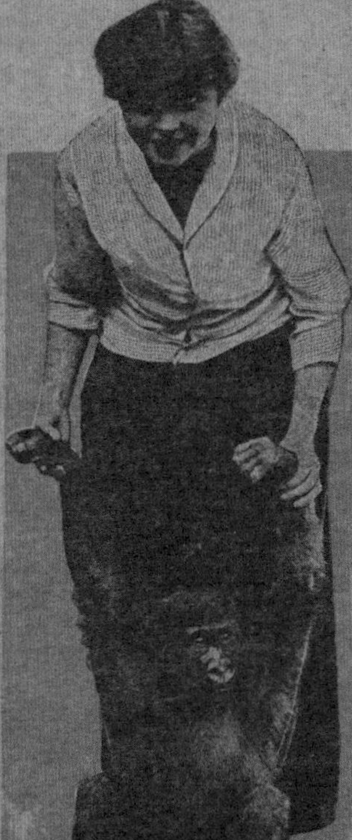

Miss Barnes playing with "Dynamite."

B)

"Nature" to "Culture": During the course of the twentieth century, numerous experiments—closely related to the language experiments from which they cannot always be clearly differentiated—were undertaken to socialize great apes within human families.

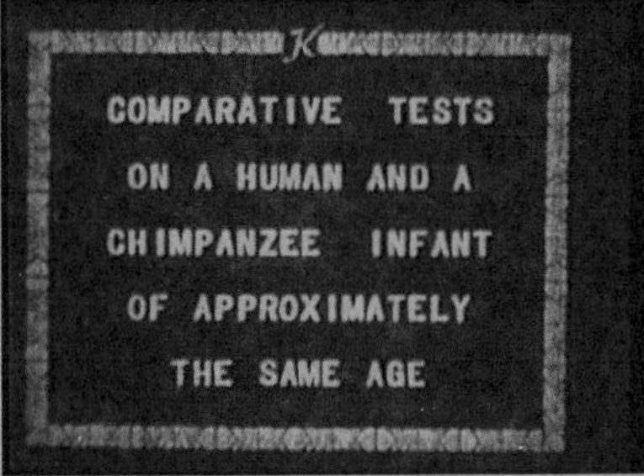

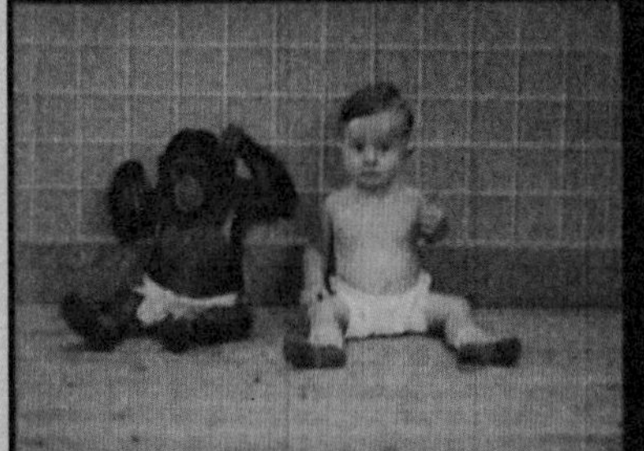

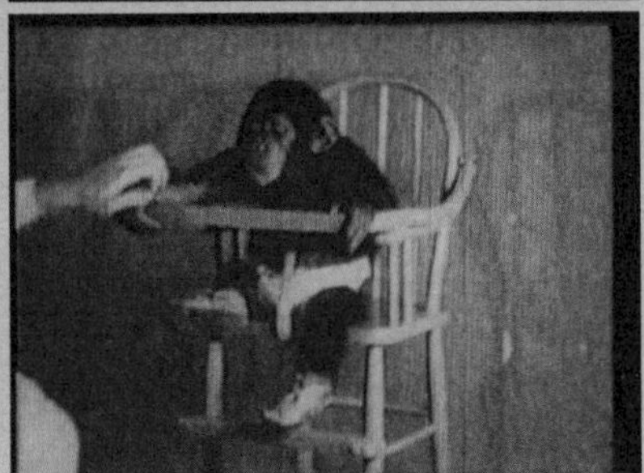

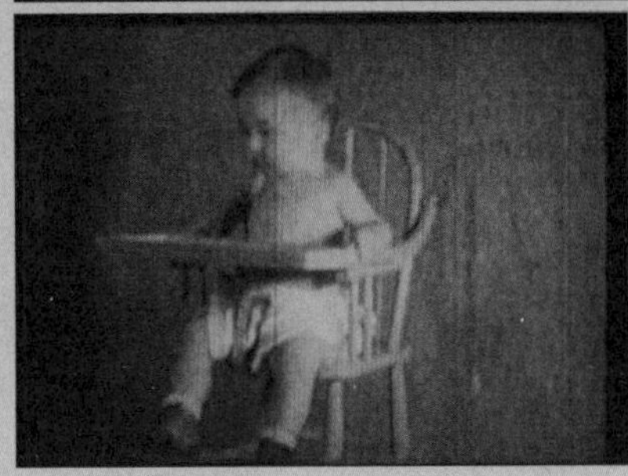

C)

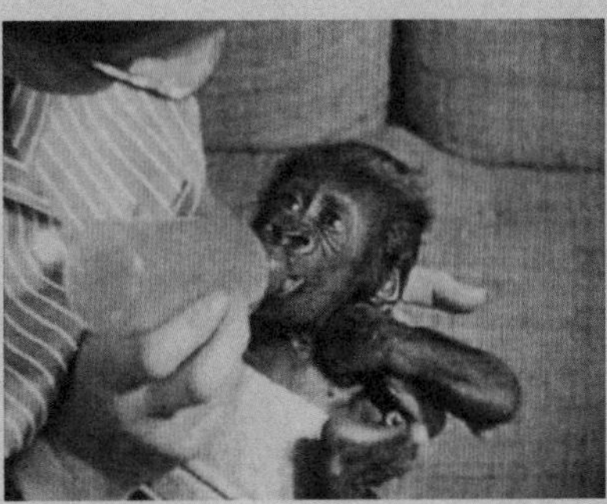

D)

B)

In 1914 the writer and journalist Djuna Barnes visited a female gorilla called Dinah in the Bronx Zoo for an article in *World Magazine*; at the time Dinah was the only living member of her species in captivity. Barnes' report was heavily laced with irony, framed as an investigation into what one could possibly learn from Dinah about new forms of femininity, for the "bush girl" appeared to be neither particularly feminine nor fragile. When Dinah failed to respond to any of her questions, Barnes began to construct a fantasy interview from the gorilla's gestures in which Dinah related her initial experiences with American culture. Barnes' report ended with the sobering assertion that Kipling's comment on the "essential stubbornness" of women applied similarly to gorillas.

Djuna Chappell Barnes, "The Girl and the Gorilla," *The World Magazine*, October 18, 1914

C)

In order to examine the influence of environmental factors on motor and cognitive development, the psychologist Winthrop Kellogg embarked on an unusual experiment in 1931: he and his wife Luella adopted the seven-and-a-half-month-old female chimpanzee Gua from the Yerkes National Primate Research Center, rearing her together with their own son Donald, who was then ten months old. Gua was dressed in nappies, fed, and pushed around in a baby carriage like a human baby. The Kellogs used the parallel development of Gua and Donald to conduct a multitude of comparative tests. Initially, Gua's motoric and perceptual capabilities developed much more rapidly. Her advantage only ended when Donald first attempted to speak at the age of sixteen months. However, when the young boy also began to imitate Gua's food calls the Kellogs became worried about his healthy development and abandoned the experiment. After nine months Gua was returned to the Yerkes Center, where she died in 1933.

Luella and Winthrop Kellogg, *Comparative tests on a human infant and a chimpanzee infant of approximately the same age*, 1931, 18 min.

D)

It was in Basel Zoo in 1959 that Goma became the first gorilla to be born on European soil. Shortly after her birth, Goma was separated from her mother and taken into care by the zoo director Ernst Lang and his family. Goma spent her first year in the Lang household, where she not only lived together with the family but was also reared like a human: she was dressed in diapers just like a small child, placed in a crib to sleep, and fenced in by a playpen. Goma's development with the Langs was documented by numerous reporters and photographers and became the focus of great public interest. After one and a half years in a human environment and the media spotlight, Goma was returned to her original gorilla family in 1961. However, she initially had difficulties integrating into the group, remaining an outsider amongst her own kind for a long time. Today, at the age of fifty-five, Goma is the oldest gorilla in Europe.

Schweizerische Filmwochenschau (SFW), *Neues von Goma, Bébé gorille a 5 mois*, February 19, 1960, 12 min.

In 1931 Maria Hoyt's husband killed the parents of a young female gorilla while hunting in French Equatorial Africa. Maria Hoyt adopted the young orphan, calling her Toto. Shortly afterwards, Hoyt moved from New York to Cuba in order to provide Toto with the optimal climactic conditions. However, the Hoyts later sold the gorilla to the circus Ringling Bros. and Barnum & Bailey.

Augusta Maria Daurer Hoyt, *Toto and I: A Gorilla in the Family*, Philadelphia / New York 1941

F)

In the 1960s and 1970s keeping great apes became very popular as a hobby. Diverse families shared their households with an ape, as was the case with two New Yorkers, Hester and Jerry Mundis. After obtaining the chimpanzee Boris from a pet store, they reared him in their apartment in Manhattan's Upper West Side. However, the Mundis' life with the "urban ape" was not motivated by the pursuit of scientific knowledge, but was intended instead as a form of literary experiment. Everyday life with the ape provided a wealth of comic material for the book *No He's Not a Monkey, He's an Ape and He's My Son*, in which the couple describe their time with Boris, from his cage in the living room to his climbing attempts on the chandelier.

Hester Mundis, *No He's Not a Monkey, He's an Ape and He's My Son*, New York 1976

G)

In 1964 the American psychotherapist Maurice Temerlin and his wife adopted Lucy, the daughter of two circus chimpanzees. In their home the couple treated the ape like a human child. They trained Lucy to perform activities such as sitting at the table, eating with cutlery, and dressing herself. Lucy also learned American Sign Language from the primatologist Roger Fouts. Lucy enjoyed great popularity in the media and was even made the subject of a title story in *Life* magazine. However, after twelve years of living with Lucy, the Temerlins found keeping a grown female chimpanzee increasingly intolerable. As a consequence, in 1976 Lucy was handed over to the Chimpanzee Rehabilitation Project in Senegal. Following a ten-year rehabilitation process she was released into the wilderness of the River Gambia National Park in Gambia by her keeper Janis Carter. Only one year later Carter discovered Lucy's skeleton in the jungle.

Maurice K. Temerlin, *Lucy: Growing Up Human; A Chimpanzee Daughter in a Psychotherapist's Family*, London 1975

H)

In 1952 the nature photographer Lilo Hess discovered a six-month-old female baby chimpanzee in a pet shop. On hearing of the animal's imminent sale to a research laboratory, she decided to buy her without further ado and bring her up on her own farm in Pennsylvania. Surrounded by toys, romper suits, and cereals, Christine's upbringing on Hess's farm clearly appeared to have more in common with that of a human child. However, Hess emphasized that she was not interested in systematically educating the ape to become a human or deliberately increasing her capabilities.

Lilo Hess, *Petra. Mein Schimpansenkind*, Stuttgart 1954 [London 1954]

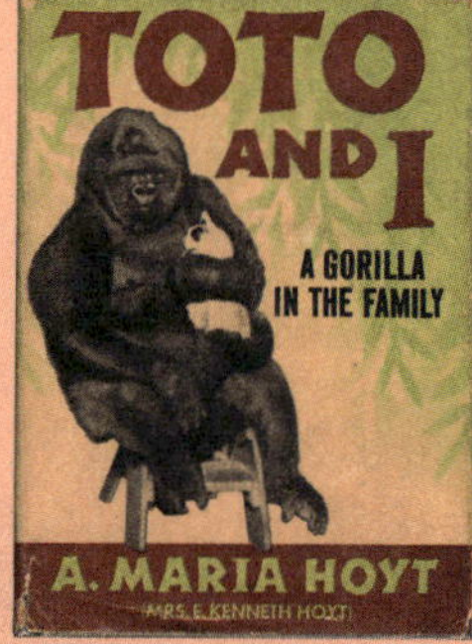
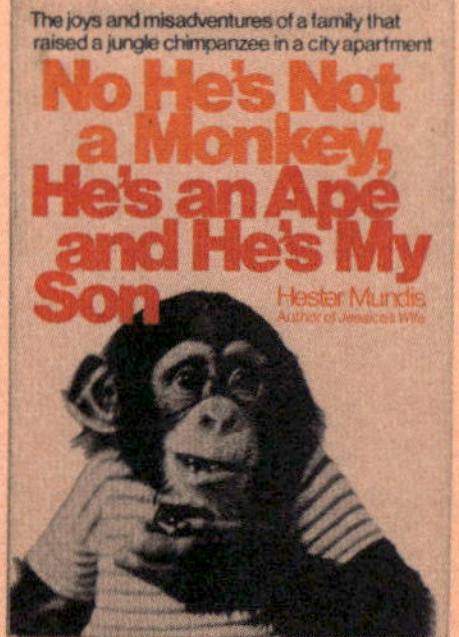
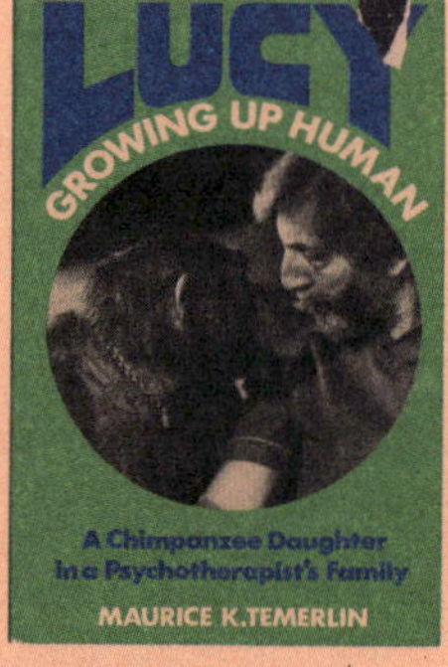
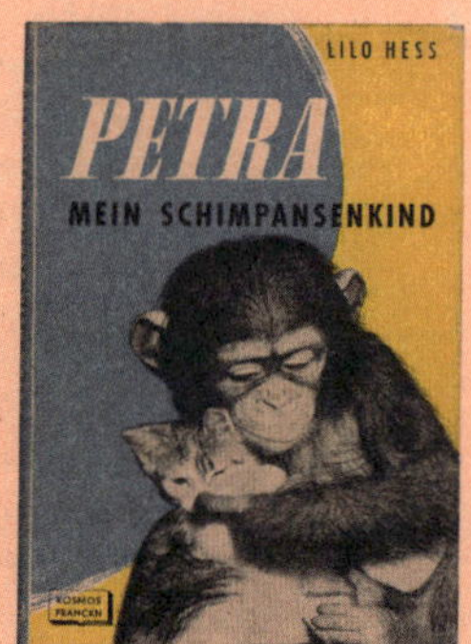

E)   F)   G)   H)

The film *Bedtime For Bonzo* (1951) tells the story of bachelor and psychologist Peter Boyd (Ronald Reagan), who, in order to obtain permission to marry a professor's daughter, must first prove that he is of suitable character. As Peter is the son of a notorious criminal, his future father-in-law, who is a strict advocate of genetic determinism, is convinced that Peter similarly has criminal tendencies. In order to prove the professor wrong, Peter devises a plan to teach Bonzo the chimpanzee human moral principles, in the hope of proving that environmental influences rather than genetic predisposition are responsible for forming people's personalities. Peter calls on the housekeeper Jane to assist him in the project, assigning her the role of Bonzo's mother, while he plays that of Bonzo's father. Thus, family life becomes a series of role-plays in which social conventions exert a greater influence than nature.

Frederick De Cordova, *Bedtime for Bonzo*, 1951, 83 min.

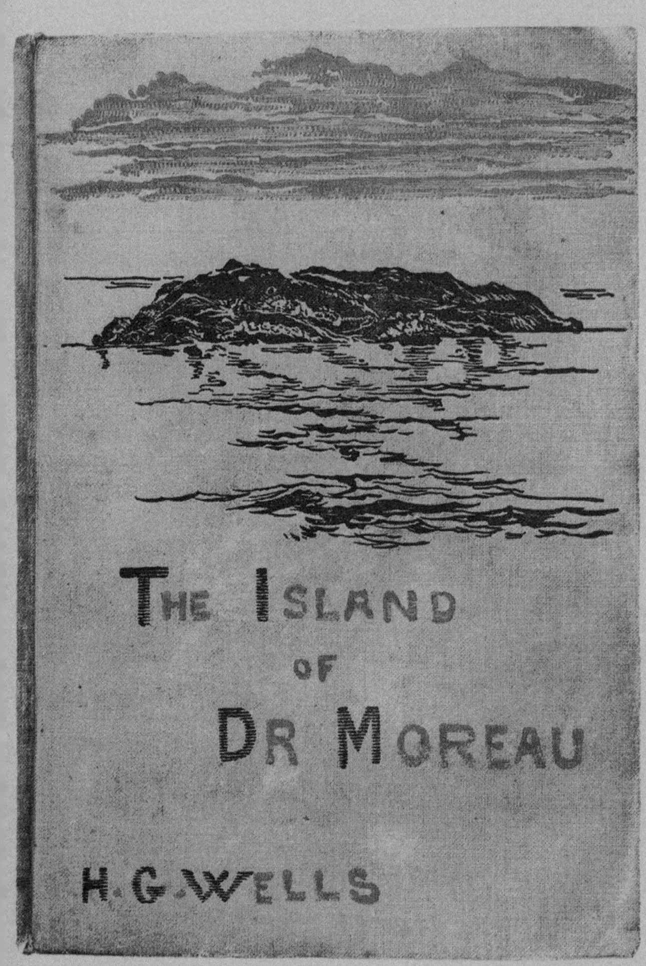

I)

[Quote]

"'*His* is the House of Pain.
  His is the Hand that makes.
  His is the Hand that wounds.
  His is the Hand that heals.'
  '*His* is the lightning flash.'
  '*His* is the deep, salt sea.'
  '*His* are the stars in the sky.'"

H. G. Wells, *The Island of Dr. Moreau*, New York 1996 [1896], p. 80

[Quote]

"Not to go on all-fours;
  that is the Law. Are we not Men?'
  'Not to suck up Drink;
  that is the Law. Are we not Men?'
  'Not to claw the Bark of Trees;
  that is the Law. Are we not Men?
  'Not to chase other Men;
  that is the Law. Are we not Men?'"

H. G. Wells, *The Island of Dr. Moreau*, New York 1996 [1896], pp. 79–80

I)

In H. G. Wells' 1896 work *The Island of Doctor Moreau*, as well as in the 1932 film adaptation, *Island of Lost Souls*, Dr. Moreau conducts secret medical experiments that turn animals into humans. A combined regime of operations (carried out without anesthesia), blood exchange, and daily training produces an array of half-human, half-bestial creatures. After their transformation, the creatures live under Moreau's surveillance, observed from a distance in their community on the side of the island opposite the laboratory. If they are guilty of breaking a law, they are brought back into the surgery, known as the "House of Pain," where Dr. Moreau continues operating on them. The slightest mention of the House of Pain almost always suffices to bring noncompliant creatures to their senses. When the creatures realise that the Law can be overturned and that their tyrannical creator Dr. Moreau is not invulnerable, they begin to revolt.

H. G. Wells, *The Island of Dr. Moreau*, New York 1996 [1896]

"[P]hilosophical narratives of the 'birth of
man' are always compelled to presuppose
such a moment in human (pre)history when
(what will become) man is no longer a mere
animal and simultaneously not yet a 'being
of language,' bound by symbolic Law; a
moment of thoroughly 'perverted,' 'denatur-
alized,' 'derailed' nature which is not yet
culture. In his pedagogical writings Kant
emphasized that the human animal needs
disciplinary pressure in order to tame an
uncanny 'unruliness' that seems to be inherent in human nature—a wild, unconstrained
propensity to insist stubbornly on one's
own will, cost what it may. Because of this
'unruliness' the human animal needs a Master
to discipline him: discipline targets this
'unruliness,' not the animal nature in man:

> 'It is discipline which prevents man
> from being turned aside by his animal
> impulses from humanity, his appointed
> end. Discipline, for instance, must
> restrain him from venturing wildly
> and rashly into danger, Discipline, thus,
> is merely negative, its action being
> to counteract man's natural unruliness.
> The positive part of education is
> instruction. Unruliness consists in
> independence of the law. By discipline
> men are placed in subjection to the
> laws of mankind, and brought to feel
> their constraint. This, however, must
> be accomplished early. Children, for
> instance, are first sent to school, not so
> much with the object of their learning
> something, but rather that they may
> become used to sitting still and doing
> exactly as they are told.[...]' "

Slavoj Žižek, *The Ticklish Subject*:
The Absence of Political Ontology,
London 2000, p. 36, quoting Immanuel Kant
[*Über Pädagogik*, 1803]

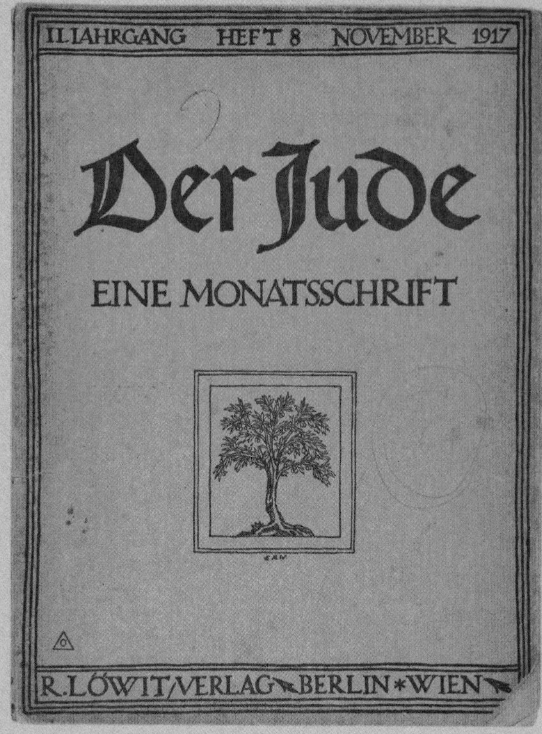

J)

J)

Franz Kafka's short story "Ein Bericht für
eine Akademie"(A Report to an Academy)
appeared for the first time in 1917 in the
magazine *Der Jude*, published by Martin
Buber and Salman Schocken. The story is
in the form of a report to an academy in
which the former ape Rotpeter describes his
transition from ape to man. With a culti-
vated use of language he describes how he
progressively became assimilated to human
society, and in the process lost all memory
of his former life as an ape. Rotpeter relates
how his primary motive for imitating humans was as a tactical "escape route" from
the discomforts of captivity. Following initial
training he went on to celebrate great suc-
cesses in vaudeville and even acquired the
"cultural level of an average European." Thus
Rotpeter's career exemplifies the civilizing
process in all its ambivalence: as the irre-
trievable loss of the past and simultaneously
as an escape route from oppression.

Franz Kafka, "Zwei Tiergeschichten:
2. Ein Bericht für eine Akademie,"
Der Jude: Eine Monatsschrift, vol. 2, no. 8,
November 1917, pp. 559–565

K)

J.M. Coetzee, *The Lives of Animals*, ed.
by Amy Gutmann, Princeton 2001, pp. 60-61

deutschen Theaters herauszugreifen — das Drama Hauptmanns und die naturalistische Schauspielkunst auf eine Epoche des Epigonendramas und des reisenden Virtuosentums, um von einer Operettenhochflut abgelöst zu werden. Die Verquickung verschiedener Kunstarten in einem theatralisch-musikalischen Spiel ist überdies für die Anfänge aller Theaterkunst kennzeichnend (Inder, Griechen). Auch im jüdischen Theater bildet diese Epoche mit all jenen szenischen Elementen, die zu jeder Zeit geistigen Verfalls ein unkultiviertes Publikum entzückten, das dramenlose Theater par excellence.

Berlin-Steglitz   Michael Weichert

ZWEI TIERGESCHICHTEN
Von Franz Kafka

2. Ein Bericht für eine Akademie

Hohe Herren von der Akademie!

Sie erweisen mir die Ehre, mich aufzufordern, der Akademie einen Bericht über mein äffisches Vorleben einzureichen.

In diesem Sinne kann ich leider der Aufforderung nicht nachkommen. Nahezu fünf Jahre trennen mich vom Affentum, eine Zeit, kurz vielleicht am Kalender gemessen, unendlich lang aber durchzugaloppieren, so wie ich es getan habe, streckenweise begleitet von vortrefflichen Menschen, Ratschlägen, Beifall und Orchestralmusik, aber im Grunde allein, denn alle Begleitung hielt sich, um im Bilde zu bleiben, weit vor der Barriere. Diese Leistung wäre unmöglich gewesen, wenn ich eigensinnig hätte an meinem Ursprung, an den Erinnerungen der Jugend festhalten wollen. Gerade Verzicht auf jeden Eigensinn war das oberste Gebot, das ich mir auferlegt hatte; ich, freier Affe, fügte mich diesem Joch. Dadurch verschlossen sich mir aber ihrerseits die Erinnerungen immer mehr. War mir zuerst die Rückkehr, wenn die Menschen gewollt hätten, freigestellt durch das ganze Tor, das der Himmel über der Erde bildet, wurde es gleichzeitig mit meiner vorwärts gepeitschten Entwicklung immer niedriger und enger; wohler und eingeschlossener fühlte ich mich in der Menschenwelt; der Sturm, der mir aus meiner Vergangenheit nachblies, sänftigte sich; heute ist es nur ein Luftzug, der mir die Fersen kühlt; und das Loch in der Ferne, durch das er kommt und durch das ich einstmals kam, ist so klein geworden, daß ich, wenn überhaupt die Kräfte und der Wille hinreichen würden, um bis dorthin zurückzulaufen, das Fell vom Leib mir schinden müßte, um durchzukommen. Offen gesprochen, so gerne ich auch Bilder wähle für diese Dinge, offen gesprochen: Ihr Affentum, meine Herren, sofern Sie etwas Derartiges hinter sich haben, kann Ihnen nicht ferner sein als mir das meine. An der Ferse aber kitzelt es jeden, der hier auf Erden geht: den kleinen Schimpansen wie den großen Achilles.

It has been agreed that O'Hearne will have three opportunities to present positions, and his mother three opportunities to reply. Since O'Hearne has had the courtesy to send her a précis beforehand, she knows, broadly speaking, what he will be saying.

"My first reservation about the animal-rights movement," O'Hearne begins, "is that by failing to recognize its historical nature, it runs the risk of becoming, like the human-rights movement, yet another Western crusade against the practices of the rest of the world, claiming universality for what are simply its own standards." He proceeds to give a brief outline of the rise of animal-protection societies in Britain and America in the nineteenth century.

"When it comes to human rights," he continues, "other cultures and other religious traditions quite properly reply that they have their own norms and see no reason why they should have to adopt those of the West. Similarly, they say, they have their own norms for the treatment of animals and see no reason to adopt ours—particularly when ours are of such recent invention.

"In yesterday's presentation our lecturer was very hard on Descartes. But Descartes did not invent the idea that animals belong to a different order from humankind: he merely formalized it in a new way. The notion that we have an obligation to animals themselves to treat them compassionately—as opposed to an obligation to ourselves to do so—is very recent, very Western, and even very Anglo-Saxon. As long as we insist that we have access to an ethical universal to which other traditions are blind, and try to impose it on them by means of propaganda or even economic pressure, we are going to meet with resistance, and that resistance will be justified."

It is his mother's turn.

"The concerns you express are substantial, Professor O'Hearne, and I am not sure I can give them a substantial answer. You are correct, of course, about the history. Kindness to animals has become a social norm only recently, in the last hundred and fifty or two hundred years, and in only part of the world.

You are correct too to link this history to the history of human rights, since concern for animals is, historically speaking, an off-shoot of broader philanthropic concerns—for the lot of slaves and of children, among others.[2]

"However, kindness to animals—and here I use the word *kindness* in its full sense, as an acceptance that we are all of one kind, one nature—has been more widespread than you imply. Pet keeping, for instance, is by no means a Western fad: the first travelers to South America encountered settlements where human beings and animals lived higgledy-piggledy together. And of course children all over the world consort quite naturally with animals. They don't see any dividing line. That is something they have to be taught, just as they have to be taught it is all right to kill and eat them.

"Getting back to Descartes, I would only want to say that the discontinuity he saw between animals and human beings was the result of incomplete information. The science of Descartes's day had no acquaintance with the great apes or with higher marine mammals, and thus little cause to question the assumption that animals cannot think. And of course it had no access to the fossil record that would reveal a graded continuum of anthropoid crea-tures stretching from the higher primates to *Homo sapiens*—anthropoids, one must point out, who were exterminated by man in the course of his rise to power.[3]

"While I concede your main point about Western cultural ar-rogance, I do think it is appropriate that those who pioneered the industrialization of animal lives and the commodification of ani-mal flesh should be at the forefront of trying to atone for it."

O'Hearne presents his second thesis. "In my reading of the scientific literature," he says, "efforts to show that animals can

---

[2] See James Turner, *Reckoning with the Beast* (Baltimore: Johns Hopkins Univer-sity Press, 1980), chap. 1.

[3] See Mary Midgley, "Persons and Non-Persons," in *In Defence of Animals*, ed. Peter Singer (Oxford: Blackwell, 1985), 59; Rosemary Rodd, *Biology, Ethics, and Ani-mals* (Oxford: Clarendon Press, 1990), 37.

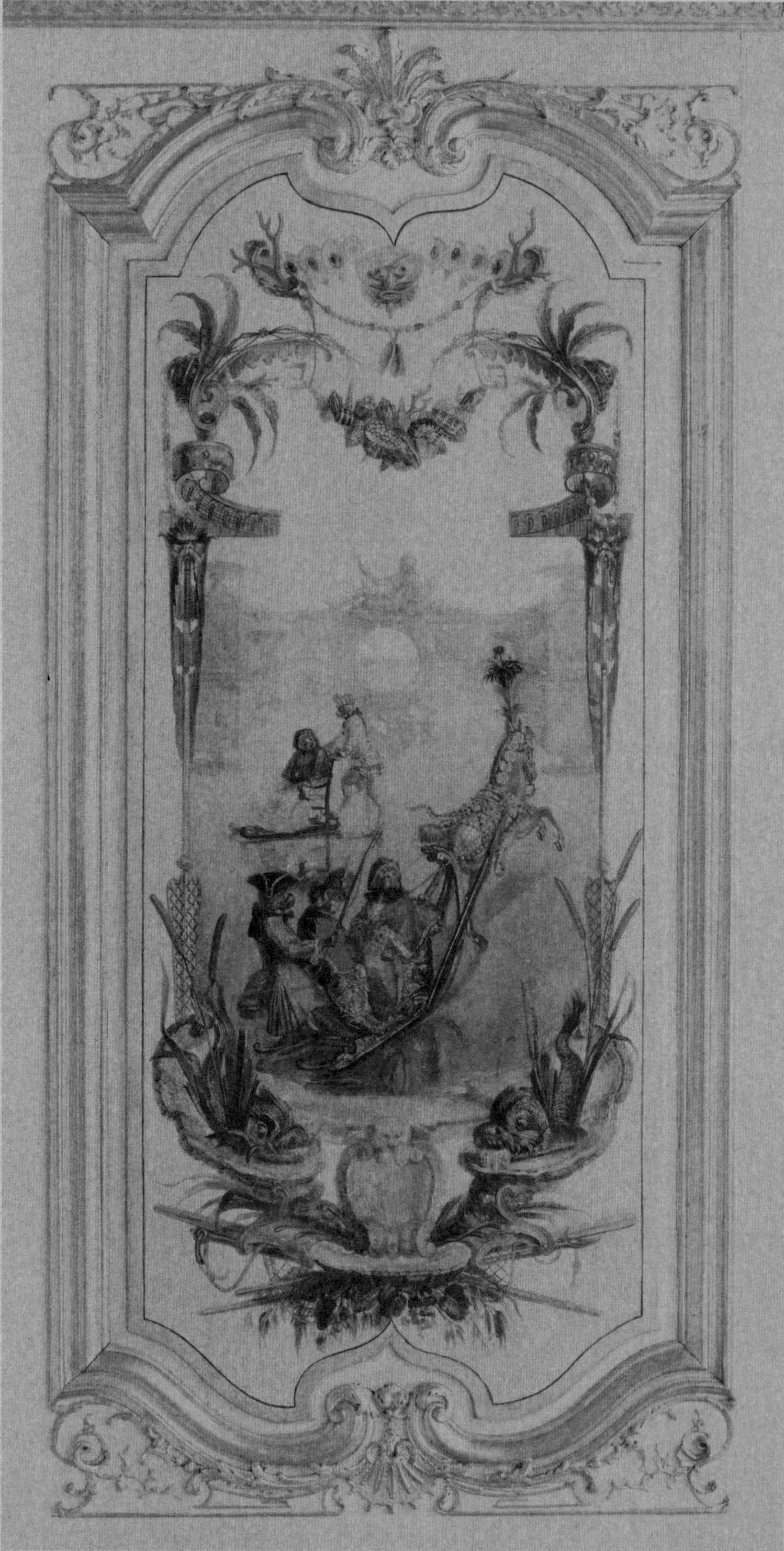

Originating in France in the early eighteenth
century, a *singerie* (which is the French term
for "monkey trick") is a genre of humorous
pictures showing fashionably attired monkeys
attired monkeys aping human behavior.
French designers and painters were inspired
by the fondness of seventeenth-century
aristocrats for dressing their pet monkeys in
outfits and teaching them tricks like pick-
pocketing for the amusement of courtiers at
Versailles. The greatest surviving example
of a room decorated in the *singerie* style is
the Grande Singerie located in the Château
de Chantilly. From 1643 to 1830, the château
was owned by the Bourbon Condé family,
cousins to Louis XIV. Christophe Huet
(1700–1759), a French painter and designer,
covered the room's six wall panels, doors,
and ceiling with monkeys incorporated into
allegories of science and the arts, the continents being represented by a crocodile,
an elephant, a horse, and a lion.

Christophe Huet, *Décor de la Petite Singerie*,
18th century, wall painting

By the mid-eighteenth century, Hannah Arendt argues, imperialism was in need of new forms of legitimization. Its resources were allocated to scientific racism, among other things. The historian Dirk Moses has called the period from 1850 to 1950 the "racial century." It was during this period that the pseudoscience of biological racism increasingly integrated policies of subjugation, enslavement, and extinction, finally fueling the political catastrophes of the twentieth century, from the genocide of the European Jews to the apartheid regime in South Africa. In the nineteenth century, Charles Darwin and a vast array of European scientists had done little to depose the pseudoscientific racism, although biological racism was incongruent with Darwinian evolutionary theory, and although Darwin had rejected the idea of hierarchy and superiority as absurd. And yet in chapter six of *The Descent of Man* (1871), Darwin predicted that the "civilised races of man will almost certainly exterminate and replace throughout the world the savage races." Herbert Spencer's use of the phrase "survival of the fittest" further anchored popular European views, neatly tied to capitalism and colonialism, within a scientific outlook.

While the equation of great apes with savage monsters and "wild men" has its roots in antiquity, biological racism has firmly established the "ape insult" in the standard repertoire of European racism. Those contesting biological racism and the naturalization of hegemony long relied on emphasizing that differences in behavior were the product of culture rather than biology, thus reinforcing the nature/culture dichotomy from the opposite end. This was the underlying situation in the 1970s, when sociobiology, a field of study suggesting that behavior is also subject to evolution, met with fierce criticism.

"An intimate connexion between the structure of the brain and the intellectual faculties in the animal kingdom cannot be doubted. As the facts which we have advanced plainly prove that there are no well-marked and essential differences between the brain of the Negro and European, we must conclude that no innate difference in the intellectual faculties can be admitted to exist between them. This has been denied by philosophers, naturalists, and travellers, who assert that the Ethiopian race is naturally inferior to the European in intellectual and moral powers. The data upon which such an opinion is based are either erroneous suppositions and false deductions from anatomy and physiology, or superficial observations on the intellectual and moral faculties of the Negroes, made by partial or prejudiced travellers. Very little value can be attached to these researches, when we consider that they have been made for the most part on poor and unfortunate Negroes in the Colonies, who have been torn from their native country and their families, and carried into the West Indies, and doomed there to a perpetual slavery and hard labour in the sugar plantations."

Friedrich Tiedemann, "On the Brain of the Negro, compared with that of the European and the Orang-Outang," *Philosophical Transactions of the Royal Society of Science of London,* London 1863, p. 520

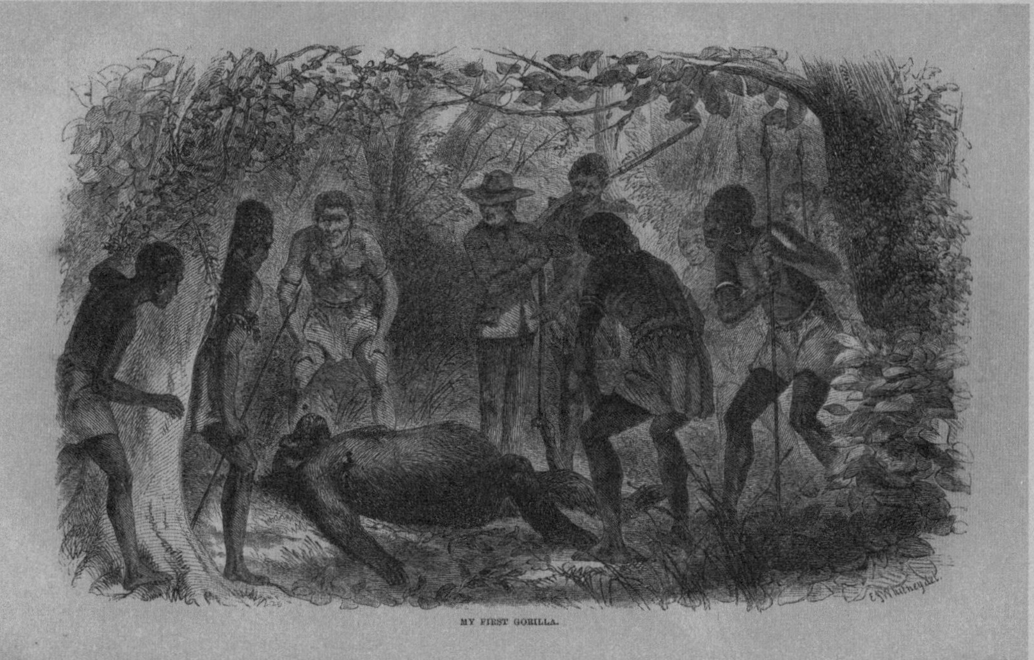

A)

A)

During a four-year expedition from 1855 to 1859, the French-American researcher Paul Belloni du Chaillu travelled the coast of West Africa, subsequently publishing his ethnological, natural historical, and geographical observations in his 1861 work *Explorations and Adventures in Equatorial Africa*. His depictions of the recently discovered species of gorilla as a dangerous beast generated great public interest, serving as the model and accompanying text for numerous magazines in Europe and the USA. Before du Chaillu, the zoological observations of Thomas Savage (1847) and Richard Owen (1859) had already contributed to visualizations of the gorilla and its demonization, as exemplified in an 1859 picture by Joseph Wolf, one of the most important animal painters of the nineteenth century, or later in the first edition of *Brehms Thierleben* from 1864. Such images can be understood as part of the debate on the relationship between man and animals, which in connection with the competition over the colonial division of Africa culminated in publicly conducted scientific racism.

Paul Du Chaillu, *Explorations and Adventures in Equatorial Africa; with Accounts of the Manners and Customs of the People, and of the Chase of the Gorilla, the Crocodile, Leopard, Elephant, Hippopotamus, and Other Animals*, New York, 1862 [1861], p. 100

B)

In July 1950 UNESCO published its *First Statement on Race*. It was the official document refuting the idea of separate and unchanging races in light of the recent catastrophes of Nazism, World War II, and the "racial century." The core concepts of the document were derived from the "modern evolutionary synthesis," whose architects defended a doctrine of natural selection and population biology that was about adaptive flexibility. While the 1950 paper met criticism as an attempt "to solve scientific questions by political manifestos," in 1964 the third version was published whose authors included biologists testifying that "it is not possible from the biological point of view to speak in any way whatsoever of a general inferiority or superiority of this or that race." However, the question of the relation between "genetic" and "cultural" factors prevailed in public debates in the second half of the twentieth century.

UNESCO/SS/1, *Statement by experts on race problems*, Paris, 20 July 1950

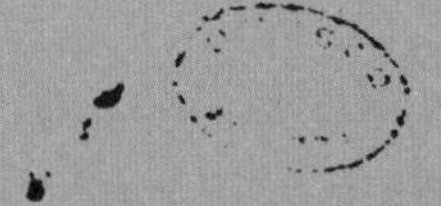

UNITED NATIONS EDUCATIONAL,
SCIENTIFIC AND CULTURAL ORGANIZATION

STATEMENT BY EXPERTS ON RACE PROBLEMS

1.   Scientists have reached general agreement in recognizing that mankind is one: that all men belong to the same species, _Homo sapiens._ It is further generally agreed among scientists that all men are probably derived from the same common stock; and that such differences as exist between different groups of mankind are due to the operation of evolutionary factors of differentiation such as isolation, the drift and random fixation of the material particles which control heredity (the genes), changes in the structure of these particles, hybridization, and natural selection.   In these ways groups have arisen of varying stability and degree of differentiation which have been classified in different ways for different purposes.

2.   From the biological standpoint, the species _Homo sapiens_ is made up of a number of populations, each one of which differs from the others in the frequency of one or more genes.   Such genes, responsible for the hereditary differences between men, are always few when compared to the whole genetic constitution of man and to the vast number of genes common to all human beings regardless of the population to which they belong.   This means that the likenesses among men are far greater than their differences.

3.   A race, from the biological standpoint, may therefore be defined as one of the group of populations constituting the species _Homo sapiens._ These populations are capable of inter-breeding with one another but, by virtue of the isolating barriers which in the past kept them more or less separated, exhibit certain physical differences as a result of their somewhat different biological histories.   These represent variations, as it were, on a common theme.

4.   In short, the term "race" designates a group or population characterized by some concentrations, relative as to frequency and distribution, of hereditary particles (genes) or physical characters, which appear, fluctuate, and often disappear in the course of time by reason of geographic and/or cultural isolation.   The varying manifestations of these traits in different populations are perceived in different ways by each group.   What is perceived is largely preconceived, so that each group arbitrarily tends to misinterpret the variability which occurs as a fundamental difference which separates that group from all others.

B)

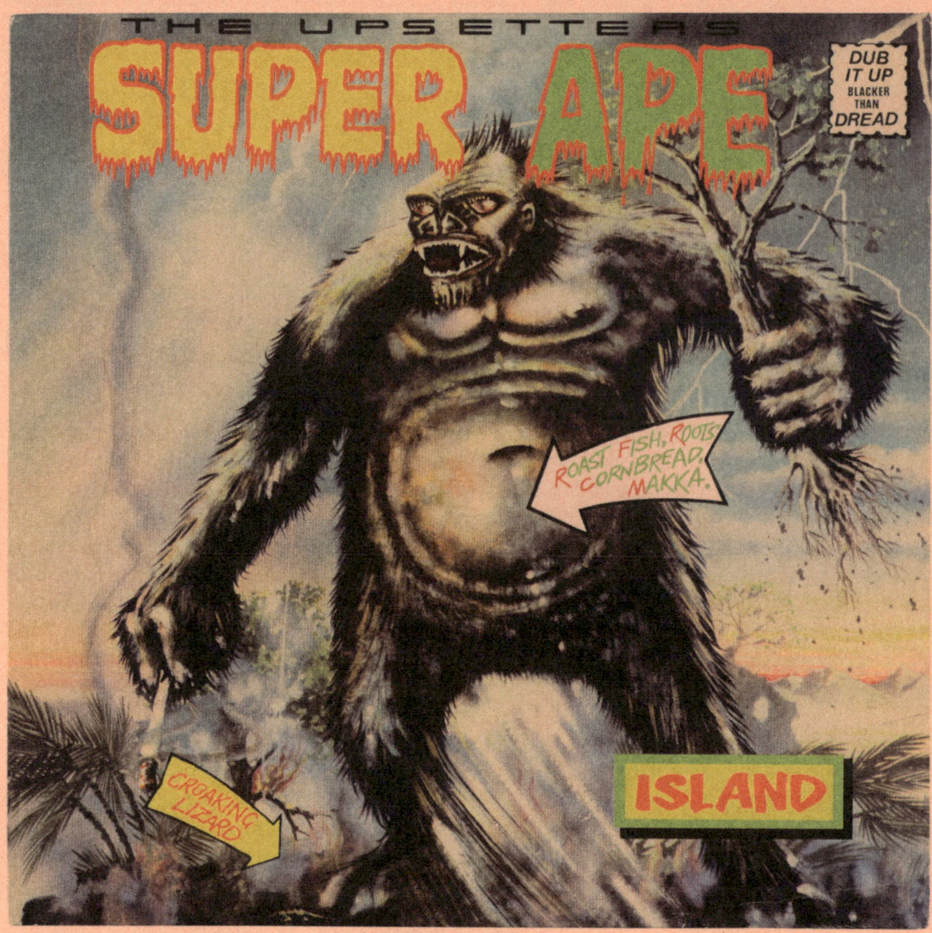

c)

c)

Super Ape (or *Scratch the Super Ape* in Jamaica) is a dub album from the Jamaican reggae artist and music producer Lee "Scratch" Perry released in 1976 and attributed to his studio band The Upsetters. Perry was renowned not only as the producer of countless Jamaican reggae musicians from the early 1970s onwards but also as a pioneer of dub music. The unique sound effects and remixing techniques he developed, his playful references from popular culture, political criticism, and religion, and his multitude of different personas are all characteristic of his style.

Record cover of: The Upsetters, *Super Ape*, The Island Def Jam Music Group 2013 [1976]

[Quote]

"This is the ape-man / Trodding through creation / Are you ready to step with I man?"

The Upsetters, *Super Ape*, Jamaica, 1976

[Quote]

"I change words, rearrange words, I am Mr. Perry, white tomorrow, black today, if you want me to."

Tobias Nagel, "Porträt Lee 'Scratch' Perry," *Frankfurter Allgemeine Zeitung*, December 20, 2001

A)

This Ethiopian painting, created ca. 1965–1975, combines the time-honored iconography of the Ethiopian Orthodox Church with folkloristic motifs. A thick line divides the larger upper half of the picture from a smaller lower half. While the upper half depicts a scene of mutual bonding and peace, the bottom part shows the same society in conflict and disharmony, juxtaposing not only order and peace with disorder and chaos, but possibly also culture with a violent and amoral natural state. Above the line is a round table around which a group of animals congregate, chaired by a lion. Inside this round table an old ape stands upright, reading from the scriptures. The picture is thus also referring to a mythical ancient era of expanded sociality and understanding among all beings, which features in many African creation myths.

Anonymous, *Assembly of the Animals*, ca. 1965–1975, oil on linen, Addis Ababa, Ethiopia

Stories of Origins

While many scientists insist that they study nonhuman primates for their own sake, few have abstained from engaging in evolutionary narratives and speculations on the origins of humanity. Especially in its popular perception in mass society and the mass media, primatology long held on to two promises: firstly, that it would provide insights into nature in its essential, pure form and into its function in determining human culture and behavior; secondly, that it would offer an understanding of the origins and first evolutionary steps of humanity and society. Together, these promises informed ideas about an original "state of nature." In primatology, this state of nature inevitably reflects Western notions of the origins of sociality.

Since early modernity, the state of nature has been a blend of ideas about the laws of nature, an archaic past, and primitive societies. It has been imagined either as "civilized life purged of its vices," that is, as a lost golden age of innocence, or as a subhuman existence of terrible hardship and deadly struggle devoid of morality: "civilized life stripped of its virtues." *

* Erwin Panofsky, "Et in Arcadia Ego: Poussin and the Elegiac Tradition," in: Panofsky, *Meaning in the Visual Arts*, New York 1955, p. 297

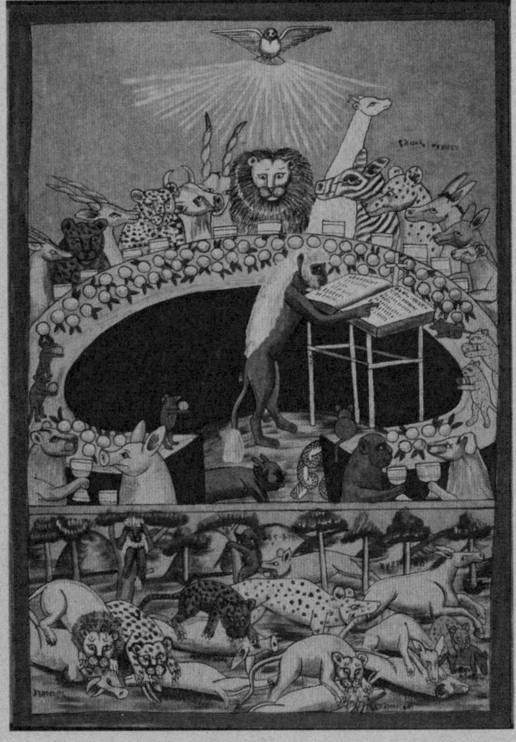

A)

B)

Solly Zuckerman's 1932 work *The Social Life
of Monkeys and Apes*, one of the very first,
and most influential studies of a nonhuman primate society, appeared to confirm
Thomas Hobbes' view that "man is wolf
to man." Zuckerman's book was the outcome
of a short-term study of hamadryas baboons
at London Zoo. Yet while Zuckerman believed he was witnessing a "state of nature,"
in actual fact he was observing a social
catastrophe unfolding in the baboon society
that had been caused on the one hand
by transferring the apes to northern Europe,
and on the other by massive overcrowding
in the colony, which provided only a hun-
dredth of the necessary space. The zoo colony had been created in 1925 with a hundred
males, at a time when scientists had no
knowledge of the behavior patterns and
social system of this species. By 1927, when
thirty females joined the group, only fifty-
six males remained; the rest had died of
injuries incurred during fights.

J. E. Saunders, "The Bigamous Family
Party of Monkey Hill," in: Solly Zuckerman,
The Social Life of Monkeys and Apes,
New York 1932, plate XII, p. 145

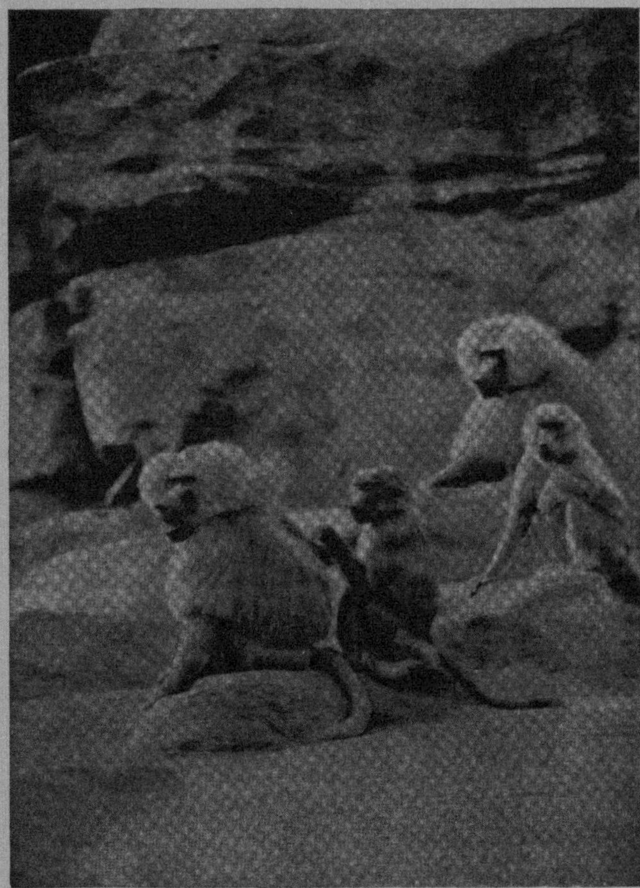

THE BIGAMOUS FAMILY PARTY OF MONKEY HILL

The male in the background was not connected with the other three
animals (See p. 144 and compare with plate XI)

B)

In primatology, the assumption of a basic primate nature was reflected in the search for a model of a "primate society" or a definitive "primate pattern." The male dominated baboon society that had first been studied by Solly Zuckerman remained the most frequent reference, with other primate societies competing only briefly. Zuckerman's claims about dominance and the central role of males captured the collective imagination more than any other work. Many people have found the resulting story of human origins a satisfying one, especially because it offers plausible explanations for many apparent "human" traits, from technological skills to the economic dependence of females. It took half a century to highlight the shortcomings of the model. (Cf. Linda Marie Fedigan)

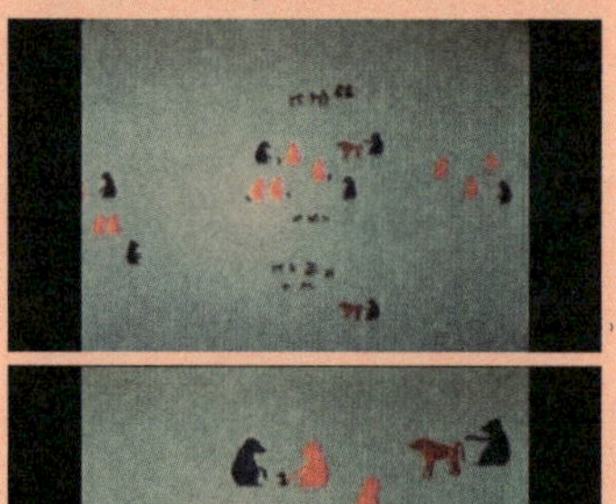
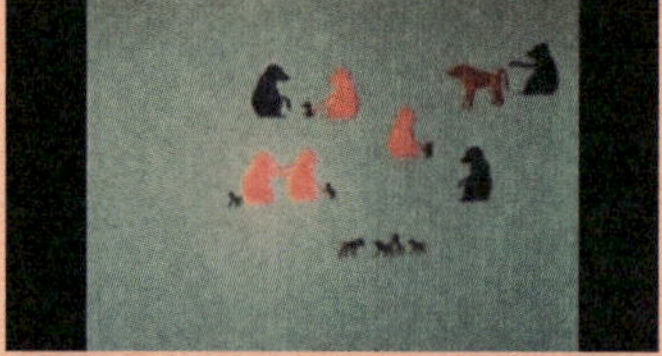
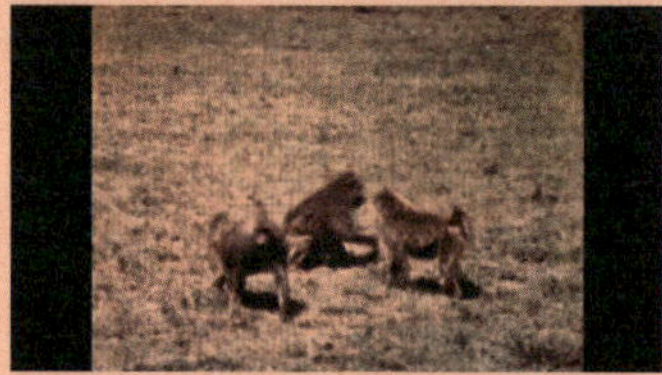
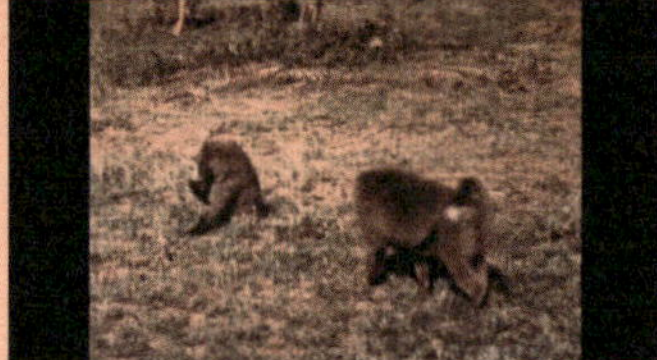
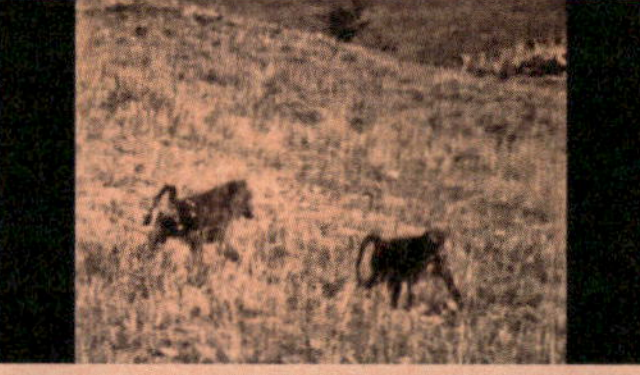
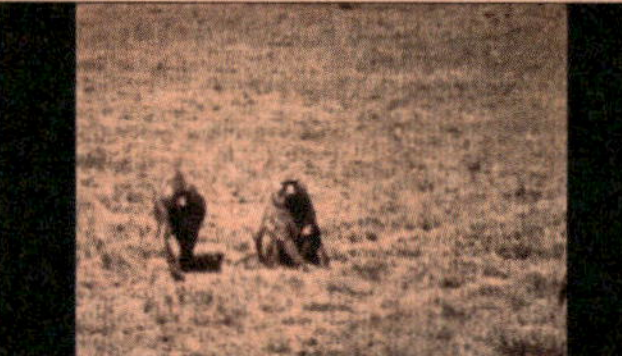
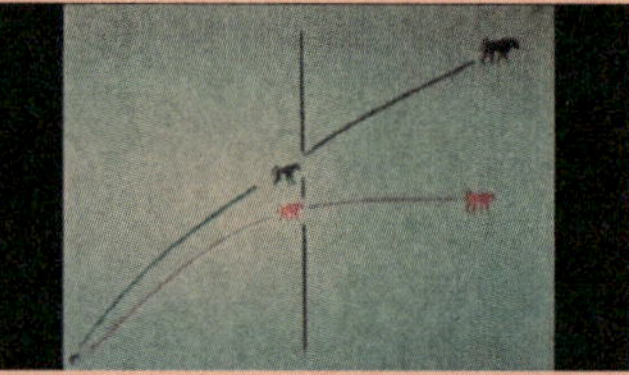
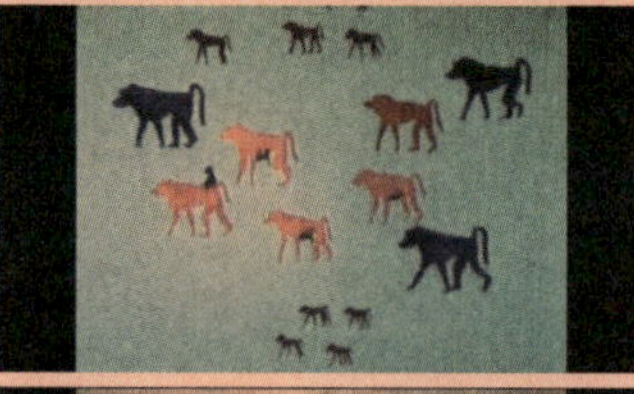
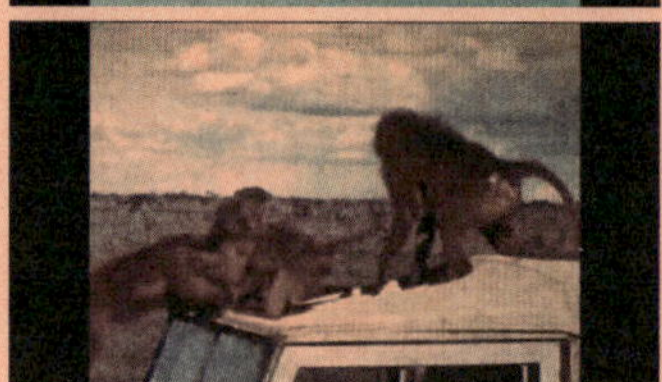

c)

Sherwood Washburn and Irven DeVore,
Baboon Social Organiziation, 1963, 17 min.

c)

"[T]ake one common baboon-type society,
add hunting and its consequences, and the
sum equals early human social life. [...]
Human behavioral characteristics which
have been traced to a hunting way of life:
1. the reduction of canines and increased skill
in the manufacture and use of tools and
weapons; 2. bipedalism (two-footed locomotion); 3. growth of the human brain and
human intelligence; 4. sharing of food;
5. sexual division of labor such that males
provide sustenance as well as protection,
and females provide sexual and reproductive
functions; 6. the human nuclear family;
7. continual sexual receptivity of the female
in order to attract and hold a provider-male
permanently; 8. the incest taboo, to avoid
disrupting nuclear families; 9. exogamy
or the exchange of females; 10. cooperation
replacing competition among males; 11. male
bonding and prominence in social, especially political life; 12. language, in order
to stalk and bring down prey cooperatively;
13. territoriality, larger home ranges and
increased mobility; 14. aesthetics, developed
from the appreciation of beautiful tools;
15. pleasure in killing. The model suggests,
then, that a prehuman ape came out of the
African forest and 'baboonized' (a term
coined by Pfeiffer 1972: 315) its social life
in order to survive the dangers of the savan-
nah, and developed extensive cognitive,
technical, and social skills as part of its adaptive complex as the best hunting species
the world has ever known."

Linda Marie Fedigan, *Primate Paradigms:
Sex Roles and Social Bonds*, Chicago 1982,
pp. 309–311

"We were born of risen apes, not fallen
angels, and the apes were armed killers
besides. And so what shall we wonder at?
Our murders and massacres and missiles,
and our irreconcilable regiments?"

Robert Ardrey, *African Genesis: A Personal
Investigation into the Animal Origins
and Nature of Man*, New York 1961, p. 348

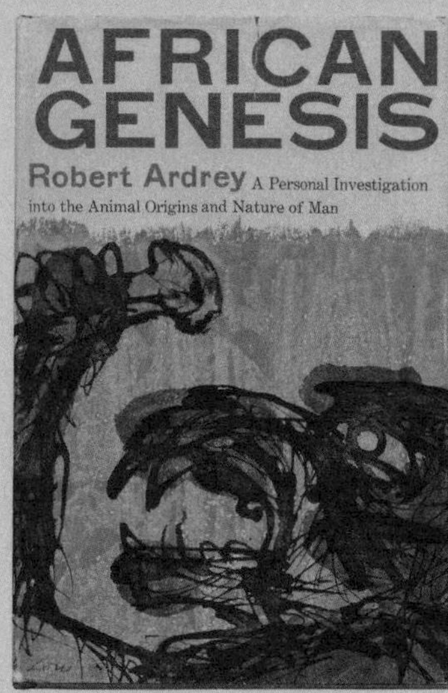

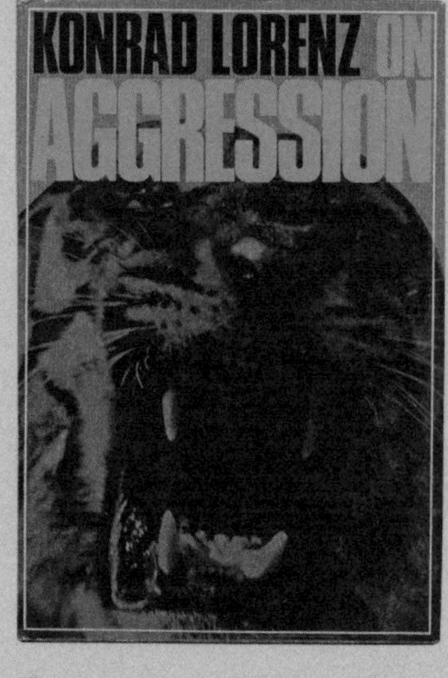

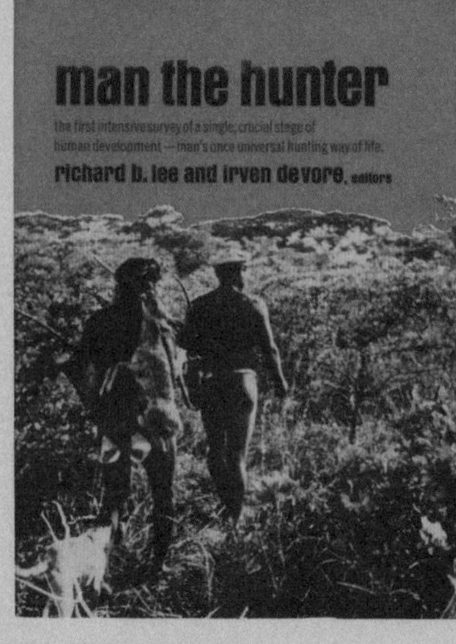

D)

E)

F)

D)

Robert Ardrey's contention is that powerful aggressiveness is one aspect of a set of biological instincts related to territory, status, and sex, and that humans merely constitute one part of a combative lineage with possessive and aggressive inclinations. The Africa hypothesis posits that humans are inherently genocidal: When bands of *Homo sapiens* migrated out of Africa, they advanced into Eurasia by supposedly murdering all other bipedal apes they ran into, including the species most similar to them, the Neanderthals.

Robert Ardrey, *African Genesis: A Personal Investigation into the Animal Origins and Nature of Man*, New York 1961

E)

In *On Aggression* Konrad Lorenz links Darwin's notion of "the struggle of the species," which drives evolution forward, with a fighting instinct in beast and man that is directed against members of the same species. According to Lorenz, this urge stems from an instinct to defend, defeat a rival for a desired female, or protect the young and defenseless of the species.

Konrad Lorenz, *On Aggression*, London 1966

F)

Man the Hunter is a compilation of articles based on a 1966 conference of the same name dedicated to hunter-gatherer studies, which was organized by Irven DeVore and Richard B. Lee. Although devoted to the masculine line of argument in the style of Solly Zuckerman, one surprising conclusion of the conference texts is the hypothesis that women, rather the male hunters, were the main breadwinners in hunter-gatherer societies.

Irven DeVore and Richard B. Lee (eds.), *Man the Hunter: The First Intensive Survey of a Single, Crucial Stage of Human Development—Man's Once Universal Hunting Way of Life*, New Brunswick 2009 [1968]

[Quote]

"Everything turned on a strategy: energy budgets, foraging patterns, genetic investment possibilities, sexual deceit payoffs, social maneuvers. Sociobiology emphasized the genetic aspects of social strategies; socioecology emphasized the intricate current market conditions of making a primate living given a particular body size, sex, species, habitat, age, and so on. Primatologists began to theorize and document complex mental and emotional capacities of simians whose lives evidenced extensive, likely conscious, strategic behavior. [...] Genes and minds are the key 'strategic' players in late capitalist bio-politics. [...] Primates became model yuppies."

Donna Haraway, *Primate Visions. Gender, Race, and Nature in the World of Modern Science*, New York 1989, p. 128

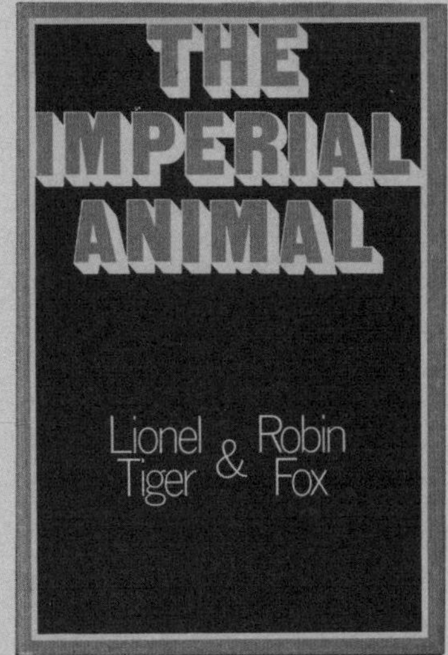

G)

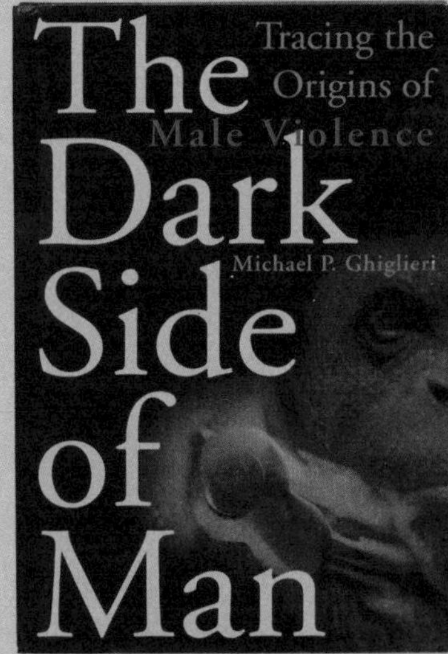

I)

G)

Lionel Tiger and Robin Fox divulge how the evolutionary past and genetic codes of human beings determine our social interactions, based on a social carnivore logic that prevails in human evolution.

Lionel Tiger and Robin Fox, *The Imperial Animal*, New York 1972

H)

Edward Wilson argues that the social behavior of humans and animals is vested in evolutionary principles, explaining social behavior entirely in terms of self-maximizing biological processes. *Sociobiology* is the first book to introduce the new scientific field. Criticism of sociobiology usually assumed the form of a contention that genes play an ultimate role in human behavior and that traits such as aggressiveness can be explained by biology rather than a person's social environment. But sociobiology not only produced questionable metaphors about trade-offs of costs and benefits, it also constituted a scientific breakthrough in being the first to acknowledge that "our very socialness antedates Hobbes and Durkheim by millions of years, that our very body, our very genes, have been shaped and selected inside some sort of social order."* Hence sociobiology is not necessarily a reductionist application of biology to society, but rather a *socialization* of biology.

* Email excerpt from Bruno Latour, quoted in: Shirley C. Strum and Linda Marie Fedigan (eds.), *Primate Encounters: Models of Science, Gender, and Society*, Chicago 2000, p. 313

Edward O. Wilson, *Sociobiology: The New Synthesis*, Cambridge, Massachusetts 1998 [1975]

I)

The Dark Side of Man develops Michael P. Ghiglieri's contention that male violence is largely innate, the product of millions of years of evolution. Taking the examples of rape, murder, and war, he draws up a map that substantiates the male proclivity for violence and then suggests strategies that would enable modern society to curb the consequences of man's natural violent instincts.

Michael P. Ghiglieri, *The Dark Side of Man: Tracing the Origins of Male Violence*, Reading, Massachusetts 1999

[Quote]

"The several theories developed under the rubric of sociobiology generated many new hypotheses, some of which were hotly contested. Reproductive strategies, including mating strategies and rearing strategies, assumed center stage. Differences in the costs of reproduction for males and females produced a 'battle of the sexes' (Dawkins 1978). Parents and offspring also had their 'battle of the generations' (Dawkins 1978; Trivers 1972). Researchers often interpreted examples of cooperation as competition in disguise."

Shirley C. Strum and Linda M. Fedigan, "Changing views of Primate Society," in: id. (eds.), *Primate Encounters. Models of Science, Gender, and Society*, Chicago 2000, p. 19

J)

Ashley Montagu analyzed and discussed the
ideas of Peter Kropotkin, republishing
the latter's 1902 work *Mutual Aid: A Factor
in Evolution* in 1955. Montagu considered
the instinct for violence to be overvalued,
and conversely, the importance of cooperation to be undervalued. Published in 1968
and edited by Montagu, *Man and Aggression*
contains a series of essays that engage
with the theoretical and methodological
inadequacies of Robert Ardrey's and Konrad
Lorenz's theses on aggression. Montagu
clearly places the accent on nurture within
the nature–nurture debate, stating in the
introduction that "the notable thing
on human behavior is that it is learned."

M. F. Ashley Montagu (ed.), *Man and
Aggression*, New York 1973 [1968]

K)

In *Woman's Evolution*, Evelyn Reed constructs
theses on sociocultural development and
goes in search of the original forms of social
organization. She advances the hypothesis
that the mother-child relationship formed the
basis of the early hunter-gatherer societies,
out of which a matrilineal clan system
emerged within a largely matriarchal society.
Reed is considered the pioneer of Marxist
feminism.

Evelyn Reed, *Woman's Evolution: From
Matriarchal Clan to Patriarchal Family*,
New York 1975

L)

Edited by Frances Dahlberg, this book examines the role of women and men in proto-
history, essentially advancing theses on the
contribution of women to the history of
human development. Sociobiological concepts
(such as kin selection) are applied to new
research findings from chimpanzee field
research, archaeological discoveries, and
contemporary hunter-gatherer societies.
The book includes an essay by Adrienne
Zihlmann entitled "Women as Shapers of the
Human Adaptation" in which she criticizes
the killer-ape and hunter hypothesis, arguing
that, firstly, women and children make
up 75 per cent of society, secondly, women
are the primary socializers, and thirdly,
the human diet is not essentially carnivorous.

Frances Dahlberg (ed.), *Woman the Gatherer*,
New Haven, Connecticut 1981

M)

In *The Descent of Woman*, Elaine Morgan
undertakes a new reading of what Desmond
Morris termed the "naked ape." She defines
the attempt to explain human development–walking upright, nudity, the use of
weapons–solely in terms of hunting as
androcentric, compiling a "housewife smart
reply to Desmond Morris"* in which she
pays tribute to the female gatherers who no
longer simply sat around naked waiting
for the men to return impassioned from the
hunt.

* Donna Haraway, *Primate Visions: Gender,
Race, and Nature in the World of Modern
Science*, New York 1989, p. 127

Elaine Morgan, *The Descent of Woman*,
London 1972

N)

Nancy Tanner focuses on the role of female
gatherers in the history of anthropogenesis
and expresses doubts in masculine fantasies.
In her study, the chimpanzee serves as a
model for the ancestral population, with the
hope that it might shed light on how the
capacity for culture evolved, i.e. intellectual
abilities, communication, and community.
Nancy Tanner and Adrienne Zihlmann
see women as essential factors in evolution,
especially with respect to capabilities
such as cooperation and communication.
Processes of sharing, appeasement, and
exchange in the mother–child relationship
promote both language development and
cognitive abilities. Tanner and Zihlmann
claim that because women select not the
strongest sexual partners, but those with the
greatest social competence, this also has
the effect of reducing the role of aggression
within the evolutionary process. Comparisons
with the social structure of chimpanzees
were designed to support this thesis.

Nancy Makepeace Tanner, *On Becoming
Human*, New York 1981

O)

"The law of competition has had to bow
before a healthy dose of cooperation, whose
crucial contributions to evolution are now
widely acknowledged, with symbiosis accepted as the very origin of multicellular life
(Margulis 1999; Nowak 2011)."*

* Brian Massumi, *What Animals Teach Us
about Politics*, Durham/New Connecticut
2014, p. 1

Lynn Margulis, *Symbiotic Planet: A New Look
at Evolution*, New York 1998

MAN
AND
AGGRESSION
SECOND EDITION
EDITED BY
ASHLEY MONTAGU

J)

WOMAN
THE GATHERER
Edited by Frances Dahlberg

L)

ON BECOMING
HUMAN
NANCY MAKEPEACE TANNER

N)

WOMAN'S
EVOLUTION
From matriarchal clan
to patriarchal family
EVELYN
REED
Author of SEXISM AND SCIENCE and
PROBLEMS OF WOMEN'S LIBERATION

K)

The
DESCENT
of
WOMAN
Elaine
Morgan

M)

"Best Biology Book of 1998" —Library Journal
SYMBIOTIC PLANET
[A NEW LOOK AT EVOLUTION]
LYNN MARGULIS

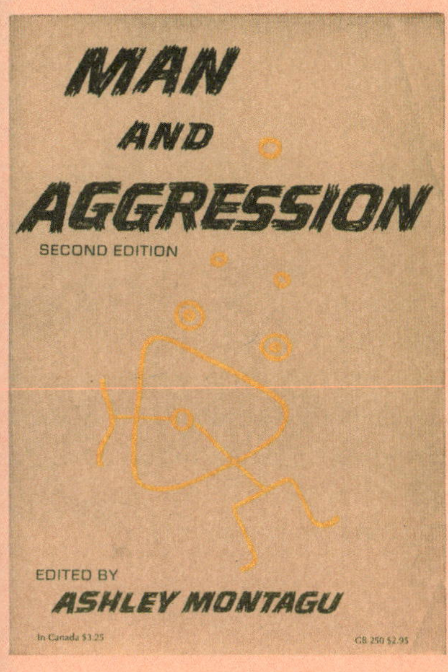

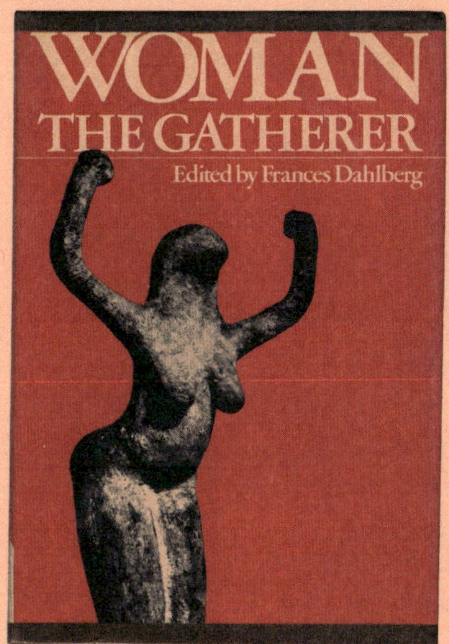

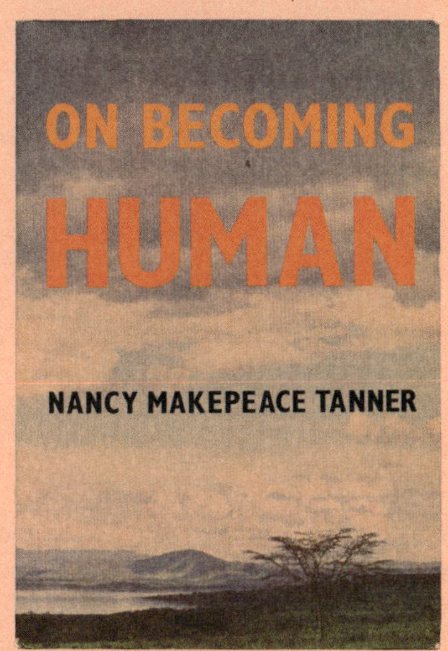

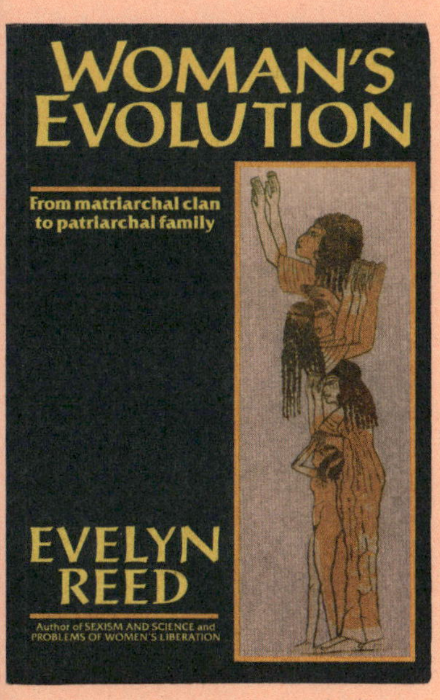

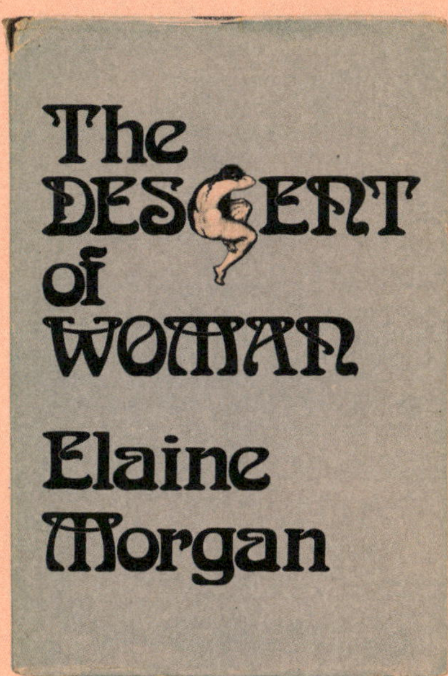

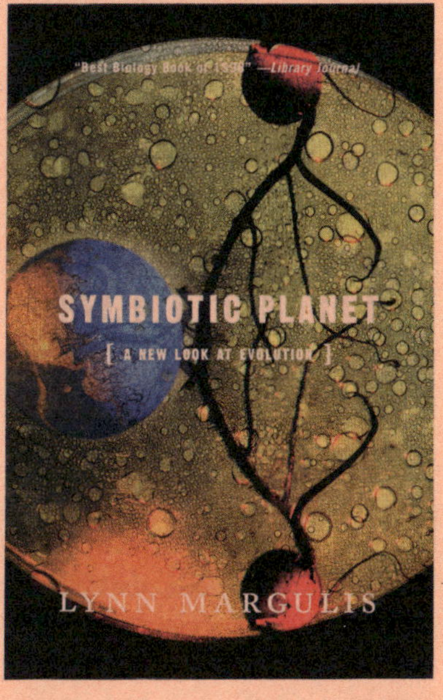

O)

In post-World War II science, monkeys and apes were used as stand-ins for people across a vast array of human problems, such as population regulation, mother-infant bonding, depression, and cooperation in corporations. In the 1960s and 1970s, research funds designated for the cold war and for psychiatry were used to support studies connecting war and aggression to stress, arousal, and territoriality, drawing biosocial lessons from the disasters of modernity by directly transferring them from the analysis of nonhuman populations. A first postwar phase focused on social stability, connecting psychiatric concerns with questions about controlling and managing mass societies. Before the war C. R. Carpenter had pioneered the study of primate society as a "semiotic project," in which researchers studied communicative behavior such as gestures and vocalizations as well as the development of symbolic social control systems. Now this gave way to a cybernetic understanding of primate societies, an approach that bridged linguistics, social psychology, biology, and, increasingly, technology and computing through the overarching concept of communication, which is seen here as a means of regulation and control. The notion of communication systems permitted the boundaries between organisms and machines to be radically questioned; where allegedly "natural" differences had hitherto existed, new distinctions and differences were now being constituted. This shift away from an initial emphasis on the primacy of sociality and the priority of "organic wholes" can be described as a "transition from an organics to a technics of control of the social body." Carpenter himself, who had pioneered "the practices enabling scientists to watch gibbons living freely in the 1930s," as Donna Haraway writes, "ended his field work surveying a braindamaged colony in a high-tech narrative of remote control."*

In the 1970s, modeling human society through primates began to take the form of a binary opposition of models, based on competition on the one hand and cooperation on the other. The weight has since shifted from initially favoring the former to increasingly emphasizing the role of the latter. This development has been inseparable from the growing number of field studies, and a recognition that a life lived in captivity often produces asocial behavior and pathologies. Moreover, it has been associated with a number of feminist scientists who, while exerting a growing influence in their field, have counteracted the male bias behind the narratives of dominance and competition.

* Donna Haraway, *Primate Visions: Gender, Race, and Nature in the World of Modern Science*, New York 1989, p. 108

C. R. Carpenter's 1940 study on gibbons
was the first time that sociometric techniques
had been used in primate research. Socio-
metry, a method of social psychology that
was widespread in the 1930s, examines
the patterns of group formation and the
self-regulation mechanisms of social organizations. Its most important tool was the
sociogram, developed by J. L. Monroe, which
was designed to provide a schematic representation of the relationship dynamics
within a group. Carpenter's sociograms thus
employ vector arrows to depict the relationships within a troop of apes, recording
all interactions, such as instances of power
being exercised, alliances being constructed,
and conflicts. The insights thereby acquired
could then be used for prognoses and
corrective interventions in group behavior.
Carpenter even envisaged this model being applied to the management of human
societies. The sociogram consequently
established a bridge between the natural and
social sciences that was extended in the
postwar period by the introduction of the
cybernetic paradigm.

Clarence Ray Carpenter, *Sociometric
diagram from Carpenter's Asiatic Primate
Expedition field notes*, 1937

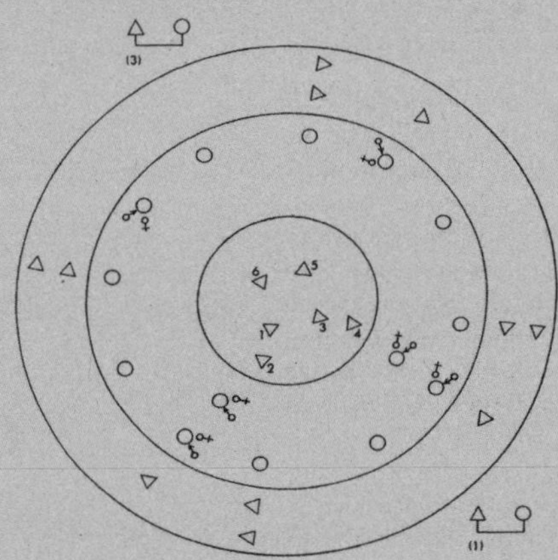
Inner circle: male hierarchy (1=α etc.)
Intermediate circle: females, infants, juveniles
Outer circle: peripheral males
Outside: consort pairs

♂♀ infants still with mother

Figure 23.1 *Multi-male group model*

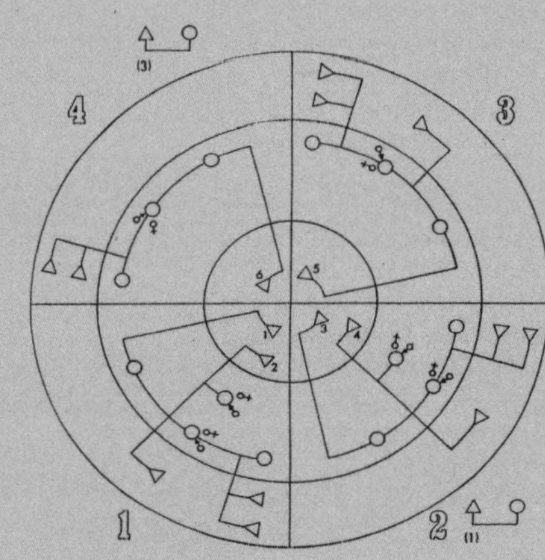
Inner circle: male hierarchy (1=α etc.)
Intermediate circle: females, infants, juveniles
Outer circle: peripheral males
Outside: consort pairs
Quadrants: matrilineages ranked 1 through 4

♂♀ infants still with mother

Figure 23.2 *Multi-male group model with kinship connections*

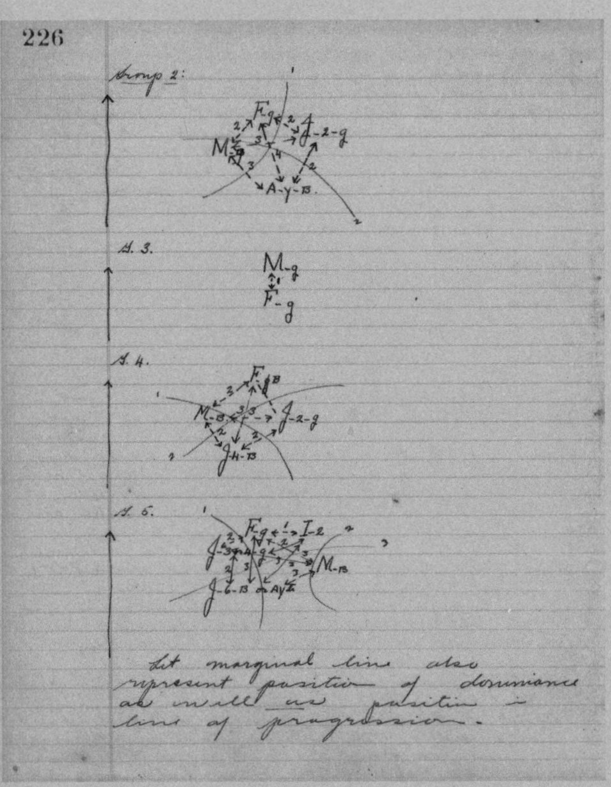

B)

Robin Fox, Multi-male group model, "Primate
Kin and Human Kinship," 1975, in: Robert
Parkin and Linda Stone (eds.), *Kinship and
Family: An Anthropological Reader*, New York
2004, p. 432

C)

Robin Fox, Multi-male group model with
kinship connections, "Primate Kin and
Human Kinship," 1975, in: Robert Parkin and
Linda Stone (eds.), *Kinship and Family:
An Anthropological Reader*, New York 2004,
p. 433

In order to depict the network of relationships within nonhuman primate societies,
Robin Fox employed diagrams in his
kinship studies. They illustrate the spatial
distribution of the apes from a bird's
eye view, with males symbolized by triangles
and females by circles. In a "multi-male"
group (B) the dominant males occupy
the center and are encircled by the females
and young animals. The young males are
banished to the periphery. Their goal is to
gradually work their way to the center
of power in order to reproduce successfully.
Connecting lines in the diagram (C) depict
the kinship relationships within the group.
They demonstrate that "multi-male" troops
are organized according to hierarchical
lines of descent, while "one-male" troops
(D) form mating groups composed of males,
each with their own permanent "harem."
According to Fox, the two models are mutu-
ally exclusive within ape societies: They
are structured according to either one model
or the other. Fox considered this recon-
ciling of two models in a common system
to be the decisive step in the development
of mankind.

Robin Fox, One-male group model, "Primate
Kin and Human Kinship," 1975, in: Robert
Parkin and Linda Stone (eds.), *Kinship and
Family: An Anthropological Reader*, New York
2004, p. 434

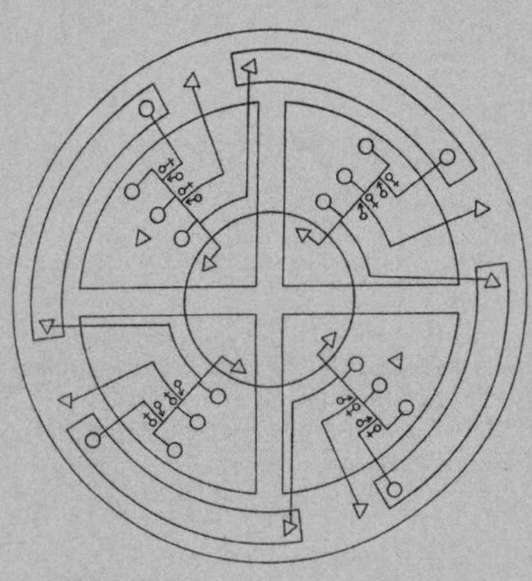

Figure 23.3 *One-male group model*

"What has gone definitively is the privileged
status attaching to life or consciousness.
Organisms become biotic components, highly
interesting, but not ontologically special,
in cybernetic systems sciences."

Donna Haraway, *Primate Visions: Gender,
Race, and Nature in the World of Modern
Science*, New York 1989, p. 103

[Quote]

"Altmann helped turn the widely felt promises
of cybernetics and communications theories
generally into technical achievements in
evolutionary animal behavior science in the
1950s. Wilson has become famous and
infamous for his versions of sociobiological
theory, while Stuart Altmann has moved
more in the direction of socioecology and
away from the communications theory-
oriented approaches that characterized his
first field study. But, Altmann's early debts
to 1940s and 1950s communications technologies illustrate an important thread in the
weave of evolutionary biology as a discourse
on technology and the organism as a natural
communication system."

Donna Haraway, *Primate Visions: Gender,
Race, and Nature in the World of Modern
Science,* New York 1989, p. 101

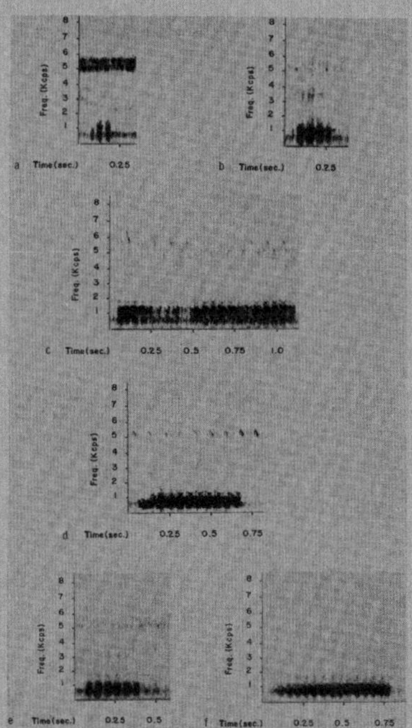

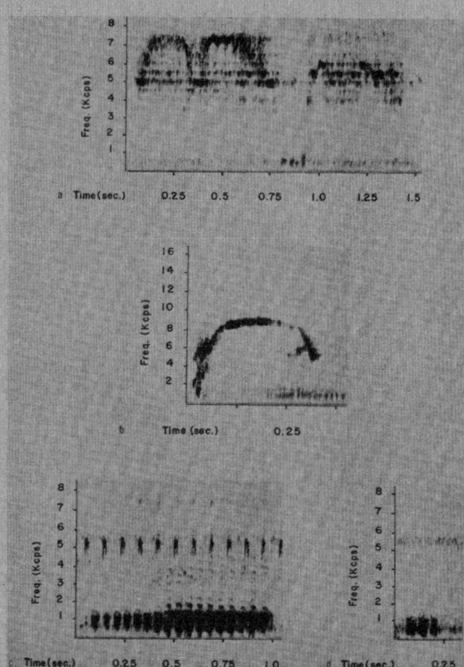

PLATE 16.4.—(a) Short *Rraugh*, (b) Short *Aarr-rraugh*, (c) Long *Rraugh*, (d) Long *Aarr-rraugh*, (e) Short *Aarr*, (f) Long *Aarr*. (Ignore background noise between 5 and 6 Kcps.)

PLATE 16.5.—(a) Weaning Scream, (b) Weaning Squeal, (c) Weaning *rrr*, (d) *Eh, eh*. (Ignore background noise between 5 and 6 Kcps.)

E)

E)

Thomas T. Struhsaker, the *rraugh* sound
and the scream, "Auditory Communication
among Vervet Monkeys," in: Stuart A.
Altmann (ed.), *Social Communication among
Primates*, Chicago 1967, Plate 16.4, 16.5,
no page

F)

Robert E. Miller, "Experimental Approaches
to the Physiological and Behavioral Concomitants of Affective Communication in
Rhesus Monkeys," in: Stuart A. Altmann
(ed.): *Social Communication among Primates*,
Chicago 1967, pp. 128–129

this discriminated avoidance-reward conditioning, however, the monkey v
first trained to avoid shock, then to obtain reward, and finally both kinds
stimuli were randomly mixed in test sessions until the animals achieved v
rigorous criteria of acquisition.

There were six categories of lever pressing to be considered in the criteria
conditioning. There were two kinds of conditioned response, for examp
the avoidance bar pulled during avoidance CS presentation or the food l
pressed during reward CS presentation. Likewise, there were two categories
error, for example, the avoidance bar pulled during presentation of a rewa
CS and vice versa—in our analysis these were called false CR's. Either l
could be operated throughout a session without regard to stimulus presen
tion. These intertrial or spontaneous responses, if they occurred (at a stead
high frequency rate) could provide a baseline from which many spurio
CR's would be expected. In order to insure that a discriminated learning v
established, criteria were required for each source of error. The number of d
served avoidance CR's in a session were compared statistically with false Cl
and with chance expected CR's (derived from spontaneous responses) ar
likewise, the same comparisons were made for reward trials. When all fo
comparisons were statistically significant for three consecutive sessions, t
monkey was judged to have acquired discriminated reward-avoidance con
tioning. Figure 1 illustrates the heart-rate responses of a group of five monke

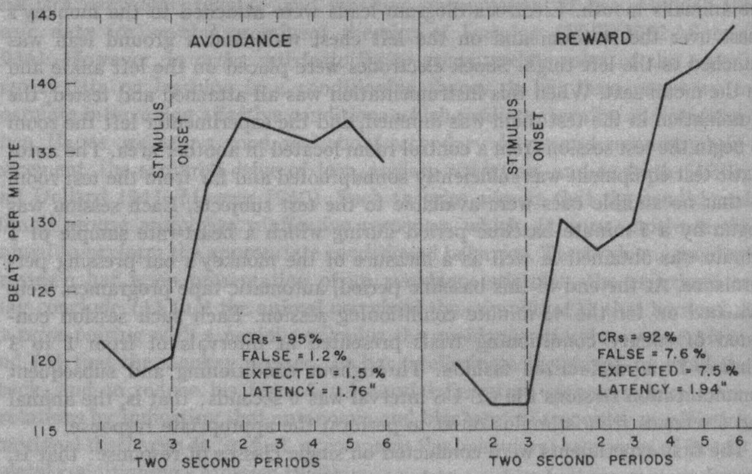

Fig. 1.—Conditioned cardiac responses in five monkeys for the final five conditioni
sessions. The heart-rate response to avoidance stimuli differs significantly in trend from t
heart-rate response to reward stimuli. Instrumental behavior is summarized in the appr
priate panel.

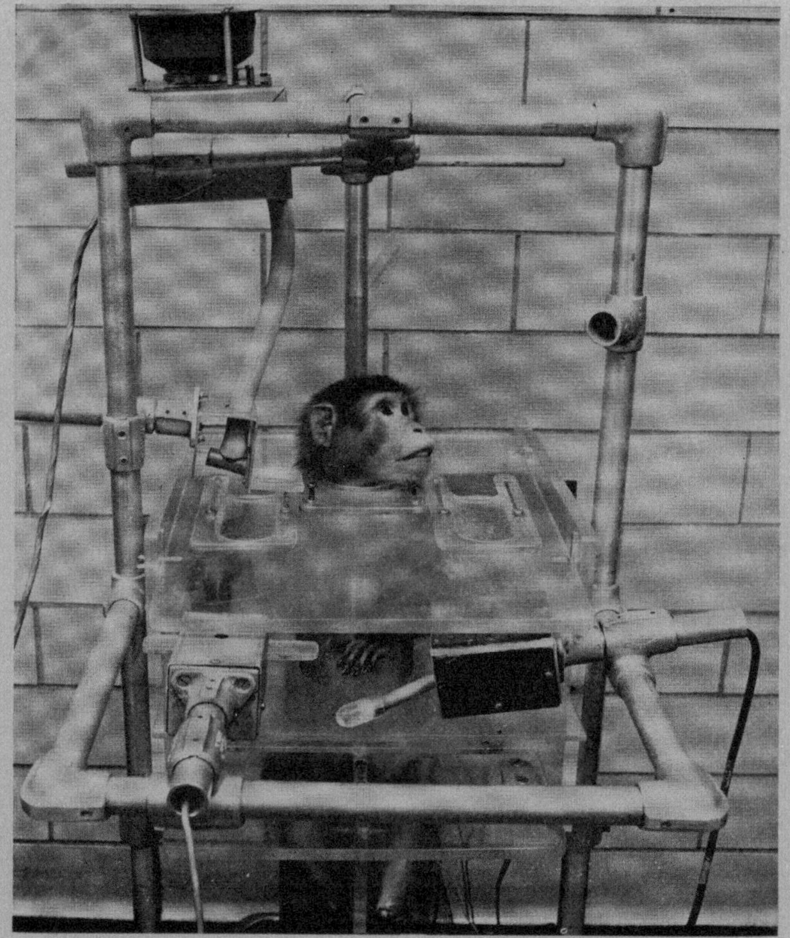

PLATE 8.1.—Front view of an animal prepared to be placed before the tunnel as a "responder." The two bars are attached to the chair and the automatic food vender is in position.

THE CIRCLE
OF EMPATHY

Empathy, once thought to be exclusive to humans,
is in fact widespread among animals. It runs from body
mimicry—yawning when others yawn—to "emotional
contagion," when the self resonates with fear or
joy as it picks up that same emotion in others. At its
most complex, there is sympathy and targeted helping.
While empathy may be most developed in humans,
several other species of animals—most notably apes,
dolphins, and elephants—display similar traits.
These animals understand the predicaments of others
well enough to offer assistance. And yet empathy is
fragile; in our close relatives it is switched on by events
within their community, such as a youngster in distress,
but it is just as easily switched off when it concerns
either those outside the "circle of sympathy" or members
of other species, such as prey.

The debate about empathic engagement centers not
only on its existence in animals, but also on the
circumstances surrounding research, especially the
devastating effects of captivity. However, the discussion
additionally explores the demands of objective science,
which tries to abstain from anthropomorphism
and subjective engagement—but in so doing produces
its own symptoms, such as yielding asocial and
pathological behavior in the research subjects. While
researchers try to find out how mind evolves from
non-mind, they cannot escape the paradox that they
themselves are not outside a social relation, for they
are always already situated within one.

Scientists as long ago as Charles Darwin and William
McDougall anticipated the current evolutionary
ideas of empathy. The latter stated that empathy must
exist in all animals living in groups, meaning those
equipped with a "gregarious instinct,"* because these
animals are innately affected by the emotions of others.
(Cf. Frans de Waal)

* William McDougall, *An Introduction to
Social Psychology*, Boston 1912, p. 296

Is a sense of justice a human privilege?
In order to address this question, in 2003 the
primatologists Sarah F. Brosnan and Frans
de Waal conducted an experiment on
the perception of injustice amongst capuchin
monkeys. This involves two monkeys in
turn being presented with a simple task to
solve. If they are successful, then they each
receive a piece of cucumber as reward.
However, if one of the monkeys witnesses
his neighbor in the next cage receiving
a bigger reward for the same work—a grape
instead of cucumber—then he refuses
to complete the task and protests loudly.
The authors interpret this reaction as
evidence that nonhuman primates also have
a well-trained sense of unfair treatment
and the unequal distribution of resources,
which can be unleashed in a display of emotion. This would form proof that "inequity
aversion," a negative reaction to the experience of inequality, arose long before
mankind in evolutionary history. It would
also mean that animals are equipped
with moral sentiments.

Sarah F. Brosnan and Frans de Waal,
Capuchin Monkeys Reject Unequal Pay, Yerkes
National Primate Research Center, Emory
University, Atlanta, Georgia 2003, 1 min.

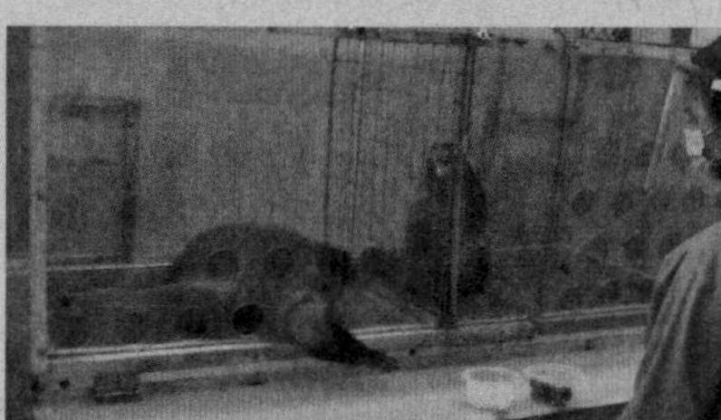

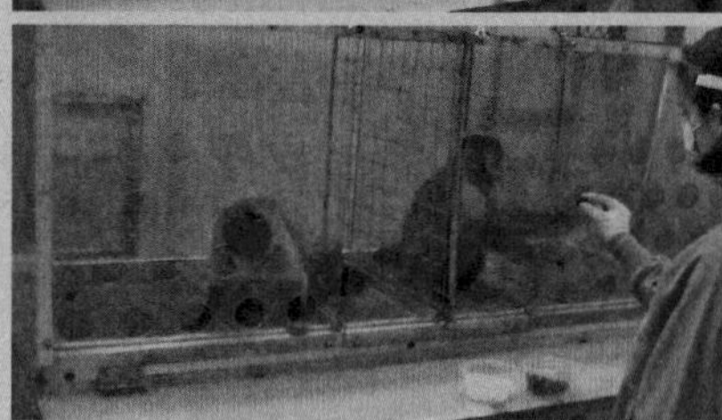

A)

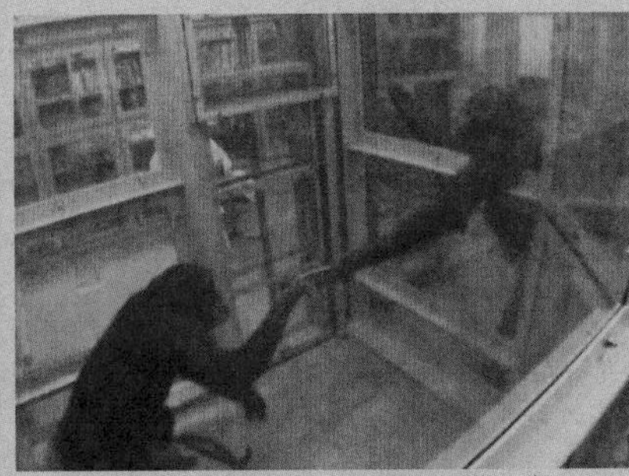

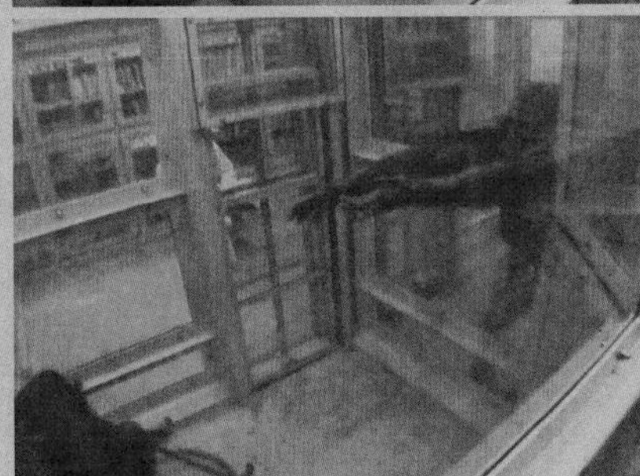

B)

B)

From 2007 to 2009, Shinya Yamamoto, Tatyana Humle, and Masayuki Tanaka of the Primate Research Institute at Kyoto University set up an experiment to test altruism in chimpanzees. In two different settings—"can see" and "cannot see" condition—chimpanzees were placed in adjacent booths with transparent or opaque panels, and each was given a different task that could only be accomplished by using a particular tool. Seven objects were located in the booth of the potential helper, and a valve was installed through which the potential recipient could put his arm to reach for the necessary tool. The researchers found that although the chimpanzees would not spontaneously pass the tool to their neighbor in the other booth, when one chimpanzee put his arm through the valve to request a tool, the other would respond by handing it over. This led the researchers to believe that chimpanzees do help each other, but only upon request.

Video stills: Experiments on chimpanzees' flexible targeted helping, Shinya Yamamoto (Kobe University), Primate Research Institute, Kyoto University 2007–2009, 2 min.

C)

Experimental setup: Experiments on chimpanzees' flexible targeted helping, Shinya Yamamoto (Kobe University), Primate Research Institute, Kyoto University 2007–2009

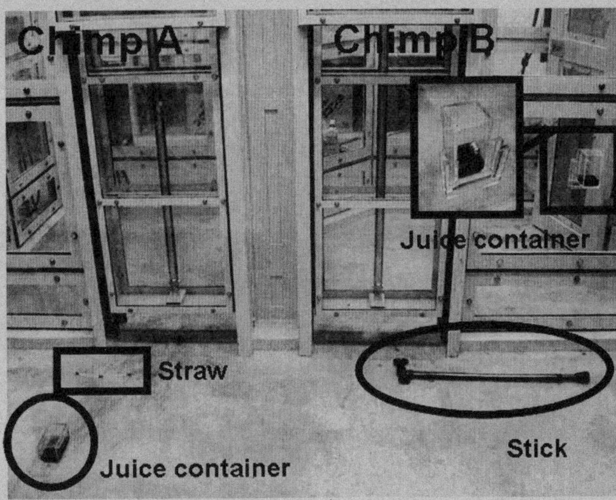

C)

[Quote]

"We would not be where we are today had our ancestors been socially aloof.
     What I see, therefore, is the opposite of the traditional image of a nature 'red in tooth and claw,' in which the individual comes first and society is a mere afterthought. One can't reap the benefits of group life without contributing to it."

Frans de Waal, *Our Inner Ape: A Leading Primatologist Explains Why We Are Who We Are*, New York 2005, p. 228

While laboratory research increasingly led scientists to view the primate's body as a technobiological "system," primatology based on field studies initiated a move away from mechanistic and deterministic explanations, resulting in a wide range of publications on the enormous complexity and variability of primate social life. Gradually, emotional bonds began to replace sex as the "glue" that holds primate societies together—an acknowledgment of the primacy of the bonds that socialization creates between group members, especially between mothers and their offspring. By the end of the 1980s, the idea of a "primate pattern" had finally been refuted. No nonhuman primate society could act as a definitive model for the nature of human society. Research into new species, and the differences among populations of the same species, had produced a picture of sheer ungovernable variability and complexity in primate social "patterns." Furthermore, the discovery and study of bonobo matriarchy undermined prevailing conceptions of human evolutionary development based on baboons or chimpanzees. The transition from mechanistic explanations, biological determinism, and reductionism towards a richer picture of variation and complexity in primate social life, establishing the primacy of social bonds, is inextricably linked to an increasingly feminist criticism that challenged the exclusive focus on the role of the male in social groups.

[Quote]

"At least on a phenomenological level, sociality in most primates is prior to individualism. It took all the resources of late-capitalist economic theory to make the autonomous, competitive individual fill the primate scientist's field of vision."

Donna Haraway, *Primate Visions: Gender, Race, and Nature in the World of Modern Science*, New York 1989, p. 405, note 38

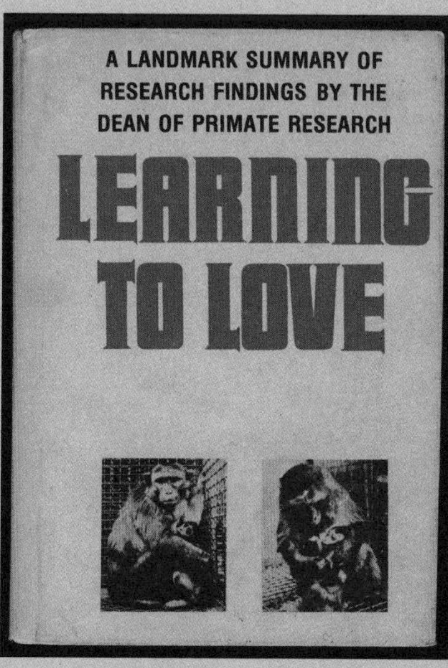

A)

A)

Harry F. Harlow, *Learning to Love*, London / New York 1974 [1971]

B)

At the beginning of the 1930s, the American behavioral scientist Harry F. Harlow established one of the first primate laboratories, where he carried out a series of now famous, albeit ethically highly contentious experiments on the maternal bond amongst rhesus monkeys. Harlow revolutionized developmental psychology at the time, believing that he had penetrated to the essence and origin of love in his experiments. The pictures from his laboratory contributed to the strengthening of the animal rights movement.

Harry F. Harlow and Robert R. Zimmermann, *The Nature and Development of Affection*, 1959, 19 min.

The Complex Affectional
Attachments Are Analyzed
By Using Cloth & Wire
Surrogate Mothers

Contact Comfort, Not
Nursing, Is The Primary
Variable Determining
Affection For The
Mother

Fear Responsiveness
Provides Another Measure
Of Infant — Mother
Attachments

Note Gradual Relaxation
Of The Clutching Response
And Subsequent Visual
Exploration Of The Fear
Stimulus

In The Cloth Mother's
Absence, These Infants
Display Signs Of Extreme
Disturbance

Monkeys Raised On A
Single Wire Surrogate
Obtain No Comfort
From Her Presence

Monkey Babies Are Happy
With Cloth Mothers...

Human Babies Are
Also Attracted!

Both Mothers Were
Constantly Available
In The Living Cage

B)

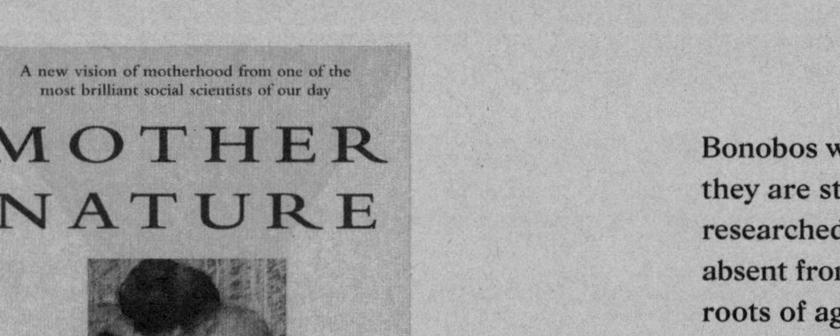

C)

C)

In its early phases primatology unreflectedly propagated the idea that the female sex merely served the reproduction of the species, and as a result had no history of its own. Up until the mid-1960s, primatology's reconstruction of the origin of mankind was based on the model of the superiority, aggressiveness, and competitive behavior of male primates. Female primates were not initially the subject of special research, appearing only as part of the small nuclear family and with respect to the bond between mother and child. It is not hard to see the extent to which this model was influenced by the patriarchal gender structure of Western societies. That the field changed so much during the 1970s and 1980s, and that primatology is now described as a "feminist" discipline, is a result of the influence of a large number of female researchers such as Linda Marie Fedigan and Sarah Blaffer Hrdy. The latter demonstrated through her research "that female monkeys and apes are not at all passive. Like male primates, the females seek a competitive advantage, are sexually active, choose their partners, compete with other females for rank and resources, and defend their offspring to the death. [...] Blaffer Hrdy's research led her to conclude that female primates are nowhere near as suppressed as they are within the species of Homo sapiens!" (Astrid Deuber-Mankowsy in this volume)

Sarah Blaffer Hrdy, *Mother Nature: Maternal Instincts and How They Shape the Human Species*, New York 1999

Bonobo

Bonobos were first discovered as a species in 1929; they are still considerably less well known and researched than other great apes, and were completely absent from the long discussion on the evolutionary roots of aggression. Although closely related to chimpanzees, their social organization is very different. In 1992 it became public knowledge that bonobo societies are matriarchal in character. Their organizational forms overturned previous assumptions about the primary role of male dominance in the evolution of primate societies.

[Quote]

"Bonobos are egalitarian primates that substitute sex for aggression: they resolve conflict through sexual contact. Females occupy prominent positions in society, and the high points of the bonobo's social life are conflict resolution and sensitivity to others. [...] I estimate that three quarters of the sexual activity I saw at the zoo had nothing to do with reproduction: it frequently involved members of the same sex or took place during the infertile portion of a female's menstrual cycle. [...] The sheer variety of erotic contacts is impressive, especially if we include the sporadic oral sex, massage of another individual's genitals, and tongue-kissing. The same within-group use of sex seems to extend to relations between groups. This is quite a contrast with chimpanzees, in which males are known to patrol the borders of their territory and occasionally invade their neighbors', setting off lethal battles."

Frans de Waal, *The Ape and the Sushi Master: Cultural Reflections of a Primatologist*, New York 2001, pp. 129–132

D)

Ian Parker, "Swingers: Bonobos are celebrated as peace-loving, matriarchal, and sexually liberated. Are they?," *The New Yorker*, July 30, 2007, cover and p. 78, 80

E)

Cynthia Moses, *The New Chimpanzees*, National Geographic Society, 1995, 57 min.

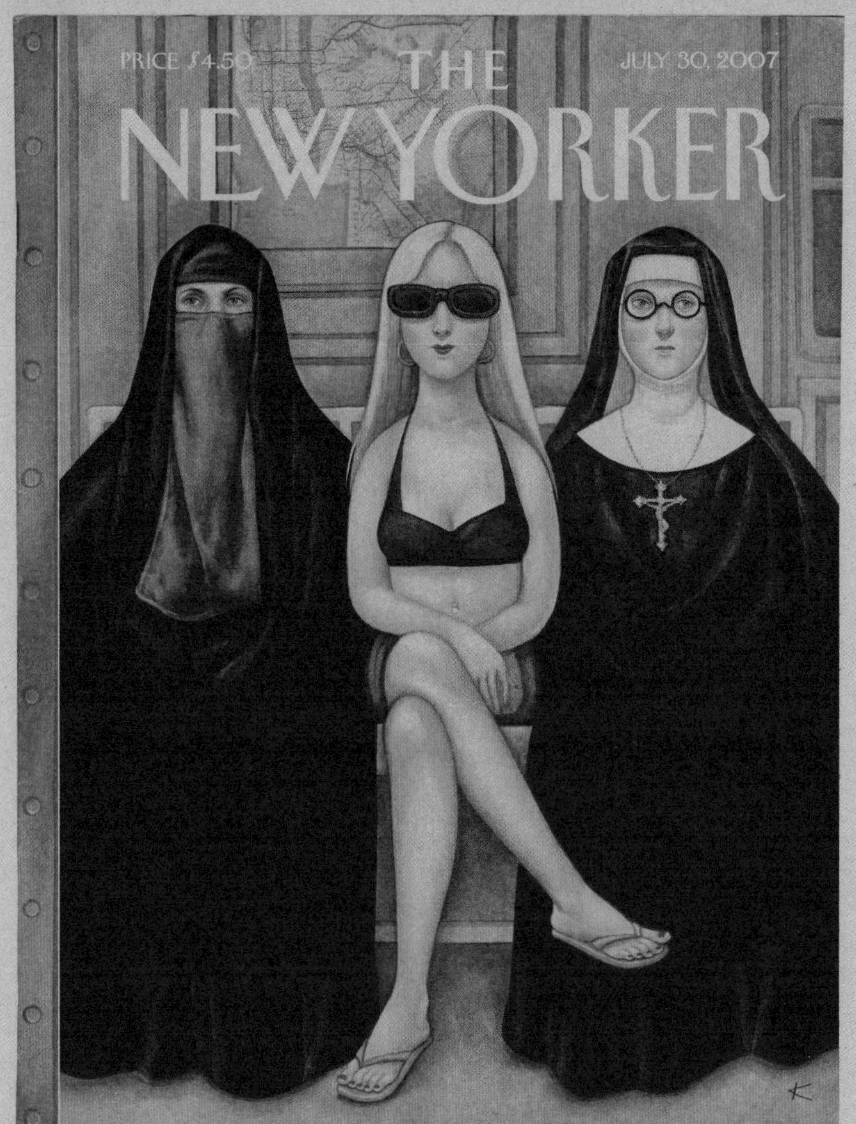

D)

SWINGERS

Bonobos are celebrated as peace-loving, matriarchal, and sexually liberated. Are they?

BY IAN PARKER

On a Saturday evening a few months ago, a fund-raiser was held in a downtown Manhattan yoga studio to benefit the bonobo, a species of African ape that is very similar to—but, some say, far nicer than—the chimpanzee. A flyer for the event depicted a bonobo sitting in the crook of a tree, a superimposed guitar in its left hand, alongside the message "Save the Hippie Chimps!" An audience of young, shoeless people sat cross-legged on a polished wooden floor, listening to Indian-accented music and eating snacks prepared by Bonobo's, a restaurant on Twenty-third Street that serves raw vegetarian food. According to the restaurant's take-out menu, "Wild bonobos are happy, pleasure-loving creatures whose lifestyle is dictated by instinct and Mother Nature."

The event was arranged by the Bonobo Conservation Initiative, an organization based in Washington, D.C., which works in the Democratic Republic of Congo to protect bonobo habitats and to combat illegal trading in bush meat. Sally Jewell Coxe, the group's founder and president, stood to make a short presentation. She showed slides of bonobos, including one captioned "MAKE LOVE NOT WAR," and said that the apes, which she described as "bisexual," engaged in various kinds of sexual activity in order to defuse conflict and maintain a tranquil society. There was applause. "Bonobos are into peace and love and harmony," Coxe said, then joked, "They might even have been the first ape to discover marijuana." Images of bonobos were projected onto the wall behind her: they looked like chimpanzees but had longer hair, flatter faces, pinker lips, smaller ears, narrower bodies, and, one might say, more gravitas—a chimpanzee's arched brow looks goofy, but a bonobo's low, straight brow sets the face in what is easy to read as earnest contemplativeness.

I spoke to a tall man in his forties who went by the single name Wind, and who had driven from his home in North Carolina to sing at the event. He was a musician and a former practitioner of "metaphysical counselling," which he also referred to as clairvoyance. He said that he had encountered bonobos a few years ago at Georgia State University, at the invitation of Sue Savage-Rumbaugh, a primatologist known for experiments that test the language-learning abilities of bonobos. (During one of Wind's several visits to G.S.U., Peter Gabriel, the British pop star, was also there; Gabriel played a keyboard, another keyboard was put in front of a bonobo, and Wind played flutes and a small drum.) Bonobos are remarkable, Wind told me, for being capable of "unconditional love." They were "tolerant, patient, forgiving, and supportive of one another." Chimps, by contrast, led brutish lives of "aggression, ego, and plotting." As for humans, they had some innate stock of bonobo temperament, but they too often behaved like chimps. (The chimp-bonobo division is strongly felt by devotees of the latter. Wind told me that he once wore a chimpanzee T-shirt to a bonobo event, and "got shit for it.")

It was Wind's turn to perform. "Help Gaia and Gaia will help you," he chanted into a microphone, in a booming voice that made people jump. "Help bonobo and bonobo will help you."

In recent years, the bonobo has found a strange niche in the popular imagination, based largely on its reputation for peacefulness and promiscuity. The Washington *Post* recently described the species as copulating "incessantly"; the *Times* claimed that the bonobo "stands out from the chest-thumping masses as an example of amicability, sensitivity and, well, humaneness"; a PBS wildlife film began with the words "Where chimpanzees fight and murder, bonobos are peace-makers. And, unlike chimps, it's not the bonobo males but the females who have the power." The Kinsey Institute claims on its Web site that "every bonobo—female, male, infant, high or low status—seeks and responds to kisses." And, in Los Angeles, a sex adviser named Susan Block promotes what she calls "The Bonobo Way" on public-access television. (In brief: "Pleasure eases pain; good sex defuses tension; love lessens violence; you can't very well fight a war while you're having an orgasm.") In newspaper columns and on the Internet, bonobos are routinely described as creatures that shun violence and live in egalitarian or female-dominated communities; more rarely, they are said to avoid meat. These behaviors are thought to be somehow linked to their unquenchable sexual appetites, often expressed in the missionary position. And because the bonobo is the "closest relative" of humans, its comportment is said to instruct us in the fundamentals of human nature. To underscore the bonobo's status as a signpost species—a guide to human virtue, or at least modern dating—it is said to walk upright. (The Encyclopædia Britannica depicts the species in a bipedal pose, like a chimpanzee in a sitcom.)

This pop image of the bonobo—equal parts dolphin, Dalai Lama, and Warren Beatty—has flourished largely in the absence of the animal itself, which was recognized as a species less than a century ago. Two hundred or so bonobos are kept in captivity around the world; but, despite being one of just four species of great ape, along with orangutans, gorillas, and chimpanzees, the wild bonobo has received comparatively little scientific scrutiny. It is one of the oddities of the bonobo world—and a source of frustration to some—that Frans de Waal, of Emory University, the high-profile Dutch primatologist and writer, who is the most frequently quoted

thority on the species, has never seen a
ild bonobo.

Attempts to study bonobos in their
habitat began only in the nineteen-sev-
enties, and those efforts have always been
intermittent, because of geography and
politics. Wild bonobos, which are endangered (estimates of their number
range from six thousand to a hundred
off and on since 1989. When I first called
Hohmann, two years ago, he didn't immediately embrace the idea of taking a
reporter on a field trip. But we continued
to talk, and in the week after attending
the bonobo fund-raiser in New York I
flew to meet Hohmann in Kinshasa,
Congo's capital. A few days later, I was
talking with him and two of his col-
with," and there were harsher judgments,
too. He lives in Leipzig with Barbara
Fruth, his wife and frequent scientific col-
laborator, and their three young children.
Three or four times a year, he flies to Kinshasa, where he charters a light plane operated by an American-based missionary group. The plane takes him into the
world's second-largest rain forest, in the

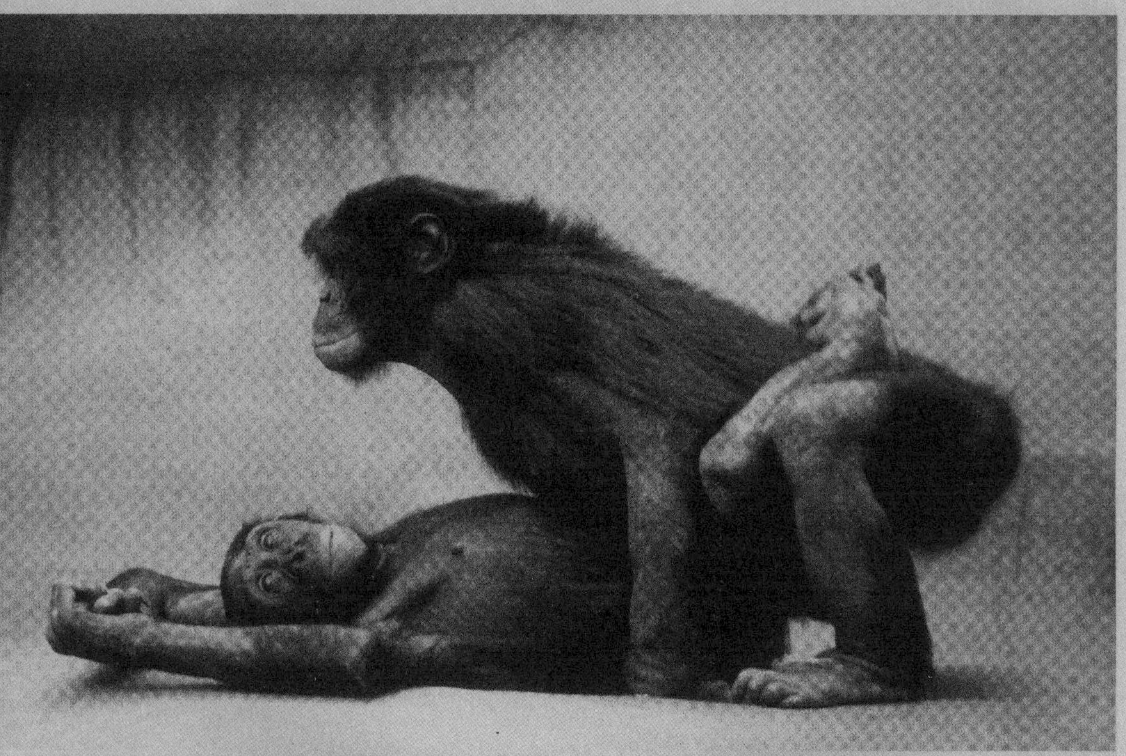

bonobos in the San Diego Zoo in 1984, photographed by the primatologist Frans de Waal.

thousand), keep themselves out of view,
in dense and inaccessible rain forests, and
only in the Democratic Republic of
Congo, where, in the past decade, more
than three million people have died in
civil and regional conflicts. For several
years around the turn of the millennium,
when fighting in Congo was at its most
intense, field observation of bonobos came
to a halt.

In recent years, however, some Congolese and overseas observers have returned to the forest, and to the hot, damp
work of sneaking up on reticent apes.
The most prominent scientist among
them is Gottfried Hohmann, a research
associate at the Max Planck Institute for
Evolutionary Anthropology, in Leipzig,
Germany. He has been visiting Congo
leagues in the shade of an aircraft hangar
in Kinshasa's airport for charter flights,
waiting for a plane to fly us to the forest.

It was a hot morning. We sat on plastic garden chairs, looking out over a run-
way undisturbed by aircraft. The airport
seemed half-ruined. Families were living
in one hangar, and laundry hung to dry
over makeshift shelters. A vender came
by with local newspapers, which were
filled with fears of renewed political violence. European embassies had been
sending cautionary text messages to their
resident nationals.

Hohmann is a lean, serious, blue-eyed
man in his mid-fifties. He has a reputation for professional fortitude, but also for
chilliness. One bonobo researcher told
me that he was "very difficult to work
Congo Basin, and puts him within hik-
ing distance of a study site called Lui
Kotal, where he has worked since 2002.
When Hohmann first came to Congo—
then Zaire—he operated from a site that
could be reached only by sweating upriver
for a week in a motorized canoe. "People
think it's entertaining, but it's not," he
told me, as we waited. "It's so slow. So
hard." He added, "You always think
there's going to be something round the
next bend, but there never is." He is an
orderly man who has learned how to
withstand disorder, an impatient man
who has reached some accommodation
with endless delay.

Hohmann makes only short visits to
Lui Kotal, but the camp is run in his absence by Congolese staff members on ro-

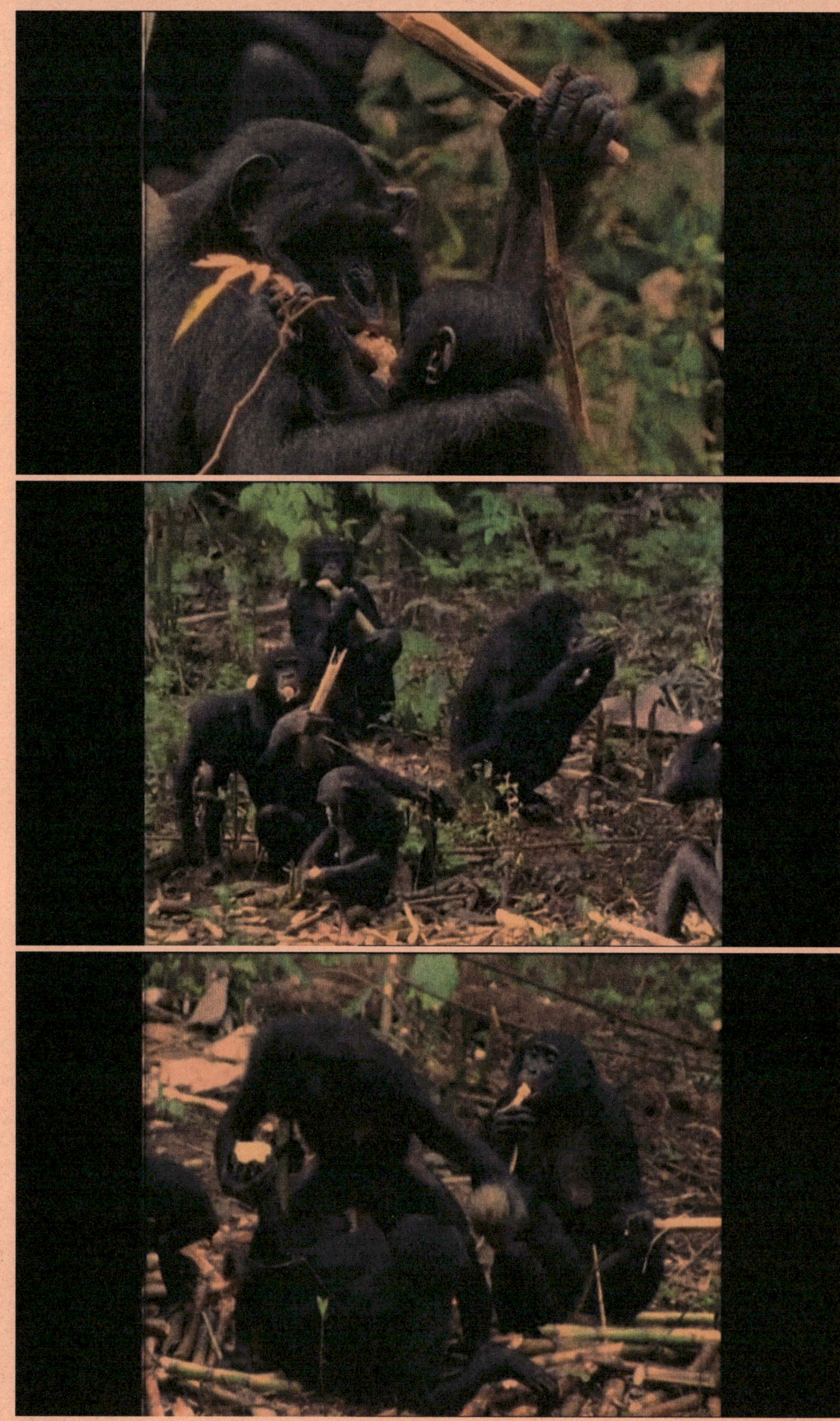

E)

SOCIAL LIFE
IN THE ENCLOSURE

A)

The Family of Chimps was filmed from July
to October 1983 at Arnhem Zoo in the
Netherlands. It is a piece of cinematographic
ethology closely related to Frans de Waal's
long-term study of the Arnhem chimpanzee
colony, which resulted in several works
including the 1982 book *Chimpanzee Politics:
Power and Sex among Apes*. De Waal, who
later became an important scholar of both
bonobos and of empathy, describes his
own account of chimpanzee society as cast
in "Machiavellian" terms, focusing on the
persistent drama in chimpanzee society,
male dominance, and power politics. The
book recounts the battle for leadership
between Nikkie and Yeroen, and later, Dandy.
The zoo reported that the screening of
Haanstra's film on public television had a
profound impact on its visitors, who learned
to distinguish between individuals and
recognize aspects of the chimpanzees' social
life. The film was reportedly also shown to
the chimps themselves, with consternation
being shown about the apparent return
of the former leader Nikkie, who had actually
died a year previously.

Bert Haanstra, *Chimps onder Elkaar*
(The Family of Chimps), 1984, 55 min.

[Quote]

"Animal play creates the conditions for
language. Its metacommunicative action
builds the evolutionary foundation for
the metalinguistic functions that will be the
hallmark of human language, and which
distinguish it from a simple code. The prehuman, preverbal embodied logic of animal
play is already essentially language-like.
It is effectively, enactively linguistic *avant la
lettre*, as humans say in French. Why then
shouldn't the opposite also be the case: that
human language is essentially animal, from
the point of view of the ludic capacities
it carries, so intimately bound up with its
metalinguistic powers? Think of humor.
Why not consider human language a reprise
of animal play, raised to a higher power?
Or say that it is actually in language that
the human reaches its highest degree
of animality?"

Brian Massumi, *What Animals Teach Us
about Politics*, Durham/New Connecticut
2014, p. 8

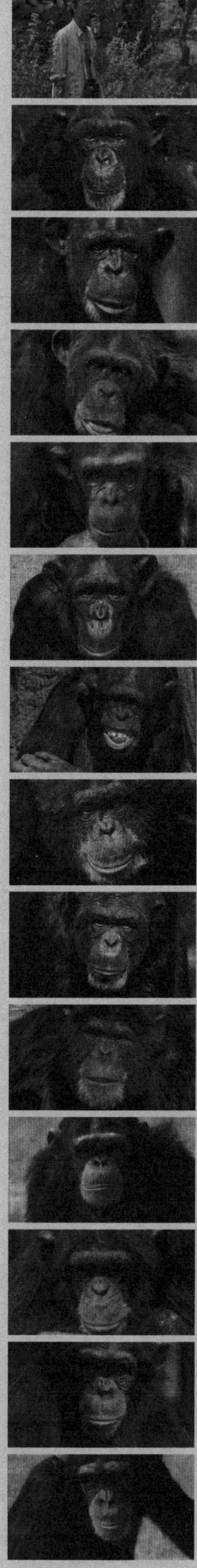

A)

APES AS SUBJECTS

A)

New York State Supreme Court,
County of Fulton, *Transcript of the Hearing
re. Tommy*, December 3, 2013

Since the 1990s, calls by proponents of the animal
protection movement for great apes to be accorded
rights have been growing louder, frequently citing
the results of the latest scientific research. For example,
the Great Ape Project, founded by the philosophers
Paola Cavalieri and Peter Singer in 1993, is demanding
that large great apes receive basic rights that have
hitherto been reserved for humans: the fundamental
right to life, individual freedom, and physical and
psychological integrity. Most recently, the Nonhuman
Rights Project has fought a number of court cases
in an effort to win recognition for chimpanzees
as legal persons. There was worldwide reporting of the
judicial proceedings before the New York State Court
in the case of Tommy, a former entertainment
chimpanzee who was being kept alone in a cage by
a private owner in New York. The lawsuit was rejected
on December 4, 2014, when the court deemed only
human individuals capable of assuming social responsibility in exchange for rights.

B)

J.M. Coetzee, *The Lives of Animals*, ed. by
Amy Gutmann, Princeton 2001, pp. 62–63

CHIMPANZEES WILL HAVE MANHATTAN COURT HEARING
TO DECIDE IF THEY'RE 'PERSONS' WITH RIGHTS

Two chimps will have their day in court— thanks to an order by a Manhattan judge that has animal rights groups going bananas. Manhattan Supreme Court Justice Barbara Jaffe has granted a hearing to decide whether a pair of chimps living at Long Island's Stony Brook University are "persons" who deserve to be released. The petition on behalf of the primates, named Leo and Hercules, was brought by the Nonhuman Rights Project, a Florida-based group that has asked several courts around the state to declare that chimps are "persons." So far, those efforts have failed.

In its latest attempt, the group wants the court to find that Leo and Hercules have been "unlawfully detained"—and to order the university to release them to an animal sanctuary.

The chimps qualify as "persons," the group says in court papers, because they show highly complex cognitive functions including "empathy," "ability to engage in mental time travel" and "capacity to suffer the pain of imprisonment." Jaffe's routine determination to consider the matter stopped short of implying that chimps are persons—as the group exuberantly proclaimed in a press release that got international attention.

"She did not say that a chimpanzee is a person,"
said David Bookstaver, a spokesman for the judge.

"She just gave them the opportunity to argue their case."

The hearing on the fate of Leo and Hercules, both males who are used in locomotion research, is slated for May 6.

There will be no monkey business in court: The chimps are not expected to attend the proceedings.

Stony Brook University declined comment.

Jaffe's order, signed Monday, initially had the animal rights group going ape.

"First Time in World History Judge Recognizes Two Chimpanzees as Legal Persons, Grants them Writ of Habeas Corpus," read the headline of the press release the group issued Monday.

It turns out the judge made a mistake, not history.

In addition to signing the order to show cause, Jaffe inadvertently signed a writ of habeas corpus.

She later signed an amended order, eliminating the writ.

The animal rights group amended its statement, too. "The issuance of the order means, we believe, that the court believes at minimum that the chimpanzees could possibly be legal persons," it said.

The group's previous attempt to free the chimps failed two years ago when Suffolk Supreme Court Justice W. Gerard Asher determined that a writ of habeas corpus "applies to persons."

Barbara Ross, Rich Schapiro,
„Chimpanzees will have Manhattan court
hearing to decide if they're 'persons' with rights",
from: *New York Daily News online*, April 20, 2015,
updated: April 21 and 22, 2015 [http://nydn.us/1aPg3tz]

updated:
JUDGE'S RULING GRANTS LEGAL RIGHT TO RESEARCH CHIMPS

Update, 21 April:
Science has learned that the court order referred to in this story has
been amended. The words "writ of habeas corpus" have been struck out,
suggesting that the court has made no decision on whether Hercules and
Leo—two research chimpanzees at Stony Brook University in New York—deserve
to be treated as legal persons. The Nonhuman Rights Project has responded
to the amendment, stating, "This case is one of a trio of cases that
the Nonhuman Rights Project has brought in an attempt to free chimpanzees
imprisoned within the State of New York through an 'Article 70-Habeas
Corpus' proceeding. These cases are novel and this is the first time that
an Order to Show Cause has issued. We are grateful for an opportunity to
litigate the issue of the freedom of the chimpanzees, Hercules and Leo,
at the ordered May hearing." Stony Brook has also issued a statement about
the case: "The University does not comment on the specifics of litigation,
and awaits the court's full consideration on this matter."

Update, 22 April:
The court hearing has been moved back from 6 May to 27 May. At that time,
the judge will hear legal arguments regarding whether Hercules and Leo
should remain at Stony Brook.

In a decision that seems to recognize chimpanzees as legal persons for
the first time, a New York judge today granted a pair of Stony Brook University lab animals the right to have their day in court. The ruling marks
the first time in U.S. history that an animal has been covered by a writ
of habeas corpus, which typically allows human prisoners to challenge
their detention. The judicial action could force the university, which is
believed to be holding the chimps, to release the primates, and could
sway additional judges to do the same with other research animals.

"This is a big step forward to getting what we are ultimately seeking:
the right to bodily liberty for chimpanzees and other cognitively complex
animals," says Natalie Prosin, the executive director of the animal rights
organization, the Nonhuman Rights Project (NhRP), that filed the case.
"We got our foot in the door. And no matter what happens, that door can
never be completely shut again."

Richard Cupp, a law professor at Pepperdine University in Malibu,
California, and a noted opponent of personhood for animals, cautions
against reading too much into the ruling, however. "The judge may merely
want more information to make a decision on the legal personhood
claim, and may have ordered a hearing simply as a vehicle for hearing
out both parties in more depth," he writes in an e-mail to Science. "It
would be quite surprising if the judge intended to make a momentous
substantive finding that chimpanzees are legal persons if the judge has
not yet heard the other side's arguments."

The case began as a salvo of lawsuits filed by NhRP in December 2013.
The group claimed that four New York chimpanzees—Hercules and Leo at
Stony Brook, and two others on private property—were too cognitively and
emotionally complex to be held in captivity and should be relocated to
an established chimpanzee sanctuary. NhRP petitioned three lower court
judges with a writ of habeas corpus, which is traditionally used to
prevent people from being unlawfully imprisoned. By granting the writ,
the judges would have implicitly acknowledged that chimpanzees were
legal people, too—a first step in freeing them.

The judges quickly struck down each case, however, and NhRP has been
appealing ever since. Today's decision is the group's first major victory.
In her ruling, New York Supreme Court Justice Barbara Jaffe orders
a representative of Stony Brook University to appear in court on 6 May to
respond to NhRP's petition that Hercules and Leo "are being unlawfully
detained" and should be immediately moved to a chimp sanctuary in Florida.

Both animals have been used to understand the evolution of human bipedalism. (Stony Brook did not immediately respond to a request for comment.)

Prosin says that even if NhRP loses the case, it will use the habeas
corpus ruling to sway judges in other jurisdictions. "It strengthens our
argument that these nonhuman animals are not property," she says. The
group plans to file another case—this one involving a captive elephant—
by the end of the year and has set its sights on other animals, including
research animals, across the country. "We have the scientific evidence
to prove in a court of law that elephants, great apes, and whales and
dolphins are autonomous beings and deserve the right to bodily liberty,"
she says.

David Grimm, "Updated: Judge's ruling
grants legal right to research chimps,"
from: AAAS ScienceInsider. April 21, 2015,
updated: April 22, 2015 [10.1126/science.aab2521].

---

18 highly sophisticated...
19 to meet the thresho...
20 to a chimpanzee.
21 And so when I say
22 anything further on...
23 this Court should re...
24 chimpanzee, specif...
25 as part of a protect...

Karen L. Kolterman...
   Official Court Re...

1 Writ of Habeas Cor...
2 of habeas corpus?...
3 regard?
4 MR. WISE: I do, Yo...
5 So, the writ of habe...
6 anyone may seek a...
7 person is being imp...
8 "human-being." It s...
9 memorandum spec...
10 "human-being" is n...
11 "person" is not a sy...
12 Throughout history,...
13 out, there have bee...
14 been legal persons...
15 and there have bee...
16 persons for purpos...
17 There is some requ...
18 though we do belie...
19 least in the year 20...
20 species homosapie...
21 condition for personhood, but there are other
22 sufficient conditions for personhood, as well; and
23 we would argue that based upon New York law common
24 law, US Supreme Court has talked about common law,
25 that indeed autonomy is one of the most highly

Karen L. Kolterman, C.S.R.
   Official Court Reporter

21
1 Writ of Habeas Corpus (12/3/13)
2 protected attributes of human-beings. Court of
3 Appeals of New York will allow you to die.
4 They'll allow you to take your own life. They'll
5 allow you to represent yourself in court, even
6 though we all know you're going to lose.
7 Autonomy is an extraordinarily important
8 attribute, and we argue that autonomy -- that a
9 being who is autonomous, who can choose, who is
10 self-aware, these, Your Honor, are essentially us.
11 They're so extraordinarily close to us.
12 We have presented 150 pages of affidavits
13 from the world's greatest primatologists who set
14 out in specific and even excruciating detail just
15 how from language to culture -- these beings have
16 cultures, there are cultures, they have language.
17 They can use human language. They can use
18 chimpanzee language. They are extraordinarily
19 similar to us. And if we focus in on not just how
20 they look, their brains are similar to us, the way
21 their brains work are similar to us. They're
22 essentially almost us. And if you focus on the
23 issue of autonomy, self-determination, choice,
24 that those are such powerful concerns of the
25 courts of New York that a being who can

Karen L. Kolterman, C.S.R.
   Official Court Reporter

22
1 Writ of Habeas Corpus (12/3/13)
2 demonstrate, which we do demonstrate, that they
3 indeed have that autonomy, that is a sufficient
4 condition for legal personhood.
5 Plus, under the Pet Trust statute, the New
6 York legislature has already determined that they
7 are legal persons, because Tommy is a beneficiary
8 of a trust that we have created. We created it
9 for him. He owns the corpus of his trust. He can
10 sue. And, indeed, Attorney Stein is the enforcer
11 of that Pet Trust statute. So he already has
12 certain kinds of rights, and we're saying that he
13 should also have the fundamental right to bodily
14 liberty that protects his fundamental interest in
15 bodily liberty.
16 Now, that is an argument as a matter of
17 liberty. We have another argument under common
18 law equality in New York that Tommy should -- the
19 only reason that someone could not issue a writ of
20 habeas corpus on behalf of Tommy is, one, that he

... section on standing, but, essentially, the writ of
25 habeas corpus is a different sort of cause of

Karen L. Kolterman, C.S.R.
   Official Court Reporter

24
1 Writ of Habeas Corpus (12/3/13)
2 action in that a person who is being imprisoned
3 generally is not able to leave the place of
4 imprisonment to come and seek a writ of habeas
5 corpus. So what happens is that the usual
6 standing requirements are exceedingly relaxed so
7 that a third party -- in fact, under the statute,
8 it says anyone can come in and seek a writ of
9 habeas corpus on behalf of a person who is
10 imprisoned. That's what we do. That's what the
11 Nonhuman Rights Project does. But even if it
12 wasn't, any person could come in and seek a writ
13 of habeas corpus on behalf of Tommy under the
14 statute as well as under the constitutional law.
15 THE COURT: The trust you say that's set up
16 for this chimpanzee, has it been used by the owner
17 of the chimpanzee or is it --
18 MR. WISE: The -- I am so sorry, Your Honor.
19 THE COURT: That's okay. Go ahead. You were
20 going to answer. Go ahead.
21 MR. WISE: The answer is the trust is for the
22 care and maintenance of Tommy, and so we have --
23 right now he's being treated as a legal thing. We
24 hope he's going to be treated as a legal --
25 THE COURT: I'm sorry. Is the trust monies

Karen L. Kolterman, C.S.R.
   Official Court Reporter

25
1 Writ of Habeas Corpus (12/3/13)
2 used for Tommy?
3 MR. WISE: Yes, Your Honor.
4 THE COURT: So the owner of Tommy has been
5 using the money?
6 MR. WISE: Nope. There is no -- the trust is
7 not for Tommy as a legal thing. Tommy cannot --
8 Tommy could not --
9 THE COURT: You said the trust is used for
10 his care.
11 MR. WISE: No. The trust shall be used for
12 his care.
13 THE COURT: So it hasn't been used yet.
14 MR. WISE: It hasn't been used for his care,
15 because the Nonhuman Rights Project has spoken
16 to -- has arranged with the North American Primate
17 Sanctuary Alliance, who has a string of primate
18 sanctuaries throughout the United States, they
19 have several of them in which they have some
20 spectacular sanctuary, they're going to take care
21 of Tommy and we're going --
22 THE COURT: Has the owner been approached and
23 will not sell Tommy, will not release Tommy? Has
24 it even been approached?

...ot been

...13)
... not been
...re. We've seen
...else? Anything
...ed representations
...sive. The Court will
...will not recognize
...as a person as a person
...s corpus under Article
...udge for any
...ngs that are done to
...nderstand what you're
...ng argument.
...the argument only
...o chimpanzees.
...I'm sorry I
...e you continue. As
...your work.
...in no way was

Karen L. Kolterman, C.S.R.
   Official Court Reporter

27
1 Writ of Habeas Corpus (12/3/13)
2 trying to avoid your answer.
3 THE COURT: No.
4 Off the record.
5 (Discussion held off the record; record
6 resumed.)
7 THE COURT: Anything further for the record?
8 MS. STEIN: No. Thank you, Your Honor.
9 MR. WISE: Thank you. We certainly
10 appreciate it.
11 THE COURT: This Court will maintain this
12 verified application and petition as part of the
13 record, and it will be held on file for a
14 reasonable period of time before it is condensed
15 and removed.
16 Thank you. Good luck.
17 (Whereupon, the proceedings held in the
18 above-entitled matter were concluded.)
19
20
21
22
23
24
25

Karen L. Kolterman, C.S.R.
   Official Court Reporter

28
1 Writ of Habeas Corpus (12/3/13)
2
3
4 C E R T I F I C A T I O N
5
6
7 I, KAREN L. KOLTERMAN, a Certified Shorthand
8 Reporter, an Official Court Reporter and Notary
9 Public in and for the State of New York, do hereby
10 CERTIFY that the foregoing record was taken by me
11 at the time and place as noted in the heading
12 hereof, was recorded stenographically by me, and
13 that the foregoing transcript is a correct and
14 accurate transcript of my stenographic notes, to
15 the best of my ability and belief.
16
17
18
19
   ____
         KAREN L. KOLTERMAN
20   Certified Shorthand Reporter
21
22
23
24
25

think strategically, hold general concepts, or communicate symbolically, have had very limited success. The best performance the higher apes can put up is no better than that of a speech-impaired human being with severe mental retardation. If so, are not animals, even the higher animals, properly thought of as belonging to another legal and ethical realm entirely, rather than being placed in this depressing human subcategory? Isn't there a certain wisdom in the traditional view that says that animals cannot enjoy legal rights because they are not persons, even potential persons, as fetuses are? In working out rules for our dealings with animals, does it not make more sense for such rules to apply to us and to our treatment of them, as at present, rather than being predicated upon rights which animals cannot claim or enforce or even understand?"[4]

His mother's turn. "To respond adequately, Professor O'Hearne, would take more time than I have, since I would first want to interrogate the whole question of rights and how we come to possess them. So let me just make one observation: that the program of scientific experimentation that leads you to conclude that animals are imbeciles is profoundly anthropocentric. It values being able to find your way out of a sterile maze, ignoring the fact that if the researcher who designed the maze were to be parachuted into the jungles of Borneo, he or she would be dead of starvation in a week. In fact I would go further. If I as a human being were told that the standards by which animals are being measured in these experiments are human standards, I would be insulted. It is the experiments themselves that are imbecile. The behaviorists who design them claim that we understand only by a process of creating abstract models and then testing those models against reality. What nonsense. We understand by immersing ourselves and our intelligence in complexity. There is something

---

[4] Cf. Bernard Williams: "Before one gets to the question of how animals should be treated, there is the fundamental point that this is the only question there can be: how they should be treated. The choice can only be whether animals benefit from our practices or are harmed by them." Quoted in Michael P. T. Leahy, *Against Liberation* (London and New York: Routledge, 1991), 208.

self-stultified in the way in which scientific behaviorism recoils from the complexity of life.[5]

"As for animals being too dumb and stupid to speak for themselves, consider the following sequence of events. When Albert Camus was a young boy in Algeria, his grandmother told him to bring her one of the hens from the cage in their backyard. He obeyed, then watched her cut off its head with a kitchen knife, catching its blood in a bowl so that the floor would not be dirtied.

"The death-cry of that hen imprinted itself on the boy's memory so hauntingly that in 1958 he wrote an impassioned attack on the guillotine. As a result, in part, of that polemic, capital punishment was abolished in France. Who is to say, then, that the hen did not speak?"[6]

O'Hearne. "I make the following statement with due deliberation, mindful of the historical associations it may evoke. I do not believe that life is as important to animals as it is to us. There is certainly in animals an instinctive struggle against death, which they share with us. But they do not *understand* death as we do, or rather, as we fail to do. There is, in the human mind, a collapse of the imagination before death, and that collapse of the imagination—graphically evoked in yesterday's lecture—is the basis of our fear of death. That fear does not and cannot exist in animals, since the effort to comprehend extinction, and the failure to do so, the failure to master it, have simply not taken place.

"For that reason, I want to suggest, dying is, for an animal, just something that happens, something against which there may be a revolt of the organism but not a revolt of the soul. And the lower

[5] For a critique of behaviorism in the political context of its times, see Bernard E. Rollin, *The Unheeded Cry* (Oxford: Oxford University Press, 1990), 100–103. On the behaviorist taboo on considering the subjective mental states of animals, see Donald R. Griffin, *Animal Minds* (Chicago: University of Chicago Press, 1992), 6–7. Griffin calls the taboo "a serious impediment to scientific investigation" but suggests that in practice investigators do not adhere to it (6, 120).

[6] Albert Camus, *The First Man*, trans. David Hapgood (London: Hamish Hamilton, 1995), 181–83; "Réflexions sur la guillotine," in *Essais*, ed. R. Quilliot and L. Faucon (Paris: Gallimard, 1965), 1019–64.

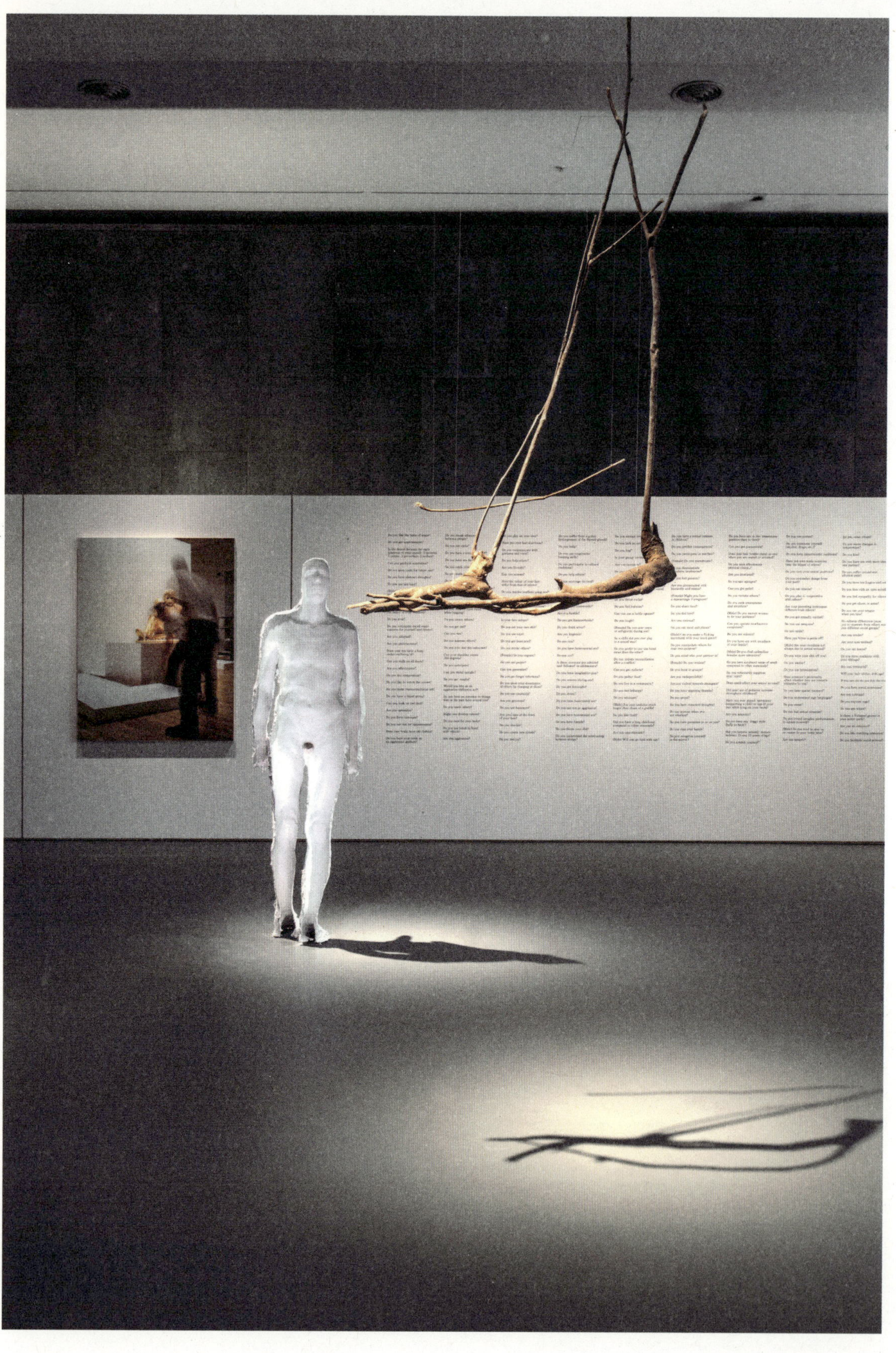

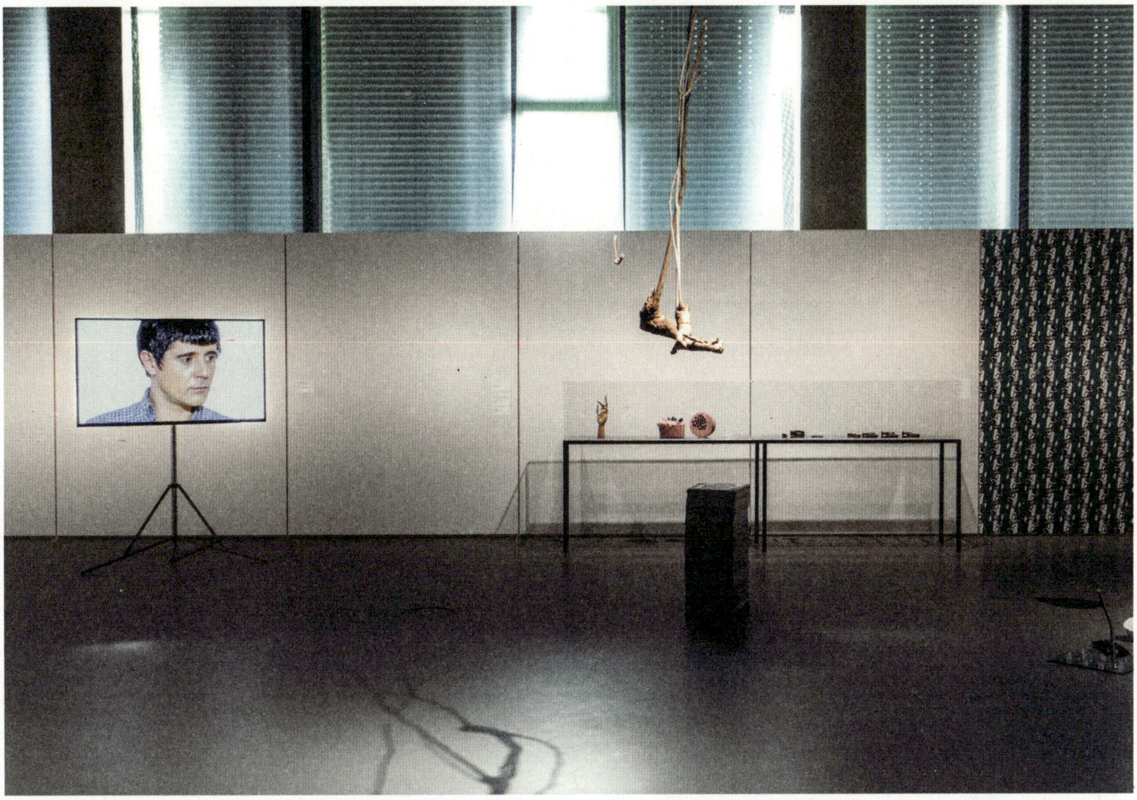

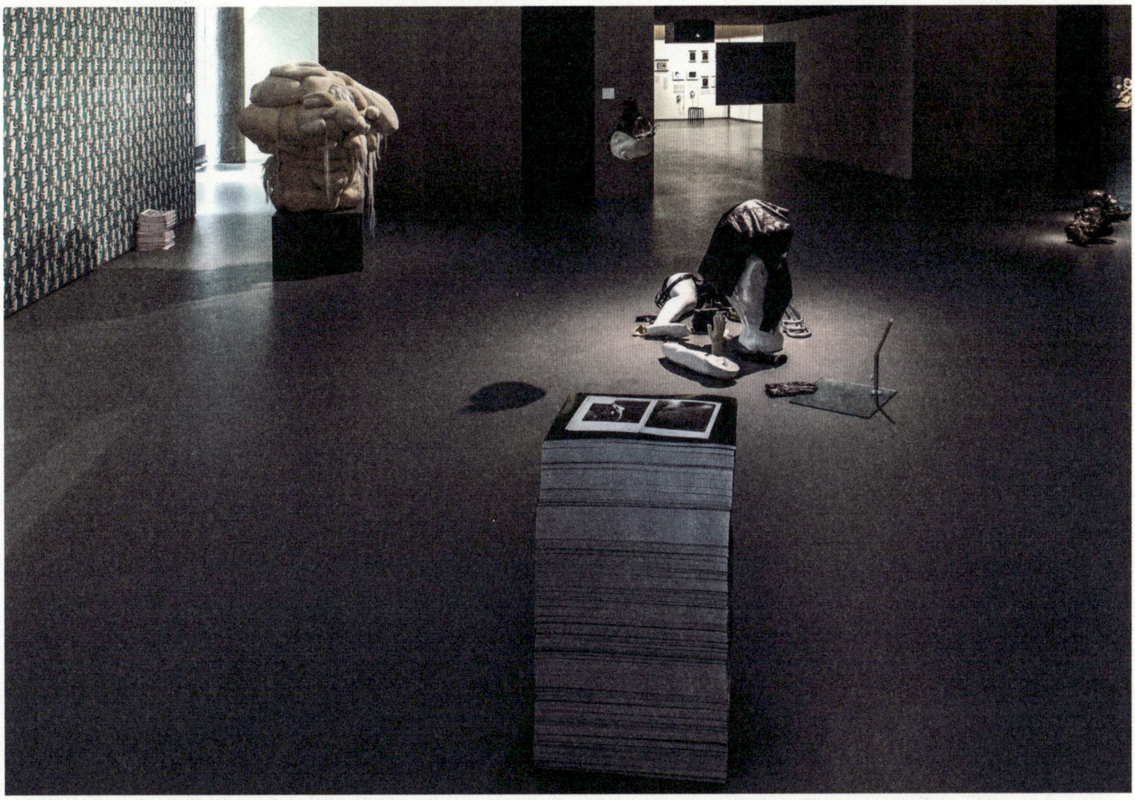

Ape Culture
Haus der Kulturen der Welt, 2015
Exhibition views
Photos: Laura Fiorio

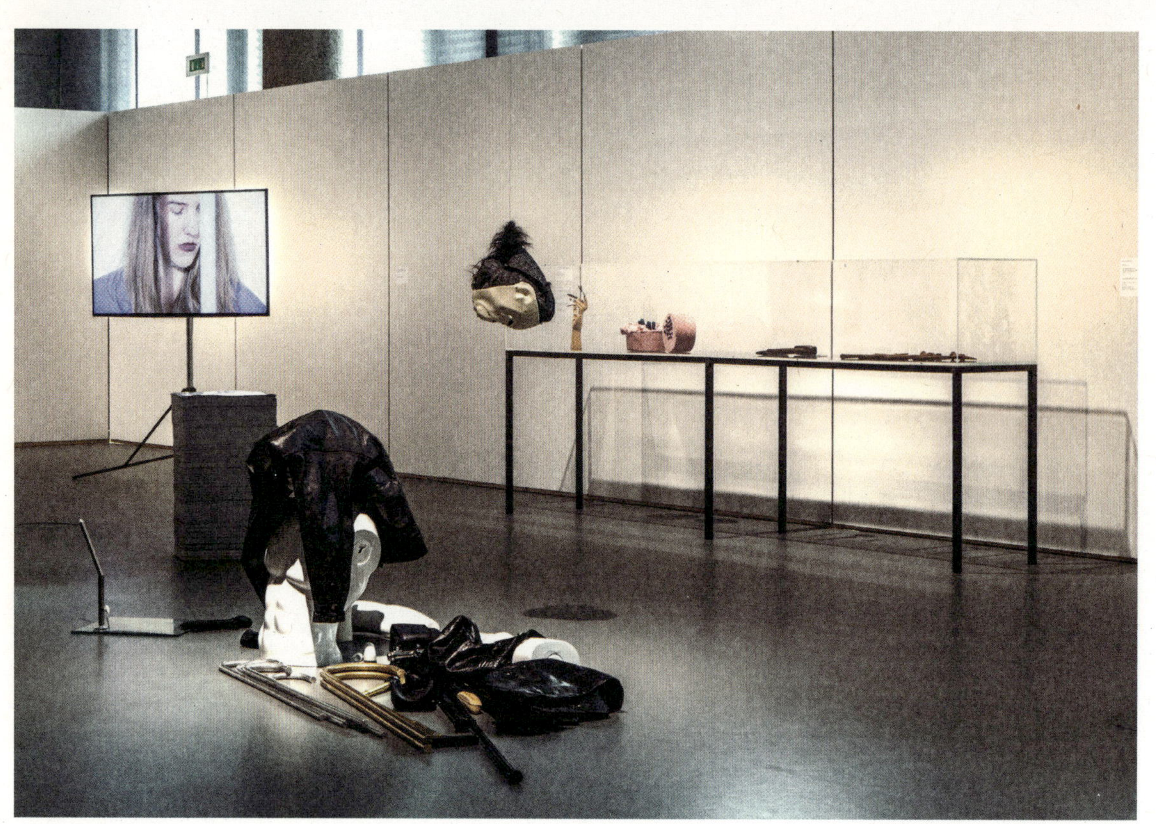

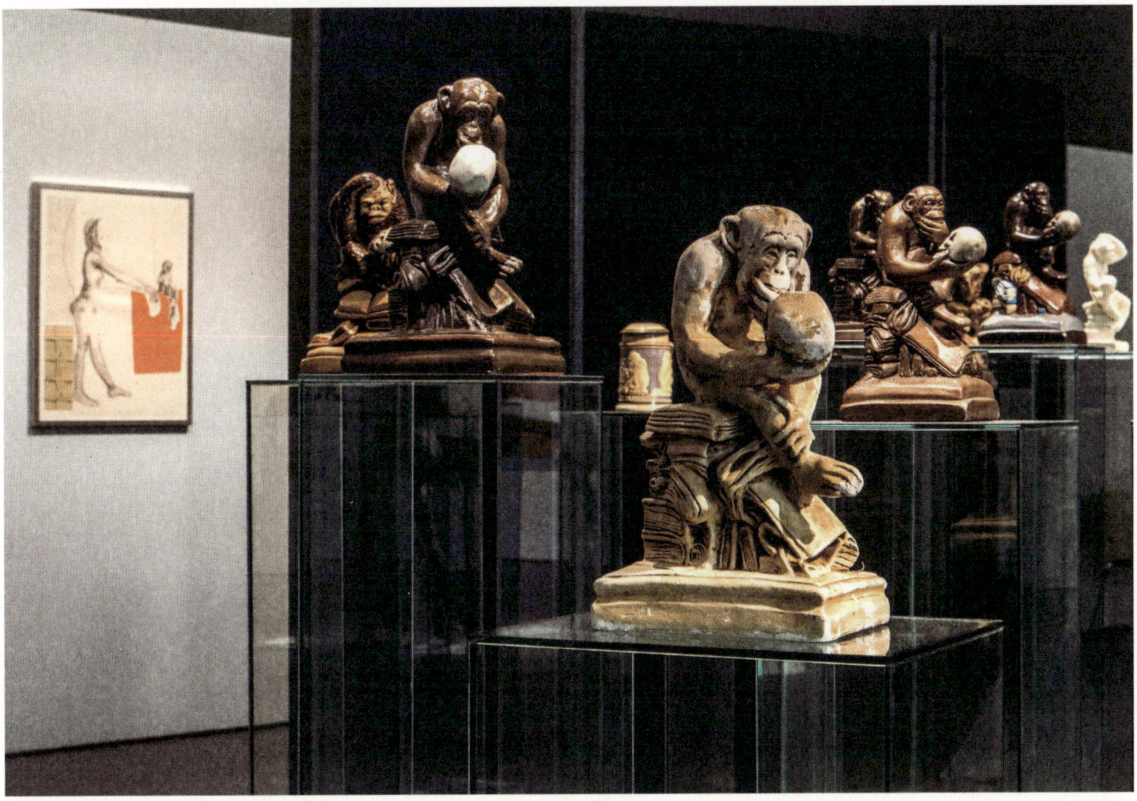

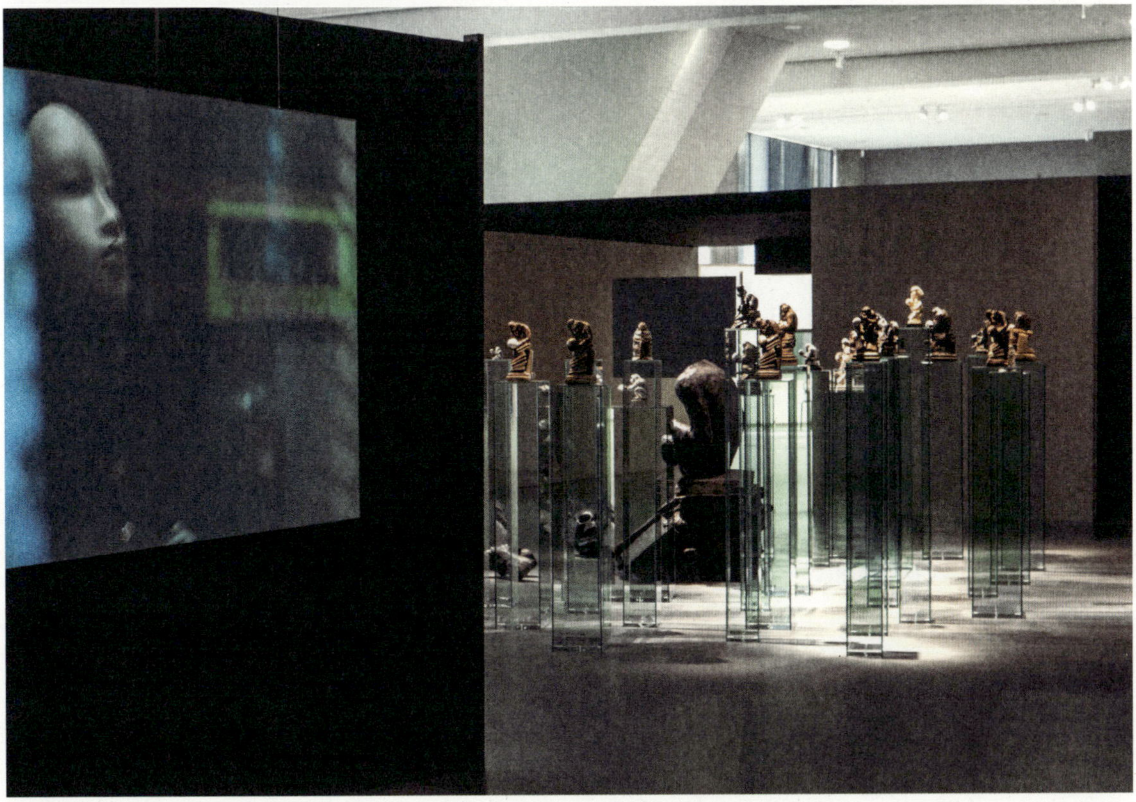

Ape Culture
Haus der Kulturen der Welt, 2015
Exhibition views
Photos: Laura Fiorio

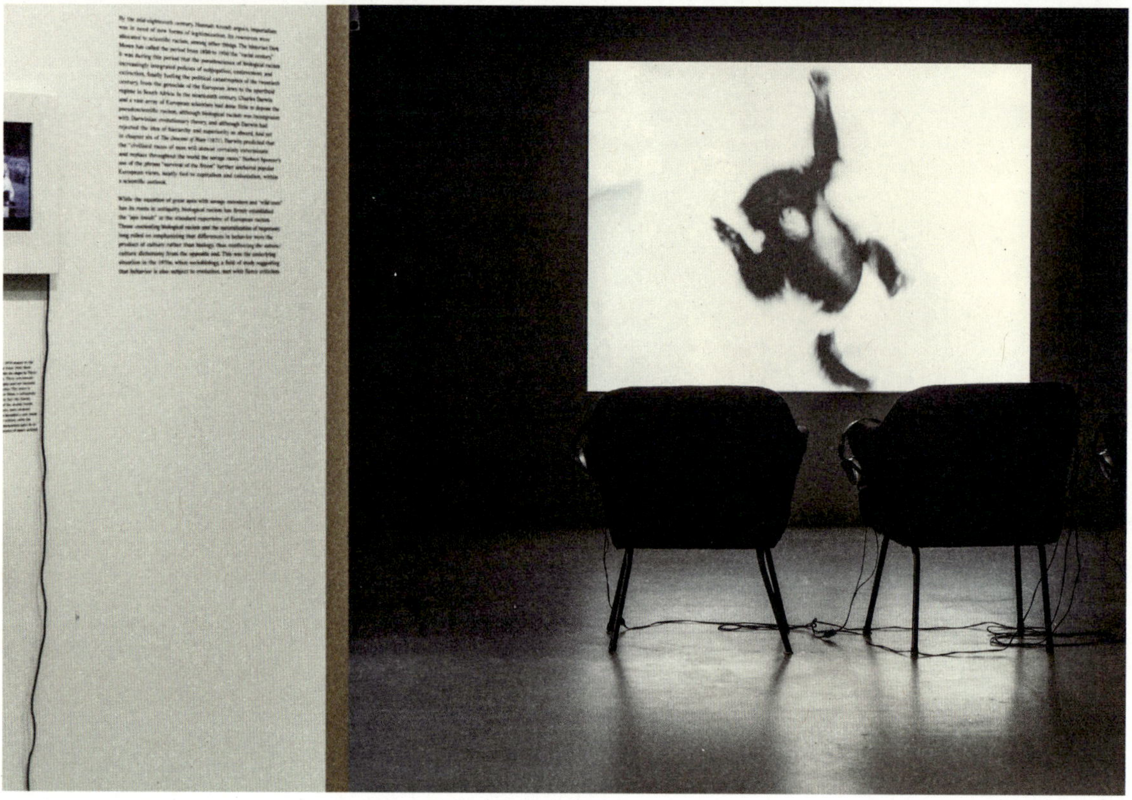

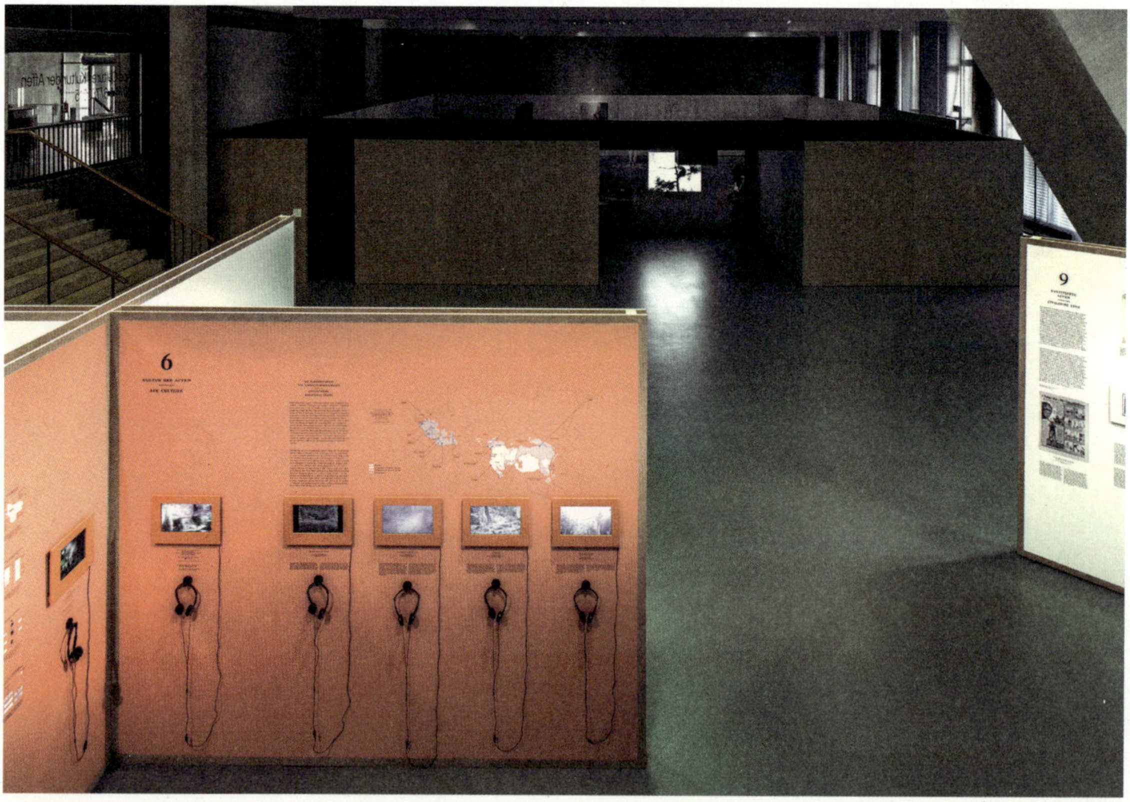

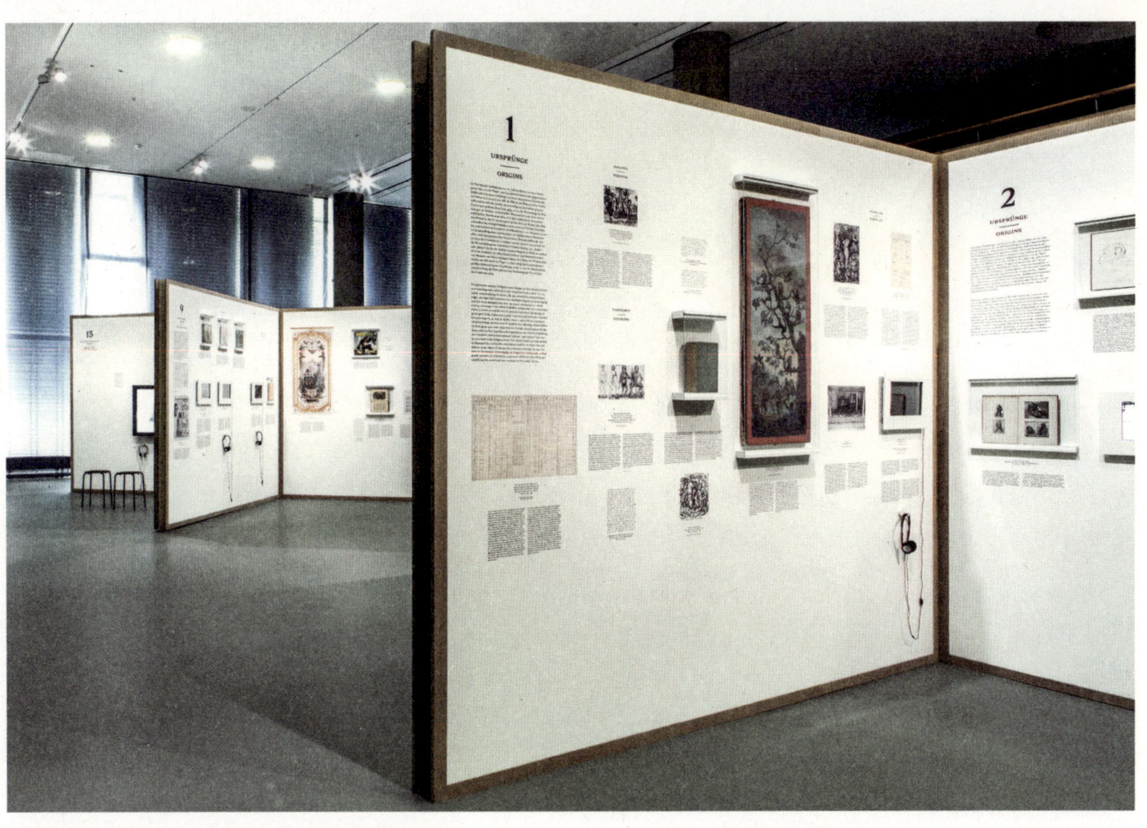

Ape Culture
Haus der Kulturen der Welt, 2015
Exhibition views
Photos: Laura Fiorio

BIBLIOGRAPHY

A

Adorno, Theodor W. et al. *The Authoritarian Personality*. New York: Science Editions, 1964 [1950].

Agamben, Giorgio. *The Open: Man and Animal*. Stanford: Stanford University Press, 2004.

Altmann, Stuart A., ed. *Social Communication among Primates*. Chicago: University of Chicago Press, 1967.

Ando, Koji et al., eds. *Primates*, vol. 1, no. 1, Kurisu: Japan Monkey Centre, 1957.

Ardrey, Robert. *African Genesis: A Personal Investigation into the Animal Origins and Nature of Man*. New York: Delta, 1961.

Ardrey, Robert. *The Territorial Imperative: A Personal Inquiry into the Animal Origins of Property and Nations*. New York: Atheneum, 1966.

Ardrey, Robert. *The Social Contract: A Personal Inquiry into the Evolutionary*. New York: Atheneum, 1970.

Asimov, Isaac. *Second Foundation*. New York, Gnome Press, 1953.

Asquith, Pamela. The Kinji Iminishi Digital Archive. Accessed May 8, 2015. http://tomcat.sunsite.ualberta.ca/Imanishi/.

B

Baratay, Eric, and Elisabeth Hardouin-Fugier. *Zoo: A History of Zoological Gardens in the West*. London: Reaktion Books, 2003.

Barnes, Djuna. "The Girl and the Gorilla." The *World Magazine*, October 18, 1914.

Benjamin, Walter. "Das Karussell der Berufe." In Walter Benjamin. *Aufsätze, Essays, Vorträge* (Gesammelte Schriften Bd.II.2), edited by Rolf Tiedemann, Hermann Schweppenhäuser. Frankfurt am Main: Suhrkamp Verlag, 1977 [1930], p. 667–676.

Berger, John. *Why Look at Animals?* London: Penguin Books, 2009.

Bhanoo, Sindya N. "Milk of human kindness also found in bonobos." *New York Times*, January 8, 2013, p. D3 [New York edition].

Biography.com, s.v. "Dian Fossey." Accessed May 8, 2015. http://www.biography.com/people/dian-fossey-9299545.

Blühm, Andreas. "Menschen und Affen: Das Bild des Affen in der Kunstgeschichte und seine Änderungen seit Charles Darwin." Lecture on October 9, 2008 at Zoo Basel as part of the lecture series "Affe, Mensch – und wir."

Boesch, Christophe. "Innovation in wild chimpanzees." *International Journal of Primatology*, vol. 16, no. 1 (1995), pp. 1–16.

Boesch, Christophe. "Three approaches for assessing chimpanzee culture." In *Reaching into Thought*, edited by A. Russon, K. Bard, and S. Parker, pp. 404–429. Cambridge: Cambridge University Press, 1996.

Boesch, Christophe. "Is culture a golden barrier between human and chimpanzee?" *Evolutionary Anthropology*, vol. 12, no. 2 (2003), pp. 26–32.

Boesch, Christophe. *Wild Cultures: A Comparison between Chimpanzee and Human Cultures*. Cambridge: Cambridge University Press, 2012.

Brown, B. Ricardo. *Until Darwin, Science, Human Variety and the Origins of Race*. London: Pickering & Chatto, 2010.

Burton, Richard F., trans. *The Book of the Thousand Nights and a Night*. Adelaide: The University of Adelaide, 2014. Last modified December 17, 2014. https://ebooks.adelaide.edu.au/b/burton/richard/b97b/index.html.

Byrne, Richard. *The Thinking Ape: The Evolutionary Origins of Intelligence*. New York: Oxford University Press, 2004.

C

Carpenter, Clarence Ray. Sociometric diagram from Carpenter's Asiatic Primate Expedition field notes, 1937. C. R. Carpenter Papers. Penn State University Archives. In Haraway, Donna. *Primate Visions*. p. 95.

Cavalieri, Paola, and Peter Singer, eds. *The Great Ape Project: Equality Beyond Humanity*. New York: St. Martin's Press, 1995.

Chomsky, Noam. *Language and Mind*. New York: Harcourt, Brace & World, 1968.

Coetzee, J. M. *The Lives of Animals*, edited by Amy Gutmann. Princeton: Princeton University Press, 2001.

Cohen, Jon. *Almost Chimpanzee: Redrawing the Lines That Separate Us from Them*. New York: Henry Holt, 2010.

Conniff, Richard. "Race, sex and the trials of a young explorer." *New York Times*, February 13, 2011.

Corbey, Raymond H. A. *The Metaphysics of Apes: Negotiating the Animal–Human Boundary*. Cambridge: Cambridge University Press, 2005.

Cordoni, G., and E. Palagi. "Ontogenetic trajectories of chimpanzee social play: Similarities with humans." *PLoS ONE*, vol. 6, no. 11 (2011), e27344.

D

Dagg, Anne Innis, and Lee E. Harding. *Human Evolution and Male Aggression: Debunking the Myth of Man and Ape*. Amherst, MA: Cambria Press, 2012.

Dahlberg, Frances, ed. *Woman the Gatherer*. New Haven: Yale University Press, 1981.

Darwin, Charles. *Charles Darwin's Notebooks, 1836–1844*. Notebooks M and N [1838–1839]. Cambridge: Cambridge University Press, 2009.

Darwin, Charles. *The Descent of Man, and Selection in Relation to Sex*. London: John Murray, 1871.

Darwin, Charles. *The Expression of the Emotions in Man and Animals*, London: John Murray, 1872.

Descola, Philippe. *Jenseits von Natur und Kultur*, Berlin: Galiani Verlag, 2013.

Despret, Vinciane. "The body we care for: Figures of anthropo-zoo-genesis." *Body & Society*, vol. 10, no. 2/3 (2004), pp. 111–134.

DeVore, Irven, and Richard B. Lee, eds. *Man the Hunter: The First Intensive Survey of a Single, Crucial Stage of Human Development—Man's Once Universal Hunting Way of Life*. New Brunswick, NJ: Aldine Transaction, 2009 [1968].

de Waal, Frans. "Without walls." *New Scientist*, vol. 172, no. 2321 (2001), p. 46.

de Waal, Frans. *Our Inner Ape*. New York: Riverhead Books, 2005.

de Waal, Frans. "Silent invasion: Imanishi's primatology and cultural bias in science." *Animal Cognition*, vol. 6, no. 4 (December 2003), pp. 293–299.

de Waal, Frans. *The Age of Empathy*, New York: Harmony, 2009.

de Waal, Frans. *The Ape and the Sushi Master: Cultural Reflections of a Primatologist*. New York: Basic Books, 2001.

de Waal, Frans, and Pier Francesco Ferrari, eds. *The Primate Mind: Built to Connect with Other Minds*. Cambridge, MA: Harvard University Press, 2012.

Diamond, Jared. *The Third Chimpanzee: The Evolution and Future of the Human Animal*. New York: HarperCollins, 1992.

Du Chaillu, Paul B. *Explorations and Adventures in Equatorial Africa; with Accounts of the Manners and Customs of the People, and of the Chase of the Gorilla, the Crocodile, Leopard, Elephant, Hippopotamus, and Other Animals*. New York: Harper & Brothers, 1862 [1861].

Dupré, John. *Humans and other Animals*. New York: Oxford University Press, 2006.

E

Ebeling, Kirsten Smilla, and Sigrid Schmitz, eds. *Geschlechterforschung und Naturwissenschaften: Einführung in ein komplexes Wechselspiel*. Berlin: VS-Verlag, 2006.

Emery, Nathan J., and Nicola J. Clayton. "Imaginative scrub-jays, causal rooks, and a liberal application of Occam's aftershave." *Behavioural and Brain Sciences*, vol. 31, no. 2 (2008), pp. 134–135.

Encyclopaedia Britannica Online, s.v. "singerie." Accessed May 8, 2015. http://www.britannica.com/EBchecked/topic/545822/singerie.

F

Fedigan, Linda Marie. *Primate Paradigms: Sex Roles and Social Bonds*. Chicago: University of Chicago Press, 1982.

Fischer, Julia. *Affengesellschaft*. Berlin: Suhrkamp Verlag, 2012.

Fossey, Dian, with photographs by Robert M. Campbell. "More years with mountain gorillas." *National Geographic*, vol. 140, no. 4 (October 1971), pp. 574–585.

Fossey, Dian. *Gorillas in the Mist*. London: Hodder and Stoughton, 1983.

Fouts, Roger. *Next of Kin: My Conversations with Chimpanzees*. New York: Avon Books, 1997.

Fragaszy, Dorothy M., and Susan Perry, eds. *The Biology of Traditions: Models and Evidence*. Cambridge: Cambridge University Press, 2003.

Fridman, Eman P. *Medical primatology: History, Biological Foundations and Applications*. Edited by Ronald D. Nadler. London and New York: Taylor & Francis, 2002.

Fromm, Erich. *Escape from Freedom*. New York: Holt Paperbacks, 1994 [1941].

Galdikas, Birutė M. F., with photographs by Rod Brindamour. "Living with the great orange apes." *National Geographic*, vol. 157, no. 6 (June 1980), pp. 830–853.

G

Galdikas, Birutė M. F. *Reflections of Eden: My Years with the Orangutans of Borneo*. Boston et al: Little, Brown, 1995.

Gardner, R. Allen, and Beatrice T. Gardner. "Teaching sign language to a chimpanzee." *Science*, New Series, vol. 165, no. 3894 (August 1969), pp. 664–672.

Garner, R. L. *The Speech of Monkeys*. New York: C. L. Webster and Co., 1892.

Gates, Henry Louis. *The Signifying Monkey*. New York: Oxford University Press, 1989.

Ghiglieri, Michael. *The Dark Side of Man: Tracing the Origins of Male Violence*. Cambridge, MA: Helix Books, 1999.

Goodall, Jane, with photographs by Baron Hugo van Lawick. "My life among wild chimpanzees." *National Geographic*, vol. 124, no. 2 (August 1963), pp. 272–308.

Goodall, Jane, with photographs by Baron Hugo van Lawick. *My Friends the Wild Chimpanzees*. Washington, DC: National Geographic Society, 1967.

Griem, Julika, ed. *Monkey Business: Affen als Figuren anthropologischer und ästhetischer Reflexion*. Frankfurt am Main: trafo Verlagsgruppe, 2010.

Griffin, Donald R. *Animal Thinking*. Cambridge, MA: Harvard University Press, 1984.

Grosz, Elisabeth: *Becoming Undone: Darwinian Reflections on Life, Politics, and Art*. Durham, NC: Duke University Press, 2011.

H

Hale, Benjamin. "The last distinction? Talking to the animals." *Harper's Magazine*, August 2012, pp. 65–70.

Haraway, Donna J. "Situated knowledges: The science question in feminism and the privilege of partial perspective." *Feminist Studies*, vol. 14, no. 3 (1988), pp. 575–599.

Haraway, Donna J. *Primate Visions: Gender, Race, and Nature in the World of Modern Science*. London and New York: Routledge, 1989.

Haraway, Donna J. *When Species Meet*. Minneapolis: University of Minnesota Press, 2007.

Harlow, Harry F. *Learning to Love*. London and New York: Aronson, 1974.

Hayes, Keith J., and Catherine Hayes. "The cultural capacity of chimpanzee." *Human Biology*, vol. 26, no. 3 (1954), pp. 288–303.

Hess, Lilo. *Christine, the Baby Chimp*. London: G. Bell & Sons, 1954.

Hohenberger, Eva, ed. *Frederick Wiseman: Kino des Sozialen*. Berlin: Verlag Vorwerk 8, 2009.

Hoyt, Augusta Maria Daurer. *Toto and I: A Gorilla in the Family*. Philadelphia and New York: J. B. Lippincott Co., 1941.

Hrdy, Sarah Blaffer. *Mother Nature*. New York: Pantheon, 1999.

Hrdy, Sarah Blaffer. *Mothers and Others: The Evolutionary Origins of Mutual Understanding*. Cambridge, MA: Harvard University Press, 2011.

Huffman, Michael A., Charmalie A. D. Nahallage, and Jean-Baptiste Leca. "Cultured monkeys: Social learning cast in stones." *Current Directions in Psychological Science*, vol. 17, no. 6 (December 2008), pp. 410–414.

Human Intelligence. "Robert Mearns Yearkes." Last modified November 7, 2013. http://www.intelltheory.com/yerkes.shtml.

I

Imanishi, Kinji. *Seibutsu no Sekai* (The World of Living Things). Tokyo: Kodansha, 1972 [1941].

Ingensiep, Hans Werner. *Der kultivierte Affe: Philosophie, Geschichte und Gegenwart*. Stuttgart: Hirzel Verlag, 2013.

K

Kafka, Franz. "Zwei Tiergeschichten: 2. Ein Bericht für eine Akademie." *Der Jude: Eine Monatsschrift*, vol. 2, November 1917, pp. 559–565.

Kellogg, Luella, and Winthrop Kellogg. *The Ape and The Child: A Comparative Study of the Environmental Influence Upon Early Behavior*. New York and London: Hafner, 1967 [1933].

Kevles, Daniel J. "Testing the army's intelligence: Psychologists and the military in World War I," *The Journal of American History*, vol. 55, no. 3 (December 1968), pp. 565–581.

Kipling, Rudyard. "The Mark of the Beast." In *The writings in prose and verse of Rudyard Kipling*. New York: Scribner, 1920.

Knapp, Margit. *Affenmensch und Menschenaffe: Geschichten und Geschichte – Der Affe in der Literatur*. Lecture on November 20, 2008 at Zoo Basel as part of the lecture series "Affe, Mensch – und wir."

Köhler, Wolfgang. *Intelligenzprüfungen an Menschenaffen*. Berlin: Springer Verlag, 1963 [1921].

Kropotkin, Petr. *Mutual Aid: A Factor in Evolution*. Boston: Extending Horizons Books, 1955 [1902].

Krüger, Gesine, Ruth Mayer, and Marianne Sommer, eds. *"Ich Tarzan." Affenmenschen und Menschenaffen zwischen Science und Fiction*, Bielefeld: transcript Verlag, 2008.

L

Ladygina-Kohts, N. N. *Infant Chimpanzee and Human Child: A Classic 1935 Comparative Study of Ape Emotions and Intelligence*, edited by Frans de Waal. Oxford: Oxford University Press, 2002.

Lange, Britta. "Repräsentation von Mensch und Tier." In *Echt. Unecht. Lebensecht. Menschenbilder im Umlauf*, edited by Britta Lange. Berlin: Kulturverlag Kadmos, 2006, pp. 85–127.

Lehrman, D. S. "A critique of Konrad Lorenz' theory of instinctive behavior." In *Foundations of animal behavior*, edited by L. D. Houck and L. C. Drickamer. Chicago: University of Chicago Press, 1996.

Lonsdorf, Elizabeth V., Stephen R. Ross, and Tetsuro Matsuzawa, eds. *The Mind of the Chimpanzee: Ecological and Experimental Perspectives*, Chicago: University of Chicago Press, 2010.

Lorenz, Konrad. *On Aggression*. London: Methuen, 1966.

M

MacClancy, Jeremy, and Agustin Fuentes. *Centralizing Fieldwork: Critical Perspectives from Primatology, Biological and Social Anthropology*. New York and Oxford: Berghahn Books, 2010.

Margulis, Lynn. *Symbiotic Planet: A New Look at Evolution*. New York: Basic Books, 1998.

Marx, Jean L. "Ape-language controversy flares up." *Science*, vol. 207, no. 4437 (March 1980), pp. 1330–1333.

Massumi, Brian. *What Animals Teach Us about Politics*. Durham, NC and London: Duke University Press, 2014.

Matsuzawa, Tetsuro, and William Clement McGrew. "Kinji Imanishi and 60 years of Japanese Primatology." *Current Biology*, vol. 18, no. 14 (2008), pp. R587–R591.

McClure, Mary Ann. "A passion to connect: The science of Jane Goodall, Dian Fossey, and Birutė Galdikas." *Research in Philosophy and Technology*, vol. 16 (1997), pp. 49–60.

McDougall, William. *An Introduction to Social Psychology*. Boston: John W. Luce & Co., 1912.

McPherson, Angie. "Zoologist Dian Fossey: A storied life with gorillas." *National Geographic* online edition, January 18, 2014. http://news.nationalgeographic.com/news/2014/01/140116-dian-fossey-google-doodle-national-geographic-gorillas-birthday/

Mercader, Julio et al. "4,300-year-old-chimpanzee sites and the origins of percussive stone technology." *Proceedings of the National Academy of Sciences*, vol. 104, no. 9 (2007), pp. 3043–3048.

Montagu, M. F. Ashley, ed. *Man and Aggression*. New York: Holt, Rinehart & Winston, 1973.

Montgomery, Sy. *Walking with the Great Apes: Jane Goodall, Dian Fossey, Birutė Galdikas*. Boston: Chelsea Green Publishing, 2009 [1991].

Morgan, Elaine. *The Descent of Woman*. London: Souvenir Press, 1972.

Morris, Desmond. *Monkey*. London: Reaktion Books, 2013.

Mundis, Hester. *No He's Not a Monkey, He's an Ape and He's My Son*. New York: Crown Publishers, 1976.

N

Nagel, Tobias. "Porträt Lee 'Scratch' Perry." *Frankfurter Allgemeine Zeitung*, December 20, 2001.

National Geographic, vol. 128, no. 6 (December 1965).

National Geographic, vol. 137, no. 1 (January 1970).

National Geographic, vol. 148, no. 4 (October 1975).

O

Ohnuki-Tierney, Emiko. *The Monkey as Mirror: Symbolic Transformations in Japanese History and Ritual*. Princeton: Princeton University Press, 1989.

P

Pan African Programme, "The cultured chimpanzee; Guidelines for research and data collection," July 2014. http://panafrican.eva.mpg.de/.

Panofsky, Erwin. "Et in Arcadia Ego: Poussin and the Elegiac Tradition." In *Meaning in the Visual Arts: Papers in and on Art History*, edited by Erwin Panofsky. New York: Doubleday Anchor Books 1955, pp. 295–320.

Parker, Ian. "Swingers: Bonobos are celebrated as peace-loving, matriarchal, and sexually liberated. Are they?" *The New Yorker*, July 30, 2007, pp. 48–61.

Parkin, Robert, and Linda Stone, eds. *Kinship and Family: An Anthropological Reader*, New York: Routledge, 2004.

Patterson, Francine. "The gestures of a gorilla: Language acquisition in another pongid," *Brain and Language*, vol. 5, no. 1 (1978), pp. 72–97.

Patterson, Francine. "Conversations with a gorilla." *National Geographic*, vol. 154, no. 4, April 1978, pp. 438–465.

Patterson, Francine, and Eugene Linden. *The Education of Koko*. New York: Holt, Rinehart & Winston, 1981.

Poe, Edgar Allan. "The Murders in the Rue Morgue." In *The Murders in the Rue Morgue and Other Stories*. Rockville, MD: Wildside Press, 2011. Originally published in *Graham's Magazine*, April 1841.

Post, Stephen G. et al. *Altruism and Altruistic Love: Science, Philosophy, and Religion in Dialogue*. Oxford: Oxford University Press, 2002.

Premack, Ann James, and David Premack. "Teaching language to an ape." *Scientific American*, vol. 227, no. 4 (October 1972), pp. 92–99.

Premack, Ann James, and David Premack. *The Mind of an Ape*. New York: Norton, 1983.

R

Radick, Gregory. *The Simian Tongue: The Long Debate about Animal Language*. Chicago: University of Chicago Press, 2007.

Reed, Evelyn. *Woman's Evolution: From Matriarchal Clan to Patriarchal Family*. New York: Pathfinder Press, 1975.

Rich, Jeremy. *Missing Links*. Athens, GA: University of Georgia Press, 2012.

Rony, Fatimah Tobing. *The Third Eye: Race, Cinema and Ethnographic Spectacle*. Durham, CT and London: Duke University Press, 1996.

Ruch, Theodore C. *Bibliographia primatologica*. Springfield, IL: Charles C. Thomas, 1941.

Rumbaugh, Duane M., and Sue Savage-Rumbaugh. "Symbolization, language, and chimpanzees: a theoretical reevaluation based on initial language acquisition process in four young Pan troglodytes." *Brain and Language*, vol. 6, no. 3 (1978), pp. 265–300.

Rumbaugh, Duane M., and Sue Savage-Rumbaugh. "Chimpanzee language research: Status and potential." *Behavior Research Methods & Instrumentation*, vol. 10, no. 2 (March 1978), pp. 119–131.

Ryan, Christopher, and Cacilda Jetha, *Sex at Dawn: The Prehistoric Origins of Modern Sexuality*. New York: HarperCollins, 2010.

S

Saito, Aya. "Byoga kodo no hattatsu to hyosho byoga no kigen: Hito to chimpanzee no hikaku" (The origin of representational drawing: Drawing behavior of chimpanzees compared with that of human children). *Japanese Psychological Review*, vol. 53, no. 53 (2010), pp. 367–382.

Savage-Rumbaugh, Sue, and Roger Lewin. *Kanzi: The Ape at the Brink of the Human Mind*. New York: Wiley, 1994.

Savage-Rumbaugh, Sue, Duane Rumbaugh, and William M. Fields. "Empirical Kanzi: The ape language controversy revisited." *Skeptic*, vol. 15, no. 1 (March 2009), p. 25.

Sebeok, Thomas A., ed. *Speaking of Apes: A Critical Anthology of Two-Way Communication with Man*. London and New York: Plenum Press, 1980.

Sebeok, Thomas A., and Robert Rosenthal. "The Clever Hans phenomenon: Communication with horses, whales, apes, and people." *Annals of the New York Academy of Sciences*, vol. 364 (1981), pp. 152–159.

Seeßlen, Georg. "King Kong, Cheetah und der Planet der Affen: Der Affe im Film." Lecture on November 6, 2008 at Zoo Basel as part of the lecture series "Affe, Mensch – und wir."

Self, Will. *Great Apes*. London: Bloomsbury, 2011. UK edition.

Seidenberg, M. S., and L. A. Petitto. "Signing behavior in apes: A critical review." *Cognition*, vol. 7 (1979), pp. 177–215.

Siegel, Joshua. *Frederick Wiseman*. New York: Museum of Modern Art, 2010.

Singer, Peter. *Animal Liberation*. New York: New York Review and Random House, 1975.

Smuts, Barbara B. *Sex and Friendship in Baboons*. Cambridge, MA: Harvard University Press, 1999.

Sokolowsky, Alexander. *Beobachtungen über die Psyche der Menschenaffen*. Frankfurt am Main: Neuer Frankfurter Verlag, 1908.

Sorenson, John. *Ape*. London: Reaktion Books, 2009.

Spalding, Linda. *A Dark Place in the Jungle*. Chapel Hill, NC: Algonquin Books, 1998.

Strum, Shirley C., and Linda M. Fedigan. "Changing views of Primate Society." In *Primate Encounters: Models of Science, Gender, and Society*, edited by Shirley C. Strum and Linda M. Fedigan. Chicago: University of Chicago Press, 2000, p. 19.

Sussman, Robert, and Joshua Marshack. "Are humans inherently killers?" Followed by a response from Richard Wrangham. Global Nonkilling Working Papers, no. 1 (2010). http://www.nonkilling.org.

T

Tanner, Nancy Makepeace. *On Becoming Human*. New York: Cambridge University Press, 1981.

Temerlin, Maurice K. *Lucy: Growing Up Human: A Chimpanzee Daughter in a Psychotherapist's Family*. London: Science and Behavior Books, 1975.

Terrace, Herbert S. et al. "Can an ape create a sentence?" *Science*, vol. 206, no. 4421 (November 1979), pp. 891–902.

Terrace, Herbert S. "How Nim Chimpsky Changed My Mind." *Psychology Today*, vol. 13, no. 6 (November 1979), pp. 65–76.

Terrace, Herbert S. *Nim: A Chimpanzee Who Learned Sign Language*, New York: Knopf Publisher House, 1979.

Thomas, Vivian. "La grande singerie," *France Today*, May 14, 2012. http://www.francetoday.com/articles/2012/05/14/la-grande-singerie.html.

Tiedemann, Friedrich. "On the Brain of the Negro, Compared with that of the European and the Orang-Outang." *Philosophical Transactions of the Royal Society of Science of London*, 1863, p. 520

Tiger, Lionel, and Robin Fox. *The Imperial Animal*. New York: Transaction, 1972.

U

Ulrich, Antonia. "Äffen und NachschAffen." *kunsttexte.de*, 2 /2005. http://www.kunsttexte.de/index.php?id=711&idartikel=12359&ausgabe=12136&zu=121&L=1.

V

Voss, Julia. *Darwin's Pictures: Views of Evolutionary Theory, 1834–1874*. New Haven: Yale University Press, 2010.

W

Wade, Nicholas. "Does man alone have language? Apes reply in riddles, and a horse says neigh." *Science*, vol. 208, no. 4450 (June 1980), pp. 1349–1351.

Wells, H. G. *The Island of Dr. Moreau*, New York: Dover Publications, 1996 [1896].

Whiten, A. et al. "Cultures in chimpanzees." *Nature*, vol. 399, no. 6737 (1999), pp. 682–685.

Wikipedia, s.v. "Killer Ape Theory." Last modified April 3, 2014. http://en.wikipedia.org/wiki/Killer_ape_theory.

Wild Chimpanzee Foundation. Accessed May 8, 2015. http://www.wildchimpanzees.org/.

Wilson, Edward O. *Sociobiology: The New Synthesis*. Cambridge, MA: Harvard University Press, 1998 [1975].

Women in Science, s.v. "Nadezhda Ladygina-Kohts." Accessed May 8, 2015. http://women-inscience.history.msu.edu/Biography/C-4A-5/nadezhda-ladyginakohts/.

Wrangham, Richard, and Dale Peterson. *Demonic Males: Apes and the Origins of Human Violence*. New York: Houghton Mifflin Harcourt, 1997.

Y

Yamamoto, Shinya, and Masayuki Tanaka. "How did altruistic cooperation evolve in humans? Perspectives from experiments on chimpanzees (Pan troglodytes)." *Interaction Studies*, vol. 10, no. 2 (2009), pp. 150–182.

Yamamoto, Shinya, Tatyana Humle, and Masayuki Tanaka. "Chimpanzees help each other upon request." *PLoS ONE*, vol. 4, no. 10 (2009), e7416.

Yerkes, Robert M. *Almost Human*. New York: Century, 1925.

Yerkes, Robert M. *Chimpanzees: A Laboratory Colony*, New York: Yale University Press, 1943.

Z

Žižek, Slavoj. *The Ticklish Subject: The Absence of Political Ontology*. London and New York: Verso, 2000.

Zuckerman, Solly. *The Social Life of Monkeys and Apes*. New York: Harcourt, Brace & Co., 1932.

FILMOGRAPHY

#

2001 – A Space Odyssey. Directed by Stanley Kubrick. 1968. 160 min. © Warner Bros. Entertainment, Inc.

A

Activity Characteristics of Gibbons (Hylobates Lar), Part III Social Behavior. Directed by Clarence Ray Carpenter. 1974. 16 min. Used with permission from Penn State University Libraries, Special Collections Library.

Algae fishing and miscellaneous excerpts. 2011 & 2014. © Pan African Programme: The Cultured Chimpanzee, Max Planck Institute for Evolutionary Anthropology, Leipzig.

B

Baboon Social Organiziation. Directed by Sherwood Washburn and Irven DeVore. 1963. 17 min. Penn State Media Sales.

Bedtime for Bonzo. Directed by Frederick De Cordova. 1951. 3 min. © Universal Pictures International.

Behavior of the Macaques of Japan. Directed by Clarence Ray Carpenter. 1969. 24 min. Used with permission from Penn State University Libraries, Special Collections Library.

Beneath the Planet of the Apes. Directed by Ted Post. 1970. 95 min. ©Twentieth Century Fox Film Corporation.

C

Capuchin Monkeys Reject Unequal Pay. Directed by Sarah F. Brosnan and Frans de Waal. 2003. 1 min. Yerkes National Primate Research Center, Emory University, Atlanta, Georgia.

Chimpanzees: Leaf Clipping / Interview with Christophe Boesch. Max Planck Institute for Evolutionary Anthropology, Leipzig. 2008. 2:04 min. © Max Planck Institute for Evolutionary Anthropology, Leipzig. Courtesy Exploratorium, www.exploratorium.edu.

Chimps onder Elkaar (The Family of Chimps). Directed by Bert Haanstra. 1984. 55 min. Courtesy Beeld en Geluid.

Comparative Tests on a Human and a Chimpanzee Infant of Approximately the Same Age. Directed by Luella and Winthrop Kellogg. 1931. 18 min. Penn State Media Sales.

D

Donna Haraway reads "The National Geographic" on Primates. Paper Tiger Television. 1987. 28 min. Courtesy Paper Tiger Television.

E

Experiments on chimpanzees' flexible targeted helping. Shinya Yamamoto (Kobe University), Primate Research Institute, Kyoto University. 2007–2009. 2 min. Courtesy Primate Research Institute, Kyoto University.

Experiments with chimpanzees, works of N. Ladygina-Kohts. Directed by Rudolf (Rudy) Kohts. Cinematography by Anatoly Anzhanov (Zhandarmov). 1962. 17 min. Courtesy Kohts family, www.kohts.com.

G

Gorillas in the Mist. Directed by Michael Apted. 1988. 129 min. © Warner Bros. Entertainment, Inc.

H

Honey harvest, termite fishing, and miscellaneous excerpts. 2013. © Pan African Programme: The Cultured Chimpanzee, Max Planck Institute for Evolutionary Anthropology, Leipzig.

I

Intelligenzprüfungen an Menschenaffen. Directed by Wolfgang Köhler. 1914–1917. 11 min. Collection of Adolf-Würth-Zentrum für Geschichte der Psychologie der Universität Würzburg.

Island of Lost Souls. Directed by Erle C. Kenton. 1932. 70 min. © Paramount Pictures.

K

Kanzi: An Ape of Genius. Directed by Genya Niio. 1993. 50:43 min. © NHK 1993 in cooperation with The Language Research Center, College of Arts & Sciences of Georgia State University.

Koko Le Gorille Qui Parle (Koko: A Talking Gorilla). Directed by Barbet Schroeder. 1978. 85 min. Courtesy Les Films du Losange.

L

Konrad Lorenz's Discussion with Richard Evans: Aggression. Directed by Richard Evans. 1975. 31 min. Penn State Media Sales.

Lucy. Directed by Luc Besson. 2014. 89 min. © Universal Pictures International.

M

Miss Goodall and the Wild Chimpanzees. Directed by Marshall Flaum. 1965. 50 min. © 1965 National Geographic Society. Courtesy National Geographic Society.

N

Neues von Goma, Bébé gorille a 5 mois.
Schweizerische Filmwochenschau (SFW).
February 19, 1960. 12 min. Schweizerisches
Bundesarchiv CH-BAR J2.143#1996/386
#898#2*.

New Chimpanzees, The. Directed by Cynthia
Moses for National Geographic. 1995.
57 min. © 1995 National Geographic Society.
Courtesy National Geographic Society.

Nut cracking and miscellaneous excerpts.
2011 & 2013. © Pan African Programme: The
Cultured Chimpanzee, Max Planck Institute
for Evolutionary Anthropology.

S

Search for the Great Apes. National
Geographic Society. 1975. 60 min. © 1975
National Geographic Society. Courtesy
National Geographic Society.

Stone throwing. 2014. © Pan African
Programme: The Cultured Chimpanzee,
Max Planck Institute for Evolutionary
Anthropology, Leipzig.

Symbolic representation and working
memory in chimpanzees. Tetsuro
Matsuzawa, Primate Research Institute,
Kyoto University. 2013. 4:50 min.

T

Too Close for Comfort? Narrated by
David Attenborough. BBC. 1992. 30 min.
Getty Images ® BBC Motion Gallery.

V

Videos on "leaf clipping." Directed by
Tobias Deschner. 2009. 4:42 min.
© Max Planck Institute for Evolutionary
Anthropology, Leipzig.

Vocalization and Speech in Chimpanzees.
Directed by Keith and Catherine Hayes.
1950. 12 min. Penn State Media Sales.

BIOGRAPHIES

CURATORS

Anselm Franke
(Berlin)
and Hila Peleg
(Berlin / Athens)

Anselm Franke is a curator and critic. Since
2013, he has headed the Department of
Visual Arts and Film at the Haus der Kulturen
der Welt, Berlin, where he co-curated the
exhibition and publication *The Whole Earth:
California and the Disappearance of the
Outside* with Diedrich Diederichsen, the exhibition *After Year Zero* with Annett Busch
(both 2013), and most recently the exhibition
Forensis with Eyal Weizman, 2014. His project
Animism was presented in different versions
in Antwerp, Bern, Vienna, Berlin, New York,
Shenzhen, Seoul, and Beirut between 2010
and 2014. Franke has edited numerous publications and regularly contributes articles
to magazines such as *Metropolis M*, *e-flux
journal*, and *Cabinet*. He was curator of the
Taipei Biennial 2012 and the Shanghai Biennale 2014.

Hila Peleg is a curator and filmmaker based
in Berlin. She has curated solo shows,
large-scale group exhibitions, and various
interdisciplinary cultural events in public
institutions across Europe, such as KW
Institute for Contemporary Art (Berlin), Extra
City Kunsthal (Antwerp), Iniva – Institute
of International Visual Arts (London), and the
Haus der Kulturen der Welt (Berlin). Peleg
was co-curator of *Manifesta 7 European
Biennial of Contemporary Art* (Trentino-Alto
Adige / Südtirol, 2008) and curator of the film
program at the *10th Shanghai Art Biennale*
(2014). Peleg is the founder and artistic
director of the *Berlin Documentary Forum*.
Initiated at the Haus der Kulturen der Welt
(HKW) in 2010, this biannual event is devoted
to the production and presentation of
contemporary and historical documentary
practices in an interdisciplinary context.
Peleg is curator of *Wohnungsfrage* (October–December 2015, HKW). Hila Peleg is curator of *documenta 14*, which will take place
in Kassel and Athens in spring / summer 2017.

ARTISTS

Lene Berg
(Berlin / New York)

Lene Berg (b. 1965), artist and filmmaker,
often draws her inspiration from documentary material. Her artistic praxis includes
installations, performance, film, photography,
and text-based works. A number of projects
have been produced in public spaces. She
frequently explores iconic, art historical concepts, where her works connect visual and
political history. The relationship between art
and propaganda as well as the representation
of truth and fiction are essential. Lene Berg
trained as a film director at the Dramatiska
Institutet in Stockholm and is a professor
of art.

Selected solo exhibitions: 55th Venice
Biennale, Norwegian Pavilion (2013); Henie
Onstad Kunstsenter, Høvikodden (2012);
Konsthall C, Stockholm (2012); Fotogalleriet,
Oslo (2008); Cooper Union, New York (2008);
Whitechapel Gallery, London (2007). Selected
group exhibitions: *The Shadow of War*,
Kunstnernes Hus, Oslo (2014); Manifesta 8
(2010); Transmediale, Berlin (2008); Sydney
Biennale (2008); *Pensee Sauvage*, Frankfurter
Kunstverein (2007).

Marcus Coates
(London)

Marcus Coates (b. 1968) explores man's relationship with animals and nature. He works
with installation, photography, sculpture, and
performance to devise processes to test
the pragmatism and insight that empathetic
perspectives and imagined realities can
offer. He studied art at the Kent Institute of
Art and Design and at the Royal Academy of
Arts in London.

Marcus Coates is the winner of several
prestigious art prizes. His international exhibitions include: *British Council Touring Exhibition* in Japan (2014–2015); Centro de Arte
Moderna, Lisbon (2013); Serpentine Gallery
(2011): Museum of Contemporary Art, Tokyo
(2010); Sydney Biennale (2010); Kunsthalle
Zurich (2009); Tate Trienniale, London (2009);
Manifesta 7 (2008); Athens Biennial (2008);
Whitechapel Gallery, London (2007).

Anja Dornieden &
Juan David González Monroy
(Berlin)

Anja Dornieden (b. 1984), filmmaker, studied
applied media studies at the Ilmenau University of Technology and New School University
in New York. Her films have been presented

at numerous international film festivals, including: Ann Arbor Film Festival in Michigan; Edinburgh International Film Festival; Visions du Réel in Nyon; Duisburger Filmwoche. Juan David González Monroy (b. 1983), filmmaker, studied anthropology at the Universidad de Los Andes in Bogota and media studies at New School University in New York. His work has been shown at venues including: Ullens Center for Contemporary Art in Peking; Image Forum in Tokyo; International Film Festival Rotterdam; Ann Arbor Film Festival in Michigan.

Anja Dornieden and Juan David González Monroy have worked together under the name OJOBOCA since 2010. Their work includes films, installations, and performances. Both filmmakers are committed to experimental film and have been using 16 mm and Super 8 film for a number of years. They are both members of Filmlabor and the artists' collective LaborBerlin.

Ines Doujak
(London and Vienna)

Ines Doujak is a feminist artist who uses various media, focusing on the political dimension of cultural exchanges. She recently received two research grants from the Austrian Science Fund *Loomshuttles / Warpaths* (2010–2014), an extensive study of textiles to investigate their global history characterized by cultural, class, and gender conflict; and *Utopian Pulse: Flares in the Darkroom* (together with Oliver Ressler, 2013–2015) which resulted in an exhibition at Secession, Vienna (2014) and a publication (Pluto Press, London).

Selected exhibitions: *Follow the Leader*, Johann Jacobs Museum, Zürich (2015); *The Potosí Principle*, Museo Nacional Centro de Arte Reina Sofía, Madrid; Haus der Kulturen der Welt, Berlin; Museo Nacional de Arte, La Paz, Bolivia (2010); *Ladies Almanack**, Tranzit CZ, Prague (2009); *Peripheral vision and collective body*, MUSEION, Bolzano (2008); documenta 12, Kassel (2007). In collaboration with John Barker: *The Beast and the Sovereign*, MACBA, Barcelona (2015); *Not Dressed for Conquering*, Royal College of Art, London (2013); *Garden of Learning*, Busan Biennale, Korea (2012).

Coco Fusco
(New York)

Coco Fusco (b. 1960), interdisciplinary artist and writer exploring the relationship between women, society, war, politics, identity, and race. She received a BA in Semiotics from Brown University, an MA in Modern Thought and Literature from Stanford University, and a PhD in Art and Visual Culture from Middlesex University. She has performed, lectured, curated, and exhibited worldwide since 1988. Coco Fusco was the MLK Visiting Professor at the Massachusetts Institute of Technology in 2014–2015. She is a recipient of a 2013 Guggenheim Fellowship, a 2013 Absolut Art Writing Award, a 2013 Fulbright Fellowship, and a 2012 US Artists Fellowship.

Coco Fusco has participated in numerous international biennials, including: Venice Biennale (2015); Whitney Biennial (2008 and 1993); Performa 05, New York (2005); Shanghai Biennale (2004). Her exhibitions include: Walker Art Center, Minneapolis (2014); Centre Pompidou, Paris (2014); New Museum of Contemporary Art, New York (2013); Contemporary Arts Museum Houston (2012); Museo Nacional Centro de Arte Reina Sofia, Madrid (2012); Tate Liverpool (2010).

Jos de Gruyter & Harald Thys
(Brussels)

The collaborative work of Jos de Gruyter & Harald Thys is rooted in a folksy, tragicomic sensibility honed into an experimental dramaturgy. For their video and photographic work they have engaged a recurring cast of nonprofessional actors as well as invented or adopted personae spanning the forms of puppets, dummies, plush animals, makeshift robots, and rejected toys. These characters continually rehearse power dynamics and emotional entanglements, creating worlds not unlike our own, yet more focused, bizarre and bleak. (Monika Szewczyk)

Jos de Gruyter (b. 1965) and Harald Thys (b. 1966) have had solo exhibitions at numerous European institutions including: Kunsthalle Wien, Vienna; M HKA, Antwerp; Kunsthalle Basel; Culturgest, Lisbon; and were included in the Venice Biennale (2013) and the Berlin Biennial (2008). This spring, CCA Wattis Institute for Contemporary Arts, San Francisco; The Power Station, Dallas; and MoMA PS1, New York have dedicated solo exhibitions to their work in the US.

Pierre Huyghe
(Paris)

The works of Pierre Huyghe (b. 1962) appear in a variety of different forms—as living systems, objects, films, photographs, drawings, and music. His films and video installations repeatedly explore the different layers of reality which become apparent, for example, through synchronization or the alteration of the social context. Pierre Huyghe studied at the École nationale supérieure des Arts Décoratifs in Paris. In 2001 he represented France at the Venice Biennale where his pavilion won a special jury prize. In 2006 he screened his film *A Journey That Wasn't* at the Whitney Biennale in New York, at the reopening of the ARC/MAM Paris, as well as at Tate Modern. In January 2011 the Kunstmuseum Basel / Museum für Gegenwartskunst devoted an exhibition to Pierre Huyghe, and at the Völklinger Hütte his neon object *Skin of Light* forms part of the permanent exhibition *GameArt*. Huyghe participated in documenta 13 (2012), as well as in exhibitions at the Museum Ludwig, Cologne (2014); Centre Pompidou, Paris (2012); Los Angeles County Museum of Art (2012). In 2013 he was awarded the Roswitha Haftmann Prize, and in 2015 the Kurt Schwitters Prize.

Louise Lawler
(New York)

Louise Lawler (b. 1947) works with photographs, material images, and installations. She completed her studies at Cornell University in Ithaca, New York, and for the past thirty years has documented the private life of art by photographing well-known works in museums, storage and auction houses, and the living rooms of art collectors. She records how works of art become projection screens for desires. Lawler's photographs show the artistic works either in sections or concealed, decentered and in detail, so that they are sometimes barely recognizable—and as a result shift further into the focus of attention.

Selected exhibitions: *No Drones*, Metro Pictures, New York; Sprüth Magers, London; Yvon Lambert, Paris (2014); *Louise Lawler: Adjusted*, Museum Ludwig, Cologne (2013/2014); *Long Term View*, Dia Art Foundation, New York (2013); *(SELECTED). Louise Lawler*, Galerie Neue Meister, Albertinum, Dresden (2012); documenta 12 (2007); *Big Bang*, Centre Pompidou, Paris (2006); *Twice Untitled and Other Pictures (looking back)*, The Wexner Center, Columbus, Ohio (2006); *Louise Lawler and Other Artists*, Museum für Gegenwartskunst Basel (2004).

Damián Ortega
(Mexico City)

Damián Ortega (b. 1967) began his career as a political caricaturist, creating his first works in parallel using everyday objects such as tools, balls, trash cans, or bricks. In his artistic works he explores specific economic, aesthetic, and cultural constellations and the connections between regional culture and the consumption of raw materials.

In 2002 he received international recognition with his work *Cosmic Thing*, a VW Beetle broken down into its individual parts and attached to the ceiling. Selected solo and group exhibitions: Institute of Contemporary Art, Philadelphia (2002); Kunsthalle

Basel (2004); Tate Modern, London; Museu
da Arte Pampulha, Belo Horizonte (2005);
Museum of Contemporary Art, Los Angeles
(2007); Centre Pompidou, Paris (2008); Institute of Contemporary Art, Boston (2009);
Barbican Curve Gallery, London (2010); Freud
Museum, London (2013); Museu de Arte Moderna do Rio de Janeiro (2015).

Nagisa Ōshima

Nagisa Ōshima (1932–2013) was a Japanese
film director, screenplay writer, and producer.
In 1959 he began work as a director at the
Shochiku film studios and soon gained a
reputation as one of the leading exponents
of *Nuberu bagu*, the New Wave. In 1976 he
had an international hit with the controversial film *In the Realm of the Senses* (*Ai
no korīda*). In 1978 *The Empire of Passion*
(*Ai no bōrei*) received its premiere, winning
the prize for best director at the Cannes
Film Festival. *Max Mon Amour* (1986) is one
of Nagisa Ōshima's late works.

Erik Steinbrecher
(Berlin)

Artist Erik Steinbrecher (b. 1963) works with
a range of different materials. By transform-
ing their appearance he produces distinct
scenarios, creating surprising connections.
His work includes works in public spaces,
sculptures, photo installations, video, graphic
and artists' books. Erik Steinbrecher studied
art and history in Basel and architecture
in Zurich under Fabio Reinhardt. In 2006 he
was visiting professor at the Hochschule
für bildende Künste in Hamburg, and since
2008 he has taught at the Zurich University
of the Arts.
Selected solo and group exhibitions:
documenta x (1997); KW Institute
for Contemporary Art, Berlin; MoMA PS1,
New York (2000–2001); Kunsthalle Wien (2004);
Museum Haus Konstruktiv, Zurich (2004),
Art Library – Berlin State Museums (2012);
Haus der Kulturen der Welt, Berlin (2012);
Graphic Collection of the ETH Zurich (2014).

Rosemarie Trockel
(Cologne)

Rosemarie Trockel (b. 1952) is a visual artist,
professor at the Kunstakademie Düsseldorf,
and a member of various academies for
science and the arts. Her multifaceted work
includes sculptures, ceramics, wool images,
and drawings, as well as video works and
large installations. Her work, which cannot
be reduced to an iconography or a specific
art theory, questions social role models and
established norms. The artist frequently
explores feminist themes, topics taken from
the animal world, and theories of sexuality,
culture, and artistic production.
In 1988 she exhibited at the Museum of
Modern Art in New York, and in 1999 she
became the first female artist to design the
German Pavilion at the Venice Biennial,
contributing again in 2013. In 1997 and 2012
she participated in the documenta in Kassel.
Selected solo exhibitions: Kunsthaus
Bregenz (2015); Museo Nacional Centro de
Arte Reina Sofía in Madrid; New Museum
in New York; Serpentine Gallery in London
(2012/2013); WIELS, Centre D'Art Contemporain
in Brussels; Culturgest in Lisbon; Museion,
Bozen (2012/2013); Kunsthalle Zurich (2010).
She is the recipient of numerous awards
including the Kaiserring Art Prize of the City
of Goslar in 2011 and the Roswitha Haftmann
Prize, Zurich 2014.

Klaus Weber
(Berlin)

Klaus Weber (b. 1967) studied fine art and
visual communication in the "Freie Klasse"
at the HdK (now UdK) Berlin. Klaus Weber's
cross-media and cross-spatial works are
frequently based on complex technological
relationships and elaborately organized
manufacturing processes. Through the inci-
sive manipulation of everyday structures,
the tracing of discrepancies, and the exploration of impossibilities, they undermine
both the metaphorical and actual power
of a functionalist rationality. Klaus Weber was
awarded the HAP Grieshaber Prize for his
life work in 2012.
Selected solo exhibitions: *Equitable Vitrines*, Welton Becket & Associates Equitable
Life Building, Los Angeles (2015); *Hybrid
Naples*, Fondazione Morra Greco, Naples
(2013); *Alle Körper fallen gleich schnell*,
Deutscher Künstlerbund, Berlin (2012); *If you
leave me I'm not coming, & Already There!*,
Nottingham Contemporary (2011); *Shape
of the Ape*, Andrew Kreps Gallery, New York
(2007).
Selected group exhibitions: Lyon
Biennale (2015); *Painting Forever! Keilrahmen*,
KW Institute for Contemporary Art, Berlin
(2013); *Painting without Paint*, David Risley
Gallery, Copenhagen (2012); *The Kaleido-
scopic Eye*, Mori Art Museum, Tokyo (2009);
The Art of Narration, Sprüth Magers, Berlin
(2011).

Frederick Wiseman
(Cambridge, Massachusetts)

Frederick Wiseman (b. 1930) is a film and
theater director. He has shot over forty documentary films and produced feature films.
His films, beginning with *Titicut Follies* (1967),
are impressive studies of institutions, for
example a prison, a school, a zoo, a primate
research center, and a museum, as in the
case of his latest film *National Gallery* (2014).
Frederick Wiseman has won numerous
scholarships and awards, including the
MacArthur Fellowship in 1982, the George Polk
Career Award in 2006, and the Golden Lion
for his life work at the Venice Film Festival in
2014. In 2012 he participated in the Whitney
Biennale in New York.

AUTHORS

John Barker, Ines Doujak, Matthew Hyland

John Barker is a writer, essayist and performer who, since the 1970s, has been focused on economics, geopolitical dynamics and the exploitation of labor. Ines Doujak is a feminist artist who uses various media. They live in London and Vienna, and work together through a common interest in the political dimension of cultural exchanges. Since 2010 they have collaborated on exhibitions such as *The Beast and the Sovereign*, MACBA, Barcelona (2015); *Not Dressed for Conquering*, Royal College of Art, London (2013); *Garden of Learning*, Busan Biennale, Korea (2012). "Matthew Hyland" is the assumed name of Clinical Wasteman. For Ines Doujak see „Artists".

Christophe Boesch

Christophe Boesch is the director of the Department of Primatology at the Max Planck Institute for Evolutionary Anthropology in Leipzig. Since 1976 he has been studying groups of chimpanzees living in the wild, for example in the Taï National Park in Côte d'Ivoire, to examine their behavior in their natural habitat—in particular social learning processes and differences between different populations, for example in the use of tools. In the face of increasing threats to chimpanzees caused by the destruction of the rainforests, in 2000 Boesch established the Wild Chimpanzee Foundation, which is dedicated to protecting their habitats. In conjunction with Hjalmar Kühl he directs the Pan African Programme: The Cultured Chimpanzee, which records the behaviors and habitats of forty different chimpanzee populations in more than twelve African countries.

Astrid Deuber-Mankowsky

Astrid Deuber-Mankowsky is currently Professor of Media Studies and Gender Studies at the Ruhr-Universität Bochum. She has published extensively on topics in feminist theory, representation and mediality, media theory and philosophy, as well as religion and modernism. Her book *Der frühe Walter Benjamin und Hermann Cohen: Jüdische Werte, Kritische Philosophie, vergängliche Erfahrung* (Berlin: Verlag Vorwerk 8, 2000]) was awarded the Humboldt University prize for best dissertation. English translations of her writings include *Lara Croft: Cyber Heroine* (Minneapolis: University of Minnesota Press, 2005, tr. Dominic Bonfiglio, foreword Sue-Ellen Case). Her more recent work from 2007 is entitled *Praktiken der Illusion: Kant, Nietzsche, Cohen, Benjamin bis Donna J. Haraway* (Berlin: Verlag Vorwerk 8). She was a visiting scholar at UC Berkeley (2007), visiting professor at the Centre d'études du vivant, Université Paris VII – Diderot (2010), Max Kade Professor at Columbia University (2012), and Senior Fellow at the Internationales Kolleg für Kulturtechnikforschung und Medienphilosophie in Weimar (2013). She is also an associate member of the Institute for Cultural Inquiry Berlin.

Cord Riechelmann

Cord Riechelmann, who was born in Celle in 1960, studied biology and philosophy at the Freie Universität Berlin, and later lectured in the social behavior of primates and the history of biological research. He writes for various newspapers including the *Frankfurter Allgemeine Sonntagszeitung*, *Merkur*, *taz*, and *Jungle World*, and has published the books *Bestiarium: Der Zoo als Welt – die Welt als Zoo* (Frankfurt am Main: Eichborn, 2003) and *Wilde Tiere in der Großstadt* (Berlin: Nicolaische Verlagsbuchhandlung, 2004). In partnership with Marcel Schwierin he curated the special program "Cinema of the Animals" at the 2011 Oberhausen Short Film Festival. In 2013, his volume *Krähen* (Crows) was published as part of the nature study series by Matthes & Seitz Berlin. Currently he is a lecturer in general studies at the Berlin University of the Arts.

CREDITS

FRONT COVER

The cover is colored in solid Pantone 2022 U, with image printed on top using black.

AFFE, 2015 (detail)
Courtesy the artist, Berlin
Photo © Andreas Meichsner

MACACA FUSCATA

• p. 60 Clarence Ray Carpenter
MACACA FUSCATA (CERCOPITHECIDAE) – Tree-Top Signaling, 1971
Courtesy Technische Informationsbibliothek (TIB), Hannover

ARTWORKS

• p. 64 Lene Berg
KOPFKINO (MINDFUCK), 2012
Courtesy the artist, Berlin / New York
Commissioned by Henie Onstad Kunstsenter (HOK), Høvikodden, Norway

• p. 68 Marcus Coates in collaboration with Volker Sommer
DEGREECOORDINATES
Shared traits of the Hominini (Humans, Bonobos and Chimpanzees), 2015
Courtesy Kate MacGarry, London; Workplace Gallery, UK

• p. 72 Anja Dornieden & Juan David González Monroy
THE MASKED MONKEYS, 2015
Courtesy the artists, Berlin

• p. 76 Ines Doujak in collaboration with John Barker and Matthew Hyland
06 KRIMINALAFFE, 2015
Courtesy the artist, Vienna / London
Produced with the support of Haus der Kulturen der Welt
p. 77 Photo © Sebastian Bolesch

• p. 80 Coco Fusco
TED ETHOLOGY: PRIMATE VISIONS OF THE HUMAN MIND, 2015
Courtesy the artist, New York
Produced at the facilities of BRIC's Community Media Center in Brooklyn
Additional production support by Haus der Kulturen der Welt

• p. 82 Jos de Gruyter & Harald Thys
DIE AAP VAN BLOEMFONTEIN, 2014
[The Ape Of Bloemfontein]
Courtesy Galerie Micheline Szwajcer, Brussels; Galerie Isabella Bortolozzi Berlin

• p. 84 Pierre Huyghe
UNTITLED (HUMAN MASK), 2014
Courtesy Marian Goodman Gallery, New York; Hauser & Wirth, London; Esther Schipper, Berlin; Anna Lena Films, Paris

• p. 86 Louise Lawler
MICHAEL, 2001
Courtesy the artist, New York;
Sprüth Magers, Berlin; Metro Pictures,
New York

• p. 88 Damián Ortega
TRANSICIÓN DEL MONO AL HOMBRE,
2015 [Transition From Ape To Man]
Courtesy the artist; kurimanzutto,
Mexico City
SHORT HISTORY OF GESTURE,
2. SYNTAX: ARMS / HANDS, 2013
© the artist, Mexico City
Courtesy White Cube, London
THE ROOT OF THE ROOT, 2011–2013
© the artist, Mexico City
Courtesy White Cube, London

• p. 90 Nagisa Ōshima
MAX MON AMOUR, 1986
© 2015 STUDIOCANAL GmbH, Berlin.
All rights reserved.

• p. 92 Erik Steinbrecher
AFFE, 2015
Courtesy the artist, Berlin
Produced with the support of
Haus der Kulturen der Welt
• p. 93 AFFE, 2015 (detail), Photo
© Andreas Meichsner
• pp. 94-95 SHE APE / APE MAN, 2015
Courtesy the artist, Berlin
Produced with the support of
Haus der Kulturen der Welt

• p. 96 Rosemarie Trockel
OHNE TITEL (part of the installation
Pennsylvania Station), 1987
Courtesy Sammlung Goetz, Munich
OHNE TITEL, 1984
Courtesy Ken & Helen Rowe, London
© Rosemarie Trockel, VG Bild-Kunst,
Bonn 2015
• p. 97 Photo © Photostudio Schaub
(Bernhard Schaub / Ralf Höffner) /
Courtesy Sprüth Magers, Köln
OHNE TITEL, 1984
Courtesy private collection

• p. 98 Klaus Weber
KOUROS (WALKING MAN), 2015
Courtesy the artist, Berlin
Produced with the support of
Haus der Kulturen der Welt; Andrew Kreps
Gallery, New York; Herald Street, London
• p. 100 SHAPE OF THE APE, 2007
Courtesy the artist, Berlin; Andrew Kreps
Gallery, New York; Herald Street, London
• p. 101 BEULEN, 2008
© Klaus Weber

• p. 104 Frederick Wiseman
PRIMATE, 1974
Courtesy Zipporah Films, Cambridge,
Massachusetts

• p. 105 WGBH TV Channel
WHAT PRICE KNOWLEDGE, 1974
Courtesy WGBH Media Library
and Archives, Boston

ESSAYS
• p. 23 From Aya Saito, "Byoga kodo no
hattatsu to hyosho byoga no kigen: Hito to
chimpanzee no hikaku" (The origin of representational drawing: Drawing behavior of
chimpanzees compared with that of human
children) in Japanese Psychological Review,
vol. 53, no. 53 (2010), pp. 375. Courtesy
Primate Research Institute, Kyoto University
• p. 28 Courtesy John Addicott
• p. 31 © Alexander Mokletsov, RIA Novosti /
Rossiya Segodnya
• p. 33 © NASA
• p. 34 © Hugo Van Lawick / National
Geographic Creative

DOCUMENTS
The pages 110-197 are colored in solid
Pantone 2022, with images printed on top
using the four-color process.

• p. 110, A) Reproduced with permission of
Koninklijke Bibliotheek, Den Haag, 388 A 6
• p. 111, B) Reproduced with permission of
Peter H. Raven Library, Missouri Botanical
Garden
• p. 112, C) Wikimedia (Public Domain)
• p. 112, D) Reproduced with permission
of Punch Limited
• p. 113, E) Courtesy Musée Buffon,
Ville de Montbard
• p. 114, F) Collection of the Ernst-Haeckel-
Archiv of the Friedrich-Schiller-Universität
Jena
• p. 114, G) Collection of the Ernst-Haeckel-
Archiv of the Friedrich-Schiller-Universität
Jena
• p. 115, H) © Naturalis Biodiversity Center,
Holland
• p. 117, B) © 1963 Julius Springer, Berlin.
With permission of Springer Science+
Business Media
• p. 117, C) Collection of Adolf-Würth-
Zentrum für Geschichte der Psychologie der
Universität Würzburg
• p. 118, E) Reproduced with permission of
Oxford University Press
• p. 119, F) Courtesy Kohts family,
www.kohts.com
• p. 119, G) Courtesy Kohts family,
www.kohts.com
• p. 122, A) Junichiro Itani Archives of the
Primate Research Institute, Kyoto University
• p. 122, B) Junichiro Itani Archives of the
Primate Research Institute, Kyoto University
• p. 122, C) Junichiro Itani Archives of the
Primate Research Institute, Kyoto University
• p. 123, D) Courtesy Primate Research
Institute, Kyoto University
• p. 123, E) The Kinji Imanishi Digital Archive,
© P. J. Asquith, 2004 (archive locator:

AFRNB 40016), http://tomcat.sunsite.
ualberta.ca/Imanishi/
• p. 124, F) Reproduced with permission of
Penn State University Libraries, Special
Collections Library
• p. 125, G) Reproduced with permission of
Penn State University Libraries, Special
Collections Library
• p. 126, H) Courtesy Tetsuro Matsuzawa,
Primate Research Institute, Kyoto University
• p. 128, A) © 1965 National Geographic Society.
Courtesy National Geographic Society
• p. 128, B) © 1965 National Geographic Society.
Courtesy National Geographic Society
• pp. 129-130, A) Reproduced with permission
of Macmillan Publishers Ltd.: Nature, vol. 399,
no. 6737, 1999, © 1999
• p. 131, B) From The Ape And The Sushi
Master: Cultural Reflections Of A Primatologist, Frans de Waal, © 2001. Reproduced with
permission of Basic Books, a member of
the Perseus Books Group
• p. 131, C) Reproduced with permission
of Cambridge University Press
• p. 131, D) Reproduced with permission
of Cambridge University Press
• p. 131, E) Courtesy Christophe Boesch,
Max Planck Institute for Evolutionary
Anthropology
• p. 132, F) Courtesy Christophe Boesch,
Max Planck Institute for Evolutionary
Anthropology
• p. 133, G) Courtesy Christophe Boesch,
Max Planck Institute for Evolutionary
Anthropology
• p. 134, H) Courtesy Christophe Boesch,
Max Planck Institute for Evolutionary
Anthropology
• p. 136, A) © 1995 National Geographic Society.
Courtesy National Geographic Society
• p. 136, B) © Tobias Deschner, Max Planck
Institute for Evolutionary Anthropology
• p. 136, C) © Pan African Programme: The
Cultured Chimpanzee, Max Planck Institute
for Evolutionary Anthropology
• p. 137, D) © Pan African Programme:
The Cultured Chimpanzee, Max Planck
Institute for Evolutionary Anthropology
• p. 137, E) © Pan African Programme:
The Cultured Chimpanzee, Max Planck
Institute for Evolutionary Anthropology
• p. 137, F) © Pan African Programme:
The Cultured Chimpanzee, Max Planck
Institute for Evolutionary Anthropology
• pp. 138-139, G) © Pan African Programme:
The Cultured Chimpanzee, Max Planck
Institute for Evolutionary Anthropology
• p. 141, B) Courtesy The Warburg Institute,
London
• p. 144, C) © Penn State Media Sales
• p. 144, D) © 1997 by Roger Fouts. Reproduced
with permission of HarperCollins Publishers
• p. 145, E) Courtesy Les Films du Losange
• pp. 146-147, F) © NHK 1993 in cooperation
with The Language Research Center,
College of Arts & Sciences of Georgia State
University

• p. 148, G) Reproduced with permission
of *Scientific American*
• p. 149, I) © 1981 by The New York Academy
of Sciences. Reproduced with permission
of John Wiley & Sons, Inc.
• pp. 150-151, J) © 1981 by The New York Academy
of Sciences. Reproduced with permission
of John Wiley & Sons, Inc.
• p. 152, A) Courtesy Paper Tiger Television
• p. 153, A) Source: Robert M. Yerkes Papers,
Manuscripts and Archives, Yale University
Library
• p. 155, C) © Penn State Media Sales
• p. 155, D) Schweizerisches Bundesarchiv
CH-BAR J2.143#1996/386#898#2*,
Schweizer Filmwochenschau, February 19,
1960. Courtesy Zoo Basel
• p. 156, E) © 1941 by A. Maria Hoyt.
Published by J.B. Lippincott Company.
Permission pending
• p. 156, F) © 1976 by Hester Mundis.
Courtesy Penguin Randomhouse LLC
• p. 156, G) © 1975 by Science and Behavior
Books Inc.
• p. 156, H) Reproduced with permission
of KOSMOS publishing house
• p. 158-159, J) Reproduced with permission
of Jüdisches Museum Berlin
• pp. 160-161, K) Reproduced with permission
of Princeton University Press, from J. M.
Coetzee, *The Lives of Animals*, Amy Gutmann
(ed.), 3rd. edition 2001; © 1999, permission
conveyed through Copyright Clearance
Center, Inc.
• p. 162, L) © bpk / RMN-Grand Palais
(domaine de Chantilly) / Michel Urtado
• p. 165, B) © UNESCO 1950
• p. 166, C) Reproduced with permission of
Universal Music Group
• p. 167, A) Courtesy Tropenmuseum,
Amsterdam
• p. 169, B) From *The Social Life of Monkeys
and Apes*, Solly Zuckerman, © 1932 and
renewed 1960 by Houghton Mifflin Harcourt
Publishing Company. Reproduced with
permission of Houghton Mifflin Harcourt
Publishing Company. Reproduced with
permission of Taylor & Francis Books UK
• p. 170, C) © Penn State Media Sales
• p. 172, D) © 1961 by Literat S.A. Published
by Atheneum Books
• p. 172, E) From *On Aggression*,
Konrad Lorenz, © 1966, published by
Methuen & Co Ltd. Reproduced with
permission of Taylor & Francis Books UK.
• p. 172, F) Reproduced with permission
of Transaction Publishers
• p. 173, G) Reproduced with permission
of Transaction Publishers
• p. 173, H) © 1975, 1980 by the President
and Fellows of Harvard College. Published
by The Belknap Press of Harvard University
Press
• p. 173, I) From *The Dark Side of Man*,
Michael P. Ghiglieri and Joshua Bilmes, © 1999.

Reproduced with permission of Basic Books,
a member of The Perseus Books Group
• p. 175, J) Reproduced with permission
of Oxford University Press
• p. 175, K) © 1975 by Pathfinder Press.
Reproduced with permission
• p. 175, L) Reproduced with permission
of Yale University Press
• p. 175, M) Reproduced with permission
of Souvenir Press
• p. 175, N) Reproduced with permission
of Cambridge University Press
• p. 175, O) From *Symbiotic Planet:
A New Look At Evolution*, Lynn Margulis,
© 1998. Reproduced with permission of
Basic Books, a member of The Perseus
Books Group
• p. 177, A) Reproduced with permission of
Penn State University Libraries, Special
Collections Library
• p. 177, B) Courtesy Robin Fox. Reproduced
with permission of John Wiley & Sons, Inc.
• p. 177, C) Courtesy Robin Fox. Reproduced
with permission of John Wiley & Sons, Inc.
• p. 178, D) Courtesy Robin Fox. Reproduced
with permission of John Wiley & Sons, Inc.
• p. 179, E) Reproduced with permission of
University of Chicago Press, from Thomas T.
Struhsaker, "Auditory Communication among
Vervet Monkeys," in *Social Communication
among Primates*, Stuart A. Altmann (ed.),
1st. edition, © 1967; permission conveyed
through Copyright Clearance Center, Inc.
• pp. 180-181, F) Reproduced with permission
of University of Chicago Press, from Robert
E. Miller, "Experimental Approaches to the
Physiological and Behavioral Concomitants
of Affective Communication in Rhesus
Monkeys," in *Social Communication among
Primates*, Stuart A. Altmann (ed.), 1st. edition,
© 1967; permission conveyed through Copyright Clearance Center, Inc.
• p. 182, A) Frans de Waal, PhD,
Yerkes National Primate Research Center,
Emory University, Atlanta, GA
• p. 183, B) Courtesy Primate Research
Institute, Kyoto University
• p. 183, C) Courtesy Primate Research
Institute, Kyoto University
• p. 184, A) © 1974 by Jason Aronson, Inc.,
© 1971 by the Albion Publishing Company
• p. 185, B) © Penn State Media Sales
• p. 186, C) © 1975 by Sarah Blaffer Hrdy.
Courtesy Penguin Random House LLC
• pp. 187-189, D) © Condé Nast. Courtesy
Ian Parker
• p. 190, E) © 1995 National Geographic Society.
Courtesy National Geographic Society
• p. 191, A) Courtesy Beeld en Geluid
• pp. 193-195, A) Courtesy the Nonhuman
Rights Project, Coral Springs, Florida,
www.nonhumanrightsproject.org
• p. 193 © Daily News, L.P. (New York).
Reproduced with permission
• pp. 194-195 Reproduced with permission
from AAAS

• pp. 196-197, B) Reproduced with permission
of Princeton University Press, from J. M.
Coetzee, *The Lives of Animals*, Amy Gutmann
(ed.), 3rd. edition 2001; © 1999, permission
conveyed through Copyright Clearance
Center, Inc.

SPECIAL THANKS

*This exhibition and catalogue would not
have been possible without the help
and generosity of* the participating artists
and authors; *as well as:*
Mimi Arandjelovic; Pamela Asquith;
Merve Ayparlar; Timothy R. Babcock;
Thomas Bach; Lars Bang Larsen;
Daniel Becker; Jason Bernth; Megan Bury;
Casper Cameraat; Ursula Davila-Villa;
Oliver Dehn; Marieke van Delft;
Tobias Deschner; Diedrich Diederichsen;
Viola Dix; Brigid Doherty; Caroline Dumalin;
Paul Feindt; Seth Flink; Robin Fox;
Simon Franzkowiak, Emily Glaser;
Achim Haigis; Jiri Heitlager; Matthias Henkel;
Lena Hofmann; Daniel Jacobs; Petya Kohts;
Oliver Könitzer; Petra Könitzer;
Matthias Kujawa; Gisela Lausberg;
Dana Liss; Julie Ludwig; Marco Majoleth;
Tetsuro Matsuzawa; Rachel Mayeri;
Patrick Munck; Ans Molenkamp;
Richard Moore; Liz Mozden; Claudia Nebel;
Sladjan Nedeljkovic; Lisa Newbern,
Ingo Niermann; Isabelle Nonain-Semelin;
Nghia Nuyen; Kayoko Ohmae;
Danilo de Oliveira Viana; Claudia Peters,
Gregory Peterson; James Quandt;
Jörg Rehder; Stephen Ross,
Ken & Helen Rowe; Felix Ruckert;
Aya Saito; Gabriele Schwab;
Sebastian Schiefner; Marcel Schwierin;
Georg Seeßlen; Elisabeth Sinn;
David Smeltzer; Volker Sommer;
Ulrike Sonnemann; Olga Starostina;
Marie Luise Stein; Armin Stock;
Norio Takasugi; Michael Taussig;
Luiza Texeira Freitas; Beatriz Waters;
Thomas Werner; Eyal Weizman;
Shinya Yamamoto; Christophe Zangerle,
Ulrich Ziemons; Margrit Zeitler.

Nor without the support from:
Adolf-Würth-Zentrum für Geschichte der
Psychologie;
The American Association for the
Advancement of Science;
Andrew Kreps Gallery;
Atelier Weber;
Cadmos;
Ernst Haeckel-Haus;
Exploratorium, San Francisco;
Galerie Esther Schipper;
Galerie Micheline Szwajcer;
Hauser & Wirth;
Herald St;
International Primatological Society;
Japan Monkey Centre;
Jüdisches Museum Berlin;
Kent State University;
The Kinji Imanishi Digital Archive,
Department of Anthropology,
University of Alberta;
Kompetenzzentrum für nicht-textuelle
Materialien (KNM), Technische Informations-
bibliothek (TIB), Abteilung Forschung
und Entwicklung;
Karen Konicek;
Koninklijke Bibliotheek;
kurimanzutto;
The Language Research Center, College of
Arts & Sciences of Georgia State University;
Louise Lawler Studio;
Max Planck Institute for Evolutionary
Anthropology, Department of Primatology;
Max Planck Institute for Evolutionary
Anthropology, Library;
Missouri Botanical Garden / Library;
Musée-site Buffon / Musée des Beaux-Arts;
National Geographic Society;
Naturalis Biodiversity Center;
Netherlands Instituut voor Beeld en Geluid;
NHK Enterprises, Inc.;
Nottingham Contemporary;
Penn State Media Sales;
Penn State University Libraries,
Special Collections Library;
Pierre Huyghe Studio;
Public Services Yale University Library;
Punch Limited;
Sammlung Goetz;
Schweizerisches Bundesarchiv BAR;
Schwelle 7 ;
Spiegel-Verlag;
Sprüth Magers Berlin / Köln;
UNESCO Division de l'information du public;
White Cube;
Wildlife Research Center, Kyoto University;
Yerkes Public Affairs.

Thank you very much!

EXHIBITION

This book was published in association with the exhibition *Ape Culture*, held from April 30 to July 6, 2015 at Haus der Kulturen der Welt.

Curators:
Anselm Franke, Hila Peleg

Exhibition Architecture:
Kooperative für Darstellungspolitik
(Jesko Fezer, Anita Kaspar,
Andreas Müller & Team)

Exhibition Graphics:
Studio Matthias Görlich
(Matthias Görlich, Anna Kraus,
Leonie Rapp)

Project and Research Coordination:
Nadja Talmi

Production Coordination:
Elsa de Seynes

Project Assistance:
Elisabeth Krämer

Interns:
Elza Czarnowski, Christopher Hupe,
Martin Siegler

Contributions and Collaboration:
Cord Riechelmann, Christophe Boesch

Research:
Heidi Ballet, Katja Kynast,
Elisabeth Krämer, Martin Siegler

HAUS DER KULTUREN DER WELT

Director:
Bernd Scherer

Visual Arts and Film Department

Head:
Anselm Franke

Program Coordination:
Sonja Oehler, Daniela Wolf

Program Assistance:
Janina Prossek

Processing:
Cornelia Pilgram

Technical Department

Technical Director:
Mathias Helfer

Technical Coordination:
Gernot Ernst, with Christian Dertinger,
Gabriel Kujawa & Team

Building Facilities:
Frank Jahn, Benjamin Brandt & Team

Video Editing:
Matthias Hartenberger, Benjamin Beck

*Communications and
Cultural Education Department*

Head:
Silvia Fehrmann

Editorial Office:
Sabine Willig, Laida Hadel

Press Office:
Anne Maier, Nabila El-Khatib

Internet:
Eva Stein, Jan Koehler, Stefan Ritscher

Public Relations:
Christiane Sonntag, Sabine Westemeier

Cultural Education Program:
Maria Fountoukis, Leila Haghighat, Eva Stein,
Josephine Schlegel

COLOPHON

Editors:
Anselm Franke, Hila Peleg

Managing Editors:
Martin Hager, Nadja Talmi

Editorial Associates:
Heidi Ballet, Elisabeth Krämer,
Katja Kynast, Martin Siegler

Editorial Assistance:
Elza Czarnowski, Christopher Hupe

Texts on Artworks:
Rachel O'Reilly

Copyediting:
Nicola Morris
Erik Empson
Colin Shepherd
Ames Gerould

Translation:
Colin Shepherd

Graphic Design:
Studio Matthias Görlich
(Matthias Görlich, Anna Kraus,
Leonie Rapp)

Image Editing:
Felix Scheu

Typeface:
Gza, Lettera Text

Paper:
EnviroTop

Printing and Binding:
DZA Druckerei zu Altenburg GmbH

First edition
Printed in Germany
ISBN 978-3-95905-006-7

© 2015 the editors, authors, artists, Haus der
Kulturen der Welt, and Spector Books

Haus der Kulturen der Welt thanks all
copyright owners for their kind permission
to reproduce their material. Should, despite
our intensive research, any person entitled
to rights have been overlooked, legitimate
claims should be compensated within
the usual provisions. Please contact
info@hkw.de.

Published by:

Spector Books
Harkortstraße 10
04107 Leipzig
www.spectorbooks.com

Distribution:
Germany, Austria: GVA, Gemeinsame Verlags-
auslieferung Göttingen GmbH&Co. KG
www.gva-verlage.de
Switzerland: AVA Verlagsauslieferung AG,
www.ava.ch
France, Belgium: Interart Paris,
www.interart.fr
UK: Central Books Ltd,
www.centralbooks.com
USA, Canada: RAM Publications+Distribution
Inc., www.rampub.com
Australia, New Zealand: Perimeter Distribution,
www.perimeterdistribution.com
Other Countries: Motto Distribution,
www.mottodistribution.com

Eine deutschsprachige Ausgabe des Buches
ist bei Spector Books unter der
ISBN 978-3-95905-000-5 erschienen.

Haus der Kulturen der Welt
John-Foster-Dulles-Allee 10
10557 Berlin
www.hkw.de

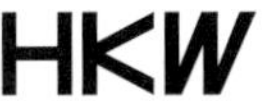

Ape Culture was produced by
Haus der Kulturender Welt, a division
of Kulturveranstaltungen des Bundes
in Berlin GmbH (KBB).

Chairwomen of the Supervisory Board:
Federal Government Commissioner
for Culture and the Media Professor
Monika Grütters MdB

Director:
Bernd Scherer

General Manager:
Charlotte Sieben

Haus der Kulturen der Welt is
supported by

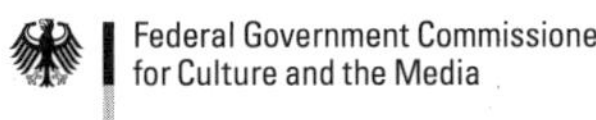

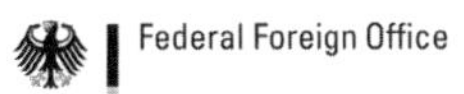